Work, Wages, and Welfare
in a Developing Metropolis

A World Bank Research Publication

Work, Wages, and Welfare
in a Developing Metropolis

Consequences of Growth
in Bogotá, Columbia

Rakesh Mohan

Published for The World Bank
OXFORD UNIVERSITY PRESS

Oxford University Press

New York Oxford London Glasgow
Toronto Melbourne Wellington Hong Kong
Tokyo Kuala Lumpur Singapore Jakarta
Delhi Bombay Calcutta Madras Karachi
Nairobi Dar es Salaam Cape Town

Copyright © 1986 by the International Bank
for Reconstruction and Development/The World Bank
1818 H Street, N.W., Washington, D.C. 20433, U.S.A.

First printing December 1986

Library of Congress Cataloging-in-Publication Data

Mohan, Rakesh, 1948–
    Work, wages, and welfare in a developing
metropolis.

    Bibliography: p.
    1. Labor and laboring classes—Colombia—Bogotá.
2. Labor and laboring classes—Colombia—Cali.
3. Bogotá (Colombia)—Economic conditions. 4. Cali
(Colombia)—Economic conditions. I. Title.
HD8310.B642M64 1986   311'.09861'4   86-18904
ISBN 0-19-520540-5

Contents

Preface

This monograph is part of a World Bank research program known as the City Study, which examined five major urban sectors—housing, transport, employment location, labor markets, and public finance—in Bogotá and Cali, Colombia. The goal of the program was to increase our understanding of the workings of these sectors in order to assess the effect of policies and projects on developing country cities in general. The overall study was directed by Gregory K. Ingram.

The work reported in this volume was undertaken almost full time, over a period of five years—from 1977 to 1980 and then in 1984. It presents the results of detailed empirical work and is perhaps unusual in the depth of its coverage of just two cities (primarily Bogotá and secondarily Cali). I owe innumerable debts to institutions and individuals who have helped in one way or another over the course of this study; if some people have inadvertently been omitted, this should be attributed to the ravages of time.

Douglas Keare must bear a large portion of the credit (blame?) for this work, for it was he who inducted me into the World Bank in December 1976 and did not let me work on anything else until I escaped to India in December 1980. Gregory Ingram must bear equal responsibility as director of the study throughout its duration. After my recapture from India in November 1983, Gregory Ingram has continued to curb my proclivities for distraction and thus induced me to finish this work. I have learned much from both of them on the arts of humane management, gentle persuasion, and the intricacies of robust empirical work.

Writing a book about a country other than one's own has many pitfalls, the chief among them being a tendency to reinvent the wheel. If I have had any success in avoiding this, I must attribute it to Ramiro Cardona, Jose Fernando Pineda, Albert Berry, Miguel Urrutia, and Jorge Garcia, all of whom contributed much to my education with regard to Colombia, as did Alvaro Pachon, Bernardo Kugler, Alberto Hernandez, and Alejandro Vivas. The generous hospitality of Ramiro and Elizabeth Cardona, Jose Fernando, and Patricia Pineda helped transform Colombia into my third home. The warm and friendly atmosphere of the Corporación Centro Regional de Población (CCRP), where the study was based in Bogotá, was also very helpful.

Some parts of the study were conducted with others. Jorge Garcia and M. Wilhelm Wagner were my coauthors on the original paper on the measurement of malnutrition and poverty; Nancy Hartline worked with me on the poor of Bogotá; and Rodrigo Villamizar on land prices. Sudhir Anand, Sherman Robinson, and Sung Yong Kang contributed to the development of the income distribution program EQUALISE. I also learned much from Gary Fields's paper on labor market segmentation for the study, and from his earlier work on Colombia.

A legion of research assistants have contributed to the computations reported. Needless to say, their assistance was indispensable. I would like to thank Yoon Joo Lee, Sung Yong Kang, Robert Marshall, Wili Wagner, Jon Roseman, Nancy Hartline, and Mark Snyderman, who gave much beyond the call of duty in computing and recomputing. It is a tribute to their patience that we have remained friends. I would also like to thank Alan Carroll and Nelson Valverde for original cleaning and documentation of raw data tapes so that they would be ready for use. Similarly, I am indebted to Ofelia Miranda, Mattie McCarter, Gladys Tivel, Anita Economides, and Mary Ann Heraud, who had to cope with the typing and retyping of text and tables. I am particularly grateful to Maria Elena Edwards, Elfreda O'Rielly-Campbell, and Myriam Bailey for preparing the final manuscript.

It is not common for economists to have been involved in the collection of the data that they eventually analyze. I had much to do with the organization and collection of data in the World Bank-DANE 1978 Household Survey sponsored by the World Bank and Colombia's National Statistical Agency, Departamento Administrativo Nacional de Estadística (DANE), and therefore realize the hard work and attention to detail that primary data collection entails. The high quality of the 1978 survey owes much to the diligence of its DANE supervisors, Roberto Pinilla and Maria Christina Jimenez. The contributions of Gary Losee, Alfredo Aliaga, Jaime Arias, Alvaro Pachon, and Jose Fernando Pineda to its design and implementation were also notable. This work would not have been possible without their efforts. I would also like to thank the authorities of DANE for providing so readily all the data sets for the study.

My intellectual debt to Sudhir Anand, Albert Berry, and Miguel Urrutia should be obvious to readers of this book. I also thank Surjit Bhalla, Francois Bourguignon, Michael Hartley, Johannes Linn, Shlomo Reutlinger, T. N. Srinivasan, Vinod Thomas, and Richard Webb for their comments on earlier versions of papers that have become incorporated here. If errors and misinterpretations remain, they must share the responsibility for them.

Finally, I must thank Peter Bocock and Venka Macintyre for their patience and excellent technical editing. They have done much to make the empirical and technical information in this book more accessible to the general reader. I have learned much from them in the art of bookmaking.

In writing this book I hope that more detailed work of this kind in developing countries will follow and that our understanding of urban labor markets will continue to improve.

I dedicate this book to my father, Ratish Mohan.

1

Introduction

The metropolis is rapidly becoming a familiar habitat to a large proportion of the world's population in developed and developing countries alike. The quarter century since World War II has been one of extremely rapid urban growth. In 1950 only three cities in the developing world had more than 5 million people. By 1980 there were more than fifteen such cities, compared with only ten in the developed countries. In the past, the word "metropolis" brought to mind names such as New York, Chicago, London, Paris, or Rome. Now it is more likely to refer to cities such as Buenos Aires, São Paulo, Mexico City, Tokyo, Manila, Seoul, Bombay, or Cairo.

Despite the rapid growth of these cities in the past quarter century, the dynamics involved have not been well understood. Whereas in the past the presence of a metropolis in a country was regarded as a matter of pride, now it is often regarded with considerable awe, if not fear. As a result, much of the explicit urban policy in most countries has been negative, often devoted to slowing the growth of large cities. This approach has seldom been successful and at times has even been counterproductive, so that large cities have continued to grow, and have usually prospered in the process. It is therefore important to understand the process of rapid city growth and its consequences. Considerable research exists on the old cities of North America and Europe, and their structures are reasonably well understood: particularly the workings of their housing markets; the locational decisions of their residents and of their employers; the patterns of their traffic and transport; and the workings of their labor markets. The stylized facts for these cities appear to have wide applicability. How well do these stylized facts fit the new cities? Should our methods of studying them be different? How have the populations in these cities responded to this rapid growth? Is there anything to fear? What do project and city planners need to know about processes and patterns in cities in order to act in an enlightened manner? How much intervention is necessary in different markets for a city to accommodate rapid growth? These are some of the questions that the City Study of Bogotá and Cali set out to illuminate.

The City Study

Researchers in the 1960s and early 1970s were optimistic about the utility and feasibility of constructing large-scale models of cities in order to understand them and hence to plan better. The idea that everything in a city is interrelated had taken hold and many felt that the best way to describe these interrelations would be to capture them in large-scale urban models. However, in designing the City Study, we were skeptical about the utility of constructing a large-scale model (see Mohan 1979), and opted instead for detailed investigations of each area of decisionmaking. The rationale was that it is more important to model the behavior of the different actors in a city rather than complex interrelationships in order to understand its overall workings. Moreover, an understanding of behavior is much more useful in designing policies. As a result, we decided to model different markets and the behavior of households, individuals, firms, and the public sector within them. In particular we focused on the responses of these different actors in the face of extremely rapid change. We asked how, for example, the poor responded in the housing market. How much did they do for themselves and how should the public sector intervene? What kind of supply resulted, given the lack of developed land? How did the public sector react, given the activities of illegal suppliers of land? What kind of transport services appeared in response to a variegated demand? How did people choose their mode of transport? How were incomes determined? How did people respond to changes in labor market conditions? How did firms respond to changing land market conditions and to a growing city? Answers to these questions are needed if planners are to design effective policies to deal with the urban growth that has become pervasive in the developing world. The answers should give some idea of what should be done as well as what should not be done, what people and firms themselves are efficient at doing, and what is in need of public intervention. This has been the approach taken in the City Study, and we have compared it and the answers found with the approaches and results known from developed countries. Thus, the broad theme of the studies constituting the City Study of Bogotá is the behavioral adaptation to rapid change.

Most urban studies concentrate exclusively on issues related to the supply of infrastructure and the provision of housing and transport services. Although these issues are also addressed in detail in the City Study, equal attention is given to understanding the working of the labor market and resulting income distribution. Since our emphasis is on understanding the behavior of people and firms in a situation of rapid growth, a prior understanding of household behavior and labor market activity of individuals and their employers is necessary before the housing, transport, and infrastructure issues can be addressed. A mapping of the spatial and overall distribution of income and explanations of its trend are crucial to understanding and predicting the nature of the demand for housing, transport, and infrastructure that is likely to arise in a growing city. This monograph is therefore devoted to the study of population growth, income distribution and its determination, and employment in Bogotá and Cali during a period of extremely rapid growth in both cities. It is designed to suggest useful approaches to the study of cities undergoing rapid growth.

Some comments are necessary on the choice of Bogotá and Cali as the cities chosen for study. Once we had decided to study one city in detail (rather than attempt to draw cross-country patterns), we quickly recognized that it had to be a Latin American city. The Latin American continent as a whole had experienced very rapid urbanization since World War II and presented a substantial number of cities with phenomena of interest. However, the largest cities (Buenos Aires, São Paulo, Mexico City) seemed far too big to study. Bogotá was finally chosen for three overriding reasons. First, it appeared to exhibit median characteristics among a cross-section of Latin American cities in a number of dimensions (see Ingram and Carroll 1981) and was therefore representative. Second, it had a rich data base on which to build. Third, the interest in careful analysis was great there. Bogotá and Colombia have a rich history of pioneering economic studies: the first World Bank mission to a developing country was to Colombia (led by Lauchlin Currie in 1950); Albert Hirschman derived the key insights for his seminal work *Strategy for Economic Development* during a three-year stint with the Colombian Planning Office; the International Labour Organisation (ILO) sent an influential employment mission headed by Dudley Seers in 1967; and the World Bank's first published country economic report, in 1972, was on Colombia. Of direct relevance to the city study was the support provided by the United Nations Development Programme (UNDP) for a major urban development study of Bogotá in 1970–74 (commonly known as the Phase II Study). This had generated a substantial amount of benchmark data. Cali was added to the study as a useful comparator since it is a city of about one million in size and is in the same country.

Income distribution and employment have also been extensively studied in Colombia. For example, Albert Berry and Miguel Urrutia (1976) conducted one of the early studies on income distribution in a developing country; similarly Nelson, Schultz, and Slighton (1971) conducted one of the early studies on income determination; and Fields did extensive work on the 1973 population census (see Fields 1975, 1977, 1978; Fields and Marulanda 1970; and Fields and Schultz 1977, 1980). The present study is distinguished from these precursors in that it concentrates on income distribution, poverty, and the operation of labor markets within Bogotá and Cali and looks explicitly at the spatial arrangements of residence and employment. In retrospect, it turns out that the years under study—1973 to 1978—were extraordinary because of unusual labor market tightening and rapid economic growth in Colombia. As a result, it was a time during which urban unemployment decreased to the point of becoming almost negligible. This period is in marked contrast to the late 1960s when the ILO mission considered urban unemployment a primary concern; the mission estimated it to be about 14 percent in 1967 along with about 12 percent underemployment. My concern in this study is much more with the decision to participate in the job market, the determination of income for those who do, and its resulting overall and spatial distribution.

Primary Concerns

In sum, this monograph is devoted to understanding the determination of labor income in urban areas in the context of rapid urban and economic growth. Colombia is a middle-income country that provides an instructive example of rapid change in a relatively short period of time. As documented in chapter 2, the 1970s brought about important changes in Colombia's labor market: income growth was accompanied by major changes in demographic variables such as fertility; there was some evidence of increasing maturity of the urbanization process as the level of urbanization throughout the country reached more than 60 percent; the education system expanded to the point that men and women had almost equal access by the end of the period; there were some signs of real increases in rural wages and a corresponding slowdown in migration; and so on.

Many studies of urban labor markets have focused on unemployment and poverty. A number of them use the "informal sector" as a shorthand expression to describe a portion of the market that is unorganized and at the same time associated with poverty. Moreover, much of the migration literature is also concerned with the likelihood that migrants will not find "formal" employment and therefore will join the informal sector, and consequently the ranks of the poor. This paradigm of urban labor markets arose from earlier dualistic theories of development: the methods of looking at phenomena were therefore dichotomous. This study emphasizes the heterogeneity that exists in the labor market, examines carefully many of the accepted impressions that exist, and questions the validity of some of these impressions. In particular, it questions the existence of easily identifiable dichotomies. The approach here is empirical, and the objective is to identify useful methods of analyzing the twin issues of income distribution and of poverty, and of classifying and analyzing labor markets in large cities.

Thus, the study examines a menu of wide-ranging questions: How segregated is the city by income? How is this changing over time? What is the extent of poverty? How much has poverty changed? What causes low earnings? Who are the people with low earnings? Are migrants different? Is there segmentation in the labor market? What are the returns to education? Are these returns changing over time? Are women treated differently in the labor market? Do they act differently? Are the data adequate to answer these questions? These are the substantive issues addressed in this monograph in order to suggest methods of looking at other cities in the developing world.

This study adds to the growing body of literature on large household surveys in developing countries that has emerged over the past decade. Colombia and Malaysia appear to be the countries most studied. The approach taken here is most similar to that of Anand (1983), but has also benefited from the work of Mazumdar (1981) and Meerman (1979) in Malaysia, and Selowsky (1979), Fields (various works), and Urrutia (1985) in Colombia.

As mentioned earlier, a great deal of information is available on Colombia, particularly on Bogotá. The last two censuses in 1964 and 1973 are readily available in computer-readable form from DANE (Departamento Administrativo Nacional de Estadística), Colombia's national statistical agency. Moreover—and this is unusual—a consistent within-city geocoding scheme has also been used in all their surveys since at least 1964. It is therefore possible to identify the location of sample households according to their neighborhood of residence. This geocoding scheme is explained in detail in appendix A, which also provides further information on the data sources used. (For a detailed description and documentation of these data sources and others used in the City Study, see Valverde 1978 and Y. J. Lee 1979, 1981). The 1964 census did not include a question on income and was therefore not utilized in this study. However, other spatial distributions such as population density, occupational distributions, and the like were compared between the two censuses and found to be consistent. DANE has also had a scheme of household surveys since about 1970; these are primarily labor force surveys in the main cities in the country, but also include some countrywide surveys on consumption. All of these are also readily available on computer tape and easily retrievable. The labor force surveys have been quarterly since 1974; the Bogotá sample usually covers between 3,000 and 5,000 households and that for Cali usually about 1,000 households. Two of these surveys—EH8E (Encuesta de Hogares Especial–Bogotá) conducted in March 1975 and EH15 conducted in March 1977—were used extensively in this study. EH15 also had comparable information on Cali.

A special multipurpose household survey (EH21) was designed and conducted as part of the City Study in December 1978 in conjunction with DANE's quarterly series. It contained detailed information on each household—including housing characteristics, travel patterns, labor force activity, and incomes—and was conducted simultaneously in Bogotá and Cali. This was superior to other surveys in a number of respects, but was especially useful for the present monograph since each worker in each household was interviewed separately. As a result, the quality of information on labor income is considered high (see appendix C).

Thus more or less comparable data were available for 1973 (census), 1975, 1977, and 1978. One objective in working with so many data sets was to test for comparability over household surveys and the difficulty involved therein; another was to trace the rapid changes taking place in urban Colombia during that period. More than usual attention is therefore paid to data comparisons.

Overview

This book is organized in two parts. Part I deals with the overall population in Bogotá and Cali: its spatial distribution, income distribution, and extent and distribution of poverty characteristics. Part II examines the characteristics of the urban labor market in Bogotá that help to explain some of the population characteristics in part I. Results for Cali are merely touched on in part II since they conform to those for Bogotá.

Chapter 2 places Bogotá in the national context, comparing its growth along with that of the country as a whole. It also briefly outlines the recent history of the Colombian economy in order to provide some background to the evolution of the labor market.

Chapter 3 introduces the cities of Bogotá and Cali by summarizing their structure in relation to the spatial distributions of population and land values and describes the changing spatial patterns by tracing the density and land value gradients as they have evolved over the past three decades. The economic and demographic structure of the two cities is also briefly described. A key finding is the great extent of spatial stratification by income—a pattern that has guided much of the city's growth.

Chapter 4 gives an anatomy of the distribution of income in the two cities. The central issue here is spatial inequality within the two cities. A measure based on the decomposition of inequality is suggested for assessing the level of intracity spatial inequality. A technical appendix to the chapter gives a brief derivation of the Theil index of inequality (and its decomposition) for measurement purposes.

Chapter 5 considers how poverty is measured and describes its correlates. Considerable attention is given to the difficulties of measuring poverty, and it is concluded that, at best, only ranges or minimum bounds of poverty levels can be derived from sources of data that are normally available. The method of measurement is described before obtaining a spatial profile of poverty. As in chapter 4, poverty is found to be concentrated in particular parts of the city. The correlates of urban poverty in various economic and demographic dimensions are then described.

Chapter 6 opens part II with a description of the characteristics of the labor force. Profiles of the work force developed from their ages, education, and income give largely conventional results. Again, as would be expected from the distribution of income found in part I, residences of poor workers are concentrated in certain parts of the city. Moreover, these workers belong to particular occupations but are spread more evenly over different industries of activity. The distribution of workers by workplace differs considerably from that by residence. Since most jobs are located in the richer parts of the city, there is considerable commuting. When the usual characteristics of the informal sector are closely examined, it appears that this sector is difficult to clearly differentiate in Bogotá.

Chapter 7 looks at the decision to participate in the labor force, particularly among women and young workers, since almost all men of prime age participate regardless of demand-side characteristics of the labor market. The econometric techniques typically used to analyze labor supply are carefully assessed and compared. Thus ordinary least squares estimates are compared with probit estimates for participation, and the tobit technique is compared with ordinary least squares and the Heckman procedure for the hours-worked decision. The supply of labor is found to be quite responsive to increasing real wages, but much of this wage elastic response is from married women. A technical appendix briefly explains the various techniques used.

Chapter 8 sets out the model used to examine earnings functions, and estimates the returns to education and experience for the Bogotá labor force. Increased education in Colombia is found to affect the returns to higher education significantly. As the supply of higher-educated labor has expanded, the marginal returns appear to have declined as might be expected but is not often quantified. The returns to firm-specific and occupation-specific experience are distinguished carefully from general labor market experience in this chapter. The issue of spatial disadvantage is addressed by analyzing the effect of background on earnings. The location of residence, which appears to be important in the descriptive chapters in terms of the characteristics of workers and their incomes, is interpreted here as a proxy for disadvantaged background with respect to the quality of education. This part of chapter 8 looks at the origin of people before they take up residence in Bogotá as well as their place of residence after arrival. Both are found to be significant, but the background effect is small after other variables such as age and education have been controlled for.

Chapter 9 uses the techniques of earnings decomposition discussed in chapter 4 to distinguish the spatial contribution to inequality in earnings. The technique is also used to decompose earnings according to the other characteristics used as explanators in the earnings functions estimates, such as age, education, firm size, occupation, and activity. This provides further insight into the determination of labor earnings supplementing the earnings functions work. It also suggests a method for distinguishing the informal sector—if one exists. It should be possible to isolate the variables characterizing the informal sector according to their contribution to earnings inequality. Once again, such a dichotomy is not easy to find in Bogotá. This issue is examined in more detail in an attempt to find the extent and reasons for segmentation in Bogotá. There is no obvious protected sector except, perhaps, for employment in government. The method used is the estimation of earnings functions according to different stratifications and testing for differences in the returns to education. Dummy variables are also used to test for shifts in earnings functions caused by segmentation.

Chapter 10 gives the earnings functions results for women and discusses the difficulties in estimation arising from interruptions in their participation. An attempt is also made to account for selectivity bias in the estimation of earnings functions for women.

The final chapter gives a summary of the main findings of the study, relates them to the overall economic environment in Colombia, and assesses their relevance to understanding the growth processes of large cities.

2

Bogotá in the National Urban Context

Because the research on incomes and employment in Bogotá reported in this book is detailed and microeconomic in nature, it seems helpful to open the discussion with a brief sketch of the economic environment in which the Bogotá labor market has operated in the past decade or so. Putting Bogotá in a wider national context also helps us to understand some of the remarkable changes that occurred in the city in the late 1970s.

The Place of Bogotá in the Colombian Urban System

Colombia is unusual among Latin American countries in that it has a well-articulated system of cities (see map 2-1). The importance of Bogotá in this system is demonstrated by the fact that it accounts for about 20 percent of the total urban population. Nevertheless, Colombia's primacy index (that is, the ratio of the population of the largest city to the total urban population of the country) is the lowest in Latin America except for that of Brazil (see Renaud 1982). Thus, although Bogotá is the dominant city in Colombia, it is less overwhelming than the largest cities in most other Latin American countries. At the same time, its share of both national population and output has been increasing over the past few decades.

Colombia has experienced rapid urbanization during the past forty years (see table 2-1). Between 1951 and 1964, there was an especially sharp rise in both population growth and the rate of urbanization. Within the space of forty years, the population has evolved from being predominantly rural to being broadly urban. In 1938, about 70 percent of the country's inhabitants lived in rural areas, but by 1982 the situation was almost reversed, with 65 percent of the population estimated to be urban inhabitants (the 1973 census figure was just under 60 percent; see World Bank 1984a). During this time, Bogotá's share of the national population grew from less than 4 percent to

Table 2-1. *Population Size and Intercensal Growth Rate*

		Population				
		Urban[a]	Bogotá	Growth rates[b]		
Year	Colombia (thousands)	(percentage of Colombia)	(percentage of Colombia)	Colombia	Urban	Bogotá
1938	8,702	31	3.8	—	—	—
1951	11,548	39	5.7	2.2	3.9	5.2
1964	17,485	52	9.5	3.2	5.4	7.3
1973	22,500	60	12.7	2.7	3.7	5.6
1982[c]	26,965	65	15.1	2.0	3.0	4.0

a. Urban areas are defined as county seats (*cabecera municipal*). A cabecera municipal can sometimes have fewer than 1,500 people, whereas other settlements sometimes have more than 1,500 people.

b. Annual intercensal compound growth rates.

c. Estimated (World Bank 1984). Bogotá growth rate of 4.0 percent a year from 1973 to 1978 assumed to continue until 1982.

upward of 15 percent. Until recently, its population was growing steadily at a rate of more than 5 percent a year, so that in a period of forty years it increased more than tenfold, from about 330,000 to about 4.0 million. It is hard to imagine that in 1938 Bogotá was no bigger than an "intermediate" city such as Bucaramanga is today.

Trends in gross domestic product for Bogotá and Colombia since 1950, which are evident in the regional income accounts compiled by the National Planning Department (Departamento Nacional de Planeación), indicate that between 1960 and 1975 Bogotá's share of national product rose from 15 to 21 percent (table 2-2). However, the fact that the ratio of Bogotá's per capita gross product to national per capita product fell from 1.8:1 in 1960 to 1.6:1 in 1975 suggests that the differential between Bogotá and the rest of the country, and, perhaps, the rural-urban income differential in general, has been falling over the past two decades. Although the relevant data are not available, it would be interesting to see if these differentials were even greater in earlier periods—in particular, during the 1930s when the process of urbanization began to pick up speed.

Bogotá's regional product grew by 7 percent a year during 1950–75; the rate for Colombia in the same period was 5.2 percent. Bogotá's per capita growth rate was much less, however: 0.6 percent as compared with 2.1 percent for the country as a whole. These data reflect high labor mobility stimulated by the large differential between Bogotá and the rest of the country. A closer look at the regional accounts reveals that the ratio of per capita personal income in Bogotá to that for the country as a whole fell from 1.78:1 to

Map 2-1. *Cities of Colombia*

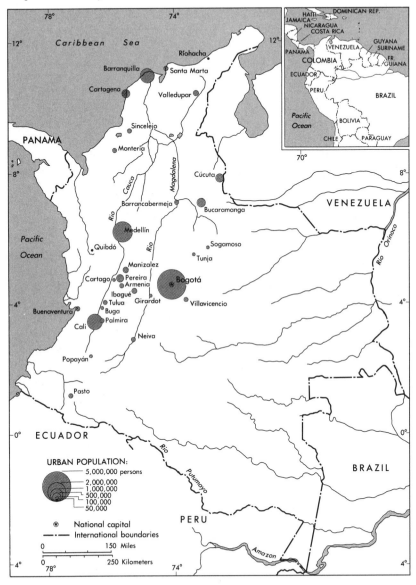

Table 2-2. *Gross Domestic Product and Per Capita Product:*
Colombia and Bogotá
(1970 Colombian pesos)

Year or period	Colombia		Bogotá		Bogotá/Colombia[a] (percent)	
	GDP (millions of pesos)	Per capita GDP (pesos)	GDP (millions of pesos)	Per capita GDP (pesos)	GDP	Per capita GDP
1960	77,714	5,088	11,996	9.220	15.4	1.81
1965	97,968	5,455	17,208	9,591	17.6	1.76
1970	130,361	6,484	25,920	10,822	19.9	1.67
1975	176,478	7,352	37,671	11,779	21.3	1.60
Average annual growth rates (percent)						
1950–75	5.2	2.1	7.0	0.6		
1960–75	5.6	2.5	7.9	1.7		
1970–75	6.2	3.2	7.8	1.7		

a. Bogotá GDP and per capita GDP as a proportion of that of Colombia.
Source: Colombia (1977).

1.53:1, a steeper decline that that for per capita product. These falling differentials indicate the workings of an equilibrating labor market. When price differences are taken into account, the current money differential may no longer be significant in real terms; we may thus expect a considerable slowdown in the rate of migration and urbanization—a slowdown that indeed seems to have been taking place in the late 1970s and early 1980s.

Bogotá has grown consistently faster than cities in other size categories (table 2-3); similarly, the cities in the next size group (Cali, Medellín, and Barranquilla) have grown faster than smaller cities, though somewhat less rapidly than Bogotá. Intermediate towns such as Buenaventura, Cúcuta, Villavicencio, Valledupar, and Bucaramanga have also grown fast (see appendix tables 2A-1 and 2A-2 at the end of this chapter), but the urbanization process has led to an increasing concentration of population in the four largest cities. According to table 2-3, the different size classes of towns grew almost proportionately up to 1964, but thereafter increasing concentration took place and created concern about the growth of Bogotá, in particular.

The National Economy

Since World War II, Colombia's economy has passed through four phases (the first three of which were suggested by Berry 1980b): effervescent growth (1946–56), stagnation (1956–65), sustained growth (1966–78), and stag-

Table 2-3. *Population Growth Rates of the Thirty Largest Cities and Metropolitan Areas in Colombia, by Size Class, 1951–73*
(percent)

Size class in 1973 (thousands)	Number of cities	Population as proportion of total urban			Intercensal average compound growth rate	
		1951	1964	1973	1951–64	1964–73
30–89	13	6.8	7.2	6.8	6.1	3.3
90–149	6	5.2	5.5	5.2	6.0	3.4
150–499	7	13.4	13.7	12.4	5.8	2.8
500–1,499	3[a]	21.0	23.2	24.1	6.4	4.3
1,500 +	1[b]	15.9	18.4	21.2	7.0	5.3
Total urban population[c] (thousands)		4,469	9,093	12,847	5.4	3.7
Urban/total (percent)		38.7	52.0	57.8	—	—
Total population (thousands)		11,548	17,484	22,264	3.1	2.6

a. Barranquilla, Cali, Medellín.
b. Bogotá.
c. Population of cabeceras municipales.
Sources: Calculated from Linn (1978), table 4; and Conroy (1976), tables A-14, A-11.

nation (from 1978–79 up to the present). The third phase is particularly interesting because during this time Colombia underwent a series of remarkable economic changes that were accompanied by major changes in the urban labor markets. From 1960 to 1980 the overall real rate of GDP growth remained at almost 6 percent a year, with the result that per capita incomes nearly doubled in this period. This kind of growth was not without precedent, however, since the rate had climbed to 5.3 percent in the first half of the 1950s, and although it slowed down in the latter half of the decade, it was still around 4.0 percent.

Because of rapid structural change in the economy, agriculture now contributes almost a quarter of national income, as does industry, while the tertiary sector contributes about half. The share of industry rose during the 1960s, but remained stationary in the 1970s and even fell toward the end of the decade, whereas the share of the tertiary sector grew considerably (tables 2-4 and 2-5). The 1967–74 period was a buoyant one in which manufacturing and construction led the overall economic boom. This period was also notable for its agricultural expansion, which continued until the end of the 1970s. Although the growth of manufacturing slowed down in the second half of

Table 2-4. *Contribution of Selected Sectors to Growth, 1960–81*
(percent)

Period	Real growth rate				Sectoral contribution to growth[a]			
	Agri-culture	Manufac-turing	Trade[b]	GDP	Agri-culture	Manufac-turing	Trade[b]	Total[c]
1960–64	3.1	5.9	6.0	4.8	21.1	20.2	20.0	100.0
1964–67	2.9	5.1	4.7	4.6	19.3	18.8	16.9	100.0
1967–74	4.3	8.6	8.3	6.7	18.0	23.1	21.4	100.0
1978–81	3.2	1.5	2.7	3.7	22.2	7.3	13.8	100.0
1960–81	4.2	6.4	6.8	5.7	20.5	20.0	21.2	100.0

a. Sectoral growth rates weighted by the corresponding sectoral shares in GDP.
b. Comprises commerce, banking, finance, and insurance.
c. The other sectors' contribution to growth is not shown; therefore the sum of agriculture, manufacturing, and trade does not add to 100 percent.
Source: World Bank (1984).

the decade (see Morawetz 1981), the tertiary sector continued to expand rapidly. It is only since 1979–80 that growth has slowed markedly in all sectors as the economy has sunk into a deep recession. This study does not analyze post-1978 changes; it remains to be seen whether the current difficulties are merely cyclical or whether they herald a longer-term structural shift.

Table 2-5. *Shares of GDP by Industrial Origin, 1960–81*
(percent at 1970 peso factor cost)

Sector	1960–64	1964–67	1967–74	1974–78	1978–81
Agriculture	32.7	30.7	28.2	26.3	25.7
Industry	24.2	25.0	26.8	26.0	24.8
Mining	2.3	2.4	2.0	1.3	1.1
Manufacturing	16.5	17.0	18.0	18.7	18.1
Construction	4.3	4.3	5.2	4.3	3.8
Electricity, gas, and water	1.1	1.3	1.6	1.7	1.8
Services	43.1	44.3	45.0	47.7	49.5
Transport and communication	6.9	7.1	7.5	8.8	9.5
Trade	16.0	16.6	17.3	18.6	19.0
Public administration	7.0	7.1	7.0	6.7	6.7
Other services	13.2	13.5	13.2	13.6	14.3
GDP	100.0	100.0	100.0	100.0	100.0

Source: World Bank (1984).

Table 2-6. *Percentage Share of Labor Force by Sector, 1925–78*

Sector	1925	1938	1951	1964	1973	1978
Agriculture	67.1	67.1	57.3	50.6	41.9	35.2
Industry[a]	15.7	17.8	16.3	17.7	20.6	22.4
Services	17.2	15.1	20.4	31.7	37.5	42.4

Note: The figures for 1973 are interpolated between 1963 and 1978—the census for 1973 contained a large proportion of unclassified activities.

a. Includes construction.

Source: Berry (1980b).

The National Labor Market

As the economy evolved, important corresponding changes took place in the structure of employment. Unlike the movements in sectoral output shares shown in table 2-5, however, which have been gradual over the past twenty-five years (and started even earlier), these changes have developed rapidly, particularly since the mid-1960s, as shown in the changing percentage shares of each sector (table 2-6). With the dramatic changes in the structure of the labor force occurring after World War II (especially after 1964), it is not surprising that urban unemployment, rural-urban migration, and the resulting explosion of urban population and unemployment were generally perceived as major problems in the late 1960s.

What could not have been foreseen was the great expansion of employment in all the main economic sectors during the 1970s (see table 2-7). In all sectors except agriculture, employment grew faster than output, producing labor-intensive expansion in the predominantly urban sectors—manufac-

Table 2-7. *Employment Change in Colombia, 1973–78*
(thousands of persons)

Sector	1973 (A)	1978 (B)	Absolute (B − A)	Percentage share in total change	Annual rate of change (percent a year)
Agriculture	2,305	2,629	324	16	2.7
Mining	68	69	1	0	0.0
Manufacturing	912	1,357	445	22	8.3
Construction	255	360	105	6	7.1
Services	2,124	3,249	1,125	56	8.9
Total	5,664	7,664	2,000	100	6.2

Source: World Bank (1984).

turing, construction, and tertiary (services)—and sharp increases in agricultural labor productivity. This is contrary to the conventional characterization of the development process, according to which the urban sectors are
capital using and agriculture is labor using. During the latter half of the
1970s, the continued expansion of urban jobs reduced unemployment to
unusually low levels, by developing-country standards.

The result has been a considerable tightening in the urban labor market,
as the following chapters show. Tables 2-8 and 2-9 show the dramatic expansion in employment in the late 1970s. Overall participation fell up to
about the mid-1970s because of the massive expansion in education, which
meant that more people were staying in school to complete secondary and
higher education. Meanwhile, the population growth rate declined considerably, but this had only a lagged effect on the labor force; thus the work
force continued to grow at a rapid rate of 3.4 percent in the second half of
the 1970s. The growth in overall employment reached 6.2 percent a year
between 1973 and 1978, and thus unemployment rates dropped sharply and
labor force participation in urban areas increased. The participation of housewives also increased, as is suggested from table 2-9, which shows labor use
in Colombia disaggregated by sex. The expansion of education has applied
equally to women. Again, what is notable is the jump in the proportion of
women employed in the latter half of the 1970s.

Measured rates of rural unemployment in Colombia have always been low,
but the general tightening of the labor market and falling urban unemploy-

Table 2-8. *Changes in Labor Use in Colombia, 1951–78*

Year or period	Total (thousands, age 15 and over)	Percentage of total			
		In school	Employed	Unemployed	Other
1951	6,910	2.4	54.1	1.7	41.8
1964	9,528	5.3	50.2	3.4	41.1
1973	12,449	9.4	45.5	5.4	39.7
1978	14,698	10.3	52.1	3.1	34.5
	Average annual rate of change (percent)				
1951–64	2.4	8.5	1.9	8.1	2.4
1964–73	3.0	7.8	1.9	8.4	2.6
1973–78	3.4	5.4	6.2	−7.7	0.5

Sources: Population censuses for 1951, 1964, 1973; 1978 DANE National Household Survey
(June); and World Bank (1984).

Table 2-9. *Sex Differences in Labor Use in Colombia, 1951–78*
(percentage of population over 15 years of age)

Year	School	Employed	Unemployed	Other	Total
			Male		
1951	2.9	90.5	2.8	3.8	100.0
1964	5.9	82.5	5.0	6.6	100.0
1973	10.4	74.3	6.5	8.8	100.0
1978	11.3	75.2	3.6	9.9	100.0
			Female		
1951	2.0	19.4	0.6	78.0	100.0
1964	4.7	19.0	1.3	75.0	100.0
1973	8.5	20.1	4.3	67.1	100.0
1978	9.4	29.1	2.7	58.9	100.0

Source: World Bank (1984), from DANE Census and Household Survey.

ment that occurred in the late 1970s are unusual for a developing country and deserve greater analysis than they have received (although more recent events have reversed these trends, at least for the time being).

Recent Colombian Urbanization: The Policy Environment

As noted earlier, the 1970s were special years in Colombian economic history. This must be understood before we can interpret the detailed findings reported here or assess the extent of their wider applicability. This section reviews some of the economic policies that contributed to the buoyancy of the 1970s and also reports on some demographic changes that helped to shape the economic environment.

Colombia's recorded periods of growth and stagnation are correlated with its terms of trade, especially the movement of world coffee prices. The years immediately after World War II saw the consolidation of the growth of the industrial sector that had begun during the war, aided by the availability of substantial foreign reserves. Consequently the demand for urban labor rose, and thus urbanization rates increased. Much of the new industry was based in Bogotá, which rapidly eclipsed Medellín as Colombia's prime manufacturing center. Then in 1956 the world coffee price fell sharply; it remained low until the mid-1960s, and per capita income remained almost constant. Migration to urban areas continued apace, however, at least in part because of *la violencia*[1] in rural Colombia (as argued by many, for example, Schultz

1. *La violencia* refers to the period of widespread violence in rural Colombia in the 1950s.

1969). Subsequently, urban unemployment rose and was perceived as perhaps the country's main economic problem along with inflation. It was also in the middle to late 1960s that people became aware of Colombia's highly skewed income distribution, as new data became available and more reliable estimates could be made. For example, Berry and Urrutia (1976) showed that wages had stagnated for at least thirty years until the mid-1960s and that income distribution had continuously worsened over that period. Such findings came as something of a surprise to many policymakers since Colombia, in comparison with other Latin American countries, had not previously been regarded as a highly unequal society.

The Lleras government (1966–70) introduced policy changes that helped to lay the foundation for some of the income and employment gains of the 1970s. There was a general opening up of the economy: a crawling peg exchange rate was adopted and export incentives introduced. The economy responded with better capacity utilization and a consequent doubling of noncoffee exports. The Pastrana government continued the export thrust, but also emphasized construction activities, including residential construction, as an engine of growth. This was a specific response to the burgeoning levels of urbanization and raised the share of construction jobs in total employment from 4.5 percent in 1964 to 5.5 percent in 1973. Much of this construction boom was concentrated in Bogotá and added to its growth tendencies and potential. (According to Lubell and McCallum 1978, as much as 90 percent of the funds went to Bogotá, Cali, and Medellín in the first two years.)

A significant component of policy in the late 1960s and early 1970s was intervention in financial markets. A new savings instrument was introduced that assured savers a real rate of return on their savings accounts through indexation. Thus, for the first time, small savers obtained a useful instrument for financial savings. The government also increasingly emphasized a pattern of public expenditures that helped the poor; expenditures on public health and education were promoted, whereas investments in infrastructure for energy and transport were relatively downgraded. The López administration (1974–78) deemphasized the strategy of support for construction and adopted an explicit urban deconcentration program in order to direct activities away from Bogotá in particular, but also from the three next largest cities—Cali, Medellín, and Barranquilla. Finally, a major tax reform was instituted to make the fiscal system more progressive. Other changes in the conduct of fiscal and monetary policy also promoted more labor-intensive industry.

During this period, world coffee prices shot up to unprecedented levels; along with unrecorded foreign exchange inflows related to the drug trade, this development caused a favorable balance of payments. As a result, the real exchange rate appreciated and noncoffee exports began to suffer; mean-

Table 2-10. *Fertility Rates, 1960–78*

Item	1960–64	1967–68	1973	1976	1978
Urban	6.0	4.6	3.6	3.5	2.9
Rural	7.9	7.4	6.7	6.3	6.1
Total	7.0	6.0	4.7	4.4	3.9

while, the large inflows probably accounted for the expansion of the tertiary sector documented earlier.

Because government policies did not discriminate against agriculture in the period after 1966, this sector experienced a sustained boom. The Turbay government (1978–82) followed essentially similar policies, but the external environment steadily worsened after 1980 and coffee prices fell, while the real exchange rate continued to appreciate. The economic situation deteriorated after 1982. The world debt crisis has had serious repercussions for Colombia, despite the prudent policies of successive governments, so that many of the gains made in the booming 1970s have been reversed (for example, unemployment has once more become very high).

Bogotá's economy has broadly evolved in line with that of the country, although its high share of the total urban population and its position as the capital city gave it more than its share of the employment boom of the 1970s; its unemployment rates, for example, were consistently below those of other cities. The constellation of policies that promoted exports since 1966 also seems to have promoted employment: by and large, export industries have been more labor-intensive than import-substituting ones.

One last important environmental feature is the drastic decline in fertility rates that took place in Colombia in the 1970s. The change was of such magnitude that it has been dubbed the demographic transition. The numbers speak for themselves (table 2-10).

Urban fertility rates have always been low, but they have been declining at a much faster rate than rural rates. With the rising urban population, the effect on the total rate has been dramatic. At least part of the fertility decline can be attributed to policy, if rising educational levels (because of education expenditures) and lower mortality rates (because of water, sanitation, and health expenditures) are taken to be causally linked to declining fertility rates. Female literacy and generally improved access to education (table 2-9) are likely to have been particularly important. Another consequence is the increased rate of female participation in the labor force—from about 23 percent to more than 27 percent in Bogotá (see chapter 7 for a detailed analysis of this issue). As other urban areas catch up with Bogotá, overall fertility rates can be expected to decline further, thus slowing the rate of growth of total and urban population alike.

Table 2A-1. *Population of the Thirty Largest Cities
and Metropolitan Areas in Colombia, 1951–73*
(population in thousands)

City (ranked by 1973 population)	1973 Population	Rank	1964 Population	Rank	1951 Population	Rank
Bogotá[a]	2,719	1	1,673	1	665	1
Medellín	1,441	2	948	2	398	2
Cali	926	3	633	3	246	4
Barranquilla	725	4	531	4	296	3
Bucaramanga	341	5	225	5	108	6
Cartagena	293	6	218	6	111	5
Cúcuta	220	7	114	10	70	10
Manizales	202	8	196	7	92	7
Pereira	202	9	179	8	90	8
Ibagué	176	10	125	11	54	11
Armenia	165	11	155	9	73	9
Palmira	140	12	107	12	54	11
Pasto	119	13	83	14	49	13
Buenaventura	116	14	70	17	35	16
Neiva	105	15	76	15	33	17
Santa Marta	102	16	89	13	37	14
Montería	90	17	71	16	24	23
Barrancabermeja	87	18	60	20	25	22
Tuluá	87	19	57	22	29	21
Valledupar	87	20	44	26	9	29
Villavicencio	83	21	45	25	17	27
Popayán	78	22	59	21	32	18
Buga	71	23	66	19	32	18
Cartago	69	24	56	23	31	20
Sincelejo	69	25	44	26	22	26
Girardot	59	26	67	18	36	15
Tunja	52	27	40	28	23	25
Sogamoso	51	28	35	29	14	28
Ciénaga	43	29	48	24	24	23
Duitama	37	30	32	30	8	30

Note: Metropolitan areas as defined in Departamento Nacional de Planeación, "Estimaciones de Población en Nivel Nacional, Departamental y de los 30 principales Centros Urbanos," Document GPRU-UER 002 (Bogotá, 1968; processed).

a. Adjusted data for Bogotá indicate a 1973 population of 2,849,000. No comparable adjusted data for the other cities are available, so the original published figure for Bogotá is used here for the sake of comparability.

Sources: Data for 1951 from Conroy (1976), table A1.4; for 1964 from "La Población en Colombia: Diagnóstico y Política," *Revista de Planeación y Desarrollo* 4 (December 1969): 19–81; and for 1973 from "Resultados Provisionales," XIV Censo Nacional de Población, *Boletín Mensual de Estadística* no. 279 (October 1974).

Table 2A-2. *Relative Intercensal Growth Rates*
of the Thirty Largest Cities in Colombia, 1951–73

City (ranked by 1973 population)	1964–73 Growth rate	Rank	1951–64 Growth rate	Rank	Ratio[a]
Bogotá	5.26	4	7.00	6	0.75
Medellín	4.53	7	6.58	9	0.68
Cali	4.12	10	7.19	5	0.57
Barranquilla	3.37	16	4.42	28	0.76
Bucaramanga	4.50	8	5.60	15	0.80
Cartagena	3.20	18	5.10	23	0.63
Cúcuta	4.36	9	5.60	15	0.78
Manizales	3.26	17	6.33	11	0.52
Pereira	1.31	26	5.25	19	0.25
Ibagué	3.70	14	6.33	11	0.25
Armenia	0.68	28	5.75	14	0.12
Palmira	2.90	20	5.11	22	0.56
Pasto	3.90	13	3.99	30	0.98
Buenaventura	5.47	3	5.25	19	1.04
Neiva	3.50	15	6.31	13	0.55
Santa Marta	1.48	25	6.67	8	0.22
Montería	2.57	22	8.28	3	0.31
Barrancabermeja	4.02	12	6.58	9	0.61
Tuluá	4.58	6	5.14	21	0.89
Valledupar	7.38	1	11.95	1	0.62
Villavicencio	6.63	2	7.37	4	0.90
Popayán	3.02	19	4.61	26	0.66
Buga	0.79	27	5.43	17	0.15
Cartago	2.26	23	4.43	27	0.51
Sincelejo	4.87	5	5.39	18	0.90
Girardot	− 1.38	30	4.74	25	—[b]
Tunja	2.84	21	4.28	29	0.66
Sogamoso	4.07	11	6.88	7	0.59
Ciénaga	− 0.90	29	5.10	23	—[b]
Duitama	1.57	24	10.75	2	0.14

Note: Growth rates are compound annual percentile rates.

a. The ratios of city growth rate during the last intercensal period to the growth rate during the earlier one are listed in this column. Ratios less than 1 indicate that a city's growth rate has slowed; ratios greater than 1 indicate an increase in growth rate.

b. Negative growth.

Source: Conroy (1976), table A1.5.

3

The Structure of Bogotá and Cali

Bogotá was founded in 1535 and Cali in 1538.[1] Bogotá has been a seat of government since 1717, originally for the Viceroyalty of Nueva Granada (which included modern Venezuela, Colombia, Panama, and Ecuador) and later for Colombia. Both cities have experienced remarkable growth rates for an extended period. Since the mid-1800s Bogotá's population has multiplied more than eightyfold and Cali's has increased fifty- to sixtyfold. More important, both cities have grown five- to sixfold since World War II (see table 3-1). In both cities, growth has been mainly concentrated in the past hundred years, after a somewhat somnolent prior record. This record is remarkable compared with some other cities in the developing countries. It outstrips that of Bombay, India, for example, which has grown only about tenfold over the past hundred years, but is close to that of Seoul and Pusan, the two largest cities in another rapidly urbanizing country, the Republic of Korea. Although growth in Bogotá and Cali has slowed since the 1950s and 1960s, the present structure and organization of these cities has been influenced by the rapid changes of that period. For both cities, the highest rate of population growth was recorded in the 1950s (table 3-1), at least partly because of the *violencia*.

To what extent growth rates will continue their present trend is difficult to predict. According to the Phase II Bogotá Urban Development Study (see Lubell and McCallum 1978, p. 30), the rate of growth for 1975–80 was forecast to have been 6.5 percent a year and was then expected to decline to 5.0 percent by 1990. This was a clear misreading of trends, since the 1964–73 rate had already fallen to 5.8 percent. Thus the forecast that Bogotá would have a population of 5.1 million by 1980 was excessive; the actual total was probably not much more than 4.0 million, our estimate based on the 1978 figures for population obtained from the dwelling unit counts done

1. Some of the information on Bogotá in this section is based on Lubell and McCallum (1978), chap. 2.

Table 3-1. *Population and Density in Bogotá and Cali, 1560–1978*

Year	Area (hectares)	Population (thousands)	Annual growth rate (percent)	Density (population per hectare)
		Bogotá		
1560	20	n.a.	n.a.	n.a.
1600	56	n.a.	n.a.	n.a.
1670	129	3	n.a.	23
1720[a]	n.a.	20	3.9	n.a.
1800[a]	n.a.	22	0.1	n.a.
1850	294	29	0.6	100
1886	610	64	2.2	105
1900	909	100	3.2	110
1928[b]	1,958	235	3.1	120
1938[b]	2,514	330	3.5	131
1951	n.a.	660	5.5	n.a.
1958	8,084	1,130	8.0	140
1964[b]	14,615	1,730	7.4	118
1973[b]	30,423	2,877	5.8	95
1978[c]	30,886	3,500	4.0	113
		Cali[d]		
1800	50[e]	6[f]	n.a.	120
1880	115[e]	14	1.1	127
1900	n.a.	24	2.5	n.a.
1918	n.a.	45	3.6	n.a.
1938[b]	400[e]	88	3.4	255
1951[b]	1,290[e]	284	9.0	187
1958	1,850[e]	428	6.0	231
1964[b]	9,100[g]	638	6.3	70
1973[b]	9,100[g]	930	4.2	103
1978	9,100[g]	1,100	3.4	121

n.a. Not available.

a. See Lubell and McCallum (1978), table 2.1.

b. Census estimates.

c. 1978 World Bank–DANE Household Survey. All others for Bogotá are from Wiesner (1980), table 1.

d. No data are available for Cali before 1800.

e. Planeación Municipal de Cali, *Plan General de Desarrollo de Cali y su Area Metropolitana, 1970–1985–2000.*

f. All Cali populations from Tabares (1979).

g. Area for Cali from Planeación Municipal de Cali (1980).

to update the sample frame for the City Study survey. Similarly, the General Development Plan for Cali projected an annual growth rate of about 5.7 percent for 1970–80 and a population of about 1.5 million by the end of that period. This was understandable, given Cali's high growth rates up to at least the 1964 census (the latest census available in 1970). In fact, Cali's rate of growth fell considerably in the 1970s and its population in 1980 was probably not more than 1.2 million. This experience illustrates the difficulty inherent in making city population projections. Unexpectedly, the urbanization problem in Colombia now is one of adaptation to slow urban growth after fifty years of extremely rapid expansion.

The data on area are probably more unreliable than other figures in table 3-1 because the area of a city is always defined somewhat arbitrarily, as the data for Cali suggest. City boundaries do, however, give some idea of the area that is regarded as belonging to a city at any given time. Despite the rapid growth of Bogotá's population, its average density has remained quite stable over the past century, with the peak occurring at the end of the 1950s, the decade of the most rapid growth. This record suggests that the juridical area of a city tends to follow its population growth, albeit with a lag. Its relatively constant average density implies that Bogotá has been decentralizing as it has grown, in the sense that the central parts of the city have housed a successively smaller proportion of the population. It would be interesting to see whether such a pattern holds for other cities since it would contradict the conventional wisdom that cities have become increasingly congested as their population has expanded (of course, this does not refer to traffic congestion). Cali's juridical area is more difficult to define and thus its density pattern is more erratic.

When compared with cities in other countries, Bogotá appears to fall somewhere between the most densely populated cities of India and the less densely populated cities of the United States (table 3-2). Such comparisons are difficult to make, however, because definitions vary as to what constitutes a city. The U.S. Census Bureau, for example, distinguishes between residents of the "central city" and the "metropolitan area," but Bogotá's population is difficult to split in this way. All the same, it is striking that, except for New York, even central cities in the United States are more sparsely settled than Bogotá (and Cali) as a whole. Interestingly, the "city proper" (as defined by Ingram and Carroll 1979) of Mexico City houses as many people as the whole of Bogotá but is twice as dense (however, Mexico City's overall population is about three times as large and its area six times as large). Although the data reported for São Paulo and Rio de Janeiro (table 3-2) are also for "city proper" (as used by Ingram and Carroll 1979), they appear to cover an area somewhere between "central city" and "metropolitan area" and indicate a density less than half that of Bogotá. Compared with the largest two cities

Table 3-2. *Characteristics of Bogotá and Some Other Large Cities*

City	Year	Population (thousands)	Area (thousands of hectares)	Density (population per hectare)	Employment (percentage of population)
Bogotá[a]	1973	2,877	30.4	95	32.4
Cali[b]	1973	930	9.1	103	32.3
North America[c]					
New York	1970	7,896	77.7	102	37.5
Los Angeles	1970	3,169	133.0	24	38.3
Chicago	1970	3,369	57.8	58	42.5
Philadelphia	1970	1,950	33.2	59	41.6
Detroit	1970	1,513	35.7	43	36.3
San Francisco	1970	1,077	25.6	42	41.6
South America[d]					
Mexico City	1970	2,903	13.8	211	n.a.
São Paulo	1970	5,979	149.0	40	n.a.
Rio de Janeiro	1970	4,252	117.0	36	n.a.
Buenos Aires	1970	2,972	20.0	149	n.a.
South Asia[e]					
Calcutta	1971	7,031	56.9	123	33.0
Bombay	1971	5,971	43.7	136	36.8
New Delhi	1971	3,647	45.0	81	30.6

n.a. Not available.

a. 1973 population census; City Study estimate.

b. Planeación Municipal de Cali.

c. See Bronitsky and others (1975). Data are for central cities.

d. Data are for "city proper" as defined by Ingram and Carroll (1979), not for metropolitan areas.

e. Misra (1978). Data are for metropolitan area.

of India (Calcutta and Bombay), Bogotá is much less dense and smaller, but is probably more similar to New Delhi. Thus Bogotá and Cali appear to be more compact than other cities of Latin America if comparable definitions are used, but other central cities might well be more densely populated than Bogotá.

As the data on area indicate, Bogotá's spatial growth has been as great as its population growth. The city was originally laid out in the traditional rectangular grid of streets and avenues with the Plaza Principal at the center. Until the early part of this century, the built-up area consisted of what is now the city center or central business district. For many years, Bogotá was primarily a commercial, political, and religious center, whereas Medellín was Colombia's industrial capital (it had more manufacturing employment than Bogotá until about fifteen years ago). Chapinero, to the north of Bogotá, was then an outlying suburb or village, but it slowly joined up with the city during the second quarter of this century (see Wiesner 1980 for more details on Bogotá's spatial growth). High- and middle-income residents began to move northward and lower- and lower-middle-income residents moved into the southern and western parts of the city (see Amato 1968). Then during the 1950s Chapinero began to replace the center of the city as the primary commercial area and Bogotá became elongated from north to south (it was bounded on the east by high mountains and in the west by valuable agricultural land as well as low-lying areas that discouraged development). It is only in the past fifteen or twenty years that the western areas have also become populated and the city has developed its present almost semicircular structure.

Cali, which is nestled in the base of the mountains on the west, has had a somewhat similar history. It began as the commercial, religious, and political center for the State of Valle del Cauca and until the early 1900s the built-up area was a compact settlement with a traditional rectangular grid of streets around the central plaza (Plaza Mayor). Before it expanded Cali was relatively small and socioeconomically well mixed. As it grew, however, the rich increasingly occupied the western part of the city and the poor the eastern areas. Like Bogotá, it developed to the north and to the south, but especially toward the south. Today the eastern part of the city consists of low-lying areas in which the poor settled during the 1950s and early 1960s. In the past thirty years Cali has filled out into a semicircular shape—almost a mirror image of Bogotá, though obviously smaller in size.

The spatial development of a city can be affected by both institutional and individual decisions, but it is often difficult to separate the two. Since this study gives importance to the spatial income pattern found in Bogotá and Cali, some of the main formal planning initiatives undertaken in Bogotá are of interest. The shape of the city was probably influenced most by Brunner (who organized a city planning department in 1935) and Le Corbusier in 1951. Many of the existing zoning and planning regulations can be attributed to Brunner. The northern part of the city was zoned for low-density residential development and the south for high-density development (see Amato 1968).[2] Le Corbusier's main contribution was the creation of an industrial zone to the west of the city; whether by accident or design, this effectively separated the poor south from the rich north.[3] As will be shown later, this pattern of somewhat segmented land use in Bogotá has become set, and the rich are

2. This is not to suggest that zoning regulations caused this pattern, but rather that the zoning is largely consistent with observed land use patterns.

3. See Kyu Sik Lee (1981a,b) for an analysis of industrial location in Bogotá.

continuing to move northward while the poor, though distributed throughout the city, are more concentrated in the extreme south.

The Economic and Demographic Structure

Like many cities of Latin America, Bogotá has more females than males because of the immigration of a large number of young women for domestic service. According to the World Bank–DANE survey of 1978 and data from censuses, this pattern has been evident since the early 1950s. If the 1978 data are accurate, the sex ratio has been starting to change in recent years:

	1951	1964	1973	1978
Percentage male	45.2	46.6	46.6	46.9
Percentage female	54.8	53.4	53.4	53.1

The age structure changed significantly between 1951 and 1964, was roughly constant up to 1973, and since then has again changed dramatically (table 3-3). The preponderance of children reflects rapid population growth rates. The decline in fertility has reduced this proportion considerably in recent years. These figures imply that the labor force is continuing to grow rapidly, even as the population growth rate declines. In addition, the persistently high proportion of children implies a lower overall participation rate in the labor force and a higher number of dependents per worker (see Mohan and Hartline 1984 for the poverty implications of Bogotá's age structure).

The male participation rate has been falling continuously since 1951 (see table 3-4), largely because a high proportion of the 15–29 age group is now

Table 3-3. *Age Structure of Bogotá's Population*
(percent)

Age group	1951	1964	1973	1978
0–14	34.8	42.1	41.4	32.2
15–24	24.1	21.0	21.7	26.4
25–34	16.8	15.3	16.1	16.4
35–44	11.4	9.8	9.5	10.9
45–54	6.9	6.1	5.8	7.2
55–64	3.6	3.5	3.3	3.8
65 +	2.4	2.2	2.2	3.1
All	100.0	100.0	100.0	100.0

Note: Percentages may not add to 100 because of rounding.
Sources: Data for 1978 from World Bank–DANE Household Survey; others from censuses.

Table 3-4. *Participation Rates in Bogotá, 1951–78*
(percent)

| | Male | | Female | |
Year	Aged 15–59	All	Aged 15–59	All
1951[a]	89.0	56.6	38.9	28.1
1964[a]	84.5	46.7	37.6	22.9
1970[b]	78.3	n.a.	47.3	n.a.
1973[a]	68.6[c]	47.7	32.8[c]	23.8
1978[b]	65.2[c]	47.5	33.5[c]	24.4

n.a. Not available.
a. Data for these years are from the respective population censuses.
b. From household surveys.
c. These rates are for all those over the age of 12.
Source: Except for 1978 figures, table is from Berry (1980b).

continuing in school and college. Interestingly, the growth rate for the 15–59 age group has increased somewhat during this period. A closer examination of age-specific rates reveals that the participation rate for the youngest age group, those between 15 and 20 years, fell from about 50 percent to about 33 percent but rose for almost all other age groups, except the oldest. (For more details on participation rates, see chapter 7.)

As for unemployment in Bogotá, it appears that the labor market there had tightened considerably since the early 1970s and that unemployment rates in the late 1970s were probably below those observed in North American cities in those years (table 3-5). In Medellín and Cali, however, the rates appear to have increased during this period (except for 1978). Women have

Table 3-5. *Unemployment Rates in Bogotá, Medellín, and Cali, 1964–78*
(percent)

| | Bogotá | | | | |
Year	Male	Female	Total	Medellín	Cali
1964	9.6	5.2	8.0	n.a.	n.a.
1970	10.4	16.7	13.0	5.9	12.4
1973	8.3	12.7	9.9	13.9	11.9
1977	6.3	8.5	7.2	13.7	11.9
1978[a]	4.7	4.3	4.5	5.5	n.a.

n.a. Not available.
Note: Number of unemployed in the labor force.
a. From 1978 World Bank–DANE Household Survey.
Source: Berry (1980b).

had higher rates of unemployment in these years, which may indicate their increasing desire to work; their participation rate might have been still higher if unemployment rates had not been so high.

The structure of employment in Bogotá has remained fairly stable since 1951, except that manufacturing has increased its share of employment somewhat (table 3-6). In comparison with noncapital cities elsewhere—for example, Calcutta, Bombay, and São Paulo—Bogotá has a larger proportion of employment in services, presumably because government sector employment is higher there. It also has a much lower proportion of people in manufacturing. All the cities listed in table 3-6 have more than 20 percent in manufacturing—except for Jakarta, which has a correspondingly higher proportion in commerce—and all but Calcutta and Bombay have more than 5 percent of their employment in construction. Overall, Bogotá and Cali seem to have evolved from largely administrative, religious, and commercial centers into well-balanced metropolitan areas, and their structure of employment is similar to that in other large cities. Cali has a higher proportion of employment in manufacturing and a lower one in the service sector than Bogotá; in neither case, however, is service employment overrepresented as it is in the two African cities in the sample.

Since data on the changing structure of output are typically available only at the state and national levels, it is not possible to compare Bogotá with other cities. At any rate, it appears that the structure of output in Bogotá did not change appreciably between 1960 and 1975 (table 3-7). There is some indication that the share of manufacturing may have decreased slightly, but the data are not reliable enough to warrant a firm conclusion. If, however, manufacturing output has indeed fallen while the sector's share of employment has increased, then perhaps manufacturing has become more labor-intensive over the years (as suggested in chapter 2). In any case, Bogotá is clearly a well-balanced city, in the sense that it is dominated by neither administrative nor manufacturing activities.

The Spatial Distribution of Population and Income

The primary spatial unit of analysis in this study is the "comuna" (see appendix A for a detailed description of the geocoding system used for Bogotá throughout the City Study). Maps 3-1 and 3-2 (see pp. 34–37) represent Bogotá and Cali according to the spatial schemes used. The smallest (two-digit) divisions shown are comunas. The size and population of these comunas vary significantly. In Bogotá, for example, the smallest comuna consists of 174 hectares and the largest is more than twenty times as large (3,680 hectares). Comuna populations also vary greatly—from about 23,000 to

Table 3-6. Structure of Employment in Selected Cities and Bogotá
(percent)

				SIC code					
City	Agriculture and mining 1,2	Manufacturing 3	Construction 5	Transport 7	Commerce 6	Utilities 4	Services 8,9	Other	Total
East Asia									
Seoul (1970)[a]	2.3	22.7	7.1	4.3	28.9	1.5	33.0	—	100.0
Kuala Lumpur (1970)[a]	7.0	20.5	6.0	6.6	17.6	1.4	35.5	5.3	100.0
Manila (1970)[a]	3.5	22.1	6.5	9.7	13.8	0.8	37.3	6.2	100.0
Jakarta (1971)[b]	4.1	9.6	7.4	11.4	29.2	0.7	37.5	—	100.0
South Asia									
Bombay (1971)[c]	0.8	43.9	0.4	8.3	18.5	0.9	27.3	—	100.0
Calcutta (1961)[d]	2.5	38.4	2.9	9.8	19.2	—	27.2	—	100.0
Africa									
Tunis (1972)[a]	1.8	18.9	5.9	6.0	17.5	1.4	39.2	9.3	100.0
Abidjan (1970)[a]	4.6	22.5	10.4	10.1	18.6	1.0	42.8	—	100.0
United States									
Small MLM (1960)[a]	7.1	25.1	6.0	3.9	28.4	1.4	28.8	3.1	100.0
Large MLM (1960)[a]	1.0	30.2	4.8	4.6	32.6	1.3	24.8	5.3	100.0

South America									
São Paulo (1970)[e]	1.9	44.2[i]	—	5.9	12.2	—	27.1	8.6	100.0
Cali (1978)[f]	1.6	28.6	5.8	6.2	24.3	0.6	32.9	—	100.0
Bogotá[g]									
1938	3.4	23.9	10.7	5.3	13.9	—	40.1	2.5	100.0
1951	3.1	23.8	8.5	6.2	11.6	0.5	38.3	8.0	100.0
1964	4.1	23.3	7.9	6.1	14.6	0.4	35.7	7.9	100.0
1973[h]	1.8	20.1	6.4	4.8	16.3	0.5	32.1	18.1	100.0
1978[f]	1.4	23.7	7.4	5.9	23.4	0.5	37.8	—	100.0

— Not applicable.

Note: sic = Standard Industrial Classification. mlm = Metropolitan labor market. Percentages may not add to 100 because of rounding.

a. Renaud (1982), table 3.3.

b. See Sethuraman (1976).

c. Harris (1978).

d. Lubell (1974).

e. Schaefer (1976).

f. 1978 World Bank–dane Household Survey.

g. 1951, 1964, and 1973 censuses.

h. Published data from dane. Note the high unclassified figure of 18.1 percent.

i. Includes construction.

Table 3-7. *The Changing Structure of Output in Bogotá, 1960–75*
(percent)

SIC code	Sector	1960	1965	1970	1975
1,2	Agriculture, fishery, mining	1.0	1.0	1.2	1.4
3	Manufacturing	24.1	22.9	21.6	21.8
5	Construction	5.8	5.3	7.4	7.1
6	Commerce	18.1	19.1	21.5	17.3
7	Transport and communica-tion	8.8	8.5	8.5	9.6
4	Utilities	1.4	1.4	1.5	1.6
8	Banking	5.8	6.1	6.6	8.7
8	Housing	12.9	12.7	11.8	11.6
9	Personal services	10.8	10.2	10.3	10.9
9	Government	11.3	12.9	9.6	9.8
Total		100.0	100.0	100.0	100.0
Total product (millions of 1970 Colombian pesos)		11,996	17,208	25,920	37,671

Source: Colombia (1977).

400,000 (see appendix tables D-3 and D-4 for more data on the spatial distribution of population and density in Bogotá).

Population distribution and densities in Bogotá can be better grasped from map 3-3 (pp. 38–39). As might be expected, the outskirts are sparsely populated and the center more dense. Three other features stand out: the south of the city is more densely populated than the north; the business center (comuna 31) is less dense than some of the immediately surrounding areas; and the densest comuna is more than ten times as dense as the least dense, but some of the outlying comunas are about as dense as some of the inner areas. This last feature is of considerable interest in that density functions are often used to summarize the structure of the populations in cities (as in the next section). It is generally believed that densities fall exponentially from the center toward the outskirts of the city. My disaggregated breakdown of the pattern for Bogotá shows that such a statement can be somewhat misleading when it comes to particulars, though still valid at a more general level. The high-density area is spread around both sides of the central business district and is roughly bounded by the Avenida Ciudad de Quito. Quite a large part of the city has uniformly high densities; those in the southern outskirts are higher than the mean. This result is consistent with the finding that overall densities in Bogotá are high even when compared

Table 3-8. *Growth of Population and Density in Bogotá, 1964–78*

Division	Area[a] (hectares)	Population, 1978 (thousands)	Annual average growth rate of population and density (percent)	
			1964–73	1973–78
Ring				
1	398	82	−1.8	2.4
2	1,357	280	−0.2	−0.3
3	2,575	426	3.2	3.4
4	5,960	923	5.7	0.7
5	14,329	1,592	14.6	6.3
6	5,804	189	37.6	13.8
All rings	30,423	3,492	7.2	3.9
Sector				
1	398	82	−1.8	2.4
2	4,357	696	5.8	7.1
3	5,313	859	8.3	2.8
4	1,914	250	7.1	−2.7
5	3,066	213	7.4	0.2
6	5,673	680	10.9	6.0
7	5,064	325	5.7	−1.9
8	4,638	388	7.1	14.5
All sectors	30,423	3,493	7.2	3.9

a. The 1973 area has been used for all the years in these tables.
Sources: 1964 and 1973 population censuses; and 1978 World Bank–DANE Household Survey.

with densities at the center of other cities. Density patterns are discussed further in the next section.

The comuna is too disaggregated a unit to give an overall view of population changes. The two natural ways of analyzing a city spatially are to divide it into concentric rings or into radial sectors. These divisions have been used throughout the City Study and are delineated for Bogotá and Cali in maps 3-1 and 3-2. Table 3-8 shows the growth of population and densities by ring and sector in Bogotá from 1964 to 1978. Both population size and density fell slightly in the center of the city during the period. The highest density was in the central business district (ring 1 and sector 1) in 1964, but ring 2 (about 1 to 3 kilometers from the center) became the densest in 1973, even though its population declined between the two census years. It is striking that ring 3 (between 3 and 6 kilometers) and ring 4 were similar in 1973 and 1978. The fastest growth occurred in rings 5 and 6. Indeed, ring 5 accommodated twice as much of the incremental population during those years as the rest of the city put together. As the next section shows, land

(*Text continues p. 40.*)

Map 3-1. *Bogotá: Ring and Sector Systems Based on 1973 Comunas*

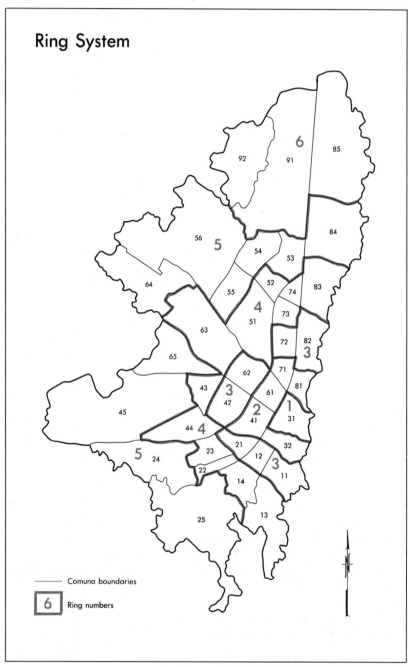

Ring System

Comuna boundaries

6 Ring numbers

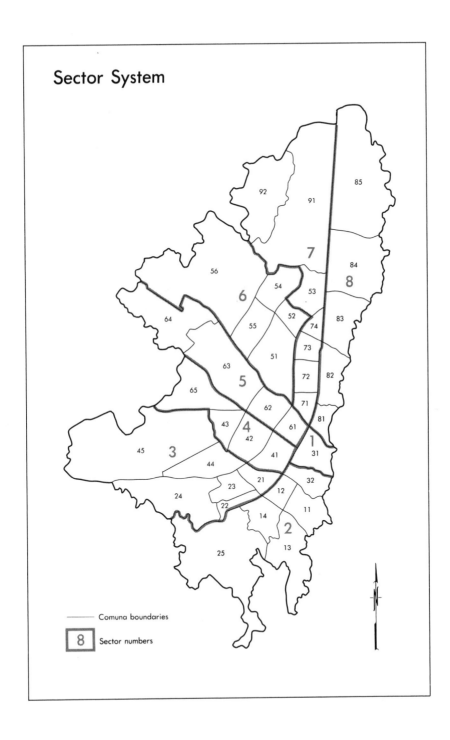

Sector System

Comuna boundaries

8 Sector numbers

Map 3-2. *Cali: Ring and Sector Systems*

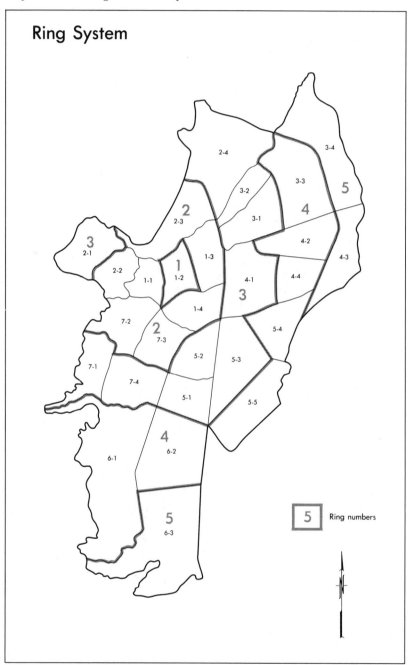

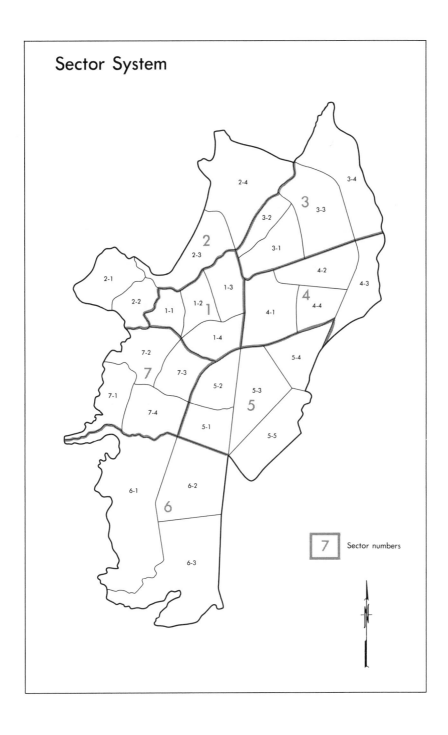

Sector System

2-4
3-4
3
3-3
3-2
2
3-1
2-3
4-2
2-1
4-3
1-3
4
2-2
1-2
4-4
1-1
1
4-1
1-4
7-2
5-4
7
7-3
5-2
5-3
7-1
5
7-4
5-1
5-5
6-1
6-2
6
6-3

7   Sector numbers

Map 3-3. *Bogotá: Population Density by Comuna*

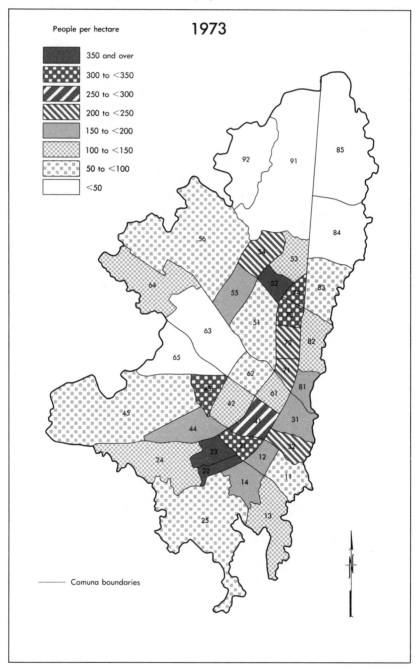

People per hectare

350 and over

300 to <350

250 to <300

200 to <250

150 to <200

100 to <150

50 to <100

<50

1973

——— Comuna boundaries

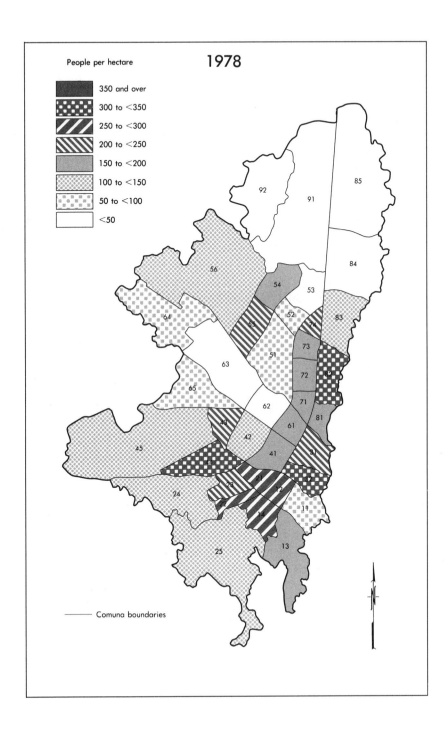

People per hectare

1978

350 and over
300 to <350
250 to <300
200 to <250
150 to <200
100 to <150
50 to <100
<50

——— Comuna boundaries

prices also increased the most in ring 5. Ring 6 was almost uninhabited in 1964. Thus population growth in Bogotá in recent years has been mainly in the outlying rings—partly as a result of decentralization of the population (because of an absolute decline of population in the two inner rings), but more because of incremental additions in the outskirts.

The bottom half of table 3-8 gives the same information for Bogotá's radial sectors. Sector 1, which is identical to ring 1, represents the central business district. The southern sectors (2, 3, 4) are almost twice as densely populated as the northern sectors (6, 7, 8). They have grown somewhat uniformly, except that sector 6 has grown faster than the others. This corroborates the earlier statement that the city had largely been a north-south strip stretching along the mountains until the early 1960s, and that the western part of the city has begun to develop only recently. Sectors 4 and 5 form the industrial corridor that le Corbusier initiated in 1951. Note that average densities in sectors 3 and 4 are very similar to those in rings 3 and 4. The northern part of sector 8 is even more sparse than the average.

The spatial distribution of incomes is investigated systematically in chapter 4; here I will simply establish its overall pattern. Again, analysis by comuna is far too disaggregated to obtain a useful picture, but the wide variations in income are apparent—that of the poorest comuna is only one-twelfth of the richest. Each comuna is relatively homogeneous within itself. The distribution of household income per capita (HINCAP) by comuna for 1973 and 1978 indicates that mean income varies across the city quite regularly, increasing clockwise from the south to the north (see map 3-4, pp. 42–43). There is little discernible pattern as one moves from the center to the periphery.

When household and income distributions are considered over rings and sectors of the city, only a faint pattern is discernible over the rings: although incomes first do rise somewhat and then decline as one moves from the center toward the periphery (see table 3-9). The differences are small, however, and the coefficients of variation are large, although ring 5 is poorer than the rest. In general, the proportion of households in a ring is not much different from its share of income—again, except in ring 5, which receives much lesss income than its share of households. Thus, the spatial distribution of incomes in Bogotá is quite different from that typically found in U.S. cities, for example, where income generally rises as one moves from the center to the periphery. The data from Bogotá partly support the view that the poor in cities in developing countries tend to be pushed out to the periphery.

Variations in income by spatial unit are more pronounced when viewed by sectors. The richest sector (8) has a mean HINCAP more than five times that of the poorest (2). Except for sector 6, which is relatively poor, income increases progressively as one moves from sector 2 to sector 8. The most heterogeneous zone is the central business district, which has a very high coefficient of variation. (Note also from table 3-9 and 3-10 that the intraring and intrasector variation is significantly less in the 1978 sample.) The share of income received by the poor sectors is much smaller than their share of households. The ranking of the sectors does not change between 1973 and 1978.

Thus a spatial analysis of Bogotá by radial sectors appears to produce more interesting variations than one by rings, although the rings do exhibit some interesting characteristics. Most notably, household size increases as one proceeds from the center to the periphery:

Ring	Household size (1978)	Ring	Household size (1978)
1	3.83	4	4.68
2	3.94	5	5.28
3	4.47	6	4.92
		Average	4.80

Larger households require greater space and hence are more likely to be located away from the center. Furthermore, the higher total incomes typically earned by larger households are still insufficient to offset the increase in household size (see table 3-11). Thus household income per capita falls with increasing household size. The periphery of Bogotá therefore contains households that are both larger and poorer in per capita terms.

The Changing Structure of Population Densities and Urban Land Values

Consider now the consequences of the recent rapid growth for population densities and land values in Bogotá and Cali (see table 3-10 for data on changing population densities by ring in both cities from 1964 to 1978). As mentioned earlier, both cities are semicircular in shape since the mountains constrain growth on one-half of the circle. Thus each ring is semicircular, too. The maximum distance from the city center (ring 1) to the periphery is about 15 kilometers in Bogotá (to ring 6), and about 10 kilometers in Cali (to ring 5). The two cities are strikingly similar in structure and growth patterns. In both cases, population density in the central business district has tended to decline from about 200 persons per hectare. As the cities have grown in population, settlement has occurred on the fringes of the existing cities, with concurrent densification of the inner rings (except for the central business district). This process is somewhat different from the growth pattern observed in most U.S. cities earlier in this century. Bogotá and Cali have decentralized with growth in the sense that a smaller proportion of the total population now lives in any central area of constant radius (while absolute population may have increased in that area). In contrast, the population in the central cities of the United States has actually declined substantially.

Map 3-4. *Bogotá: Mean Household Income Per Capita by Comuna*

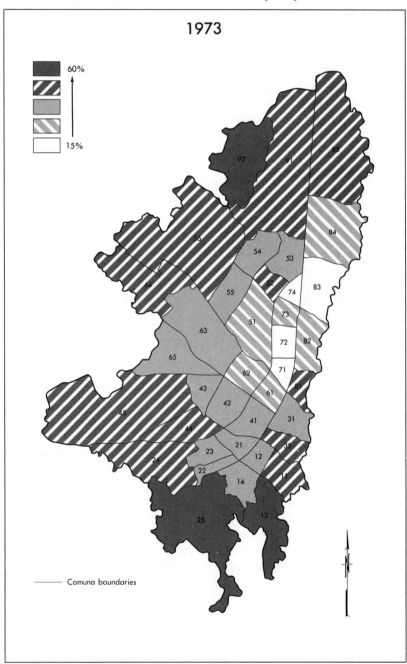

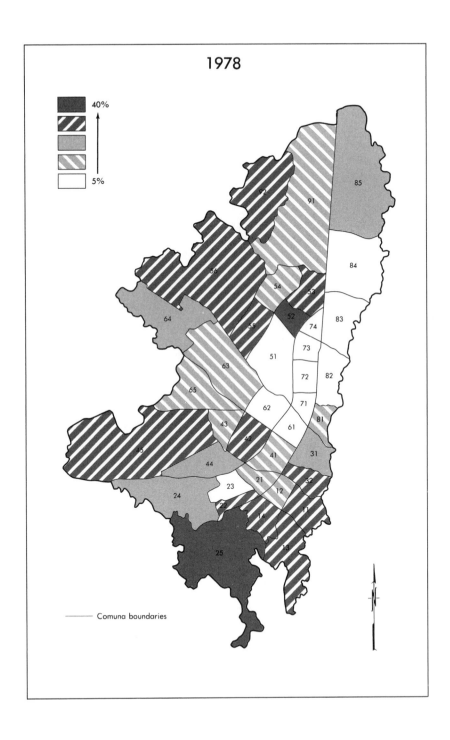

Table 3-9. *Spatial Distribution of Population and Monthly Income in Bogotá, 1973 and 1978*

Division	1973				1978			
	Mean household income (1973 pesos)	Mean household income per capita (1973 pesos)	Share of households (percent)	Share of income (percent)	Mean household income (1978 pesos)	Mean household income per capita (1978 pesos)	Share of households (percent)	Share of income (percent)
Ring								
1	2,114 (2.10)	884	3.5	2.6	8,343 (1.03)	2,490	3.0	1.8
2	2,976 (1.92)	1,016	10.8	11.5	16,047 (1.04)	5,570	9.8	11.4
3	3,722 (1.59)	1,073	12.7	16.9	19,928 (0.93)	5,913	13.1	19.0
4	3,046 (1.94)	788	30.7	33.5	14,772 (1.40)	4,105	27.2	29.1
5	2,264 (1.86)	533	39.1	31.7	10,818 (1.10)	2,277	41.6	32.6
6	3,202 (1.93)	753	3.3	3.8	15,999 (1.26)	3,178	5.3	6.1
All rings	2,791	751	100.0	100.0	13,805	3,629	100.0	100.0

Sector								
1	2,114 (2.11)	884	3.5	2.6	8,343 (1.03)	2,490	3.0	1.8
2	1,583 (1.44)	414	18.1	10.2	6,833 (0.52)	1,585	19.9	9.9
3	2,002 (1.41)	484	24.4	17.5	9,930 (0.86)	2,234	24.6	17.1
4	2,347 (1.68)	646	9.8	8.2	12,843 (0.88)	2,800	7.2	6.4
5	2,453 (1.68)	700	7.7	6.8	13,893 (1.04)	3,067	6.1	6.0
6	2,349 (1.66)	5,561	17.0	14.3	12,801 (0.98)	2,744	19.5	16.3
7	45,791 (1.61)	1,265	12.6	20.6	16,163 (1.07)	3,750	9.3	11.6
8	7,895 (1.50)	2,258	7.0	19.7	32,804 (0.90)	11,354	11.1	31.0
All sectors	2,791 (1.89)	751	100.0	100.0	13,805 (1.22)	3,629	100.0	100.0

Note: Coefficient of variations in parentheses. Percentages may not add to 100 because of rounding.
Sources: 1973 population census sample; and 1978 World Bank–DANE Household Survey.

Table 3-10. *Evolution of Population Density by Ring,*
Bogotá and Cali, 1964–78
(persons per hectare)

	Bogotá				Cali			
	Area	Density			Area	Density		
	(hundreds				(hundreds of			
Ring	of hectares)	1964	1973	1978	hectares)	1964	1973	1978
1[a]	5	220	180	205	1.4	210	150	160
2	15	210	210	220	15	140	125	135
3	25	100	140	140	30	95	135	160
4	60	90	150	155	30	25	70	100
5	140	25	80	110	15	25	50	70
6	60	1	17	32				
All rings	305	50[b]	95	115	91	70[b]	103	121

Note: All figures are rounded.

a. Central business district.

b. City area has been kept constant for all these calculations. In fact, both cities have grown during the period covered and many peripheral areas included here were outside the city boundaries in 1964.

Sources: Data for Bogotá are from 1964 and 1973 population census; and 1978 World Bank–DANE Household Survey. Data for Cali are from Tabares (1979).

What has happened to land values during the same period? Good land value data are notoriously difficult to obtain, in part because the value of land is difficult to separate from that of the structures built on it, and most land transactions observed in cities are of plots with buildings on them. We were fortunate in obtaining from the files of the long-established real estate firm of Wiesner and Cia Ltd. a unique set of data consisting of about 6,000 transactions in Bogotá between 1955 and 1978. Guillermo Wiesner had kept meticulous records for almost forty years because of his own interest in land valuation. We were able to choose the vacant land transactions only and therefore did not have to separate land values from built-up property values. Naturally, there are more transactions near the city center in earlier years and fewer in later years, while the converse is true for the outer rings. The overall quality of the data is high, but land values in the central business district may possibly be on the low side for later years.[4]

The data for Cali were obtained from the Cali Municipal Planning Office. The overall patterns are summarized in table 3-12, which gives land price

4. See Mohan and Villamizar 1982; Villamizar 1981; and Wagner 1984. The quality of the Cali data is probably less uniform since the methods of collection were different in different years. The planning office has kept files on land value averages for each barrio, or neighborhood. In 1964 there were 84 such observations and in 1978–79 about 170.

Table 3-11. *Distribution of Households by Household Size in Bogotá, 1973 and 1978*
(income in current Colombian pesos)

Household size	1973			1978		
	Percentage of households	Mean household income	Mean household income per capita	Percentage of households	Mean household income	Mean household income per capita
1	10.7	1,372	1,372	5.3	10,432	10,432
2	13.9	1,927	964	10.6	13,518	6,759
3–4	32.4	2,508	723	34.4	11,397	3,236
5–6	23.3	3,261	602	29.4	15,521	2,866
7–9	15.9	3,858	503	16.0	16,075	2,111
10–25	4.0	4,925	435	4.4	17,708	1,560
Total	100.0	2,791	751	100.0	13,805	3,629

Note: Percentages may not add to 100 because of rounding.
Sources: 1973 population census sample; and 1978 World Bank–DANE Household Survey.

data by ring for Bogotá and Cali from 1964 to 1978. The prices are given in constant 1978 Colombian pesos; earlier nominal values have been converted to 1978 prices by using the consumer price index. Overall land prices near the center have been relatively stagnant, whereas prices have increased more markedly near the periphery. This is consistent with the evolving density patterns described earlier. There are some surprises, however: land prices in the center of Bogotá have not risen appreciably in real terms, but have lagged behind the consumer price index in rings 1 to 3, and have been ahead of it in rings 4, 5, and 6.

The picture for Cali is broadly similar, but some differences exist. First, it is interesting to note that Cali land prices are as high as those in Bogotá. Central business district prices and their growth rates seem higher in Cali than in Bogotá, and despite problems with the data, we can conjecture that at least prices are unlikely to be lower than in Bogotá.[5] That land prices have reached similar levels in the two cities is consistent with the fact that their densities are also similar. Mills and Song (1979) found that in Korea the growth in land values in the three largest cities was less than in the next nine largest, and thus argued that the growth of land values need not be higher in larger cities.

Our main findings in this regard may be summarized as follows: (1) land values and population densities decline away from the city center in Bogotá

5. Note that the data for Bogotá for the last period are an average for 1975–77, and those for Cali are from 1979. If it is true, as some believe, that there was an inflationary spurt in land values in the late 1970s, absolute values in Bogotá would not be less than those in Cali.

Table 3-12. *Evolution of Land Values in Bogotá and Cali, 1964–78*
(1978 Colombian pesos per square meter)

		Bogotá					Cali			
Ring	Average distance from center (kilometers)	1963–65	1972–74	1975–77	Annual growth rate 1964–78 (percent)	Average distance from center (kilometers)	1963	1974	1979	Annual growth rate 1963–79 (percent)
1	0	4,250	3,900	3,100	−2.3	0	5,900	4,600	6,400	0.6
2	2.2	1,850	1,660	1,550	−1.3	1.8	1,100	1,100	2,400	5.6
3	3.8	1,350	1,350	1,320	−0.2	3.4	520	480	1,030	4.9
4	6.5	870	1,080	1,130	1.9	5.4	380	410	960	6.6
5	9.8	570	800	850	2.9	6.9	150	370	810	12.0
6	15.4	370	700	730	4.9					

Note: 1978 exchange rate US$1 = 38.00 pesos.
Sources: Data for Bogotá calculated from Villamizar (1981); data for Cali from Velasco and Mier (1980).

48

and Cali; (2) land values and densities increase throughout the two cities along with urban growth—but proportionately less so in the center (the rotation of the land value surfaces is measured below); and (3) Bogotá and Cali have rising average land values—in Bogotá they have grown at about 3 to 4 percent a year in real terms since 1955. To conclude, although average land values should be interpreted with some caution, it can be said with confidence that land prices have increased in real terms on the periphery, but at best have remained constant in the center.

Changes in land value and density patterns can be measured more systematically by measuring changes in densities and land value gradients. The patterns may be expressed in simple exponential equations:

(3-1) $$D_x = D_0 \, e^{-gx}$$

and

(3-2) $$V_x = V_0 \, e^{-hx}$$

where D_x is the population density at x kilometers from the center, V_x is the land value at x kilometers, and D_0, V_0, g, and h are the parameters to be estimated from the data. In fact, D_0 and V_0 estimate the density and land value at the center (when $x = 0$, $D_x = D_0$, $V_x = V_0$); and g and h estimate the two gradients, which can be interpreted as the percentage decrease in density and land values, respectively, per kilometer (tables 3-13 and 3-14).

First, consider the density gradients for Bogotá and Cali for 1964, 1973, and 1978 (table 3-13). The unit of observation is the barrio, or neighborhood. As expected, g declines over time for both cities and is higher for Cali than for Bogotá. For purposes of comparison, in 1970 g was -0.08 for New York, about -0.13 for Atlanta, -0.22 for Seoul, -0.17 for Mexico City, -0.12 for Buenos Aires, and -0.08 for Tokyo. (Data on South American cities are from Ingram and Carroll 1980; others from Mills and Tan 1980. See also Mills and Ohta 1976 for data on Japanese cities.) Thus Bogotá's gradient is similar to that of other large cities. Among smaller cities such as Cali, we have information on Monterrey (-0.27) and Guadalajara (-0.41), Mexico; Belo Horizonte (-0.27) and Recife (-0.17), Brazil; Sapporo (-0.23), Japan; and Pusan ($-.13$), Korea, all of which suggests that Cali is not atypical. In general, the larger the city, the higher the income; and the lower the transportation costs (Mills and Tan 1980), the lower g will be. This also implies that g depends on the age of the city (Harrison and Kain 1974). Older cities were built when intracity transportation costs were high and therefore had very dense central areas. Consequently, they had very high land values in the center, and this pattern tended to persist over time. It follows that the fast-growing cities in Latin America would have relatively flatter density gradients.

Table 3-13. *Population Density Patterns in Bogotá and Cali, 1964–78*

City and year	Population (thousands)	Density (D_0) at central business district (thousands per square kilometer)			g^d	R^2	N^e
		Actual[a]	Estimate[b]	Estimate[c]			
Bogotá							
1964	1,730	22	23	20	−0.18	0.12	292
1973	2,878	18	27	10	−0.15	0.22	453
1978	3,500	17	24	10	−0.12	0.19	465
Cali							
1964	640	21	39	17	−0.51	0.21	131
1973	930	16	24	11	−0.44	0.09	195
1978	1,100	16	29	11	−0.25	0.11	193

a. Residential population density for central business district.

b. Equation estimated was $D_x = D_0 e^{-gx}$ where D_x is population density in people per square kilometer at distance x in kilometers, and D_0 is estimated population density at central business district.

c. Estimate of D_0 from $D_x = D_0 e^{(g_1 x + g_2 x^2)}$ (other results not reported here).

d. g is the density gradient, the percentage decrease in density per kilometer; all estimates significant at the 1 percent level.

e. Number of data points in regressions.

Sources: Bogotá barrio population data from City Study files; Cali barrio population data from Tabares (1979).

Now observe the estimates for D_0—the hypothetical density at the center of the city (see table 3-13). Note that central densities have remained relatively constant, except for a small decline, a phenomenon at least consistent with the behavior of land values in Bogotá. The estimated values are consistently higher. The central business district contains a large proportion of commercial economic activity and a relatively small residential population. Therefore estimated D_0 can be expected to be higher than the actual values. Now consider comparable land value patterns for Bogotá and Cali (see table 3-14). Once again, as expected, the estimates for land value gradients decline with time in both cities, and those for Cali are steeper than those for Bogotá. Their similarity to the density gradients is remarkable, as the following figures show:

	Bogotá		Cali	
	Land value	Density	Land value	Density
1964	−0.15	−0.18	−0.51	−0.51
1973	−0.08	−0.15	−0.25	−0.44
1978	−0.07	−0.12	−0.23	−0.25

Figure 3-1 graphically illustrates these similarities.

Table 3-14. *Land Value Patterns in Bogotá and Cali*
(prices in 1978 Colombian pesos per square meter and distances in kilometers)

City and year	Population (thousands)	Price (V_0) at central business district Actual[a]	Estimate[b]	Estimate[c]	h[d]	R^2	N[e]
Bogotá							
1959	n.a.	6,300	2,400	n.a.	−0.18	0.56	38
1964	1,730	5,600	2,500	2,470	−0.16	0.55	38
1973	2,878	5,500	1,900	2,290	−0.08	0.39	38
1977	3,500	4,300	1,760	2,240	−0.07	0.35	38
Cali							
1959	n.a.	5,000	2,240	n.a.	−0.55	0.44	n.a.
1964	640	5,000	2,030	4,700	−0.51	0.41	84
1974	940	3,700	1,030	2,130	−0.25	0.30	155
1979	1,100	5,300	2,070	4,950	−0.23	0.27	171

n.a. Not available

Note: Equation run was $V_x = V_0 e^{-hx}$, where V_x is price at distance x, and V_0 is estimated price at the central business district.

a. Approximate average for central business district. Highest observed values are about three times these values.

b. Estimate of V_0 from above equation.

c. Estimate of V_0 from $V_x = V_0 e^{(h_1 x + h_2 x^2)}$ (other results not reported here).

d. h is the land value gradient, which can be interpreted as the percentage decrease in land value per kilometer; all estimates significant at the 1 percent level.

e. Number of data points in regressions.

Sources: Population from table 3-1; Bogotá estimates from Villamizar (1980); Cali estimates based on Velasco and Mier (1980).

According to standard urban economic theory, the pattern of land value gradients might be expected to be similar to density gradients. The former are in fact consistently lower than the latter. Mills and Song (1979) found similar patterns in Korea. A comparison of estimated V_0 (land value at the center of the city) with actual V_0 reveals that my estimates are consistently lower than the actual values. This implies that the gradient of the curve should in fact be much steeper at the center of the city than has been estimated. Because of the high concentration of economic activity at the center, land values are probably determined much more by employment density than by residential density. Since the former falls rapidly from the center, it is quite plausible that land values will exhibit a similar decline. Estimated V_0 is therefore likely to be lower than this central peak, with the result that the land value and population density functions need to be slightly revised. The estimated densities were found to be consistently higher for the central business district than the actual ones, whereas land values were consistently lower. Indeed, we would expect residential densities to increase

Figure 3-1. *The Changing Urban Structure of Bogotá and Cali,*
1964–78

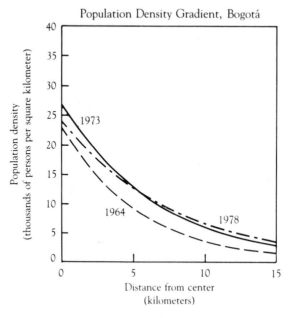

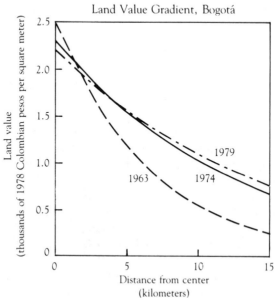

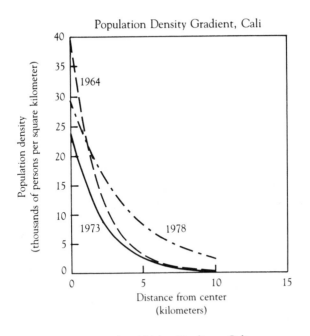

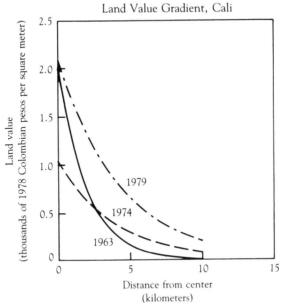

Source: Tables 3-13 and 3-14.

somewhat from the central business district and then to fall, while land values should fall rapidly from the city center, but then should slow down. Thus land price reflects the intensity of demand for land at a particular location. Residential and employment densities are merely imperfect proxies for demand, but they are usually easy to measure and help to explain the land value patterns in cities.

Both population density and land value gradients have flattened, but it would be premature to conclude that these cities have decentralized in the sense that their central areas have actually lost population. Among large European cities, decentralization has been taking place for a long time: the population of central London reached its peak in 1930–40, that of Paris in 1920, that of Vienna in 1910, and those of Rotterdam, Zurich, Hamburg, Glasgow, and Amsterdam in 1950–60 (see Mitchell 1978, p. 12). All have declined since those dates, but suburban populations have risen. To explain these changes, we need a better understanding of the processes that bring people together to improve economic opportunities for themselves and thereby impart higher values to land. With the low transport costs (despite the energy crisis) and changing manufacturing technology, there is reason to believe that more and more manufacturing jobs are locating in peripheral locations (Lee 1981a,b). The volume of these jobs is not yet large enough to affect the commercial primacy of the city center, but greater movement of commerce and service jobs along with manufacturing ones can be expected in the future, together with obvious improvements in the access characteristics of peripheral locations.

Summary

Bogotá has experienced a remarkably long period of unbroken and rapid expansion, with population increasing eightyfold over the past hundred years and an astonishingly high sustained growth rate of almost 5 percent a year over the last forty years. Despite this expansion, the average population density of the city has remained surprisingly constant. Compared with other cities, Bogotá is relatively densely inhabited (though less so than some Asian cities).

The demographic structure of the city is much like that of other Latin American cities: it has high proportions of women and of children under 15 years of age, the latter comprising more than 40 percent of the population. As a result of increasing female participation rates and the predominance of young people in the age structure, the city's labor force can be expected to continue to expand rapidly, even after population growth slows down. Despite the expansion in the labor force, unemployment fell to what might be called internationally acceptable rates during most of the 1970s. The city now has a balanced economic structure, which is not dominated by manufacturing, services, or administration, as it is in some other large cities in the world. As Jacobs (1961) has persuasively argued, such a balanced and diversified economic structure is important for the sustained stability and growth of cities.

The population has expanded most in the outer rings. In contrast, the inner rings have had a relatively stable population—unlike the central cities of North America, which have tended to lose population as they have become decentralized. As a result, densities are now high throughout Bogotá except in the outermost rings, but the south of the city is much more densely inhabited than the north. A detailed examination of income levels reveals no strong pattern by rings, although income tends to rise as one first moves away from the center, and then to fall again. Household size, however, does increase monotonically with distance from the city center. Furthermore, average household income increases as one moves clockwise from the south to the north, except that one sector in the northwestern part is poor. Population density is lower in rich areas than in poor ones.

The density and land value patterns in the city conform broadly to theory, in that an exponential decline is observed from the city center toward the periphery. However, the rate of decline in densities varies greatly in different parts of the city, although density is uniformly high in the south, where most of the poor live. These patterns are similar for Cali, except that it is a mirror image of Bogotá, and the rich live in the south.

The extreme differences in income among the sectors in the city are analyzed in greater detail and more systematically in the following chapters, which are concerned with inequality and poverty and their spatial components.

4

The Distribution of Income

As noted earlier, one of the main objectives of this book is to improve our understanding of how urban incomes are determined in the context of dynamic economic and population growth. Thus, trends in income distribution in Bogotá and Cali between 1973 and 1978—a period that well exemplifies the above kinds of growth—are of particular interest. The first part of this chapter tries to answer two broad questions: Historically, how unequally has income been distributed in Bogotá and Cali? and how, if at all, did this distribution change under the boom conditions of the mid- to late 1970s?

Like the overall City Study, this book is especially concerned with the evolution of urban structure along with overall economic development. This emphasis has led me to examine the spatial aspects of income distribution in Bogotá and Cali. It has already been suggested that striking patterns of income inequality are discernible among the geographical zones in both cities; in the second part of this chapter, I examine these patterns in some detail and address a number of conceptual and measurement issues: How does one measure spatial inequalities in urban labor incomes? What is the extent of these inequalities in Bogotá and Cali? Has spatial inequality grown or shrunk over the study period? In attempting to answer these questions, I undertake a systematic decomposition of spatial inequality in the two cities, developing indices that in turn provide a way of assessing spatial income inequality in most urban areas—a topic on which little information is currently available in the literature on urban economics.

In this study, I was fortunate to have access to sets of micro data for four years from 1973 to 1978, and thus was able to estimate inequality indices for this entire period. As a result of this unusual situation, the comparisons between years give a sense of the robustness of the estimates derived. Although it is important to avoid over-interpreting small changes in the indices derived from different surveys, some comparisons have been made between the estimates for 1973–78 and those available for earlier years.

Most income distribution studies use grouped data to calculate inequality

56

indices. Sometimes, only published data are available that typically give information about the distribution of population by specific income groups, and there is no choice but to use such grouped data. Even when micro data are available, computation is usually done after the data are grouped because of the expense involved in making direct calculations from the micro information (see, for example, Altimir 1977, and Altimir and Piñera 1977). A similar procedure is used here, but the computer program EQUALISE (available in Mohan 1984), uses micro data as direct input and permits any level of disaggregation desired for the computation of inequality indices. An extension of the same program is used to decompose inequality.[1]

Methodology

Inequality indices have been computed for both household income (HHY) and household income per capita (HINCAP), and later for earned incomes. The concepts and methodology used are laid out below; subsequent sections present the findings.

Income Concepts and Population Units Used

Appendix A briefly describes the sources of data used in this study. All incomes are current monthly incomes derived from the surveys described in the appendix; caution therefore needs to be exercised in interpreting them as measures of welfare. Household consumption expenditures are usually considered better proxies for permanent income (and hence for welfare levels of households and individuals) than monthly money incomes. There was little choice in this matter, however, since no recent surveys of consumption in Colombia were available.

A further problem arises in computing inequality on the basis of current monthly household income (HHY) or household income per capita (HINCAP). The differential incidence of taxes on different incomes under a specific taxation system is not accounted for, nor is any consideration given to the differential accrual to different income groups of the benefits that flow from public expenditures on services such as health, education, sanitation, and water. It has not been possible to account for these adjustments in this study, owing to the lack of data. (see Selowsky 1979 for explicit consideration of these adjustments in the computation of inequality in Colombia). Although somewhat different income questions were asked in the four data sources—

1. Parts of the program were originally developed by Sherman Robinson (1976) and Sudhir Anand (1983) in earlier studies of income distribution for the World Bank.

the 1973 census, the 1975 and 1977 DANE household surveys, and the 1978 World Bank–DANE Household Survey (see appendix A)—the basic income concepts used here are monthly household income[2] and monthly household income per capita. HINCAP is merely the HHY divided by household size (HHSIZE). In principle, HHY covers the labor earnings of all members of the household, including earnings in kind and nonlabor income. (Estimates of earnings in kind do not extend to imputation of earnings for household work.) The coverage of labor earnings in all the surveys is much better than the coverage of nonlabor income. The 1978 survey included detailed questions on specific categories of nonlabor income, but I suspect that the coverage was still less than desirable. HHY does not include imputed income from housing for owner-occupied households.

All households with zero incomes were excluded in the computation of income inequality, as were other households with miscoded location. The term "workers" was taken to mean individuals who indicated that their primary activity is working and those who worked at least fifteen hours a week; the households with zero incomes were essentially those whose members happened to be unemployed. As noted in appendix B, income was systematically imputed to workers who were employed but who did not give information on their incomes.

Studies of inequality must choose the *population unit* as well as the *income concept* by which data are to be ranked in order to derive income distributions. The most common practice is to rank households by household income, but this approach has been increasingly criticized in recent works (for example, Anand 1983; Datta and Meerman 1980) for not providing a good indication of differences in living standards. As Anand argues, our general concern should be with the welfare of *individuals* rather than of households. Second, households vary in size as well as in the age and sex of their members, and therefore comparisons between households should account for these variables. Some studies that have measured poverty on the basis of nutrition levels have attempted to make such adjustments by deriving "adult equivalent" measures of consumption. Although it may be possible to develop adult equivalent norms for food consumption on the basis of age and sex, this is hard to do for consumption as a whole. For example, a child may well require less nutrition than an adult, but expenditures on his or her education and health exceed those for adults. In view of this difficulty, I have adopted the "next best" strategy of using HINCAP (household income adjusted for house-

---

2. Households are defined as commensal units in these censuses and surveys. Although live-in domestic servants are enumerated with and counted as members of their employing households, the computation of household income and household income per capita excludes them.

hold size) to rank households and individuals for welfare comparisons. This approach is certainly better than using HHY, even though economies of scale in consumption are also ignored in the computation of HINCAP. It is implicitly assumed that the distribution of welfare within the household is even— although some might argue that this is usually not the case. In any event, there is no information with which to make any other assumption.

Although I am mainly interested in individual welfare, the basic income concept from which HINCAP is derived is HHY. There is no other option, since the household is the basic unit within which consumption allocations are typically made. Furthermore, nonlabor income usually accrues to the household rather than the individual. As a result, the analysis here is concerned with the following distributions: (1) households ranked by household income, (2) households ranked by household income per capita, and (3) individuals ranked by household income per capita. (The distribution of workers ranked by labor income, which includes income in kind, is taken up in chapter 9.)

Measures of Income Inequality

Various inequality measures have been used in this study. Those displayed in the tables are the Gini coefficient, the Theil inequality index, the standard deviation of logarithms, the Atkinson index, and the coefficient of variation. The Gini coefficient, the standard deviation of logs, and the coefficient of variation are widely used and need no explanation here. Although the Theil (1967, 1972) and Atkinson (1970) measures are now well known, they are still not widely used in computing inequality. (These last two measures are briefly explained in the appendix to this chapter; for a detailed account of all the measures listed above, see Anand 1983.)

Two properties of inequality measures that are regarded as important and desirable are

1. They should be mean-independent (that is, their value should remain unchanged if everyone's income is increased by the same proportion).
2. They should satisfy the Pigou-Dalton condition, which requires that any transfer from a richer to a poorer person (that does not change their relative ranks) should be reflected in a reduction of the inequality index.

The Gini coefficient satisfies these two conditions, as does the coefficient of variation (the square root of variance divided by the mean). Although the variance of incomes, which would be an obvious measure of the inequality in a distribution, satisfies the Pigou-Dalton condition, it is not mean-independent. The log variance of income does, however, satisfy both these conditions:

$$\text{Var}(y) = \frac{1}{n} \sum_{i=1}^{n} (y_i - \mu)^2$$

hence $\text{Var}(\lambda y) = \lambda^2 \text{Var}(y)$

but $\text{Var}(\lambda y) = \text{Var}(\log y)$

where y_i is income of unit i, μ is the mean, and λ is the proportionate change in all incomes. The log variance of incomes is therefore a convenient measure to use,[3] except that it is not defined when a sample contains zero incomes. Hence all zero incomes have been excluded from my sample. Nevertheless, the log variance is an attractive measure because of its decomposition properties.

The Theil index also satisfies both the desirable properties defined above and is decomposable. Therefore both the log variance and Theil measures are used here to decompose inequality. (See the appendix to this chapter for a brief derivation of the Theil index and its decomposition properties, along with an introduction to the Atkinson index.)

The Decomposition of Inequality

In this study I am particularly interested in measuring spatial inequality, but there is a generic problem in measuring inequality between groups as opposed to interpersonal inequality. The traditional method of doing this has been to measure differences between the mean incomes of different groups, but this ignores the distribution of incomes within each group and thus fails to capture the contribution of intragroup inequality to total inequality. It is quite possible, for example, for intragroup inequality to be so large within each group that, even with widely differing intergroup means, the contribution of the latter to total inequality would be small. This was found to be the case, for example, for interregional inequality in Colombia (Fields and Schultz 1977).

Obviously the more homogeneous the groups, the higher the contribution of intergroup inequality. The decomposition of inequality between and within groups can therefore also be used to test for the degree of homogeneity within a group. For example, the decomposition of labor earnings by occupation and other personal characteristics (see chapter 9) is useful in analyzing the

---

3. The Pigou-Dalton condition is satisfied for log variance over the whole range of incomes. It does not hold for incomes over $\bar{\mu} e$, where $\bar{\mu}$ is the geometric mean and e is the base of natural logarithms.

homogeneity of earnings within occupations. Essentially, the intergroup component of inequality is the value of the inequality index when the intragroup inequality is suppressed. In the methodology used to calculate the Theil index (see the appendix to this chapter), for example, as in EQUALISE, the population is divided into quantiles. The index basically represents the intergroup inequality between quantiles, if it is assumed that everyone in the quantile earns the mean of the quantile. Overall inequality is therefore somewhat understated—but the larger the number of quantiles, the smaller the error.

Similarly, the intragroup component of inequality is the inequality under the assumption that there is no intergroup inequality—for a mean-independent index, it is simply a weighted average of intragroup inequalities. The weights used in the Theil index are the income shares of each group, and those in the log-variance are population shares. Both the log-variance and Theil indices are additive decomposable; that is, the sum of the intergroup and intragroup inequalities gives the overall inequality. This is not true for the Gini coefficient.

Trends in the Distribution of Income in Colombia

Reliable data on the distribution of income in Colombia have become available only in the last fifteen years or so. In fact, the 1973 census was the first even to include a question on income. Although the early household surveys—which were conducted by Centro de Estudios sobre Desarrollo Economico (CEDE), Universidad de los Andes (Center for the Study of Economic Development)—date back to the mid to late 1960s, they were largely confined to urban areas. DANE's 1970 nationwide household survey probably gave the first estimates of income distribution for the country as a whole. It is therefore difficult to compare the current distribution of income with historical trends. However, in a pioneering book on the subject, Berry and Urrutia (1976) pieced together information from a multitude of sources in an attempt to identify trends since the late 1930s. They used 1964 as their benchmark year and derived the distribution of income for the economically active population. Using the generally accurate distribution of occupations and activities from the 1964 census together with income estimates for urban areas derived from the 1967–69 CEDE unemployment survey, they obtained a general idea of the distribution of earnings in urban areas. For rural areas, they used the agricultural census of 1960 and various later sources for the distribution of land and of agricultural production.

Table 4-1 summarizes Berry and Urrutia's findings for rural areas, urban areas, and the country as a whole. Their results are somewhat surprising, in that they reveal a distribution of income that was among the most unequal

Table 4-1. *Distribution of Income in Colombia, 1964–74, and Malaysia, 1970*
(percentage of total income)

Category	Economically active population, 1964[a]			Population, 1974[b]			Malaysia, 1970 total[c]
	Urban	Rural	Total	Urban	Rural	Total	
Bottom 20 percent	2.5	4.1	4.5	3.2	5.4	3.6	4.3
Bottom 40 percent	9.8	10.8	9.6	9.9	15.8	10.8	12.3
Top 20 percent	49.9	63.5	63.1	60.6	49.4	60.2	54.8
Top 5 percent	27.1	40.4	33.7	31.5	24.4	32.8	28.5
Gini coefficient	0.55	0.57	0.57	0.54	0.42	0.50	0.50

a. From Selowsky (1979), table 2.2; (see also Berry and Urrutia 1976). Economically active population ranked by earnings.

b. From Berry and Soligo (1980), table 1.1; see also Selowsky (1979). Population ranked by household income per capita (HINCAP).

c. From Anand (1983), table 3.2, for individuals ranked by HINCAP.

in the world at the time. The top 5 percent of the economically active population earned as much as 30–40 percent of total income and the Gini coefficient ranged from 0.55 to 0.57. Inequality, which was somewhat higher in rural areas than in urban areas, reflected a highly skewed pattern of landholdings. In an international comparison reported by Berry and Urrutia, only one estimate (for Brazil) indicated an income distribution more unequal than that for Colombia.

Contrary to the Berry-Urrutia estimates for 1964, Selowsky (1979) found in a 1974 nationwide survey that income distribution for the population as a whole (ranked by household income per capita, see table 4-1) was substantially more equal for rural areas than for urban areas. Few conclusions can be drawn about trends from these two studies, however, because the Berry-Urrutia data were estimates pieced together from diverse sources and the Selowsky estimates are based on only one survey. Furthermore, Selowsky's sample was small—4,000 households were sampled and rural areas were somewhat underrepresented (Selowsky 1979, p. 15)—and questions have also been raised about the quality of responses to the sole question in his survey about income. The two estimations agree, however, on the consistently high degree of income inequality in Colombia; the Gini coefficients range from 0.50 to 0.57 for the country as a whole. For purposes of comparison, table 4-1 also gives estimates for Malaysia in 1970.

Berry and Urrutia also examined the available data going back to the 1930s. They compiled wage series for various groups of workers and then attempted to derive the income distribution for the population. Their main conclusions (Berry and Urrutia 1976, p. 89) were that (1) income distribution in agriculture has worsened steadily since the mid-1930s, and (2) the non-agricultural income distribution probably worsened from the mid-1930s until sometime in the early 1950s, then improved until sometime in the mid-1960s, and then tended to level off.

Berry and Urrutia speculated that the distribution of income generally tends to worsen during periods of rapid growth, whereas it improves during periods of slow growth. The economic background given in chapter 2 is reexamined now in the light of this suggestion. It will be remembered that the late 1940s and the early 1950s were a period of rapid industrialization, when new industries were created under conditions of substantial protection. If it is assumed that these protected industries were highly capital intensive, such a pattern of industrialization would be expected to lead to a lower labor share of total earnings. Moreover, protected industries would tend to generate monopoly profits. With the ownership of capital being highly skewed, such industrialization might indeed lead to a worsening of income distribution.

Rural-urban migration was also very high at that time (Mohan 1980), particularly during the period of the *violencia* from the late 1940s to the mid-1950s. Thus unskilled, blue-collar wages may have been kept down during this period because of the relatively unlimited supply of labor that resulted from migration into the cities. At the same time, the burst of industrialization created a sudden demand for highly skilled and educated workers, with the result that real earnings rose rapidly between 1945 and 1953. Thus, between the 1930s and the mid-1950s the Colombian economy underwent major structural changes, the most important of which was a shift from a rural and predominantly agricultural economy to an increasingly urban, industrial, and service one.

These structural changes continued apace until the mid-1960s, but blue-collar wages increased dramatically in the latter part of the period. Berry and Urrutia hypothesize that by then the degree of protected import substitution may have declined and that competitive small-scale enterprises may have become more successful. The rapid expansion of primary education in the 1950s may have also contributed to the higher skill levels of average workers. The years between the mid-1950s and mid-1960s witnessed a slowing down of economic growth and may be regarded as a period of consolidation. That the incomes of less skilled workers rose so rapidly is surprising, since the rate of rural-urban migration continued to be high.

Since the mid-1960s, Colombia has achieved a relatively high and sustained real rate of growth of GNP (about 5.5 percent a year), but it is difficult to draw any firm conclusions about the trend of the distribution of income from the available data. Now that fertility rates have fallen and a progressively smaller proportion of the population remains in rural areas, the rates of rural-urban migration and urbanization are declining. With the coffee boom and the "success" of the drug trade, it may be that the incomes of unskilled rural workers have been rising—and consequently those of their urban counterparts as well. As chapter 5 points out, the earnings of the most unskilled categories of the urban labor force did indeed rise relatively fast between 1973 and 1978. It is possible that a slowdown in urbanization rates has begun to improve the overall distribution of incomes.

The Distribution of Income in Bogotá and Cali, 1973–78

Unlike most studies of income distribution, which usually take an entire country as the unit of observation, this study concentrates on urban income distribution within a country, as reflected in data from Bogotá and Cali. According to shares of income for Bogotá households, ranked by household income for different years (see table 4-2), the evidence is mixed but there is some indication that the distribution of income may have improved between 1973 and 1978. The principal problem in comparing estimates from different years is that the overall coverage of income differs from survey to survey (see appendix C). The 1973 census, for example, seems to have covered only about 50 percent of total personal income, whereas the 1978 survey may have covered as much as 90 percent. It is difficult, however, to determine whether undercoverage is consistent across income groups or if it is skewed toward particular groups. The evidence is conflicting, but if the labor earnings of the least-skilled occupational categories are any indication, it seems that the census may have covered the earnings of poor male workers well. At the same time, many working females apparently were not captured by the census. Female participation rates as given in the census are substantially lower in 1973 than in other years. If this undercoverage is in fact greater for women in lower-income households, then the income coverage of these households would be lower compared with groups that are better off. Since we know that there is substantial undercoverage overall, undercoverage at the lower end of the household income scale, because of the neglect of some female workers, probably does not cause atypical undercoverage of income among those households. Moreover, participation rates at low household income levels are low anyway.

The shares of income received by selected decile groups between 1973 and 1978 reflect the striking inequality that exists in Colombia (see table 4-2). The income share of the bottom 40 percent of households in these years is less than half of the share received by the top 5 percent. Moreover, even in 1978, when the income coverage is estimated to have exceeded 90 percent, it appears that undercoverage of income from capital was substantial. Since

Table 4-2. *Distribution of Income in Bogotá and Cali:*
Income Shares, 1973–78
(percentage shares of total monthly income)

Category	Bogotá				Cali		
	1973	1975	1977	1978	1973	1977	1978
Households ranked by household income							
Bottom 20 percent	3.3	3.8	4.0	4.0	3.4	4.5	4.1
Bottom 40 percent	9.8	11.0	11.6	11.9	10.4	13.0	12.4
Top 20 percent	62.5	56.9	56.3	55.5	60.0	53.1	54.1
Top 5 percent	30.2	24.9	23.8	25.1	31.7	23.9	25.0
Individuals ranked by household income per capita							
Bottom 20 percent	3.3	3.9	4.2	4.0	3.4	4.5	4.2
Bottom 40 percent	9.9	11.5	12.0	11.5	10.5	13.0	12.4
Top 20 percent	62.6	57.4	56.0	58.0	60.5	54.4	55.5
Top 5 percent	30.8	24.0	24.5	29.0	31.4	24.5	27.3

Sources: 1973 population census; 1975 DANE Household Survey EH8E; 1977 DANE Household Survey EH15; and 1978 World Bank–DANE Household Survey EH21.

this income is likely to accrue to richer households, the actual distribution may be even more unequal than that shown in the table. The poor have, however, obtained gains from economic growth that are at least proportionate to, if not somewhat higher than, those made by the rich.

The picture for Cali is quite similar. There appears to be a slight worsening between 1977 and 1978, but it is difficult to distinguish real changes from changes due to sample errors. The possibility that the changes may have been real is supported by the similarity between the two cities with respect to the worsening. The high degree of inequality in Bogotá and Cali can be gauged by looking at comparable information for other countries. The share of the bottom 40 percent of households (ranked by household income) in developed countries—both capitalist and socialist—for example, is typically of the order of 15–20 percent, and the share of the top 20 percent is between 35 and 45 percent (Morrison 1984).

The results are similar when individuals are ranked by household income per capita (HINCAP), as shown in the lower panel of table 4-2. Datta and Meerman (1980) have demonstrated that the rank of particular individuals changes substantially when ranked by HINCAP as opposed to household income (HHY), but the overall result does not. The particular rank is clearly important when the aim is to determine the characteristics of the poor (as, for example, in Mohan and Hartline 1984) or of the rich in order to design policies that might alleviate poverty. The distribution itself does not appear to be different. There seems to be an overall improvement between 1973 and 1978.

Table 4-3. *Inequality Indices for Bogotá Households, 1973–78*

Inequality index	Ranked by monthly household income				Ranked by monthly household income per capita			
	1973	1975	1977	1978	1973	1975	1977	1978
Gini	0.565	0.514	0.507	0.507	0.581	0.555	0.511	0.558
Theil	0.610	0.467	0.453	0.458	0.682	0.634	0.468	0.589
Standard deviations of logs	1.023	0.951	0.914	0.926	1.040	0.995	0.935	0.996
Atkinson	0.654	0.586	0.556	0.569	0.671	0.644	0.581	0.626
Coefficient of variation	1.403	1.142	1.131	1.146	1.618	1.640	1.155	1.351
Mean household income (pesos)[a]	3,323	5,692	8,229	13,405	—	—	—	—
Mean household income per capita (pesos)[a,b]	—	—	—	—	895	1,249	1,800	3,683
Sample size (number of households)	41,282	3,620	2,934	2,991	—	—	—	—
Expanded sample size[c]	440,000	n.a.[d]	636,000	696,000	—	—	—	—

n.a. Not available.

— Not applicable.

a. Current prices. Consumer price index (1970 = 100, approximately): 1973 = 150; 1975 = 240; 1977 = 380; 1978 = 400.

b. Mean taken over households.

c. Estimated number of households in Bogotá.

d. Not expanded because expansion factors were not available.

Source: See table 4-2.

The inequality indices for Bogotá and Cali presented in tables 4-3, 4-4, and 4-5 are surprisingly consistent across different income concepts and ranking procedures. The Gini coefficient, for example, ranges from 0.57 to 0.50 and the Theil index from 0.68 to 0.44 (table 4-3). The distribution of households appears to be worse if ranked by household income per capita rather than household income itself. Anand (1983) obtained a similar result for Malaysia, but found that the plotted Lorenz curves for the two distributions (by HHY and by HINCAP) intersected each other. He therefore concluded that the HINCAP distribution could not be considered unambiguously worse and that different indices could produce different results. Here it may be noted that all the indices used yield higher inequality when ranked by HINCAP. This implies that even though households with higher income tend to be larger, the additional income is not compensating enough and the distribution of HINCAP becomes worse than HHY. (The ordering of households by HINCAP differs from that by HHY.)

Table 4-4. *Inequality Indices for Bogotá's Population Ranked by Household Income Per Capita, 1973–78*

Inequality index	1973	1975	1977	1978
Gini	0.568	0.515	0.499	0.522
Theil	0.649	0.499	0.442	0.508
Standard deviation of logs	1.007	0.949	0.911	0.920
Atkinson	0.646	0.601	0.561	0.570
Coefficient of variation	1.582	1.309	1.117	1.255
Mean household income per capita (pesos)[a]	697	1,012	1,573	2,844
Sample size (number of households)	41,282	3,620	2,934	2,991
Expanded sample size (thousands of individuals)[b]	2,892	n.a.[c]	3,328[d]	3,279[d]

n.a. Not available.

a. Mean taken over individuals. Current Colombian pesos. See table 4-3, note a, for consumer price indexes from 1973 to 1978.

b. Estimated population of Bogotá.

c. Not expanded because expansion factors were not available.

d. The estimated population for Bogotá is less in 1978 than in 1977 because of differences in the expansion factors used. The 1978 survey estimates are based on a new sample frame during that year, whereas the 1977 estimates relied on an old sample frame.

Source: See table 4-2.

Table 4-4 presents inequality data for individuals (as opposed to households) in Bogotá. A ranking by HINCAP is of greater interest here than one by HHY. (Anand 1983, among others, has also argued that HINCAP is a better measure of welfare than HHY.) As might be expected, table 4-4 shows that inequality among individuals is somewhat less than that for households ranked by HINCAP, but it is greater than that for households ranked by HHY. As Mohan (1980) has shown, household income increases with household size, but HINCAP decreases. The larger number of income earners does not, on the average, compensate adequately for the increase in dependents. Nonetheless, these results are reassuring from a methodological point of view. The level of inequality deduced from either of these income concepts and ranking criteria gives somewhat similar results. Moreover, the changes for different years and income concepts are also consistent for the different indices. All show an improvement between 1973 and 1977 and a slight worsening between 1977 and 1978.

Table 4-5 gives comparable estimates for Cali but reports only the Gini and Theil indices. The conclusions are similar to those for Bogotá, although there seems to be less overall inequality in Cali. A larger city with a diversified

Table 4-5. *Inequality Indices for Cali, 1973–78*

Category	Inequality index	1973	1977	1978
Households ranked by house- hold income	Gini Theil	0.553 0.601	0.475 0.403	0.487 0.429
Households ranked by house- hold income per capita	Gini Theil	0.568 0.665	0.487 0.430	0.524 0.510
Individuals ranked by household income per capita	Gini Theil	0.554 0.632	0.481 0.420	0.500 0.470
Mean household income (pesos)[a]		2,632	7,192	11,321
Mean household income per capita (pesos)[b]		594	1,350	2,425
Sample size (number of house- holds)		11,520	1,016	974
Expanded sample size[c]				
Households		n.a.[d]	191,421	216,633
Individuals		n.a.[d]	1,019,766[e]	1,011,209[e]

n.a. Not available.

a. Current Colombian pesos. See table 4-3, note a, for consumer price indexes from 1973 to 1975.

b. Mean taken over individuals.

c. Estimated number of households and population in Cali.

d. Not expanded because expansion factors were not available.

e. See table 4-4, note d. The same applies to Cali.

Source: See table 4-2.

economic structure might be expected to have more higher-paid specialized professionals and more people with high nonlabor incomes. As mentioned earlier, however, the coverage of nonlabor income is poor in the sources of data considered; consequently, the former reason is probably the more likely explanation (as is corroborated by the analysis of the distribution of labor earnings in chapter 9).

One technical detail worth noting about the computation of inequality indices is that the population is usually grouped in quantiles and then the resulting piecewise linear Lorenz curve is used to calculate the relevant indices. Data on income distribution are generally available in one of two formats: income shares of different quantile groups or population (or household) groups falling within specified income ranges. An approximation of the Lorenz curve can be obtained from either. The essential point is that data are usually available in a form that allows only a small number of observations (10 to 20) to be plotted on the Lorenz curve. What is unusual about the present study, as noted earlier, is that income data on individual households were available from as many as four surveys, one of which was a census sample. It is therefore interesting to determine the error involved when as many as 3,000 available observations on income are grouped into 10–20 quantile groups. The EQUALISE program permits flexibility in the number of observations that must be used on the Lorenz curve.

It is expensive to use all the information available from a sample survey since all observations need to be ranked when an index is to be computed. Typically, quantile averages are taken and the relevant indices calculated. Table 4-6 gives some idea of the error that arises when 20 quantiles are used rather than all observations. As would be expected, inequality is slightly understated by the use of quantiles. The Gini coefficient and the standard deviation of logarithms appear to be relatively insensitive to the number of observations used. The Theil and Atkinson indices are also affected, but not as much. Although it is difficult to find the optimal level of aggregation, the errors caused by the use of 20 quantiles are probably tolerable for most purposes (table 4-6).

In summary, the overall levels of inequality in Bogotá and Cali are not substantially different from estimates reported earlier in the chapter. There is no marked movement toward greater equality, although some tendencies toward a slight improvement are apparent. The distribution of income in Cali is somewhat better than that in Bogotá. The use of different indices, income concepts, or ranking procedures does not alter these general conclusions.

The Spatial Distribution of Income

Consider now how incomes are distributed geographically within these two cities and whether there are any discernible patterns of spatial inequality. As this section shows, Bogotá and Cali exhibit distinct patterns. The ratio between mean incomes in different spatial zones is as much as 1 to 6, with means being taken over relatively large zones. Since little information of this type is available for other cities, I cannot say whether such a pattern of income differentiation within a city is unusual. This extent of spatial disparity in mean incomes *is* unusual among regions in most countries (although it does exist among the regions in Colombia, as documented by Fields and Schultz 1977). Merely observing differences between the means for different populations can be misleading, however, and therefore the full distributions should be examined.

The extent of spatial inequality within a city is difficult to determine because a city—unlike the world, which can be divided into countries, or

Table 4-6. *Inequality Indices for Bogotá, 1978: Results from Using Different Numbers of Observations in the Lorenz Curve*

Inequality index	Households by household income		Households by HINCAP		Individuals by HINCAP	
	20 observations	All observations[a]	20 observations	All observations[a]	20 observations	All observations[b]
Gini	0.507	0.511	0.558	0.570	0.522	0.528
Theil	0.458	0.477	0.589	0.704	0.508	0.559
Standard deviation of logs	0.926	0.953	0.996	0.994	0.920	0.932
Atkinson	0.569	0.647	0.626	0.688	0.570	0.637
Coefficient of variation	1.146	1.229	1.351	2.097	1.255	1.646

a. About 3,000 observations.
b. About 17,000 observations.

Source: My estimates from 1978 World Bank–DANE Household Survey.

a country, which can be divided into states—has no generally accepted or natural administrative divisions. In the United States, central cities are often compared with suburbs—but even here, there is no standard definition of what constitutes a central city. Whatever city divisions are used, they are inevitably arbitrary. Thus an analytically appropriate zoning system must be found.

Two geometric patterns suggest themselves as possible methods of zonification. A circular city can be divided either into rings or into radial sectors. In the United States, for example, suburbs are conventionally considered to be distinct from the central city; more generally, urban economic theory (e.g., Muth 1969) suggests that under certain assumptions the poorest population groups can be expected to locate in the center and that incomes will therefore rise as one proceeds outward from the center. Thus it would seem appropriate to divide the city into rings and to study the spatial distribution of income among these rings. The other obvious pattern, that of radial sectors, was suggested by Homer Hoyt (1939, 1966), for one. Using these divisions to trace the historical development of a large number of North American cities, Hoyt concluded that income groups tend to locate themselves near like groups. Hence, if the rich historically located themselves in one section of the city, the city grew in such a way that the rich continued to locate in the same direction, and different pie slices or radial sectors emerged having their own distinctive characteristics. Amato (1968, 1969, 1970, 1980), focusing on the elite of Bogotá, showed that the rich there have tended to locate predominantly in the north of the city and have continued to move in that direction.

Consider now the geography of Bogotá and Cali (see maps 3-1 and 3-2) and the spatial disaggregation system described in appendix A. Both cities can be divided conveniently into semicircular rings and radial sectors, although there is no special reason why Bogotá should be divided into eight radial sectors and six rings other than the fact that the DANE geocoding system makes these numbers the obvious choices. The rings and sectors are made up of smaller units—comunas—of which there are thirty-eight in Bogotá and twenty-five in Cali. The following analysis is based on these geographical divisions; although the spatial disaggregations employed are particular to these two cities, the analytical principle involved can be generalized to other cities.

Tables 4-7 and 4-8 describe the distribution of mean incomes and of the population in Bogotá and Cali by radial sectors from 1973 to 1978. As noted earlier, according to the surveys analyzed, the proportion of the population in each sector remains similar in all the years and therefore increases confidence in the sample distribution of these household surveys. The sample frame for the 1978 survey was updated and the resulting distribution indicates that the population in sector 8 may have risen over the period 1973 to 1978.

Table 4-7. *Spatial Distribution of Income in Bogotá by Sector, 1973–78*

	1973		1975		1977		1978	
Sector	Population (percent)[a]	Mean HINCAP[b]	Population (percent)[a]	Mean HINCAP[b]	Population (percent)[a]	Mean HINCAP[b]	Population (percent)[a]	Mean HINCAP[b]
1[c]	2.3	1.07	1.2	2.05	1.9	1.38	2.4	0.80
2	18.2	0.57	16.5	0.66	18.6	0.56	20.6	0.50
3	26.0	0.68	28.2	0.71	25.5	0.76	25.2	0.73
4	9.3	0.90	9.0	0.92	8.2	1.08	7.2	0.98
5	7.3	0.93	6.5	1.45	6.5	1.11	6.2	1.03
6	18.2	0.80	20.0	0.95	19.0	0.87	20.0	0.91
7	12.0	1.71	10.3	1.38	13.5	1.39	9.1	1.44
8	6.6	2.87	8.2	1.90	7.0	2.33	9.1	2.66
All sectors	100.0	697[d]	100.0	1,012[d]	100.0	1,573[d]	100.0	2,843[d]

Note: Percentages may not add to 100 because of rounding.

a. Percentage of the city's total population living in the sector.

b. Mean monthly household income per capita taken across individuals in the sector as a multiple of overall mean HINCAP.

c. Central business district.

d. Mean monthly household income per capita taken across individuals for Bogotá in current Colombian pesos. See table 4-3, note a, for consumer price indexes for 1973 to 1978.

Sources: See table 4-2.

72

Table 4-8. *Spatial Distribution of Income in Cali by Sector, 1973–78*

Sector	1973 Population (percent)[a]	1973 Mean HINCAP[b]	1977 Population (percent)[a]	1977 Mean HINCAP[b]	1978 Population (percent)[a]	1978 Mean HINCAP[b]
1[c]	4.3	1.03	3.2	1.12	1.1	1.78
2	4.2	3.68	7.3	2.63	4.8	2.36
3	19.5	0.89	13.4	0.68	15.2	0.88
4	21.2	0.69	16.8	0.79	17.8	0.64
5	35.1	0.68	37.1	0.78	42.2	0.73
6	11.1	1.61	16.5	1.29	12.8	1.42
7	4.5	1.37	2.7	.80	6.0	2.13
All sectors	100.0	594[d]	100.0	1,350[d]	100.0	2,425[d]

Note: Percentages may not add to 100 because of rounding.

a. Percentage of total population living in the sector.

b. Mean monthly household income per capita taken across individuals in the sector as a multiple of overall mean HINCAP.

c. Central business district.

d. Mean monthly household income per capita taken across individuals in Cali in current Colombian pesos. See table 4-3, note a, for consumer price indexes for 1973 to 1978.

Sources: See table 4-2.

The 1975 and 1977 surveys used samples from the same basic sampling frame, so no conclusions can be drawn from them about changes in the spatial distribution of the population. The mean household income per capita is expressed as a multiple of the overall mean. The multiples remain broadly similar over the entire period. In the poorest sector (sector 2 in the south of the city) HINCAP is about one-fifth or one-sixth of that in the richest (sector 8 in the north). With the exception of sector 6, mean incomes rise as one moves clockwise from the south to the north (sector 1 is the city center). The poor southern sectors 2, 3, and 6 account for almost 65 percent of the total population. There is no noticeable trend toward a narrowing of the differences in mean income between the sectors.

In contrast, the division between rich and poor in Cali seems to run along an east-west rather than a north-south axis, with the eastern sectors 3, 4, and 5 being relatively poorer than the western sectors 2, 6, and 7. Moreover, the data for Cali suggest that the degree of inequality may be changing over time. Mean HINCAP in the poorest sector was about one-sixth of that in the richest in 1973, and about one-quarter in 1974. This could also be the result of smaller sample sizes and hence larger sampling errors. It does appear, however, that sector 2 is becoming relatively less rich and, if the changes in sector 1 are not the result of sampling errors, the city center may be gaining higher-income people.

These broad patterns have already been established for Bogotá (Mohan 1980), so that the question that needs to be addressed now is how much these patterns hide. Are there large variances around the means or do they capture the essential characteristics of different sectors? I decompose the variance in incomes into two parts. Households or people are grouped by sectors or rings. Overall inequality in the city is then decomposed into its intragroup and intergroup components. The intragroup component is essentially a weighted average of the indices of inequality within each group, and the intergroup component is a measure of the differences in group means, appropriately weighted by group populations for log variance, and by group shares in income for the Theil index.

In both Bogotá and Cali, income patterns are more distinct in the radial sectors than in the rings, as is documented in table 4-9, which ranks households by both HHY and HINCAP and analyzes inequality by means of both Theil and log variance indices. For Bogotá, more than one-quarter of overall inequality as measured by the Theil index is attributable to space; as measured by log variance, the figure is about 20 percent. The spatial contributions are somewhat lower for Cali; in particular, the intergroup component is very small when households are grouped by rings. Note that the intergroup contribution of rings increases substantially when households are ranked by HINCAP; this is due to the fact that average household size is larger at the periphery than in the center (Mohan 1980), and hence differences between the rings are greater for HINCAP than for HHY. The intergroup contribution can be regarded as an *index of spatial inequality in incomes*: it may be termed an *index of spatial income segregation* (ISIS).

Table 4-9 also shows ISIS according to location of residence for individuals ranked by HINCAP as well as for workers ranked by labor earnings. The ISIS for workers is substantially lower than the comparable indices for households and for individuals. This finding indicates that some of the spatial differences in income inequality are due to locational patterns arising from differences in household characteristics rather than spatial distinctions in the labor market.

Tables 4-10 and 4-11 give the pattern of income inequality between and within radial sectors in Bogotá and Cali, respectively. The Theil index is shown for each sector as well as for the city as a whole. (Examples of the log variance used as the inequality index are given in appendix tables 4A-1 and 4A-2.) Tables 4-10 and 4-11 reveal some interesting trends. First, the level of inequality within each sector is less than overall inequality. Second, the city center (sector 1) is the most heterogeneous in both cities. Third, the poorest sectors (sector 2 in Bogotá and sector 4 in Cali) show low indices of inequality, as do the richest sectors, sector 8 in Bogotá and sector 2 in Cali. In Bogotá, ISIS clearly appears to be increasing over time, from about 22 percent in 1973 to 27 percent in 1978 (with lower figures in intervening

Table 4-9. *Spatial Distribution of Income by Ring and Sector,
Bogotá and Cali, 1978*

| | Intergroup contribution to inequality (percent) | | | |
| | Bogotá | | Cali | |
Ranking criterion and zonification system	Theil	Log variance	Theil	Log variance
Households by household income				
Rings	4	5	6	4
Sectors	26	17	23	13
Households by HINCAP				
Rings	9	6	10	9
Sectors	32	22	21	14
Individuals by HINCAP				
Rings	6	4	11	9
Sectors	27	17	23	14
Workers by labor earnings				
Rings	6	4	3	3
Sectors	20	12	15	6

Source: My estimates from 1978 World Bank–DANE Household Survey.

years). The last line in both tables shows the ISIS if comunas are used as the spatial division. The fact that intergroup contribution rises to 35–40 percent indicates that comunas are relatively homogeneous units: differences between comunas account for almost 40 percent of the overall inequality. ISIS for these also increases over time.

It is difficult to get an intuitive feel for this kind of spatial inequality. I have seen no similar indices for other cities, but Anand's (1983) work on Malaysia again provides some estimates for comparison. He found interstate and rural-urban contributions to inequality in Malaysia (in terms of HINCAP for individuals) to be 9.1 and 13.7 percent, respectively, for the Theil index. By this standard, the spatial inequality in Bogotá and Cali seems extremely high.

These results strongly indicate that the pattern of spatial income differentiation in Bogotá is deteriorating with time: there is certainly no evidence that spatial disparities are improving. At the same time, overall inequality does not appear to be increasing. If spatial differentiation of income groups has long-term adverse effects on the chances of the poor in the labor market, as will be suggested later, then Bogotá's increasing spatial differentiation by income is a cause for concern. Inasmuch as policymakers themselves are relatively richer, increasing differentiation can, over the longer term, make them oblivious to the conditions of the poor in the city. Moreover, job

Table 4-10. *Spatial Inequality in Bogotá (Theil Index), 1973–78: Individuals Ranked by* HINCAP

Sector	Income rank (1978)[a]	1973		1975		1977		1978	
		Theil index	Rank[b]	Theil index	Rank	Theil index	Rank	Theil index	Rank
1	3	0.635	8	0.678	8	0.612	8	0.458	8
2	1	0.429	3	0.440	4	0.283	2	0.286	1
3	2	0.390	1	0.309	2	0.347	3	0.309	2
4	5	0.407	2	0.273	1	0.413	6	0.362	4
5	6	0.553	5	0.504	6	0.426	7	0.418	5
6	4	0.514	4	0.439	3	0.366	4	0.426	6
7	7	0.572	6	0.462	5	0.372	5	0.444	7
8	8	0.602	7	0.542	7	0.281	1	0.357	3
All sectors		0.649		0.499		0.442		0.508	
Intergroup contribution									
Sectors (Theil index)		0.140		0.069		0.087		0.137	
Sectors (percent)		21.6		13.7		19.6		26.9	
Comunas[c] (percent)		32.6		26.1		30.5		37.8	

a. Ascending order of income by mean HINCAP.
b. Ranking by ascending order of inequality.
c. Intergroup contribution if grouped by comunas.
Source: See table 4-2.

Table 4-11. *Spatial Inequality in Cali (Theil Index), 1973–78: Individuals Ranked by* HINCAP

Sector	Income rank (1978)[a]	1973		1977		1978	
		Theil index	Rank[b]	Theil index	Rank	Theil index	Rank
1	5	0.573	5	0.449	6	0.549	7
2	7	0.368	2	0.184	1	0.257	2
3	3	0.429	3	0.228	2	0.315	3
4	1	0.328	1	0.313	4	0.251	1
5	2	0.435	4	0.323	5	0.337	4
6	4	0.731	6	0.498	7	0.495	6
7	6	0.781	7	0.239	3	0.463	5
All sectors		0.632		0.420		0.470	
Intergroup contribution							
Sectors (Theil index)		0.143		0.325		0.106	
Sectors (percent)		22.7		22.7		22.5	
Comunas[c] (percent)		37.3		41.3		40.6	

a. Ascending order of income by mean HINCAP.

b. Ascending order of inequality.

c. Intergroup contribution if grouped by comunas.

Source: See table 4-2.

opportunities are generally greater in richer areas than in poorer ones. Increasing segregation might then also mean that, on the average, the poor who work in the richer areas of town will have to do more commuting. If such trends continue, a spatially based dualistic economy will become a reality.

If the methods employed here to analyze the spatial distribution of income were applied to other cities, one could establish whether Bogotá and Cali are atypical in their degree of income segregation. If enough such studies were carried out, it might become possible to explain higher and lower levels of spatial differentiation between cities and their effects on labor markets and on social welfare as a whole.

Summary

According to the data available, the distribution of income in Bogotá and Cali appears to have improved somewhat between 1973 and 1978. The quality of the data is not robust enough to be able to state this conclusively but such a tendency would be consistent with other changes in the national economy during that period. With more than 60 percent of the population now in urban areas, the rate of urbanization is naturally falling, as is evident in the growth of both Bogotá and Cali. To the extent that such a slowdown in the growth of these cities implies a tightening of the labor market which pushes up unskilled wages, the distribution of income can be expected to improve. Furthermore, although more than half of the population in these cities has only a primary-level education or less, the level of education of the labor force has been rising. As inequalities in educational levels decline, so should inequalities in the distribution of earned income. If, however, the coverage of nonlabor income in all the surveys is poor, as is suspected, some of the improvement in the distribution of income could be illusory.

Despite any improvement that may have occurred in income distribution, the level of inequality in the two cities remains high by world standards. Measured in any way—by households ranked according to household income or household income per capita, by individuals ranked according to household income per capita, or by workers ranked according to labor earnings—the Gini coefficient is between about 0.55 and 0.50 (although it showed signs of improvement between 1973 and 1978). These results are robust across different samples, indices, income concepts, and ranking procedures. As might be expected, the overall level of inequality is higher in Bogotá than in Cali, which is a smaller city.

A special feature of this study is the calculation of isis—the index of spatial income segregation—which is defined as the percentage contribution of spatial zones to overall inequality in a city. Interzonal variations in income levels in Bogotá and Cali are reflected in the differences between radial sectors rather than between concentric rings, as is the case in the cities of North America. That the isis in Bogotá and Cali is substantially lower for labor earnings than for household income per capita suggests that some of the inequality is due to locational differences in the composition of households. The most disquieting feature of these findings is that isis appears to be increasing over time while inequality within sectors is declining. Thus both richer and poorer sectors are becoming more homogeneous and the city more spatially differentiated by income over time.

If, as some suspect, greater segmentation by income has adverse effects on social welfare, mainly through the operation of labor markets, the increasing spatial disparities in Bogotá are of concern. That this variable is a significant factor in the determination of labor earnings becomes clear in chapter 8, which discusses the influence of background on earnings and uses a location of residence variable as a proxy for family background, educational quality, and other similar determinants of earnings. The contribution of intersectoral differences to overall inequality in labor earnings supports that finding. If the deficiencies in environment faced by a poor child are reinforced by higher segregation, then an increase in isis can be expected to have an adverse effect on the future distribution of earnings.

In most cities, richer areas are much better served by public utilities than poorer ones. If, on the one hand, the richer and poorer areas are mixed— as is the case in many cities—then the poorer areas also benefit from the pressures brought by the rich for improved sanitation, water supply, roads, and the like. If, on the other hand, very few people are better off in very large areas, such as the southern segment of Bogotá and the eastern segment of Cali, then the likelihood of neglect by public authorities increases. In turn, such segregation affects schooling, by lowering the quality of teachers and students alike. Thus the spatial disadvantages suffered by children living in these areas could increase over the long term and be self-perpetrating and could later manifest themselves in the labor market. (Although the lack of consistent zonification remains a problem in intercity comparisons, isis can be used as a measure of income segmentation and could easily be applied to different cities. If the same numbers of quantiles and zones were used, the results would be quite comparable across cities.)

Overall, Bogotá exhibited higher inequality and a higher isis than Cali. This is a suggestive finding from the point of view of the characteristics and roles of large and smaller cities respectively. Thus it appears that a larger city might be expected to have a much more variegated and heterogeneous labor market, and consequently higher inequality. Since the highest professional and other skills can only be utilized in the largest cities, the highest professional incomes will only be found there. Thus there would also be more pressure for greater spatial segmentation, particularly where overall inequality is high. The relatively rich would want to live near others like themselves— and in a large enough city, there would be a critical mass for them to be able to do so.

Appendix. Introduction to the Theil Index and the Atkinson Index of Inequality

The Theil Index

The Theil index is based on the concept of expected information in a distribution. That is to say, when the probability of an event occurring is low, the information contained in a message stating that it has occurred is high. Intuitively, then, information can be regarded as the converse of probability. As a precise measure of information contained in a message that states that an event with prior probability p has occurred, the function suggested is:

$$(4A\text{-}1) \qquad\qquad h(p) \;=\; \log \frac{1}{p}$$

which ranges from infinity (when p is small, the event is unlikely and hence when it does occur, information in the message stating that it has occurred is high) to zero (when $p = 1$, the event is certain). For a distribution of events, each with probability p_i ($i = 1, \ldots n$) and

$$\sum_{i=1}^{n} p_i = 1$$

the expected information of the message on the occurrence of one of these events is

(4A-2) $$H = \sum_{i=1}^{n} p_i \log \frac{1}{p_i}$$

that is, the weighted average of the information contained in each message. The minimum of this distribution occurs when

$$p_i = 1$$

and all $p_i = 0$ ($i \neq j$)

that is, $$H = \log 1 = 0$$

and the maximum occurs when

$$p_i = \frac{1}{n} \text{ for all } i.$$

Then $$H = \sum_{i=1}^{n} \frac{1}{n} \log \frac{1}{1/n}$$

$$= \log n.$$

   H is also known as entropy. In its application to the measurement of income distribution, it can be interpreted as a measure of uncertainty. The higher the uncertainty in a distribution, the greater the expected information in the message stating that an event has occurred from the distribution of possible events; hence the entropy of a distribution may be said to measure the "amount of uncertainty" in it. It is similar to variance, which is the more common measure used to measure uncertainty.

   Now consider an income distribution,

$$z_1, z_2 \cdots z_n$$

that is, n individuals with income z_i. Let

$$Z = \sum_{i=1}^{n} z_i.$$

Then $$\sum_{i=1}^{n} \frac{z_i}{Z} = 1.$$

The entropy of the income distribution can then be defined. Let

$$q_i = \frac{z_i}{Z}$$

hence $$\sum q_i = 1$$

and all $q_i \geqslant 0.$

Then $$H(q) = \sum_{i=1}^{n} q_i \log \frac{1}{q_i}$$

as for any distribution of probabilities

$$H(q) = \sum \frac{z_i}{Z} \log \frac{1}{z_i/Z} \qquad \text{(all summations are from 1 to } n\text{)}$$

but $$Z = n\bar{z}$$

where $\bar{z}$ is the mean of the distribution.

$$\text{Then } H(q) = \sum \frac{z_i}{n\bar{z}} \log \frac{1}{z_i/n\bar{z}}$$

$$= \frac{1}{n} \sum \left(\frac{z_i}{\bar{z}} \log \frac{n}{z_i/\bar{z}} \right)$$

$$= \frac{1}{n} \sum \left(\frac{z_i}{\bar{z}} \log n + \frac{z_i}{\bar{z}} \log \frac{1}{z_i/\bar{z}} \right)$$

$$= \frac{1}{n} \cdot n\frac{\bar{z}}{\bar{z}} \log n + \frac{1}{n} \sum \left(\frac{z_i}{\bar{z}} \log \frac{1}{z_i/\bar{z}} \right)$$

(4A-3) $$= \log n + \frac{1}{n} \sum \left(\frac{z_i}{\bar{z}} \log \frac{1}{z_i/\bar{z}} \right).$$

Now, if $z_i = z_j$ for all $i = j$

$$z_i = \bar{z}$$

and $H(q) = \log n$, and if all income is earned by one individual j,

$$z_j = Z = n\bar{z}$$

and $H(q) = 0.$

Hence entropy is high when inequality is low, and low when inequality is high. Intuitively then, if we want an index that is low for low inequality and high for high inequality, we can arbitrarily define

(4A-4) $$T = \log n - H(q)$$

to measure the departure of an income distribution from an even distribution.

In fact, the Theil index (T) of income inequality is defined as "the expected information of the message which transforms population shares into income shares." Consider again an event E with prior probability p. If a message is now received that the probability of this event has changed to q, what is the information contained in this message? The prior probability of the event occurring is p and the posterior probability is q. When the event does occur, the information provided by that message will be $h(q)$. Hence, if the information content of the intermediary message changing the probability to q, is I,

$$I + h(q) = h(p)$$

$$\text{or } I = h(p) - h(q) = \log \frac{q}{p}.$$

Again, this can be applied to a distribution of probabilities

$$(p_1, p_2 \cdots p_n)$$

being changed to $$(q_1, q_2, \ldots q_n).$$

The expected information or entropy of the message changing the probabilities is then

$$I(q{:}p) = \sum_{i=1} q_i \log \frac{q_i}{p_i}$$

that is, a weighted average of the information for each event—the weighting being done by the posterior probability. "I" may be regarded as a measure of the "differentness" of the second distribution (q_i) from the first (p_i).

Note that if $p_i = 1/n$, the case of equiprobability,

$$I(q{:}p) = \sum_{i=1} q_i \log \frac{q_i}{1/n}$$

$$= \log n - \sum q_i \log \frac{1}{q_i}$$

which is the same form as T in equation (4A-4). The interpretation is that T is a measure of the departure from complete equality. Since an individual's share in a population of n is $1/n$, the distribution of population shares (p_i, p_2 . . . p_n) is an even distribution. When we are then provided with their income distribution, their share of income may be regarded as the posterior distribution and we arrive at the original definition of the Theil index as "The expected information of the message which transforms population shares into income shares."

Methodology Used in EQUALISE

It is clear that the value of the Theil index varies from zero for perfect equality to log n for the extreme case where one individual gets all the income and the other ($n - 1$) individuals earn nothing. This raises a problem of comparability of the Theil index between different populations, since it is dependent on the magnitude of n. One method of normalization is to compute T as a proportion of log n, its feasible maximum value for the population at hand. That approach has not been attempted in this study since all the calculations have been based on 20 quantiles drawn from each sample. The procedure adopted in EQUALISE is to compute each inequality index on the basis of the income share received by each quantile of population. As mentioned earlier, the program makes it possible to use all the observations available or to aggregate them into quantiles. Experiments were done using different numbers of quantiles and 20 was chosen because it is large enough to give reasonable accuracy in the computation. As is evident from equations (4A-3) and (4A-4), the only information needed for the calculation of the Theil index is income shares and population shares for a defined number of population groups. In the case of 20 quantiles, $n = 20$ and, in principle, the index is calculated as if there were no individuals in the population. *The magnitudes of the Theil indices for the different years and different-size samples are therefore directly comparable in this study.*

Decomposition of the Theil Index

Recall the derivation of the Theil index as an information expectation (see Theil 1972, pp. 20–22). Consider n events E_1, E_2 . . . E_n and G sets of events S_1, S_2, . . . S_G such that each set S_g has k_g events where

$$n = \sum_{g=1}^{g} k_g.$$

The probability of the set S_g occurring is

(4A-5) $$P_g = \sum_{i \varepsilon S_g} p_i$$

and the entropy at the level of sets is

$$(4A\text{-}6) \qquad\qquad H_o = \sum_{i=1}^{g} P_g \log \frac{1}{P_g}.$$

This is intergroup entropy—analogous to intergroup inequality.

Now "total" entropy at the level of events is

$$H = \sum_{i=1}^{n} p_i \log \frac{1}{p_i}$$

$$= \sum_{g=1}^{g} \sum_{i\varepsilon S_g} p_i \log \frac{1}{p_i}$$

$$= \sum_{g=1}^{G} P_g \sum_{i\varepsilon S_g} \frac{p_i}{P_g} \left(\log \frac{1}{P_g} + \log \frac{P_g}{p_i} \right)$$

$$= \sum_{g=1}^{G} P_g \sum_{i\varepsilon S_g} \left(\frac{p_i}{P_g} \log \frac{1}{P_g} \right) + \sum_{g=1}^{G} P_g \left(\sum_{i\varepsilon S_g} \frac{p_i}{P_g} \log \frac{P_g}{p_i} \right)$$

$$= \sum_{g=1}^{G} P_g \log \frac{1}{P_g} + \sum_{g=1}^{G} P_g \left(\sum_{i\varepsilon S_g} \frac{p_i}{P_g} \log \frac{1}{p_i/P_g} \right)$$

that is,

$$(4A\text{-}7) \qquad\qquad H = H_o + \sum_{g=1}^{G} P_g H_g$$

where

$$(4A\text{-}8) \qquad\qquad H_g = \sum \frac{p_i}{P_g} \log \frac{1}{p_i/P_g}.$$

H_g is the entropy within set S_g and hence $\Sigma P_g H_g$ is the average intragroup entropy. The total entropy is then the sum of intergroup entropy H_o and the average intragroup entropy—exactly analogous to the intra- and intergroup inequality decomposition.

This result can be extended to the decomposition of information expectation of a message transforming prior probabilities p_i to q_i. Let

$$P_g = \sum_{i\varepsilon S_g} p_i, \qquad Q_g = \sum_{i\varepsilon S_g} q_i$$

with $p_i(i = 1, \ldots n)$ and $q_i(i = 1, 2, \ldots n)$ being the prior and posterior probabilities that are aggregated into G sets correspondingly. At the set level, the information expectation is then

$$(4A\text{-}9) \qquad I_o\,(q{:}p) \;=\; \sum_{g=1}^{G} Q_g \log \frac{Q_g}{P_g}$$

but

$$
\begin{aligned}
I(q{:}p) &= \sum_{i=1}^{n} q_i \log \frac{q_i}{p_i} \\
&= \sum_{g=1}^{G} Q_g \sum_{i \in S_g} \frac{q_i}{Q_g} \left(\log \frac{Q_g}{P_g} + \log \frac{q_i/Q_g}{p_i/P_g} \right) \\
&= \sum_{g=1}^{G} Q_g \log \frac{Q_g}{P_g} + \sum_{g=1}^{G} Q_g \sum_{i \in S_g} \frac{q_i}{Q_g} \log \frac{q_i/Q_g}{p_i/P_g}
\end{aligned}
$$

that is,

$$(4A\text{-}10) \qquad I(q{:}p) \;=\; I_o(q{:}p) + \sum_{g=1}^{G} Q_g I_g(q{:}p)$$

where

$$(4A\text{-}11) \qquad I_g(q{:}p) \;=\; \sum_{i \in S_g} \frac{q_i}{Q_g} \log \frac{q_i/Q_g}{p_i/P_g}$$

hence the expected information of a message transforming prior probabilities to posterior probabilities is decomposable in an exactly analogous manner as the entropy for groups.

We can now return to income inequality where the p_i are population shares and q_i are income shares with p_i now being aggregated into groups of individuals with population shares P_g and income shares Q_g. Now

$$P_g = \frac{n_g}{n}$$

where n_g is the number of individuals in the group and n the total number of individuals in the population.

$$Q_g = \sum_{i \in S_g} q_i$$

is the income share of the group. Hence, using (4A-9), (4A-10), and (4A-11)

$$(4A\text{-}12) \qquad T = T_o + \sum_{g=1}^{G} Q_g T_g$$

where T_o is the intergroup Theil index, T_g is the intragroup Theil index, and T is the overall Theil index,

(4A-13)
$$T_o = \sum_{g=1}^{G} Q_g \log \frac{Q_g}{P_g}$$

and

(4A-14)
$$T_g = \sum_{i \in S_g} \frac{q_i}{Q_g} \log \frac{q_i/Q_g}{p_i/P_g}.$$

Q_g is the income share of group S_g, and P_g is the population share of group S_g.

Thus the overall Theil index is the sum of the intergroup Theil index (or contribution to inequality) and a weighted average of the intragroup Theil indices—the weights used being the income shares Q_g. Income shares are used because they are regarded as the posterior probabilities. When the groups used are quantiles, the intragroup inequality is obviously suppressed and regarded as zero because everyone is taken to receive the mean income within the quantile. The decomposition of log variance may be done just like the decomposition of any variance into intergroup and intragroup components (see Anand 1983 for an exposition of the derivation of the decomposition). However, the weighting of the intragroup components, unlike that for the Theil decomposition, is by the population shares of each group.

Log variance is also additively decomposable such that total inequality is the sum of intergroup and intragroup inequality. The log variance is highly sensitive to small changes at low-income levels—hence the inclusion of one or a few low incomes in a sample would tend to heighten inequality as measured by log variance. One advantage of using log variance is that the ratio of intergroup and intragroup variance follows an F-distribution. Hence the ratio can be tested for statistical significance. The measures described here are essentially descriptive—they have no normative content. It is difficult to find any means of evaluating the comparative magnitudes of the percentage intergroup contributions to total inequality as measured by the Theil index and the log variance. Hence both measures are given in this study: the closeness of results between the two then gives greater confidence in the results.

The Atkinson Index

Atkinson's index (originally suggested by Atkinson 1970; also see Anand 1983) is different in that it is based on a social welfare function evaluating alternative income distributions. The principle is to measure the departure from the existing per capita income from that "equally distributed income" that would achieve the same level of social welfare as the given distribution. The definition is independent of the social welfare function chosen, but Atkinson restricts his set of welfare functions to additively separable and symmetric functions. The "equally distributed income" z_E is defined by

(4A-15)
$$n\, U(z_E) = \sum_{i=1}^{n} U(z_i)$$

where the right-hand side U is the social welfare function chosen. Then the Atkinson index

(4A-16)
$$A = 1 - \frac{z_E}{\bar{z}}$$

where $\bar{z}$ is the mean income of the distribution of incomes

$$(z_1\, z_2, \ldots z_n)$$

as before.

If the function is to satisfy the first condition—that is, be mean-independent—$U(z)$ must be of the constant marginal utility form, that is,

$$U(z) = \left\{\frac{1}{1-\varepsilon}\right\}z^{1-\varepsilon} \qquad \varepsilon \neq 1$$

$$\log z \qquad\qquad \varepsilon = 1$$

For values of $\varepsilon \geq 0$, $U(z)$ is concave and $z_E \leq \bar{z}$; ε measures "inequality aversion": the greater that ε is, the more weight is attached to income transfers to the poor. As reported by Anand (1983), there seems to be general agreement that the value of ε should be placed between 1.5 and 2.5: EQUALISE uses $\varepsilon = 2.0$. (The Atkinson index cannot be computed for values of $\varepsilon \geq 1$ if there are zero incomes in the sample.)

Now
$$A = 1 - \frac{z_E}{\bar{z}}.$$

Hence, the lower the z_E, or greater the departure of z_E from $\bar{z}$, the greater is the implied welfare loss from inequality.

Table 4A-1. Log Variance of Spatial Inequality in Bogotá, 1973–78: Individuals Ranked by HINCAP

Sector	1973 Log variance	Rank[a]	1975 Log variance	Rank	1977 Log variance	Rank	1978 Log variance	Rank
1	1.101	6	1.514	8	1.301	8	0.645	3
2	0.718	2	0.767	3	0.551	1	0.474	1
3	0.686	1	0.629	2	0.599	2	0.546	2
4	0.769	2	0.590	1	0.819	4	0.694	4
5	0.917	5	1.062	5	0.886	5	0.750	6
6	0.822	4	0.814	4	0.639	3	0.715	5
7	1.247	7	1.054	6	0.905	6	1.001	7
8	1.990	8	1.439	7	0.970	7	1.282	8
All sectors	1.013		0.901		0.830		0.846	
Intergroup contribution								
Sectors (log variance)	0.109		0.066		0.115		0.147	
Sectors (percent)	10.7		7.3		13.9		17.3	
Comunas[b] (percent)	20.3		18.3		23.9		28.5	

a. Ascending order of inequality.
b. Intergroup contribution if grouped by comunas.
Source: See table 4-2.

Table 4A-2. *Log Variance of Spatial Inequality in Cali, 1973–78: Individuals Ranked by* HINCAP

Sector	1973		1977		1978	
	Log variance	Rank[a]	Log variance	Rank	Log variance	Rank
1	0.925	4	1.117	7	1.212	7
2	0.970	5	0.446	1	0.604	3
3	0.792	3	0.502	2	0.534	1
4	0.616	1	0.526	3	0.573	2
5	0.774	2	0.578	4	0.626	4
6	1.472	7	1.042	6	1.047	5
7	1.128	6	0.615	5	1.144	6
All sectors	0.973		0.767		0.809	
Intergroup contribution						
Sectors (log variance)	0.121		0.119		0.116	
Sectors (percent)	12.4		15.5		14.4	
Comunas[b] (percent)	26.5		32.1		30.2	

a. Ascending order of inequality.
b. Intergroup contribution if grouped by comunas.
Source: See table 4-2.

5

Poverty in Bogotá and Cali

Chapter 4 described the overall distribution of income in Bogotá and Cali, suggested some ways of looking at the problem of income distribution in a developing urban economy, and demonstrated the extensive spatial segmentation of incomes in the two cities. Not only were specific areas found to be particularly rich and others particularly poor, but it was also found that homogeneity was tending to increase *within* zones just as differences were tending to increase *between* them. Much of the discussion was concerned with ways to measure these differences. Similarly, much of this chapter's discussion of poverty deals with ways of measuring it. Later chapters analyze the determinants of participation in the labor market, and of the earnings of those who do participate.

This chapter identifies the correlates of poverty by examining the composition and characteristics of the poor in Bogotá and Cali. Before these characteristics can be described, however, poverty itself needs to be defined so that the people "in poverty" can be identified. Since descriptive data about the poor tend to become lost in analytical work, this chapter tries to redress the balance by identifying some of the more interesting ways by which the poor can be described through the cross-tabulation of characteristics. I identify the poor largely by comparing their characteristics with those of the population as a whole.

Measuring poverty and malnutrition is a difficult task that is often surrounded by controversy, and estimates of the two phenomena often span a very large range. This can be true even of estimates for the same country and sometimes even when based on the same source material. To determine the characteristics and correlates of poverty (and its relationship to the operation of the labor market), the appropriate variables must be carefully defined and measured. The next section addresses some of the conceptual and empirical problems inherent in the measurement of poverty and malnutrition, and the chapter appendix describes the method used here to identify the poor. Considerable attention is given to these topics in order to clarify what is being measured and what is not. The discussion emphasizes the difficulties inherent in poverty measurement, and reader is encouraged to be wary of accepting poverty estimates whose assumptions are not made clear. In the remainder of the chapter I look at the range of estimates of poverty and malnutrition for Bogotá and Cali and their spread in the two cities, the characteristics of the poor and some popular notions of the correlates of poverty, and some data on unemployment and participation rates among the poor.

Most of the questions addressed in this chapter are fairly standard ones for this kind of inquiry: Who are the poor, and what do they do? Are they unemployed, underemployed, or overworked? Are they young or old? Are they predominantly male or female? Are they concentrated in certain occupations or industries of activity? Are they migrants or nonmigrants? The additional dimension investigated here, as in the rest of this book, is that of the geographical distribution of poverty in Bogotá and Cali—where do the poor live?

The Measurement of Malnutrition and Poverty

Measuring poverty involves a number of conceptual problems. One key concern is to develop a working definition that is purged of all relative notions of poverty. To take an extreme example, if the household income definition of poverty used in the United States was to be applied to developing countries, poverty would include all but the wealthiest households in most of these countries. To avoid problems such as this, analysts have sought some yardstick that will yield a more widely applicable absolute definition of poverty. Most attempts at measuring absolute poverty have used malnutrition as their criterion, both for various countries and for the world. Appropriately enough, this approach was pioneered in India (Ojha 1970; Dandekar and Rath 1971), and soon gained widespread attention when used to estimate the extent of malnutrition in the world (Reutlinger and Selowsky 1976). In what follows here, I try to estimate the extent of malnutrition and poverty is Bogotá and Cali and to locate it spatially within the two cities.

In carrying out this exercise, however, I have found that estimating malnutrition and poverty is fraught with conceptual and empirical difficulties. It is hard to measure the extent of malnutrition directly, or to define poverty accurately enough to make precise estimates. Nonetheless, as this chapter shows, ranges can be estimated for malnutrition and poverty, and hence upper and lower limits can be placed on their incidence and scale. The breadth of the ranges that result from sensitivity tests reflects the uncertainty surrounding these calculations and demonstrates the difficulties involved in estimating the level of poverty and malnutrition even when the quality of the data is above average, as it is in Bogotá and Cali. Thus any specific magnitudes estimated for global or countrywide malnutrition and poverty warrant skeptical examination; concrete measures of their extent are more appropriately expressed in ranges and distributions that clearly state the assumptions made. Given current methods, it is best to place lower bounds on estimates of poverty and malnutrition; this can be done with a reasonable degree of confidence.

In the present study, it had been somewhat naively assumed that the analysis would be able to indicate with some precision the extent of malnutrition in the two cities, to identify the worst-off neighborhoods, and to find the appropriate cutoff levels of income below which people could be identified as poor according to a definition of nutrition. As just noted, however, the estimates derived are much more diffuse than had been hoped; nevertheless, the results are helpful for tracking welfare trends in the two cities.

The first point to clarify is what is being measured in this study. It is difficult to estimate the actual prevalence of malnutrition in a community—that is, to make a definitive statement asserting that y percent of a population is malnourished.[1] Instead, the statement must be much weaker: z percent of a population simply does not have adequate income to purchase enough food to achieve w percent of the average nutrition requirements for that population. As Sen (1980) argues, "Considerations of average nutritional requirements can be used for one perspective of poverty even when nutritional requirements vary from person to person." Recognizing this variation, we have to admit that an estimate z has a probability distribution around some mean $\bar{z}$, as does w around $\bar{w}$. Put in simple terms, the objective here is to find a lower bound for an estimate of malnutrition or poverty such that one can state with a relatively high degree of confidence that $\bar{z}$ percent of the population *must* be malnourished since they simply do not receive adequate incomes; however, there may well be more people who are in fact malnourished.

Malnutrition is essentially a biological or medical condition and thus its most direct expression involves clinical types of measurement. But even these measurements are actually indirect expressions since they measure the consequences of malnutrition, such as "below normal" heights or weights, the "state of health," and level of cognitive ability. At the heart of the problem is the question of how to define "normal." If that task is relegated to the medical profession and its judgments accepted, economists can at least conceive of a data set that gives "independent" estimates of the prevalence of

---

1. For an overview of the variables most likely to help in identifying the groups at risk, see Austin (1980).

malnutrition and then proceed to estimate its determinants. This procedure would be empirically convenient, although it begs the conceptual question of what is "normal."

In view of the difficulty of measuring malnutrition directly, the procedure usually adopted has been to measure a single index of nutrition rather than a vector of attributes; the underlying assumption is that nutrition is determined by energy intake and expenditure, which can largely be measured by the caloric content of foods. Although this simplification has been attacked on the grounds that protein deficiencies are as important or more important than calorie deficiencies, Sukhatme (1978) has persuasively defended the use of calorie intake, noting that "protein malnutrition . . . is for the most part the indirect result of inadequate energy in the diet." Moreover, as Sukhatme (1970, 1977a, 1977b, 1978) and Srinivasan (1980) have pointed out, the focus on calorie intake has itself led to further problems. In reducing the measurement problem to that of calorie intake in foods, the problem of defining the caloric norm against which to compare the intake of individuals remains.

Problems in Measuring Calorie Requirements

As Sukhatme and Srinivasan have pointed out, positing a "normal" level of calorie requirements opens the procedure to two types of error. The first is the *interindividual* variation in requirements and the second is the *intraindividual* variation in the requirements.[2] Thus, if μ is a communitywide norm for per capita calorie requirements, then the norm for an individual i will be

$$(5\text{-}1) \qquad\qquad \overline{\mu}_i = \mu + a_i + b_t$$

where a_i represents the individual i's deviation from the community norm and b_t the individual's own deviation over time from his own norm. Now, if a_i and b_t are independent random variables with mean 0 and variance $\sigma^2_{a_i}$ and $\sigma^2_{b_t}$, the total variance can be written as [3]

$$(5\text{-}2) \qquad\qquad \sigma^2 = \sigma^2_{a_i} + \sigma^2_{b_t}.$$

2. They emphasize the *intraindividual* variation. According to Srinivasan (personal communication): "A person is likely to be in nutritional stress if his energy intakes are *beyond* the limits imposed by the homeostasis mechanism. And this stress appears to be similar to a threshold effect. Everything is all right if intakes are within these limits: sustained intake below the lower limit or above the upper limit leads the system to fall apart. Sukhatme identifies these limits for a given individual as his long run mean intake plus or minus twice the intraindividual standard deviation of intakes."

3. Assumes that a_i and b_t are uncorrelated; that is, Cov $(a_i, b_t) = 0$.

Good estimates for $\sigma_{a_i}^2$ and $\sigma_{b_t}^2$ do not exist but Sukhatme suggests that

$$\frac{\sigma}{\mu} = 0.15$$

in approximate terms.

Thus, at any given time the requirements of an individual can be said to be in the range $\mu \pm 2\sigma$ with 95 percent of confidence. If σ is approximately 0.15, then there is very low probability (approximately 0.025) that an individual's requirements at any given time would be lower than 0.7μ.

It is therefore crucial to establish the minimum level of calorie requirements in determining the degree of malnutrition. Since there are a large number of people whose calorie consumption is around the usual requirement levels, a small percentage change in requirements can lead to substantial changes in the estimate of malnourished people. The energy requirements of individuals depend on four variables that are interrelated in a complex way: physical activity, body size and sex, age, and climatic and other ecological factors (FAO 1973). Requirements are then specified by age, sex, body weight, and nature of activity. Unfortunately, many agencies still disagree strongly as to the minimum level of requirements. Consider for example, the differing recommendations given by the U.S. Food and Nutrition Board and the Food and Agriculture Organization (see table 5-1).

The Colombian Institute of Family Welfare (Instituto Colombiano de

Table 5-1. *U.S. and FAO Calorie Requirements for Different Ages*

Age	United States	Food and Agriculture Organization
Male		
1–3	1,300	1,360
4–6	1,700	1,830
7–10	2,400	2,240
11–14	2,700	2,750
15–18	2,800	3,060
19–22	2,900	3,000
23–50	2,700	3,000
Female		
11–14	2,200	2,425
15–18	2,100	2,380
19–22	2,100	2,200
23–50	2,000	2,200

Sources: FAO (1973) and Food and Nutrition Board (1980).

Bienestar Familiar, ICBF) is the agency responsible for monitoring nutrition in Colombia. Over time, it has revised its recommendations for the minimum adequate level of calorie intake from an average of 2,150 calories a day in 1972 to 1,970 calories a day in 1977 (assuming that the age and sex distribution of the Colombian population remains unchanged). Such changes have major implications for estimates of malnutrition. García (1980) estimated that about 70 percent of the Colombian population would be undernourished if 2,150 calories were taken as the requirement level, whereas only about 29 percent would be so classified if 1,970 calories were taken as the appropriate level.

Another example is reported by Bhalla (1980), who examined the results of the Health and Nutrition Examination Survey (HANES) for the United States. He found that "according to the FAO requirements, 67% of American males and 80% of American females have a calorie intake which is below the requirement level." If U.S. recommendations are imposed, the corresponding "malnutrition" figures are 46 percent for men and 70 percent for women. Bhalla adds, "Can these figures be believed, i.e., is it possible that approximately half the American population is malnourished (below 80% of FAO requirements) in terms of calories?" Clearly, estimates of malnutrition depend greatly on the level of calorie intake chosen as the cutoff point.

Thus far this discussion has focused only on the calorie intake of individuals. We need to recall that malnutrition is a wider concept. The prevalence of chronic stomach diseases, such as those caused by amoebic infections, makes the magnitude of energy ingested somewhat irrelevant. This is where the concept of the human body as a servomechanism or a self-regulating control system becomes important. Not only do diseases make the body an inefficient energy converter, but the control system itself becomes ineffective; as a result, intake of the required number of calories no longer ensures adequate nutrition. Stated another way, under conditions of poor sanitation, impure water, tardy garbage removal, or even bad and overcrowded housing, malnutrition can occur regardless of calorie intake. Thus the quality of public services such as medical care, sanitation, and garbage removal can often have a greater effect than low earning on actual malnutrition in a population.

This point is particularly relevant to current conditions in middle-income, semi-industrialized countries where urban malnutrition may often have more to do with neighborhood environmental factors than with low income. In many Latin American and East Asian middle-income countries, average earnings are now approaching levels at which most people have at least the *potential* to enjoy adequate nutrition. As incomes move closer to these levels, as they are doing in Colombia, estimates of malnutrition will have to be arrived at more carefully. In such cases, estimates of malnutrition based on low incomes could be misleading unless the prevalence of low incomes is closely correlated with neighborhood and environmental conditions. Otherwise, it will be necessary to make direct estimates of the effects of sanitation, hygiene, and housing on nutritional standards. Rapid increases in urbanization will make such estimates more and more important, as Basta (1977) has shown for selected urban areas. The encouraging point here is that if low income ceases to be the critical determinant of malnutrition, then improvements in these other areas might be brought about more easily by direct public policy actions.

The estimates in this chapter, like those in most other studies, do not take into account neighborhood effects, although an effort has been made to focus on the problem areas of Bogotá and Cali. However, the estimates do take into account inter- and intraindividual variations in daily calorie intake requirements by considering estimates of the proportion of individuals who consume less than 0.7μ or 0.8μ. Using these procedures, the probability that well-nourished individuals will be misclassified as malnourished is small. The probability that malnourished individuals will be misclassified as well nourished increases, but this is in keeping with the objective of finding lower-bound estimates of malnutrition.

Calorie intake by a population can be measured in different ways. Reutlinger and Selowsky (1976), Reutlinger and Alderman (1980), García (1979, 1980, 1981), and various others have estimated total energy consumption by means of nationwide food balance sheets. They estimate the total amount of food consumed in a country and then attempt to distribute it over various income groups in order to identify groups that are malnourished. At the national level it is important to take into account the particular age and sex distribution at a given time in order to arrive at a representative per capita (or per "reference adult," or per "adult equivalent") measure of the consumption of calories. Thus, the total estimate of calories consumed ought to be disaggregated by income groups and by age and sex groups to obtain meaningful results. This has not been done in the studies mentioned above. It is easy to adjust the per capita needs of a population by its age and sex distribution, but harder to adjust its consumption. Nonetheless, if comparisons are made over time, these adjustments also need to be made, particularly when the age and sex composition of a population is changing rapidly. Such adjustments are clearly difficult to make in practice.

A second approach is to measure calorie intake on the basis of household survey data on consumption, expenditure, and income. This procedure has been used for Brazil, for example (World Bank 1979), and Sri Lanka (Visaria 1979; Gavan and Sri Chandrasekhara 1979), and in various studies conducted in India. Since information on food consumption is available for each household, its calorie intake can be calculated. This procedure can give rise to several types of error, however.[4] The first of these is the familiar reporting error that may arise as a result of memory lapses when the household reports retrospectively on food consumed over a reference period (day, week, month, year); that may occur because of a desire to understate (or overstate) consumption when the household keeps a diary of food consumption over a period; or that may occur because of divergences from the "normal" consumption pattern when the surveyors themselves make the measurements. Whichever method is used, we can expect measurement errors to occur. The second error stems from intraindividual variation in consumption. Consumption is measured over a reference period; the longer the period, the smaller this problem should be. (But the first type of error might actually increase when the reference period is increased.) Third, errors can be caused by variations in the caloric content of food. A commodity typically comes in a variety of forms, but a standardized or "normal" caloric content is used to estimate its contribution to household consumption. If there is a systematic correlation between the caloric content of different varieties and the varieties typically bought by the rich or the poor, estimates will inevitably be biased.

In addition to the methods of estimation that start at the national level and those that focus on the household level are ones that use published grouped data from household surveys, as did Knudsen and Scandizzo (1979). Here, average diets must be attributed to each group in order to estimate its consumption of calories, and thus intragroup variation is unavoidably lost.

The objective of most of these studies is to estimate a relationship between calorie consumption and income in order to derive bases for cutoff incomes that characterize absolute poverty. Whereas estimates of poverty based on household-level data can suffer from errors due to the understatement of income (a well-known feature of most surveys), estimations that use grouped data from household surveys face the problem that either everyone in a given group is classified as malnourished or no one is, since only averages can be dealt with. This problem is clearly more serious the smaller the number of groups being considered. (Reutlinger and Alderman 1980 solve this problem in part by assuming a normal distribution of intakes and requirements within income groups.)

In general, researchers try to establish the income level that corresponds to the minimum daily calorie requirement, and then classify everyone below that income level as malnourished. If deciles are used, for example, each requirement level is associated with a decile. A small variation in the re-

---

4. This is not meant to imply that these errors are greater than those that arise when national food balance sheets are used—indeed, the converse is true, since surveys constitute the only source of direct observations on the distribution of intakes among households.

quirement level could easily cause the malnutrition estimate to jump one decile. In fact, income data are often grouped in such a way that the bottom half of the population falls in the bottom two or three groups and the top half is divided into many more groups. This type of problem is illustrated in table 5-2, which is based on earlier studies that relied on published data only (Garcia 1980, 1981). As mentioned earlier, a 10 percent change in the average calorie requirement causes a much larger change in the estimate of malnutrition.

In summary, measuring calorie consumption is just as difficult as estimating calorie requirements. This study tries to deal with both these problems by conducting various simulations in order to obtain some idea of the magnitude of possible error. The methods used to estimate malnutrition and poverty are given in appendix 5A to this chapter. The next section reports the results for Cali and Bogotá, which will give some indication of the lower bounds of malnutrition in the two cities. The range of these results reflects the difficulties inherent in this kind of estimation.

Estimates of Malnutrition and Poverty

The existing estimates of malnutrition and poverty in Colombia range from 18 to 100 percent of the population, depending on the reference population, the level of calorie requirements, and methodology (see Betancourth 1977;

Table 5-2. *Calorie Consumption per Day and Distribution of Population in Colombia, 1972*

Income bracket	Calorie consumption	Cumulative distribution of population
I	1,530	6.49
II	1,796	28.52
III	1,974	52.00
IV	2,116	68.49
V	2,292	76.18
VI	2,441	83.33
VII	2,577	89.29
VIII	2,810	94.45
IX	3,045	97.58
X	3,325	100.00

Source: García (1980, 1981) for calorie consumption and distribution of population, respectively.

Lemoine and Becerra 1978; Garcia 1980, 1981; and Pinstrup-Anderson and Caicedo 1978, among others). As mentioned earlier, the Instituto Colombiano de Bienestar Familiar (ICBF) had been in charge of the main nutrition programs up to 1974; since then, the Special Food and Nutrition Program has been implemented by several government agencies coordinated by the Colombian National Planning Office. Thus a considerable body of data and studies based on them exist, but there is little agreement on the extent of malnutrition and poverty for the reasons discussed in the preceding section. The estimates of malnutrition in Bogotá and Cali given below demonstrate that it is possible to obtain some idea of the magnitude of the problem but that the range of uncertainty is very wide. The estimates are of *the proportion of the population whose income is inadequate to cover food and nutrition needs, given existing food and consumption habits and prices.* This approach thus indicates approximate magnitudes with respect to the number of people who lack even the potential for being well nourished.

Although results are given for both 1973 and 1978, the two sets of estimates are not strictly comparable in that almost 10 percent of the respondents in the 1973 sample did not report their incomes. They have been excluded from this calculation, as have any households who have even one working individual whose income is not reported. Live-in maids are excluded from both samples because it is difficult to assign them to any household other than single-member households of their own.

In the 1978 survey, almost all households reported their incomes; only about 3 percent of the sample provided no information. As already noted, income coverage for the 1973 census was only about 50 percent, but was about 90 percent for the 1978 sample. Thus, estimates of malnutrition are somewhat high for 1973, but an effort has been made to account for underreporting by means of various sensitivity tests.

Table 5-3 indicates the range of estimates of malnutrition in Bogotá and Cali. As might be expected, the extent of malnutrition is systematically higher for the WHO requirements than for the ICBF requirements. The percentage malnourished (hereafter PCM) at 0.7R (70 percent of requirements) and 0.8R are higher according to method 2 (M2), but at 1.0R the PCM is higher according to method 1 (M1). (M1 and M2 refer to different ways of calculating calories consumed; see appendix 5A.) For Bogotá, the total range of estimates is from 17.2 percent malnourished (at 0.7R) to 75.0 PCM (at 1.0R) for 1973 and from 5.5 to 58.1 PCM for 1978. This is the range in the sense that there is no general agreement as to the level of requirements. Note that 1.0R itself is lower than the actual WHO-FAO recommendations. The estimates are highly sensitive to the level of requirements and somewhat less so to the method of calculation used.

The picture is muddied further when attempts are made to correct for the

Table 5-3. *Extent of Malnutrition in Bogotá and Cali: Proportion*
of Population below Requirement Levels

	Categories of requirements[a]					
	0.7R		0.8R		1.0R	
Method[b]	WHO	ICBF	WHO	ICBF	WHO	ICBF
	Bogotá					
1973						
M1	24.6	17.2	42.8	31.9	75.0	66.4
M2	38.2	34.0	46.3	41.6	59.0	55.2
1978						
M1	9.5	5.5	21.3	14.7	58.1	47.0
M2	18.3	16.0	25.1	21.1	36.6	33.1
	Cali					
1973						
M1	26.9	19.1	45.1	34.8	77.3	68.6
M2	41.1	36.9	48.5	44.6	61.1	57.2
1978						
M1	11.0	7.3	22.9	15.9	60.7	50.6
M2	19.7	16.7	25.7	22.1	40.3	36.4

	Range of estimates	
	1973	1978
Bogotá		
Total range	17.2 to 75.0	5.5 to 58.1
0.8R	31.9 to 46.3	14.7 to 25.1
Cali		
Total range	19.1 to 77.3	7.3 to 60.7
0.8R	34.8 to 48.5	15.9 to 25.7

a. R is requirements according to WHO/FAO and the ICBF as detailed in table 5A-1; 0.7R, 0.8R, 1.0R refer to percentage receiving less than 70 percent, 80 percent, and 100 percent of requirement levels.

b. Method refers to the calculation of calories consumed. See chapter 5, appendix.

understatement of income referred to earlier.[5] This procedure serves two purposes. It provides an idea of PCM, corrected for underreported incomes, and it also offers some basis for estimating the feasibility of eliminating malnutrition through income growth alone. How long will it take to eliminate malnutrition under current income trends, given optimistic assumptions of real per capita income growing at a rate of 3–4 percent a year and of income

5. See table 5-5 for the results of these income experiments.

distribution remaining unchanged, that is, everyone's income increasing by the same proportion?

What can be concluded from table 5-3? If a compromise is made between two kinds of errors—type I (misclassifying well nourished as malnourished) and type II (misclassifying malnourished as well nourished)—0.8R may be regarded as the "correct" requirement level, which takes into account interindividual variations. The *intraindividual* variations are implicitly accounted for in this method, since either annual or monthly expenditures are being used to calculate calorie consumption. The maximum type I error at 0.8R (if we assume a normal distribution of individuals around R with standard deviation about 15 percent) is about 10 percent. It is probably not unreasonable to assume that the type II error might be about 5 percent (but there is no rigorous basis for this assumption). One can therefore subtract 5 percent from the PCM at 0.8R. From table 5-3 it can then be concluded that the proportion of the population that was malnourished in 1973 was 25–35 percent in Bogotá and 30–40 percent in Cali; and that the proportion in 1978 was 10–16 percent in both cities. These results would hold if incomes at the low end were fully reported in both the samples.

In order to examine the extent to which income was underreported at low income levels, the reported wages of selected low-wage occupations were compared for the two samples. Table 5-4 shows that the real incomes of people in these occupations rose by about 8 percent a year. Surprisingly, the minimum wage increased in real terms at a similar rate: 8.8 percent a year. It is remarkable that the relative structure of wages has remained stable and that the relationship between the minimum wage and wages in poorly paid occupations has been constant. Two conclusions can be drawn from these wage patterns. First, if we assume that there was very little underreporting of low wages in the 1978 survey, the coverage of incomes in the 1973 census appears to have been good, at least at the low end. Second, poorly paid groups in the population made considerable gains in their real incomes between 1973 and 1978. The fact that average real wages reported in these occupations were more than twice the minimum wage gives us further confidence in these conclusions. The overall undercoverage of income in the 1973 census must therefore be attributed to undercoverage at the higher end of the income scale.

The estimates of malnutrition given above do not suffer greatly from the underestimation of incomes. Nonetheless, income experiments were conducted (see table 5-5). The income of every household was augmented by fixed percentage levels and the malnutrition estimates were recomputed. If it is assumed that the low end of the 1973 income distribution was really 30 percent higher (that is, underreported by about 20 percent), the estimate of malnutrition becomes about 30 percent according to M2 at the 0.8R level.

Table 5-4. Real Wage Trends for Males in Low-Income Occupations in Bogotá, 1973–78

ILO code	Occupation	Wages as proportion of minimum wage		Monthly wages in constant 1970 pesos		Annual rate of growth (percent)
		1973	1978	1973	1978	1973–78
37	Mail distribution clerk	1.9	1.9	543	835	8.9
53	Cooks, waiters, and bartenders	2.7	2.5	745	1,094	8.0
58	Protective service	2.8	2.7	787	1,170	7.9
77	Food and beverage processors	2.6	2.5	724	1,106	8.5
93	Painters	2.5	2.7	709	1,170	10.0
95	Construction	2.5	2.2	692	966	6.7
97	Transport equipment operators	2.1	2.0	580	879	8.3
	Monthly minimum wage	1.0	1.0	279	434	8.8

Note: Consumer price index (1970 = 100): 1973 = 150 and 1978 = 400.
Sources: 1973 population census sample; and 1978 World Bank–DANE Household Survey.

Table 5-5. Income Experiments for Bogotá: Percentage of Population below ICBF Requirements (Methods 1 and 2)

	Categories of requirements					
	0.8R			1.0R		
Percentage increase in income[a]	1973	1978		1973	1978	
	M2	M2	M1	M2	M2	M1
0	41.6	21.1	14.7	55.2	33.1	47.0
10	37.5	17.5	12.4	51.4	29.6	43.0
20	33.9	16.0	10.3	47.2	26.4	39.0
30	30.4	13.7	7.8	43.8	22.9	35.1
50	24.6	9.3	5.7	37.3	18.1	29.0
70	20.2	6.7	3.6	32.3	15.2	23.8
100	15.3	4.0	2.7	25.3	10.1	17.8

a. The income of each household was augmented by these percentages and the calories consumed were then calculated at these incomes.
Source: My estimates from 1978 World Bank–DANE Household Survey.

If income is assumed to be underreported by 10 percent in 1978, the comparable figures are 18 percent by M2 and 12 percent by M1. The new estimates of malnutrition are therefore *25–30 percent for 1973 and 12–18 percent in 1978* for Bogotá; the estimates for Cali are similar.

One other adjustment needs to be made. As mentioned earlier, the poor are more efficient in their consumption of calories than the rich. The foods they buy are probably lower in quality than those bought by the better-off, but similar in calorie content—so that the prices they paid per calorie are lower than those paid by higher-income groups. According to the price experiments (see table 5-6), if prices paid by the poor are 20 percent less than the average, the estimate of malnutrition is reduced by about 10 percent for each year.

It is difficult to specify precisely what adjustments should be made to the estimates on account of underreporting of income and price variations between the rich and the poor. Nevertheless, by combining the two kinds of adjustments, using M2 at 0.8R of ICBF requirements, and taking into account type I and type II errors, *one can say with a high degree of confidence that the proportion of malnourished in Bogotá in 1973 could not have been much less than about 25 percent.* The same procedure gives an estimate of about *12 percent* for 1978. Thus it is probably fair to say that malnutrition and absolute poverty in Bogotá fell from about 25 percent in 1973 to 12 percent in 1978—give or take 5 percent. The estimates for Cali are similar.

The above statements sound more definitive than they are meant to be. The estimates really refer to lower bounds: there must be *at least* this number

Table 5-6. *Price Experiments for Bogotá: Percentage of Population below ICBF Requirements (Method 2)*

| Percentage change in calorie price | Categories of requirements | | | |
| | 0.8R | | 1.0R | |
	1973	1978	1973	1978
−50	9.9	2.1	17.0	4.7
−40	15.6	4.1	25.4	9.4
−30	22.1	7.4	34.6	10.6
−20	28.8	11.2	41.6	21.1
−10	35.6	16.7	49.2	27.9
0	41.6	21.1	55.2	33.1
10	48.6	26.2	60.7	38.4
20	52.9	30.9	65.0	45.1
30	57.6	35.1	69.2	49.9

Source: See table 5-5.

of people who simply do not have incomes that would allow adequate nu-trition. There might well be more who have adequate incomes but suffer from malnutrition for other reasons. As the income experiments in table 5-5 show, even if average household income was to grow by 5 percent a year for the next ten years, at least 5 percent of the population would still be malnourished. The high average incomes produced by such a growth rate ought to make it possible to eliminate malnutrition completely; in practice, however, income growth alone cannot eliminate malnutrition and poverty over the medium term. The problem must be attacked directly. The bottom 5–10 percent on the income scale are likely to consist disproportionately of the old, the infirm, and those who are too malnourished to be able to work; the aggregate growth of employment income does them no good.

Mapping Malnutrition, Poverty, and Incomes

When Mohan and Hartline (1984) examined the correlates of poverty in Bogotá, the 1978 survey data were not yet available and they had to work from household surveys conducted in 1975 and 1977. They approached the problem by looking at the bottom 30 percent of the income distribution ranked by household income per capita (HINCAP), but some might question whether it is appropriate to define the poor (or the malnourished) on the basis of some arbitrary division of incomes such that everyone below a certain level is characterized as poor or malnourished. That question is taken up in this section, which demonstrates the kind of errors that arise as a result of such a simple mapping procedure.

Table 5-7 gives a number of characteristics of the population of Bogotá by income deciles. The ranking criterion is household income per capita for all individuals. Row 1 gives the breakdown of people with PCM less than 0.8R by decile for Bogotá in 1978. Virtually all of those defined as malnourished on this basis fall in the bottom three deciles. If, however, the third decile is defined as the malnutrition cutoff point, about 9 percent of the popula-tion—as many as 32 percent in the second decile and 58 percent in the third decile—are misclassified as malnourished. Conversely, one can be sure that only in the top five deciles is there no malnutrition due to income deprivation. The fact that household size declines monotonically with income deciles (see row 7)[6] suggests that the malnourished belong predominantly to large families with high dependency ratios.

Rows 8 and 9 give average household income per capita and household income by decile. It is useful to compare the minimum wage with these

6. Note that the deciles are ranked by *household income per capita*. As mentioned earlier, household size increases if households are ranked by *household income*.

average incomes. The 1978 monthly minimum wage was 1,738 pesos. Since the majority of the second decile and part of the third decile are malnourished, a rule-of-thumb estimate for the household income necessary for minimum adequate nutrition might be somewhere between the averages for these two deciles—that is, about 4,000–5,000 pesos a month. This in turn translates into a per household employment level of roughly 2.5 workers at the minimum wage. In fact, poor households have characteristically high dependency ratios—they have fewer than 2.5 workers per household (Mohan and Hartline 1984). Viewed in this way, the minimum wage is not unduly high: indeed, it should be higher than it is, if the objective of a minimum wage is to ensure that everyone has at least the potential to consume a minimally adequate diet.[7]

It is clear from the above that one must be wary of malnutrition estimates reached by simple income cutoff levels.[8] The present results differ from those in other studies because household size and intrahousehold age and sex composition have been taken into account. Moreover, although these calculations are also based on income, they have been appropriately adjusted for estimating food expenditures.

To sum up, taking the whole of the bottom 30 percent as poor (according to HINCAP) would misclassify some nonpoor households as poor in 1978. At the same time, there is clearly almost zero probability of any malnourished households being in the top five deciles; while there are only a few in the fourth and fifth deciles who are malnourished, they would be missed if only the bottom 30 percent were taken as poor. This is true for 1978, when the overall incidence of 0.8R is 21 percent. In 1973, the proportion was higher (about 42 percent by M2 according to ICBF requirements). After the corrections made earlier, the 1973 estimate for the proportion almost certainly living in poverty was reduced to 25–30 percent. Moreover, the structure of the poorest workers' relative wages was found to be very stable between the two years. In view of all these considerations, it turns out to be reasonable to use the bottom 30 percent as a poverty cutoff point for Bogotá and Cali in the 1970s. There would be some misclassification (involving omission of some of the poor in the early part of the period and wrong inclusion of some

7. This ignores other labor market effects of imposing a higher minimum wage. Table 5-5 shows that mean wages even in the occupations receiving the lowest pay were substantially higher than the minimum wage. In current conditions, it would be difficult to argue that the minimum wage in Bogotá is the cause of unemployment, as is often suggested.

8. These problems have led to the wide variation in estimates for Colombia: Pinstrup-Andersen and Caicedo (1978) estimated that 18–30 percent were malnourished in Cali in 1969–70; Garcia (1980) estimated 40 percent for Colombia as a whole in 1972; Betancourth (1977), 60 percent for Colombia in 1972; and Lemoine and Becerra (1978), almost 100 percent for all of Colombia in 1974–76. See Mohan, Garcia, and Wagner (1981) for more details.

Table 5-7. Mapping Malnutrition into Income Deciles in Bogotá, 1978: ICBF Requirements (Method 2)

Category					Income decile						
	1	2	3	4	5	6	7	8	9	10	Total
1. Percentage of 0.8R in decile	46	32	20	1	1	0	0	0	0	0	100.0
Percentage of decile in each category											
2. 0.8R	100	68	42	2	2	0	0	0	0	0	21
3. 0.8R to 1.0R	0	28	35	40	16	3	0	0	0	0	12
4. 1.0R+	0	4	23	58	82	97	100	100	100	100	67
5. Total	100	100	100	100	100	100	100	100	100	100	100
6. Percentage of population in decile	9.8	10.0	9.8	9.7	10.0	10.4	9.8	10.1	10.3	10.3	100[c]
7. Average household size	6.1	5.5	5.4	5.3	5.2	4.8	4.6	4.3	4.1	3.5	4.8
8. Average household income per capita[a]	440	720	925	1,200	1,470	1,810	2,300	3,110	4,780	12,640	2,980
9. Average household income[b]	2,580	3,980	5,050	6,340	7,680	8,710	10,675	13,400	19,670	51,790	18,140

Note: The population is ranked according to household income per capita.
a. Monthly income in 1978 pesos.
b. Minimum monthly wage in 1978: 1,738 pesos.
c. 3.5 million people.
Source: See table 5-5.

of the nonpoor in the latter part); overall, however, the characteristics obtained would not be misleading. In particular, a profile of poor workers based on this procedure would be quite accurate.

The Age Distribution of Malnutrition and Poverty

One of the more interesting findings in Mohan and Hartline (1984) is a distinctly higher incidence of poverty among children, despite the fact that income was assumed to be distributed evenly within households (this assumption is implicit in ranking persons by household income per capita). The same phenomenon is found in the estimates of malnutrition. This finding should not be surprising since basically a transformation of income is being used to define malnutrition here. If anything, malnutrition among children is even more pronounced. Note once again that in this study the nutrition level is assumed to be the same for all members of the same household, so no comment is being made on the intrafamily distribution of nutrition.

Table 5-8 presents the age distribution of malnutrition in Bogotá and Cali calculated at 0.8R and 1.0R of ICBF requirements by both M1 and M2. The PCM(M2) of children in the 5–14 age group is 14–16 points higher than

Table 5-8. *Extent of Malnutrition in Bogotá and Cali by Age Group,*
1973 and 1978: ICBF Requirements
(percent malnourished)

Age group and year	Bogotá				Cali			
	0.8R		1.0R		0.8R		1.0R	
	M1	M2	M1	M2	M1	M2	M1	M2
1973								
0–4	25.5	44.3	59.7	58.9	31.2	48.7	63.5	62.9
5–9	41.5	55.8	75.0	69.5	45.3	59.9	78.8	73.1
10–14	49.9	57.7	81.1	70.5	47.3	55.6	76.4	66.7
15–54	28.0	35.3	63.8	48.8	31.1	38.6	67.0	51.5
55–99	23.0	27.8	53.5	39.4	26.4	33.3	57.4	44.1
Total	31.9	41.6	66.4	55.2	34.8	44.6	48.6	57.2
1978								
0–4	8.6	19.7	35.0	32.1	12.0	22.1	36.6	37.1
5–9	18.0	28.4	51.7	43.7	21.7	31.7	56.5	47.9
10–14	26.9	34.1	69.7	49.9	26.5	33.4	70.0	51.3
15–54	12.9	17.7	44.6	28.8	13.6	18.3	48.8	31.7
55–99	12.0	15.4	36.5	21.9	11.9	15.3	41.4	27.2
Total	14.7	21.1	47.0	33.1	15.9	22.1	50.6	36.4

Source: See table 5-5.

the citywide PCM in 1973 and 7–13 points higher in 1978 at the 0.8R level. The levels for the 0–4 age group are near the mean. This finding is somewhat reassuring since these earliest years are the ones in which malnutrition produces the maximum irreparable damage (as reported, for example, by McKay and others 1978). Nevertheless, the high estimate for the 5–14 age group is disturbing. One can expect the schooling of these children to be adversely affected, and hence their chances in the labor market and their lifetime earnings. As a result of these low earnings, the children in the next generation would be similarly disadvantaged and the vicious cycle would continue.

A word of explanation is in order here concerning these children and why they are badly off when nutrition is evenly distributed within the household. As is well known (and as will be shown for Bogotá in chapter 8), the age-earnings profile is relatively flat for less-educated, low-income workers. Thus, for households headed by these workers, income per capita falls as household formation progresses and more children appear. As the children grow up and leave home, income per capita rises again. What is being observed may therefore be termed a life-cycle phenomenon. Visaria (1980) observed the same thing when looking at poverty across detailed household data sets for six countries in Asia. Malnourished children therefore come from the larger households headed by less-educated, low-income workers. If these children are indeed as malnourished as these calculations indicate, their handicap in the labor market (which already exists because of their low socioeconomic background) is magnified by the effects of malnutrition on their schooling.

These ideas gain further support when malnutrition in Bogotá is disaggregated by family size for 1978. From the data in table 5-9 it is clear that the incidence of malnutrition increases monotonically with family size and that as many as 50 percent of those in the largest families are likely to be malnourished. Although economies of scale in food consumption are probably not being fully accounted for, M2 does so in principle. The differences between family sizes are so marked, however, that the results are unlikely to change substantially even if economies of scale are taken into account. As Mohan (1980) has pointed out, larger households have fewer workers per dependent—and therefore proportionately lower incomes—than smaller ones. Larger families have proportionately more children, and hence those results show up in the age distribution.

To summarize the picture so far, the poor and malnourished come from low-income households that typically have high dependency ratios and income earners with flat age-earnings profiles. Children in these households are thus disproportionately disadvantaged and can be said to be caught in a low-income poverty trap. Over the past decade, trickle-down, or normal income growth, has done much to reduce the numbers of people who have no chance to achieve even minimally adequate nutrition. Given the long-

Table 5-9. Extent of Malnutrition in Bogotá by Family Size, 1978: Percentage of Population below ICBF Requirements (Method 2)

| | Categories of requirements | | | | | |
| | Bogotá | | | Cali | | |
Household size	0.8R	1.0R	Percentage of population	0.8R	1.0R	Percentage of population
1	1.8	3.2	1.1	5.4	5.4	1.3
2	3.7	5.7	4.7	4.3	10.3	4.8
3, 4	6.9	13.8	28.2	6.3	14.3	25.3
5, 6	18.2	30.1	31.2	20.0	31.7	31.9
7–9	33.0	49.0	24.8	36.1	58.9	27.2
10+	50.9	73.4	10.0	41.6	63.0	9.6
All categories	21.1	33.1	100.0	22.1	36.4	100.0

Source: See table 5-5.

term consequences of malnutrition in growing children, however, it would be desirable to intervene directly to reduce the incidence of malnutrition among them, in order to break the vicious cycle sketched above. Normal income growth alone raises their nutritional status too slowly.

The Spatial Distribution of Malnutrition

A major concern in the City Study was the spatial distribution of socio-economic characteristics. Chapters 3 and 4 have shown that in Bogotá incomes rose slightly with distance from the city center up to ring 3 and then fell, but the pattern with respect to mean household income per capita was not distinct. Table 5-10 shows a much stronger pattern. In 1973, per capita malnutrition (PCM) in the two outer rings was about 7–13 points higher than in ring 1 (the central business district), whereas in ring 3 it was about 6 points lower. This difference is proportionately even stronger in 1978. There is also a major change in 1978 compared with 1973. Ring 6, which lies entirely in the extreme north, has apparently changed from being a particularly poor area to a relatively rich one. Because the better-off have moved toward the north, average incomes in northern areas have naturally increased, but some of the poor may also have moved to the south.

In Cali, apart from the central business district, PCM increases consistently with distance from the center. Thus in Cali, it is much more correct to say that the poor live on the periphery and the relatively rich are more centrally located.

According to table 5-11, the distribution of malnutrition by radial sectors

Table 5-10. *Distribution of Malnutrition by Rings, 1973 and 1978: Percentage Malnourished at 0.8R of ICBF Requirements*

	Bogotá				Cali			
	1973		1978		1973		1978	
Ring	M1	M2	M1	M2	M1	M2	M1	M2
1	30.1	36.2	18.1	21.4	32.6	39.3	0.0	22.9
2	27.4	33.7	10.9	15.3	20.8	26.4	9.8	11.4
3	23.9	30.8	9.8	11.6	35.0	45.3	12.9	18.1
4	28.7	38.0	12.2	17.2	47.0	59.6	21.5	30.8
5	37.1	48.6	17.6	26.8	48.4	63.4	26.8	34.3
6	37.2	49.5	17.2	20.7	—	—	—	—
All rings	31.9	41.6	14.7	21.1	34.8	44.6	15.9	22.1

— Not applicable. There is no ring 6 in Cali.
Source: See table 5-5.

is even more distinct than it is by rings. Malnutrition in Bogotá is much higher in the southern sectors 2 and 3 and in sector 6, as one would expect from the income patterns mapped in chapters 2 and 4 and in Mohan and Hartline (1984). Once again, the differences are magnified when compared with the spatial distribution of income. Cali has a less distinct sectoral pattern. In general, the western part of the city is better off than the north and sector 2 stands out as being particularly well off.

Table 5-11. *Distribution of Malnutrition by Sectors, 1973 and 1978: Percentage Malnourished at 0.8R of ICBF Requirements*

	Bogotá				Cali			
	1973		1978		1973		1978	
Sector	M1	M2	M1	M2	M1	M2	M1	M2
1	30.1	36.3	18.1	21.4	32.6	39.3	0.0	22.9
2	43.0	55.4	22.6	32.7	4.6	8.5	6.7	6.7
3	34.5	45.9	13.6	20.6	30.5	39.3	11.0	14.5
4	26.0	33.1	13.2	16.9	37.0	48.8	21.3	28.5
5	30.6	39.1	10.2	15.1	42.0	53.2	19.3	26.0
6	33.3	44.3	15.1	23.5	33.4	41.5	10.5	18.3
7	19.9	25.3	11.2	12.8	32.3	42.2	9.8	13.4
8	20.0	26.4	7.1	8.1	—	—	—	—
All sectors	31.9	41.6	14.7	21.1	34.8	44.6	15.9	22.1

— Not applicable. There is no sector 8 in Cali.
Source: See table 5-5.

Map 5-1 provides a more disaggregated and better picture of the distribution of malnutrition and poverty in Bogotá. The darker shades, which represent higher PCM levels, illustrate the concentration of PCM in the periphery and in the south of Bogotá. It was also shown earlier that larger households are more likely to be located at the periphery. Thus the observed malnutrition map underscores the effects on PCM levels of low incomes and larger household size in the darkly shaded areas of the city.

As noted earlier, malnutrition is accentuated by disease, crowding, poor sanitation, and the practice of bad hygiene. Thus the estimates of malnutrition due to lack of income are likely to be understated in poor neighborhoods. In these areas, even people who have somewhat higher incomes and can afford more food may suffer from malnutrition because of chronic stomach disorders and other neighborhood-related problems, as was found to be the case in a recent detailed clinical nutrition study of Cali (personal communication, Luis Fajardo, Universidad del Valle). This possibility gives cause for further concern about the excessive PCMS found among children. These children were inferred to belong to large, poor families. In Bogotá such families are concentrated mainly in southern and peripheral locations on the basis of spatial patterns of poverty and family size. Children who are malnourished because their families lack the income to buy food are then even more likely to be affected by infectious diseases spread by bad sanitation and crowding. One thus begins to see how the nutrition of children is affected by a combination of life cycle and spatial or neighborhood factors and how these trends are perpetuated.

Further evidence of the spatial pattern of malnutrition in Bogotá is given by an index of the incidence of malnutrition by age group for each ring and sector (table 5-12). The index gives a sense of the relative incidence of malnutrition in a particular age group in a particular sector or ring, compared with the overall incidence for the age group. Thus indices in excess of 100 mean that the incidence of malnutrition is particularly high in that sector or ring for that age group. As table 5-12 shows, rings 1 and 5, and to a lesser extent ring 6—that is, the center and the periphery, respectively—are particularly hard hit. In ring 5 in particular, children are not disproportionately affected but the adults in these areas are relatively badly off compared with the overall city average. The sectoral distribution tells a similar story. The poor southern sector 2 has a much higher incidence in all age groups, but it is proportionately higher among adults, particularly among old people.

The earlier summary of the pattern of malnutrition and poverty in Bogotá can therefore be restated: southern and peripheral areas of Bogotá have a much higher incidence of malnutrition than the rest of the city. Interestingly, the adults in these areas are more disproportionately affected than the children. This pattern tends to bear out the idea that malnutrition is higher in

Map 5-1. *Bogotá: Percentage of the Population Who Are Malnourished by Comuna*

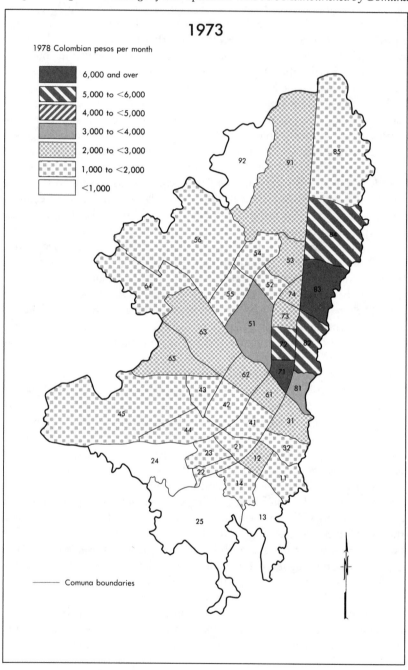

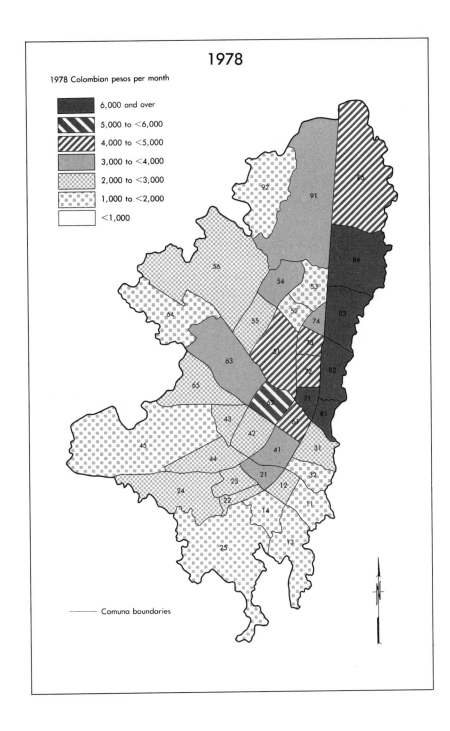

1978

1978 Colombian pesos per month

- 6,000 and over
- 5,000 to <6,000
- 4,000 to <5,000
- 3,000 to <4,000
- 2,000 to <3,000
- 1,000 to <2,000
- <1,000

—— Comuna boundaries

these areas because of larger household sizes and higher dependency ratios, which tend to accentuate the degree of malnutrition of families whose income earners have relatively flat age-income profiles.

If nutrition programs are to be organized, they should be targeted at these areas, particularly at the children living there, so that the vicious cycle alluded to earlier can be broken. The obvious intervention point is the school system. Better education and the provision of day care centers in these areas would enable women to participate in the labor force and thereby reduce dependency ratios. Given the poor sanitation and crowding in these areas, actual malnutrition must be even higher than our calculations suggest. Thus environmental programs concerned with improving public services should certainly be focused on these areas.

Characteristics of Poor Workers

Many studies have given considerable attention to the "urban informal sector," and much energy has gone into efforts to define this elusive concept.[9] This sector has been variously taken to include all those earning less than a minimum wage; all those working in small (or unenumerated) establishments; all those working in service occupations; and so on. This issue is examined in depth in chapter 9, in which I attempt to identify determinants of segmentation through the estimation of earnings functions. An appropriate policy, however, will seek to identify and remove poverty regardless of whether people work in small or large establishments, whether they are enumerated in economic censuses or not, or whether they work in manufacturing or service occupations. Such criteria should only be important if poverty is found to be systematically related to the characteristics of certain employment conditions. This section is therefore concerned with identifying the correlates of poverty among those who work.

As the last section showed, Mohan and Hartline's (1984) definition of the poor—those in the bottom 30 percent of individuals ranked according to household income per capita (HINCAP)—can be justified for Bogotá in the mid-1970s and it gives rise to very little misclassification. This section reports the main results of their analysis of the labor force characteristics of the poor, that is, the characteristics of those among the poor who work as determined from household surveys conducted in Bogotá in 1975 and 1977.

The fact of working at all does much to alleviate poverty. Thus, among men, only about 20 percent of the workers and, among women, only 15

9. For studies of the informal sector, see Mazumdar 1979; Webb 1977; Sethuraman 1974, 1976; Schaefer 1976; Joshi, Lubell, and Mouly 1976; Lubell 1974; and Lubell and McCallum 1978, among others.

Table 5-12. *Distribution of Malnutrition by Age Group, Ring, and Sector in Bogotá, 1978: Malnutrition at 0.8R of ICBF Requirements (Method 2)* (index of malnutrition)

Age group	Ring						Total percentage of malnourished in age group
	1	2	3	4	5	6	
0–4	160	92	54	77	117	101	19.7
5–9	28	76	77	81	120	112	28.4
10–14	126	82	76	86	112	98	34.1
15–54	77	65	45	84	133	92	17.7
55+	131	97	51	68	140	88	15.4
Total	101	73	55	82	127	98	21.1

Age group	Sector								
	1	2	3	4	5	6	7	8	
0–4	160	147	94	54	81	103	75	40	19.7
5–9	28	144	98	73	55	96	70	77	28.4
10–14	126	147	95	88	67	94	70	58	34.1
15–54	77	156	97	85	71	120	57	29	17.7
55+	131	188	108	83	141	84	51	23	15.4
Total	101	155	98	80	92	111	81	38	21.1

Note: The index of malnutrition:

$$A_{ij} = \frac{\text{Percentage malnourished in age group } i \text{ in sector } j}{\text{Percentage malnourished in age group } i}.$$

Source: See table 5-5.

percent fall in the overall bottom 30 percent. The majority of women are secondary workers; just bringing a second income into a household makes that household better off. As might be expected, almost one-half of all male workers with no education and about one-third of those with primary education belong to the poor. Furthermore, as pointed out in the last section, children suffer disproportionately from poverty. An analysis of poverty by age and education groups provides some corroborating evidence of this phenomenon. Among both males and females, workers in the 35–44 age group typically belong to the poor. Thus, although about 20 percent of all male workers are classified as poor, more than one-third in the 35–44 age group are classified as such. The majority of these people have no education or only primary schooling, but they also include about 15 percent of all those who have secondary education. As will be shown in chapter 6, workers with little education have relatively flat age-income profiles. It is this set of workers—whose households expand and whose children are in school during this phase of their life cycle—who appear to fall among the poor at this point. As a result, it is easy to see the economic hardship the poor suffer in educating their teen-age children rather than sending them out to work. Notice, too, that the relatively small sample of those in the 12–14 age group who work includes very few who are in poverty. Those who work clearly contribute to household income and thus, perhaps, help to lift the household out of poverty.

Poor workers are concentrated in a few occupations and corresponding industries. As might be expected, blue-collar occupations account for about 70–75 percent of poor workers. This may be compared with the 55–57 percent share of blue-collar occupations among all workers. It is interesting that production workers are atypically poor, as are construction, transport, and service workers. These four categories constitute about 70 percent of all poor male workers. Among women, it is notable that maids (domestics)— who comprise about 20 percent of the female labor force—are not particularly poor (the household income of live-in domestic servants is taken as their own income). Among women, almost one-third of the poor workers are service workers (excluding maids). Among production workers, traditional industries such as textiles and footwear, lumber and wood products, and printing and publishing account for the majority of the poor. Females participate in production activities mainly in textiles and footwear, and do not seem to be paid well there.

In addition, it is striking that the poor are overrepresented among workers who work long hours. About 20 percent of poor male workers put in more than 60 hours a week, whereas only 15 percent of all male workers work such hours. Sales, construction, and transport workers who are poor appear to work particularly long hours. Among the poor, only professional and technical workers have relatively short hours. Only about 8 percent of the poor work less than 40 hours and about 55–60 percent work the "normal" 40- to 48-hour week. In general, sales and transport workers work the longest hours.

The story is somewhat different for female workers. They appear to be overrepresented among those working shorter hours. It is mainly the sales workers and maids who work very long hours. Apparently many poor women working part-time would like more work but have difficulty finding it, or cannot work longer hours because of responsibilities at home.

Overall, it appears that poor male workers are not lacking for work since there is little overt or open underemployment. If anything, the poor are overworked but locked into low-productivity occupations. The sales workers may actually be underemployed, that is, idle for a substantial part of their working hours. But they constitute only about 25 percent of all poor workers. Almost half of the poor overworked men are transport or construction workers. It is unlikely that they are idle during much of their working day. On the other hand, a substantial portion of the women are either genuinely underemployed (that is, they are willing and able to work more hours) or are unable to work longer hours. Poverty will therefore not be alleviated simply by expanding employment opportunities. Among the men, training programs may be needed for the least skilled and overworked. For women, more employment opportunities may be needed, along with day care programs, so that they can participate in income-producing activities. The provision of day care is itself an employment-generating activity.

It is often alleged that recent migrants earn less than others and have to take up very low-paid jobs while waiting for better opportunities to appear. The evidence to this effect is mixed. In Bogotá, 22 percent of the most recent arrivals seem to earn less than the minimum wage, compared with about 38 percent overall in 1975. At the same time, as many as 20 percent of those who have been in Bogotá for 11–20 years, earn less than the minimum wage. Those earning low wages seem to be fairly evenly spread among workers of all ages, and experience in the city does not appear to count for much. This is confirmed more systematically in chapter 8 in the context of estimating earnings functions. For women, there is strong evidence that a smaller proportion of recent migrants earn less than the minimum wage compared with those who have lived in Bogotá longer. It is difficult to explain this; the answer may lie in the large number of maids (domestics) who are recent migrants. Although these women are not particularly well off, this study has consistently found that a large proportion of them are not among the poorest. The income in kind that they receive accounts for this result. On the whole, it is clear that recent migrants have no monopoly on poverty; indeed, 60–70 percent of all workers with earnings below the minimum wage have been in Bogotá for more than ten years.

Unemployment and Participation Rates among the Poor

Having examined the correlates of poverty among those who work, I now look at those who do not work. I have just shown that the working poor often work long hours and thus do not suffer from underemployment. This section shows in addition that the unemployed fall disproportionately among the poor and hence that unemployment is a major cause of poverty. A caveat should be entered here, however: it is difficult to distinguish between people who are unemployed because they are poor and those who are poor because they are unemployed. The ideal income concept would be some index of permanent income. It would then be possible to distinguish between these two groups of people. In this study the measure used is current income, and the results are therefore subject to the problems arising from its use. But looking at primary and secondary workers separately can also suggest some insight into the direction of causation between poverty and unemployment.

Table 5-13 gives decile-specific unemployment rates for three years—1975, 1977, and 1978. All three years are shown so that cyclical changes in the labor market can be accounted for. This table reflects the fact that the Colombian urban economy experienced a boom in late 1978, with the result that unemployment rates were very low (see chapter 1). As might be expected, the unemployed are concentrated in the bottom five deciles, particularly in the bottom two. Unemployment rates decline quite regularly as income increases for both males and females, though less regularly for the females. Almost half of all the unemployed males fall in the bottom 30 percent (table 5-13). The unemployed females are more evenly distributed; only about 35–40 percent fall among the poor. Since most women are secondary workers, this gives some indication of whether people are poor because they are unemployed. If a large proportion of the unemployed who fall in the bottom 30 percent are poor because they are transitorily unemployed, we would expect the majority of them to be primary workers (heads of households). The data on women indicate that this is not so. More detailed information on this point follows.

Table 5-14 shows the unemployed in 1975 and 1977 disaggregated into primary and secondary workers. More than half of the poor are secondary workers, although the majority of the primary workers who *are* unemployed fall in the bottom 30 percent. Even if all the primary workers who are unemployed are taken to be transitorily unemployed and not "normally" poor, we are still left with rates of unemployment among the bottom 30 percent that would be substantially higher than in higher deciles. Therefore the probability of unemployment *is* higher among those who are chronically poor.

The picture becomes clearer if one examines participation rates by decile (see table 5-15). Not only do the poor have higher unemployment rates, but they also have more discouraged workers and hence substantially lower participation rates. Thus the bottom deciles have a substantial proportion of people who are not working in one way or another. Male participation rates rise and then flatten out. Female participation rates rise regularly until the last decile (except for the bottom two deciles in 1978). The low participation rates in the bottom decile indicate the presence of discouraged workers along with the old, infirm, or incapacitated who cannot work and are therefore poor.

The somewhat different results for 1978 are related to the fact that the labor market tightened up considerably toward the latter part of the 1970s. Moreover, as discussed in the preceding section, the incidence of poverty declined considerably in 1978 compared with 1973. The remarkable increase in female participation in the bottom two deciles in table 5-15 is consistent with Urrutia's (1985) conjecture that the improvement in the urban income

Table 5-13. *Percentage Distribution of Unemployment in Bogotá by Income Group and Sex, 1975–78*

Sex and year	Income decile[a]										Overall	Total (thousands)
	1	2	3	4	5	6	7	8	9	10		
	Unemployment rate (percent)											Labor force[b]
Male												
1975	30.8	11.4	7.3	8.7	8.0	5.2	3.8	2.5	2.6	0.4	6.9	624
1977	30.2	12.2	6.2	6.5	6.6	5.5	3.9	4.4	2.7	0.5	6.2	782
1978	19.8	10.2	6.1	5.6	4.2	2.7	2.0	2.9	0.7	0.6	4.7	753
Female												
1975	29.2	12.1	12.7	9.6	7.9	7.8	6.1	3.7	1.9	1.1	6.4	337
1977	16.3	11.1	9.4	9.5	7.7	6.4	5.8	4.2	1.7	2.1	5.8	469
1978	6.2	7.3	5.1	8.9	7.3	4.3	2.5	1.9	1.7	0.4	4.3	463

(Table continues on following page.)

Table 5-13 (continued)

Sex and year	Income decile[a]										Overall	Total (thousands) Unemployed
	1	2	3	4	5	6	7	8	9	10		
	Percentage of total unemployed											
Male												
1975	23.8	15.5	11.2	14.2	12.4	8.1	6.6	3.7	4.0	0.6	100.0	43
1977	23.2	15.0	9.0	10.7	10.3	10.2	7.1	8.1	5.0	1.5	100.0	49
1978	30.9	16.2	10.3	11.2	9.4	6.0	4.7	7.9	1.8	1.6	100.0	35
Female												
1975	13.0	11.8	13.0	12.4	11.2	12.4	10.6	8.1	4.3	3.1	100.0	21
1977	15.1	10.0	11.0	10.7	11.1	10.5	11.0	9.7	5.1	6.0	100.0	28
1978	21.9	16.7	9.5	13.6	13.8	7.9	5.5	5.0	5.2	1.0	100.0	20

Note: Percentages may not add to 100 because of rounding.

a. Ranked by household income per capita.

b. As explained in appendix D, the estimated population of Bogotá was lower than expected in 1978. The estimated labor force in 1978 is also low since the estimates to 1975 and 1977 use the original DANE expansion factors.

Sources: 1975 DANE Special Bogotá Household Survey EH8E; 1977 DANE Household Survey EH15; and 1978 World Bank–DANE Household Survey EH21.

Table 5-14. Composition of the Unemployed in Bogotá, 1975 and 1977

	Male						Female					
	Bottom 30 percent		Top 70 percent		Total		Bottom 30 percent		Top 70 percent		Total	
Year	Number	Percent	Number	Percent	Number	Percent	Number	Percent	Number	Percent	Number	Percent
Primary workers[a]												
1975	10,108	47	2,926	14	13,034	31	665	8	399	3	1,064	5
1977	8,264	36	2,033	8	10,297	21	1,452	15	840	5	2,292	8
Secondary workers												
1975	11,571	53	18,221	86	29,792	69	7,448	92	12,901	97	20,349	95
1977	15,009	64	24,047	92	39,056	79	8,487	85	16,806	95	25,293	92
Total												
1975	21,679	100	21,147	100	42,826	100	8,113	100	13,300	100	21,413	100
1977	23,273	100	26,080	100	49,353	100	9,939	100	17,646	100	27,585	100

a. Primary workers are those who are household heads.
Source: See table 5-13.

Table 5-15. *Distribution of Participation Rates in Bogotá by Income Group and Sex, 1975–78*
(percent)

| Sex and year | Income decile | | | | | | | | | | Overall |
	1	2	3	4	5	6	7	8	9	10	
Male											
1975	49	59	66	66	66	70	73	68	72	77	67
1977	37	60	64	69	66	71	71	72	70	71	66
1978	52	60	58	67	68	66	69	69	69	69	65
Female											
1975	11	19	20	24	27	31	33	41	43	54	31
1977	17	21	25	24	29	34	37	42	50	50	34
1978	39	34	27	25	29	26	33	36	43	40	33
Total											
1975	26	29	43	45	47	52	53	55	59	60	49
1977	26	39	43	45	47	52	53	55	59	60	49
1978	44	45	41	44	47	45	50	53	53	55	48

Note: Participation rates are in relation to all individuals over 12 years of age.

Sources: 1975 DANE Special Bogotá Household Survey EH8E; 1977 DANE Household Survey EH15; and 1978 City Study/DANE Household Survey EH21.

distribution in Colombia in the latter part of the 1970s was partly attributable to the increased participation of women among lower income groups.

A composite picture thus emerges. In the bottom decile, that is, among the very poorest, only about 40–50 percent of males (and only 15 percent of females) over 12 years of age participate in the labor force, whereas the overall participation rate is about 70 percent for men and about 30 percent for women (as explained above, this was not true for women in the tight labor market conditions of 1978). Almost 30 percent of those in the bottom decile who do participate are out of work. Consequently, in the bottom decile only about 35 percent of all males who are 12 or older have jobs, and only about 8–10 percent of the females. Of the remainder, some are discouraged workers and others are incapacitated by sickness or injury. Employment generation is therefore only partly the answer. Many of the poor are probably unemployable and their poverty must be attacked directly.

Summary

This chapter has attempted to provide estimates of the extent of malnutrition and poverty in Bogotá and Cali in order to better understand who constitute the poor. However, conceptual and empirical difficulties arise in attempting such an estimation. The kind of methods used in the literature can, at best, provide some bounds on the magnitude of the problem of malnutrition and poverty. Specifically, what such methods do is provide lower-bound estimates of the number of people who simply do not receive adequate income for even the barest minimum of nutritional requirements.

Previous estimates of malnutrition in Colombia range from about 18 to 100 percent of the population. The range for Bogotá in this study is 17–75 percent in 1973 and 6–58 percent in 1978, depending on the level of requirements assumed and the method used for calculating calories consumed. The ranges for Cali are not very different. Despite misgivings about making point estimates from such ranges, the proportion of malnourished owing to lack of income could not have been much less than 25 percent in 1974 and about 12 percent in 1978 in both cities.

Although an attempt has been made here to rectify some of the shortcomings of earlier studies, a few problems remain. The use of household-level data has made it possible to adjust for age and sex distributions and size of household on the requirements side, but the adjustment has not been as satisfactory on the consumption side. Method 2 (M2) implicitly adjusts for this problem since all calculations for consumption are done at the household level—the commensal unit. This adjustment would have been worked out better if data were available on actual consumption for each household.

Since few authorities agree on the appropriate level of requirements, findings about the incidence of malnutrition are presented at the 70, 80, and 100 percent (0.7R, 0.8R, and 1.0R) levels of calorie requirements. This clarifies the basis of the range of estimates and indicates the extent of the measurement problem. Such a procedure also corrects for interindividual variation in requirements if certain assumptions are made about the distribution of requirement levels. Since monthly or annual income estimates are used, intraindividual variations in the level of requirements are implicitly accounted for. Furthermore, although only income information is available, total consumption or food expenditures are estimated, and these can be assumed to be better proxies for permanent income than the observed current income. The estimates should therefore not suffer seriously from this bias. Through income experiments, an attempt is made to account for the understatement of income that is characteristic of most household surveys. The evidence suggests that the understatement of income is probably not a very serious problem at the low-income end.

In calculating the price of an average diet or the average number of calories consumed, a balanced diet as observed in Colombia was assumed. If the costs of calorie intake are not minimized, the preference structure of Colombians is preserved with respect to the food consumed. This procedure cannot correct for changes in relative prices, however, unless more frequent diet and cost of food surveys become available. Price experiments make it possible to account for the allegedly more energy efficient consumption of food by the poor. If the poor do spend less per calorie consumed, the price experiments give the possible ranges of malnutrition.

It was assumed that food is distributed evenly within the family since there is no information to the contrary. Similarly, any neighborhood effects such as lack of sanitation, prevalence of disease, and the like cannot be accounted for. More direct estimates of malnutrition are needed to account for these factors, which will probably soon become important determinants of malnutrition in the middle-income countries, if current income trends continue. Income inadequacy will then be a secondary consideration in the fight against malnutrition.

The areas of Bogotá and Cali with high levels of malnutrition and poverty that have been delineated are characterized by large low-income families with high dependency ratios because of the presence of many children. In view of the important role that adequate nutrition plays in the development of cognitive ability, malnutrition can be expected to impair the schooling of these children, and consequently to have an adverse effect on their future earnings potential and chances in the labor market. Thus poverty is likely to set in motion a vicious cycle if direct nutrition and health measures are not taken in the most seriously affected parts of the city.

Spatially, malnutrition closely follows the income patterns in Bogotá and Cali, although the differences are somewhat magnified. In Bogotá, malnutrition is high at the periphery of the city and at the center. Malnutrition clearly increases with distance from the center in Cali.

Most estimates of malnutrition, since they are based on calorie-income relationships (or variants thereof), should be viewed with some skepticism. More careful work is needed to produce better estimates and to delineate ranges of estimates rather than specific estimates. It has been shown that income growth in Bogotá and Cali from 1973 to 1978 was substantial even for people at low levels of income. Malnutrition solely due to income inadequacy has certainly decreased. Nonetheless, even now at least 10–12 percent of the people in Bogotá and Cali must be malnourished because they simply do not earn enough to maintain an adequate diet: in round numbers, they make up about half a million people in the two cities.

As might be expected, the characteristics of poor workers indicate that workers with little or no schooling are most likely to be poor. For workers with flat age-earnings profiles, the expansion of their families during middle age pushes them into poverty and, as a result, as many as 40 percent of children are found in the poverty group. Most poor workers are not underemployed; if anything, they appear to work significantly long hours (they are concentrated in the traditional manufacturing industries and the construction and transport sectors). Among women, maids (who constitute 20 percent of the female labor force) are not found to be particularly poor. Contrary to popular belief, recent migrants do not seem to be especially poor. At the lowest end of the income range, it is lack of work—through nonparticipation or unemployment—that pushes people into poverty.

Appendix 5A. Method Used to Estimate Malnutrition and Poverty

The Data

As in other estimations in this study, the 1973 population census sample (about 7 percent of the total population) and the 1978 World Bank–DANE Household Survey for Bogotá and Cali are used to obtain estimates of malnutrition at two points in time. These detailed data sets make it possible to avoid some but not all of the pitfalls involved in such an estimation. Specifically, these data sets do not include any expenditure data and therefore only household income, suitably transformed, needs to be used for the calculation. As is shown in appendix C of this book, the 1973 census accounted for only 50 percent of total personal income in Bogotá, whereas the 1978 survey captured more than 90 percent of personal income. Both data sources allow the identification of the location of each household within the two cities; a malnutrition-poverty map of Bogotá can therefore be drawn.

Calculating Calorie Requirements

Various institutions have published calorie requirements for adequate nutrition in Colombia. Three sources are utilized here (summarized in table 5A-1).

- World Health Organization and Food and Agricultural Organization Ad Hoc Committee of Experts. Their mean weights for men and women have to be adjusted downward to adapt their recommendations to the likely Colombian norm.
- Instituto de Investigaciones Tecnológicas (IIT). This institute did a special study (1972) to estimate the level of requirements appropriate for Colombia. Its estimates were, in general, lower than the WHO-FAO recommendations.
- Instituto Colombiano de Bienestar Familiar (ICBF). This is the governmental agency responsible for nutrition policy in Colombia. It has carried out surveys on diet and nutrition that have covered food expenditures,

Table 5A-1. *Daily Calorie Requirements by Age and Sex for Colombia*

| | WHO and FAO[a] | | Male and female | |
	Male	Female	ICBF[b]	IIT[c]
0–1	1,090	1,090	860	540
1–3	1,360	1,360	1,140	1,300
4–6	1,830	1,830 ⎫	1,710	1,870
7–9	2,190	2,190 ⎭		
10–12	2,600	2,350 ⎫	2,270	2,470
13–15	2,670 (0.97M)[d]	2,260 (1.13F)[e] ⎭		
16–19	2,815 (1.02M)	2,100 (1.05F)	2,450	
20–39	2,760 (1.00M)	2,000 (1.00F) ⎫	2,290	
40–49	2,620 (0.95M)	1,900 (0.95F) ⎭		2,290
50–59	2,480 (0.90M)	1,800 (0.90F)		
60–69	2,210 (0.80M)	1,600 (0.80F) ⎫	1,985	
70+	1,930 (0.70M)	1,400 (0.70F) ⎭		

a. From WHO-FAO ad hoc expert committee.

b. Instituto Colombiano de Bienestar Familiar (1977).

c. Instituto de Investigaciones Tecnológicas, Bogotá.

d. Numbers in parentheses are minimum daily calorie requirements for average-weight males and females, where M = average male body weight (BWM) × 46, and F = average female body weight (BWF) × 40. I have assumed BWM = 60 kilograms; BWF = 50 kilograms. WHO-FAO assume BWM = 65 kilograms and BWF = 55 kilograms. I have taken lower numbers for Colombia to account for lower average weight.

e. Requirements for lactating mothers are higher in all the sources but have been neglected here.

food prices, and other such variables in various years. Starting from WHO-FAO recommendations, the ICBF has gradually reduced the level of calorie requirements appropriate for adequate nutrition in Colombia. Its recommendations (from 1977), which average out to 1,970 calories per capita per day (age and sex adjusted), have been used.

The total calories required by each household have been calculated according to each of these three sources. HCALR1, HCALR2, and HCALR3, denote the total calories required by each household according to WHO-FAO, the ICBF, and the IIT, respectively.[10] In this way, the age and sex composition of each household are fully accounted for on the requirements side of this procedure.[11] This detail is usually neglected in other studies.

10. Only the results for HCALR1 and HCALR2 are reported, since HCALR3 is quite similar to HCALR2.

11. For example (using table 5-3), for a household of three people consisting of a man aged 41, a woman 35, and a boy 10 years old, HCALR1 = 2,620 + 2,000 + 2,600 = 7,220 calories.

Calculating Calorie Consumption

METHOD I (M1). The overall objective is to calculate the calories consumed by each household and then compare them with the household's
requirements, as computed above. It is assumed that the distribution of food
within the household is proportional to each member's requirements, and
that each household member is equally well nourished or malnourished. Since
only income data are available, the calculations must move through a number
of steps to reach calorie consumption from the household's income.

This study takes García's earlier work as its point of departure and uses
some of his results for Colombia to estimate malnutrition in Bogotá and Cali.
A brief review of García's method for Colombia (García, 1979, 1980, 1981)
follows. García used essentially the Reutlinger-Selowsky method and applied
it to Colombian data. Calorie consumption is regarded as an increasing
function of income (expenditure):

(5A-1) $$C = f(Y) \qquad \frac{\partial f}{\partial Y} > 0, \frac{\partial^2 f}{\partial Y^2} < 0 \quad \text{or}$$

(5A-2) $$C = f(EX) \qquad \frac{\partial f}{\partial EX} > 0, \frac{\partial^2 f}{\partial EX^2} < 0$$

where C is calorie consumption per capita per day, Y is annual income per
capita, and EX is annual per capita expenditure on food.

Two functional forms that satisfy the marginal conditions above are

(5A-3a) $$\text{Semilog: } C = a + b(\ln Y) \quad \text{or}$$

(5A-3b) $$C = a + b(\ln EX)$$

(5A-4a) $$\text{Inverse: } C = a + \frac{b}{Y} \quad \text{or}$$

(5A-4b) $$C = a + \frac{b}{EX}$$

The log-log function $\ln C = a + b(\ln Y)$ suffers from the problem that
the calorie-income (expenditure) elasticity is constant. For (5A-3) and
(5A-4) the elasticities are

$$\text{Semilog: } \eta_{C/Y} = \frac{b}{C}$$

$$\text{Inverse: } \eta_{C/Y} = -\frac{b}{CY}.$$

García used data from 1958 to 1975 to estimate the calorie income-expenditure relationship. The entire population was assumed to have the same diet.[12] Food balance sheets for each of the major categories were used[13] to estimate total food consumption in the country; appropriate allowances were made for animal feed and effective food content (that is, elimination of seeds, cortex, and so on). Estimations were made for three time periods—1958–1975, 1960–75, and 1962–75. The fit was best for the 1962–75 estimation.

The estimated calorie-income-expenditure equations were then applied to grouped data from the 1972 survey in order to estimate the proportion of malnourished in the country according to income groups. The precision of these estimates obviously depended on the number of income groups described in published data. As noted earlier, although ten income groups were provided, more than half of the population fell in the bottom three groups. As a result, depending on different assumptions about calorie requirements, malnutrition afflicted 28 percent of the population (the bottom two income groups), or 52 percent (the bottom three), or 68 percent (the bottom four) (see table 5-2).

In estimating the calorie-income (expenditure) relation from national average time-series data, it is implicitly assumed that income is distributed uniformly and that everybody in the country has the same nutrition level. This is clearly not true. The problem is further compounded by the fact that calorie consumption in a population is obviously distributed much more uniformly than the distribution of income (the ratio between highest and lowest incomes can be as great as 1,000 to 1 whereas the ratio between highest and lowest calorie consumption is unlikely to be greater than 4 to 1). The estimated function should therefore be highly nonlinear and is likely to be most accurate around the requirements range.

It is also necessary to establish whether expenditure or income is the more appropriate determining variable. As mentioned earlier, household surveys characteristically underestimate income. In Colombia, the last income-consumption survey was undertaken in 1972 (DANE, Encuesta de Hogares 6 [EH6], Ingresos y Gastos). García estimated that it accounted for about 77 percent and 91 percent of per capita personal income and private consumption expenditures, respectively, compared with the national income accounts. The permanent-income hypothesis also implies that permanent income is a better explanator of food consumption than current income and that expenditure from household surveys would then be a more reliable proxy for

12. Average diet for Colombia according to ICBF (1972). Since Bogotá falls in the Cundinamarca-Boyaca region, the average diet for this region was used here, and is shown later in this appendix.

13. These have been prepared by the FAO and the ICBF since the early 1960s. They are not mutually consistent. García prepared his own balance sheets.

permanent income than measured current income. Expenditures also capture the life cycle effect. A third reason for using expenditure per capita rather than income per capita from national income accounts as an explanator of calorie consumption has to do with patterns of income distribution. Income is highly concentrated in Colombia, and the share of labor in national income is only about 40 percent. This proportion is lower than the share of total personal expenditure. But capital income goes to only a small proportion of the population; hence the use of GNP per capital would vastly overstate average consumption. Total expenditure per capita is therefore a more appropriate variable to use. Furthermore, in most household surveys of consumption the total expenditure reported by low-income households is greater than their incomes. Aggregated expenditures from such surveys are then more consistent with total personal expenditure in national income accounts. Transferring calorie expenditure estimates derived from national time-series data to cross-sectional data then becomes somewhat more defensible. In this study, García's calorie-expenditure estimates are utilized in M1 rather than the calorie-income ones. García's estimates for equation (5A-3b), $C = a + b \ln EX$, are utilized for Colombia, where C is the calories consumed per capita and EX is the annual expenditure per capita (in 1970 pesos). His estimate for 1960–75 data was

(5A-5)   (M1) $C = -3,088 + 609 \ln EX.$

García obtained better goodness fit of characteristics for his 1962–75 equation, but regarded the parameters of equation (5A-5) as more robust.[14]

If 1,800–2,000 calories per day are regarded as the approximate requirement level, the calorie expenditure elasticity for equation (5A-5) (at the requirements level) is

$$\eta_{C/EX} \approx \frac{600}{1,800} \text{ to } \frac{600}{2,000} \quad \left(\frac{b}{c}\right)$$

$$= 0.33 \text{ to } 0.3.$$

Since the data sets used here exclude data on expenditures, a relationship between "expenditure share" and household income, estimated from the 1972 DANE Consumption Survey (appendix 5B), generates the data on which this estimation was based. The estimated equation is

(5A-6) $\dfrac{EXH}{YH} = 2.2666 \quad - \quad 0.1546 \ln YH \qquad R^2 = 0.936$

$\qquad\qquad\qquad\qquad\qquad\quad (-10.8) \qquad$ (t statistic in parentheses)

---

14. The estimated equation for 1962–75 was $C = -4,622 + 790 \ln EX$, which implies an $\eta_{C/EX}$ at 2,000 calories of about 0.4.

where *EXH* and *YH* are monthly household expenditure and income, respectively (in 1973 pesos). Equation (5A-6) is used to derive the expenditure for each household in the 1973 and 1978[15] data sets and thence household expenditure per capita (*EX*).[16] The derived *EX* is then used to derive the M1 (method 1, equation 5A-5) estimate of calorie consumption per capita per day in each household. The total household calorie intake per day (CALM1) thus obtained can then be compared with household calorie requirements (HCALR1, 2, and 3).

This method (M1) has a few shortcomings. First, a time-series countrywide relationship is applied to cross-sectional household data from urban households only. Second, expenditure per capita is used to derive calories consumed per capita in the household without accounting for the age-sex distribution within households. Third, the estimation of total expenditure from income does not allow for variation in expenditures between households with the same income. We attempt to overcome these problems in our second method of estimation.

METHOD 2 (M2). This method also takes several steps to arrive at the calories consumed by each household. The 1972 household survey results were again used to derived the food share of total expenditure as a fraction of total household income. The equation estimated (see appendix 5B) was

$$(5A-7) \quad \text{FSHARE} = 1.6998 - 0.1486 \quad \ln YH \qquad R^2 = 0.971$$
$$\qquad\qquad\qquad (16.5) \qquad\qquad (t \text{ statistic in parentheses})$$

where
$$\text{FSHARE} = \frac{\text{Food expenditure}}{YH}$$

and *YH* is total monthly household income, as before (1973 pesos).

This procedure for calculating food share in total expenditure (or income) could be improved if household size were also taken into account. Since no three-way tabulations were provided between income groups, household size, and food share, this could not be accomplished. Surprisingly, however, household size does not appear to make much difference inasmuch as the proportion

15. Incomes were adjusted to account for inflation so that equations (5A-5) and (5A-6) could be applied to the 1973 and 1978 data. Incomes quoted in 1973 pesos were used to estimate equation (5A-6) and incomes in 1970 pesos were used to estimate the calorie consumption measure of equation (5A-5). Note that Garcia's estimates are in constant 1970 pesos. In summary, all calculations have accounted for price changes.

16. See figures 5B-1 and 5B-2, which depict the expenditure-income relation and mark off the 1973 and 1978 deciles. Note that households up to the seventh decile spend more than their income.

Table 5A-2. *Food Expenditure as Percentage of Total Expenditure by Household Size in Colombia, 1967 and 1972*

Household size	1972	1967
1–2	42 ⎱	44
3	38 ⎰	
4	43 ⎱	46
5	37 ⎰	
6	40 ⎱	48
7–8	39 ⎰	
9+	41	47

Sources: DANE 1972 Household Consumption Survey EH4; and Musgrove (1978), calculated from ECIEL 1967 Household Consumption Survey.

of food expenditure to total expenditure from two sources turns out to be remarkably consistent (see table 5A-2). The picture might not be as clear if the data in table 5A-2 were organized by income groups. Nonetheless, the results here indicate that these estimations do not suffer from a major error. Economies of scale in food consumption perhaps account for this as well as the correlation between household size and total household income.[17]

Having obtained the food share, I can now calculate the total calories consumed by the household:

$$(5A-8) \qquad (M2) \qquad CALM2 = \frac{FSHARE \times YH}{P_c}$$

where CALM2 is the total calories consumed by the household per day by method 2 (M2), FSHARE and YH are as before, and P_c is the monthly cost of consuming 1 calorie per day.

P_c clearly needs an explanation. The ICBF conducted a national survey of diets (Encuesta Nacional de Dietas) in 1972 and published an average daily diet disaggregated for each region (the results are reported in DNP 1974). Its data for the Cundinamarca-Boyaca region have been used. The information provided includes the quantity of each of twenty-five main food items, their caloric content, and price (see table 5C-1, and section below on calculating calorie price). It is therefore possible to compute the cost of this average fixed bundle of foods, hence the cost of calories implied by this diet, and consequently the monthly cost of consuming 1 calorie per day.

One point that needs to be clarified here is that the average diet should

---

17. Elsewhere (Mohan 1980) I document the fact that household income rises with household size—though not proportionately. (Household income per capita decreases.)

not be used for all households. There is good evidence from other countries that poor families generally obtain more calories per unit of expenditure; that is, P_c is lower for poor families than for richer families, as has been indicated for Brazil (World Bank 1979), Pakistan (Hammer 1978), and Sri Lanka (Visaria 1979). Hammer reports income elasticities for the demand for commodities such as wheat, rice, and sugar, on the one hand, and more preferred (or more expensive) foods such as meat and milk, on the other. On the basis of data in Visaria (1979), Bhalla (1980) estimates that the price per calorie paid by the poor in Sri Lanka can be about 30 percent less than the mean. It was not possible to obtain comparable information for Colombia, but table 5D-1 reports proportions of food expenditure by commodity for ten broad income groups that are consistent with the evidence cited above for other countries. The proportions spent on cereals and tubers decrease with increasing income, whereas those spent on meat and eggs increase. Nevertheless, the difference between the rich and poor diet is not dramatic. Although it is difficult to make an accurate estimate, this evidence suggests that P_c for low-income groups is likely to be about 20–30 percent below the mean, as in Sri Lanka. We attempt to account for this problem by conducting sensitivity tests by varying P_c.[18]

The calorie income elasticity $\eta_{C/Y}$ for M2 can be derived from equations (5A-7) and (5A-8). Writing FSHARE $= g + h \ln YH$ for equation (5A-7), we have[19]

$$\eta_{C/Y} = 1 + \frac{h}{\text{FSHARE}};$$

where $h = -0.1486$.

Here FSHARE is difficult to calculate at the requirements level because it

---

18. We need not do it differentially for the poor and rich since we are mainly concerned with the bottom end of the scale.

19.
$$\text{FSHARE} = g + h \ln YH \quad \text{and} \quad \text{CALM2} = \frac{\text{FSHARE} \times YH}{P_c};$$

that is,
$$\text{CALM2} = \frac{1}{P_c} (g + \ln YH) \times YH$$

$$\frac{\partial \text{CALM2}}{\partial YH} = \frac{1}{P} (g + h \ln YH + h) = \frac{1}{P_c} (\text{FSHARE} + h)$$

$$\eta_{C/Y} = \frac{\partial \text{CALM2}}{\partial YH} \times \frac{YH}{\text{CALM2}} = \frac{1}{P_c} (\text{FSHARE} + h) \times YH \frac{P_c}{\text{FSHARE} \times YH}$$

$$= 1 + \frac{h}{\text{FSHARE}}$$

depends on household size and composition. (Later in this appendix FSHARE is found to be in the range of 0.6 to 0.7.) Thus $\eta_{C/Y}$ = 0.75 to 0.8 in the relevant range. (This is somewhat higher than most estimates of calorie-income elasticity.)

Note that since FSHARE declines with increasing income and h is negative, $\eta_{C/Y}$ also declines, as it should. That is,

$$\frac{\partial \eta_{C/Y}}{\partial Y}$$

is negative.

Around the requirements level, therefore, the calories consumed by a household are much more income-elastic according to M2 than M1.

M2 corrects for two of the shortcomings in M1. First, all calculations for calorie consumption are done at the household level—the commensal unit. Thus, the age-sex composition is accounted for implicitly. The assumption of an even intrafamily distribution commensurate with each person's requirements is retained. Second, information on actual diets consumed is used to calculate calories consumed from the food share in expenditures. Thus, there is no jump from time-series or per capita calculations to household cross-sectional data. One problem remains: that all households at the same income level devote the same proportion of their income to food and therefore do not allow for interhousehold variation in food expenditures for households at the same income level.

ESTIMATING MALNUTRITION. Having accomplished all the above, six estimates of malnutrition are obtained for each set of data and city. Three sets of calorie requirements are calculated for each household: those according to WHO-FAO, the ITT, and the ICBF. In addition, there are two sets of estimates for calories consumed: those according to M1 and M2. Next, the nutrition level for each household is obtained:

$$(5A\text{-}9) \qquad\qquad \text{NLH} = \frac{\text{CALM}i}{\text{HCALCR}j}$$

where NLH is the nutritional level, CALMi is calories consumed by method i (i = 1,2), and HCALRj is calories required as recommended by sources j (j = 1,2,3) by the household. The household is malnourished or well nourished according to whether NLH < 1 or NLH > 1, respectively.

Each person in the household is assigned the household NLH so that the age and sex distributions of nutrition can be obtained. In order to account for interindividual as well as intraindividual variations, I also report the proportions of households whose NLH < 0.7 or NLH < 0.8.

Appendix 5B. Food Expenditure and Total Expenditure by Income Group

Ideally, one would like to have the total expenditure and budget composition for each household to estimate accurately the two calorie-consumption measures proposed in the text. Expenditure data were not available at the household level, however, so the relationship of "expenditure share" (equation 5A-6) and "food share" (equation 5A-7) with household income were estimated from the 1972 DANE Consumption Survey to derive our calorie-consumption measures. Table 5B-1 gives the data used to estimate equations (5A-6) and (5A-7). The fitted curves and actual data points are plotted in figures 5B-1 and 5B-2. These figures also show the decile cutoffs by household monthly income of the 1973 census and the 1978 Household Survey in Bogotá. The data points for the two highest income groups fall outside the ranges shown in the graphs. This was done purposely to indicate the decile cutoff. The decile ranges for monthly household income and monthly household income per capita are presented in table 5B-2.

Figure 5B-1. *Food Expenditure as Share of Household Income*

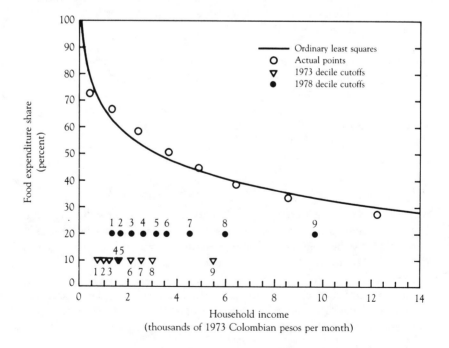

Food expenditure share (percent)

Household income
(thousands of 1973 Colombian pesos per month)

Table 5B-1. *Household Food Expenditure and Total Expenditure
by Income Group in Urban Colombia, 1972*

Monthly household income (1973 pesos)		Food expenditure as a percentage of income (used for equation 5A-7)	Total expenditure as a percentage of income (used for equation 5A-6)
Range	Midpoint		
0–921	460.5	0.727	1.2395
922–1,842	1,382.0	0.669	1.1527
1,843–3,070	2,456.5	0.584	1.1007
3,071–4,298	3,684.5	0.507	1.0521
4,299–5,526	4,912.5	0.448	0.9862
5,527–7,368	6,447.5	0.386	0.9454
7,369–9,824	8,596.5	0.336	0.8297
9,825–14,736	12,280.5	0.275	0.8071
14,737–24,560	19,648.0	0.220	0.7813
24,561–50,000	37,280.5	0.135	0.5492

Source: Adapted from DANE, *Ingresos y Gastos de los Hogares en Colombia, 1972.*

Figure 5B-2. *Total Expenditure as Share of Household Income*

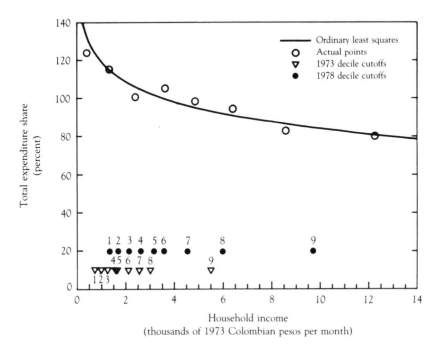

Table 5B-2. *Decile Ranges for Monthly Household Income and Monthly Household Income Per Capita in Bogotá*

| | Monthly household income | | | Monthly household income per capita | | |
| | 1973 | 1978 | | 1973 | 1978 | |
Decile	(1973 pesos)	1978 pesos	1973 pesos	(1973 pesos)	1978 pesos	1973 pesos
1	0– 732	0– 3,584	0–1,344	0– 124	0– 592	0– 222
2	773–1,009	3,585– 4,529	1,345–1,698	125– 179	593– 816	223– 306
3	1,010–1,249	4,530– 5,741	1,699–2,153	180– 233	817–1,057	307– 396
4	1,250–1,594	5,742– 7,041	2,154–2,640	234– 299	1,058–1,338	397– 502
5	1,595–1,649	7,042– 8,471	2,641–3,177	300– 359	1,339–1,624	503– 609
6	1,650–2,113	8,472– 9,578	3,178–3,592	360– 450	1,625–2,000	610– 750
7	2,114–2,556	9,579–12,133	3,593–4,550	451– 598	2,001–2,625	751– 984
8	2,557–3,002	12,134–15,940	4,551–5,977	599– 831	2,626–3,704	985–1,389
9	3,003–5,493	15,941–25,872	5,978–9,702	832–1,498	3,705–6,340	1,390–2,378
10	5,494+	25,873+	9,703+	1,499+	6,341+	2,379+

Note: Decile ranking is by household income per capita.
Sources: 1973 census and 1978 World Bank–DANE Household Survey.

Appendix 5C. Calculating Calorie Price

Three pieces of information are required to calculate the price of consuming one calorie a day: the composition of the diet, the caloric content of each food item, and its price. Fortunately, this information was available (see table 5C-1). The steps leading to the estimated monthly cost of consuming one calorie a day are discussed below.

First, the caloric content and cost of each food item are calculated in terms of the same numeraire, taking account of the importance of each foodstuff in the representative diet. By multiplying columns 1 and 2 of table 5C-1 I obtain the caloric content of each food item weighted by its share in 100 grams of the average diet. Similarly, by multiplying columns 1 and 3, I obtain the cost of each food item weighted by its relative importance in 100 grams of the average diet.

Second, adding overall food items and dividing the total cost by total calorie intake in 100 grams of average diet gives an approximate measure of the cost per day of one calorie of diet a day.

To make the estimate comparable to monthly income, the daily cost of one calorie of diet a day is multiplied by the average number of days in one month (30.5) to obtain the monthly cost (in 1973 pesos) of one calorie a day.

(1) Calorie content of 100 grams of average diet = 169.12 calories

(2) Cost of 100 grams of average diet = 0.6148 pesos

Monthly cost of one calorie a day $\left(\dfrac{(2)}{(1)} \times 30.5\right)$ = 0.1108763 pesos per month

Appendix 5D. The Diet in Urban Colombia by Income Group, 1972

In developing countries, the staples of the general population, particularly the poor, are cereals and tubers. The situation is not much different in urban Colombia. Table 5D-1 presents the share in food expenditure of various commodities for ten income groups in 1972. Although the differences are not dramatic, low-income households spent proportionately more on cereals and tubers than their richer counterparts. Conversely, the proportions spent on meat and dairy products rise with incomes. Note also the high expenditure share of meat in the food budget across all income groups and the rising expenditure share with increasing income of more preferred (or more expensive) fruit.

Table 5C-1. *Calculating Calorie Price*

Food item	Share of food item in the diet by weight[a] (percent)	Calorie content per 100 grams of food item[a] (calories)	Cost per 100 grams of food item in Bogotá[b] (1973 pesos)	Calorie content of food item in 100 grams of average diet (calories)	Cost of food item in 100 grams of average diet (1973 pesos)	Per capita calories per day[a] (calories)
Potatoes	33.46	91	0.392	30.44	0.1312	325
Milk	19.12	61	0.478	11.66	0.0914	124
Wheat	7.50	315	0.600	23.55	0.0450	251
Panela[c]	7.40	312	0.418	23.09	0.0309	246
Meat	5.72	227	2.400	12.98	0.1373	138
Rice	5.72	359	0.588	20.53	0.0336	219
Plantain	3.00	142	0.358	4.26	0.0107	45
Banana	2.62	94	0.330	2.46	0.0086	26
Maize	2.44	328	0.600	8.00	0.0146	85
Yuca (cassava)	2.16	146	0.372	3.15	0.0080	34
Sugar	1.41	384	0.576	5.41	0.0081	58

138

Lard	1.22	870	1.510	10.61	0.0184	113
Oranges	1.03	35	0.292	0.36	0.0030	4
Green peas	0.94	308	1.240	2.90	0.0117	31
Tomatoes	0.94	170	0.918	0.16	0.0086	2
Arracacho	0.84	100	0.560	0.84	0.0047	9
Carrots	0.84	36	0.236	0.30	0.0020	3
Eggs	0.66	163	1.170	1.08	0.0077	11
Onions	0.66	54	0.264	0.36	0.0017	4
Fish	0.56	111	3.000	0.62	0.0168	7
Cooking oil	0.47	900	2.520	4.23	0.0118	45
Cabbage	0.47	24	0.238	0.11	0.0011	1
Sweet peas	0.37	297	0.560	1.10	0.0021	12
Guayabe (guava)	0.19	36	0.216	0.07	0.0004	1
Total	100.00			169.12	0.6148	1,803

a. ICBF, Encuesta Nacional de Dietas, 1972. The last column is the ICBF finding of the average calorie consumption per day for the Cundi-Boyacense region of the country. The diet for this region was assumed to be representative of Bogotá on account of food availability and social custom. Comparable data for Cali were unavailable. Thus, the diet and commodity prices for Bogotá were used as proxies for those of Cali. Percentages may not add to 100 because of rounding.

b. DANE, consumer price index tabulations, 1971–74.

c. Unrefined brown sugar.

Table 5D-1. *Percentage of Food Expenditure by Commodity for Ten Income Groups in Urban Colombia, 1972* (percent)

	Monthly household income (1972 pesos)										
Foodstuff	0–921	922–1,842	1,843–3,070	3,071–4,298	4,299–5,526	5,527–7,368	7,369–9,824	9,825–14,736	14,737–24,560	24,561+	Total
Cereals	16.1	16.3	15.8	15.1	14.4	14.3	13.4	12.0	11.7	10.4	13.9
Tubers, roots, plantain, dry legumes	13.4	14.3	14.8	14.5	13.7	12.6	12.5	10.1	8.6	7.4	12.4
Vegetables, fresh legumes, fresh seasoning	5.4	5.2	6.4	6.8	6.1	7.1	6.6	6.7	7.1	6.5	6.5
Fruit	2.2	3.2	3.4	3.7	4.5	5.3	5.2	8.1	7.5	7.1	5.1
Meat	17.3	20.3	22.6	25.3	23.2	24.0	26.3	25.2	24.5	24.0	24.0
Milk, dairy products, eggs, fat	11.4	13.3	13.9	15.0	15.3	16.5	16.7	16.7	17.7	14.8	15.4
Other foodstuffs	15.1	13.4	12.5	12.6	11.3	11.1	10.9	10.4	9.4	8.9	11.4
Food and drinks consumed or prepared out of the house	6.6	6.5	3.1	2.2	3.9	5.5	3.3	5.0	5.7	4.7	4.2
Food and drink received in kind	12.5	7.5	7.5	4.8	7.6	3.6	5.1	5.8	7.8	16.2	7.1
Total	100.0	100.0	100.0	100.0	100.0	100.0	100.0	100.0	100.0	100.0	100.0

Source: DANE, Ingresos y Gastos de los Hogares en Colombia, 1972.

6

Characteristics of the Labor Force

Studies of urban labor markets in developing countries tend to fall into three distinct but related groups: those that concentrate on the causes of migration to urban areas and its consequences for labor markets at both the issuing and receiving ends;[1] those that use labor market data to test the validity of the human capital model of labor earnings in developing countries;[2] and those that are based on a dualistic model that assumes that urban labor markets are composed of formal and informal sectors.[3] The connecting thread between these groups is an underlying preoccupation with the causes of poverty and its amelioration. The overall conclusions of these types of analyses can be summarized as follows: the human capital model, which essentially explains variations in earnings by investments in education and on-the-job experience, "works" but characteristically accounts for 30–45 percent of the observed variation of incomes in developing countries. The rest is explained by other systematic economic variables that are not easily measurable (such as skill levels); structural imperfections that impede the functioning of the market, such as social welfare regulations; or the existence of merely random processes that reward some and not others. Those who believe that dualism exists in urban labor markets—as formal and informal sectors—attribute it to structural imperfections; they posit the existence of a "protected" sector that "artificially" keeps wages high in one sector and restricts entry to newcomers. The "experience" variable is called in to support these arguments, the suggestion being that a major part of the informal sector consists of new entrants who are migrants who are inexperienced in various ways and must therefore

1. See, for example, Harris and Todaro (1970), Mazumdar (1976b), Todaro (1976a, b), and Yap (1977).

2. See, for example, Fields (1977, 1978), Jallade (1974), and Psacharopoulos (1973).

3. See Mazumdar (1976a), Joshi, Lubell, and Mouly (1976), Lubell (1974), Merrick (1976), and Sethuraman (1978).

acquire experience, skills, and passports to entry in the form of certification before they can penetrate the curtain of the protected sector.

This study finds merit in most of the above ideas but suggests that the operation of labor markets cannot be fully understood unless the heterogeneous nature of the labor force is explicitly recognized and, possibly, its members' preferences as well. My aim is to step back somewhat and to explore additional areas of taxonomy that might add something to the analysis of urban labor market behavior. The main additional dimension examined here is that of spatial differences within a large city. Are workers living in one part of a city disadvantaged (or advantaged) by virtue of their location? How homogeneous are different sectors of a city with respect to labor force characteristics? How useful is such a classification for understanding the operation of urban labor markets?

As this book shows, these questions can be addressed systematically by modeling labor force participation and estimating earnings functions. This chapter describes the characteristics of the labor force so as to throw additional light on the nature of the labor market in Bogotá and to pave the way for the systematic analysis of subsequent chapters. As a first step, the next section provides a conventional age-education profile of the labor force, but also disaggregates the data spatially.

A connecting thread in much of the discussion in this chapter is the idea that different geographical areas of the city have sharply different socioeconomic characteristics. This phenomenon has been described in terms of income distribution and poverty in earlier chapters and is now extended to the labor market. Nevertheless, the overall judgment that emerges from the analysis that follows is that the labor market works relatively well in Bogotá.

Age-Education-Income Profile

This section presents an age-education-income profile of workers[4] in Bogotá, both at the city level and disaggregated by the eight spatial sectors. The human capital model seems to work well in general and the results obtained here are much as would be expected. (See Fields 1977 for a systematic treatment of education and earnings for all of Colombia.) As will be seen, however, spatial disaggregation of the data provides evidence of significant spatial differences.

Tables 6-1 and 6-2 show the conventional distribution of workers by age

---

4. The definition of workers that I have adopted is all those whose principal activity is reported as "working" for 1973. For 1978 I have added all others (for example, students) who work more than 15 hours a week.

Table 6-1. *Distribution of Workers in Bogotá by Age Group, 1973 and 1978*
(percent)

Age group	1973			1978		
	Male	Female	Total	Male	Female	Total
12–14	1.3	2.3	1.6	0.8	1.2	1.0
15–24	29.5	42.6	34.0	25.7	37.5	30.2
25–34	32.9	27.4	31.0	30.6	29.0	30.0
35–44	19.2	16.4	18.2	22.4	17.3	20.4
45–54	11.0	7.7	9.9	12.8	11.0	12.1
55–64	4.7	2.7	4.0	5.7	3.0	4.7
65–99	1.5	0.9	1.3	1.9	0.8	1.5
Total	100.0	100.0	100.0	100.0	100.0	100.0

Note: Percentages may not add to 100 because of rounding.
Sources: 1973 population census sample; and 1978 World Bank–DANE Household Survey.

group and sex for the city as a whole. There is reasonable consistency between 1973 and 1978 except that in 1978 the age distribution has shifted toward a greater proportion of older workers, particularly among the males. That this is not due to sampling errors is supported by similar proportions reported for 1977 (Mohan 1980). That the shift is also consistent with steadily rising education levels means that more and more people now continue with school-

Table 6-2. *Mean Earnings of Workers in Bogotá by Sex and Age,*
1973 and 1978
(monthly earnings in current Colombian pesos)

Age group	1973			1978		
	Male	Female	Income ratio (female/male)	Male	Female	Income ratio (female/male)
12–14	0.30	0.28	0.68	0.40	0.68	1.48
15–24	1.00	1.00	0.75	1.00	1.00	0.86
	(1,041)	(778)	—	(4,489)	(3,874)	—
25–34	2.04	1.61	0.59	2.15	1.74	0.70
35–44	2.83	1.65	0.44	2.51	1.50	0.52
45–54	3.39	1.46	0.32	2.90	1.11	0.33
55–64	3.17	1.63	0.38	2.62	1.06	0.35
65–99	2.74	2.27	0.62	1.96	0.83	0.37
All age groups	2.10	1.32	0.48	2.04	1.31	0.55

— Not applicable.
Note: All earnings are expressed as multiples of earnings of workers in the 15–24 age group. Figures in parentheses are mean monthly earnings in current Colombian pesos for this age group.
Sources: 1973 population census sample; and 1978 World Bank–DANE Household Survey.

Table 6-3. *Distribution of Workers in Bogotá by Sex and Education,*
1973 and 1978
(percent)

Education level	1973			1978		
	Male	Female	All	Male	Female	All
None	5.1	9.2	6.5	2.3	5.7	3.6
Primary	55.0	53.9	54.7	42.0	42.3	42.1
Secondary	31.1	32.5	31.6	38.8	37.6	38.4
Higher	8.8	4.3	7.3	16.8	14.4	15.9
Total	100.0	100.0	100.0	100.0	100.0	100.0
Number of workers (thousands)	488	249	738	732	454	1,186
Number in sample	45,080	23,041	68,121	3,078	1,914	4,992

Note: Percentages may not add to 100 because of rounding.
Sources: 1973 population census sample; and 1978 World Bank–DANE Household Survey.

ing after the age of 15. Note that women workers are concentrated in the younger age groups. Male workers' earnings peak in the 45–54 age group for both years (table 6-2), whereas female earnings peak earlier. The earnings of women have a much flatter overall profile; as a result, the female-to-male earnings ratio declines with age. It might be thought that women's flat age-earnings profile could be because women, on the average, have less education than men; in fact, this is only true in the case of higher education. Indeed, as table 6-3 shows, female secondary and higher education expanded tremendously during the 1970s. One is left to hypothesize either that women acquire less on-the-job training than men (perhaps because of interruptions in their working life caused by childbearing), or that they are discriminated against or are concentrated in lower-paying occupations.

The data show a more pronounced increase in average earnings with age in 1973 than in 1978 (table 6-4); again, the results for 1978 are very close to those from the 1977 survey. With an increasing supply of better-educated people (whose incomes are mainly responsible for the higher earnings of older workers), these differentials—and the returns to higher education—can be expected to fall, as is shown in chapter 8.

Table 6-3 reports the distribution of workers by sex and education level, and table 6-4 by sex, education level, and mean incomes. As just noted, the male and female percentages are comparable for primary and secondary schooling, but a smaller proportion of female workers have higher education.[5]

5. Primary education is taken to be 1–5 years of schooling, secondary 6–11 years, and higher education 11 or more years.

Table 6-4. *Mean Income of Workers in Bogotá by Sex and Education,*
1973 and 1978
(current Colombian pesos)

Education level	1973			1978		
	Male	Female	Income ratio (female/male)	Male	Female	Income ratio (female/male)
None	0.66	0.66	0.51	0.69	0.80	0.75
Primary	1.00	1.00	0.51	1.00	1.00	0.65
	(1,175)	(595)	—	(4,903)	(3,176)	—
Secondary	2.11	2.62	0.63	1.59	1.81	0.74
Higher	6.75	6.22	0.47	4.82	3.10	0.42
All	1.83	1.72	0.48	1.87	1.59	0.55
Number of workers (thousands)	488	249	—	732	454	—
Number in sample	45,080	23,041	—	3,078	1,914	—

— Not applicable.
Note: All earnings are expressed as multiples of earnings of workers with only primary education. Figures in parentheses are mean monthly earnings in current Colombian pesos for this group.
Sources: 1973 population census sample; and 1978 World Bank–DANE Household Survey.

The fact that a much larger percentage of women workers have no education (table 6-3) probably reflects the presence of a large number of fresh female immigrants who are young domestic workers. The 1978 sample reports much higher proportions of workers with both secondary and higher education (as did the 1977 sample), again as a result of increasing education levels in the labor force as a whole.

From the data in Table 6-4 it appears that incomes rose more with the level of education in 1973 than in 1978. It may be recalled that the 1973 census income information does not distinguish between labor earnings and other nonlabor income. This may partly account for the higher multiples of earnings obtained for higher education in 1973.[6] Moreover, with a greater percentage having a higher education, the scarcity value of this group might decline and the quality of such education become diluted. The difference between the 1973 and 1978 data is very large, but the later figures are consistent with the 1977 results. The female-to-male ratio appears to have improved for all education categories except for higher education. The overall

6. However, as shown in appendix C, household surveys have difficulty capturing nonlabor income, and a census would be even less likely to do so.

ratio of 0.55 in 1978 is comparable with, but slightly above, the 0.52 ratio in 1977, possibly as a result of a continuing upward trend in female earnings.

Consider now the age-education distribution of poor workers, defined as those belonging to households in the bottom 30 percent classified by household income per capita (see chapter 5; details are available in Mohan and Hartline 1984). To summarize the findings briefly, the age distribution of poor male workers is not strikingly different from that of all male workers, except that the poor are overrepresented in the 35–44 age group. Among females as well, the poor are overrepresented in the 35–44 group. In the age-education distribution, among the workers who have only primary or less education, the poor appear to predominate in the 25–34 age group. The numbers of the poor in the 35–44 group may be unusually large because workers in this group are likely to have just finished forming their households and thus may have children who are still too young to work; in other words, dependency ratios are expected to be high for this age group. Furthermore, 40 percent of all children in the 12–14 age group come from the poorest 30 percent of the population. However, only 20 percent of all male workers and 15 percent of female workers fall in the bottom 30 percent. This evidence suggests that any kind of employment helps to alleviate poverty. The surprising finding that only 15 percent of working women come from poor households probably reflects the fact that most women are secondary workers, and that just bringing a second income into a household makes that household sufficiently better off to raise it above the poorest 30 percent. One-half of all workers with no education and one-third of those with only primary education fall in the bottom 30 percent of the population; the proportions are much lower for females.

The above patterns confirm what one might expect for Bogotá as a whole. What is interesting is that these patterns hold for individual spatial sectors of the city, although the profile differs from sector to sector.

The distribution of workers by age and education categories and the mean incomes for each group are given in appendix tables 6A-1 and 6A-2 at the end of this chapter. Figure 6-1 presents the data graphically. The age-income profile for each sector appears in figure 6-1A. If the seven sectors (excluding sector 1, the central business district) are ranked in descending order by mean income, the order is consistently 8, 7, 5, 4, 6, 3, 2 for each age group, with almost no irregularities.

The poorer sectors (2, 3, and 6) have flatter age-income profiles than the richer sectors (4, 5, 7, and 8). The poorest sectors (2 and 3) account for 50–55 percent of all poor workers. It may therefore be hypothesized that people in these areas have few expectations of improvement over time if what they observe in their neighborhoods is any guide. Presumably those who do "make good" move to more attractive locales. (Table 6A-8 shows,

Figure 6-1. *Earnings Profile of Bogotá by Age and Sector, Education and Sector, and Age and Education, 1978*

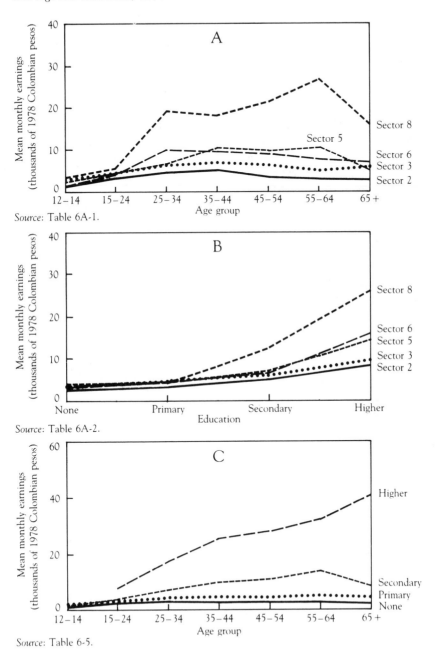

Source: Table 6A-1.

Source: Table 6A-2.

Source: Table 6-5.

however, that a large proportion of the population of every sector had lived in Bogotá for more than ten years.) Although these data do not permit us to draw any inferences about the intracity mobility of households, residents of a poor sector who have been in Bogotá for a long time are not likely to have moved "downward" from a richer sector. It is therefore reasonable to conclude that a significant proportion of people in poor neighborhoods have lived there or in other poor sections of the city for most of their lives.

Now consider Figure 6-1B, which gives the education-income profile for each sector. As with the age categories, people in the richer sectors earn more than their counterparts in the poorer sectors *at every level of education*; moreover, the same sectoral ranking prevails (although there is some crossing over at the higher education level). The differential between the sectors increases with higher levels of education. These patterns also hold up with multivariate analysis (chapter 8).

Why should returns to schooling differ for people living in different locations? Some of the variation evident in figure 6-1B is no doubt caused by differing mean years of schooling between the sectors since the various years of schooling are grouped into four levels. Except for sector 2, earnings appear to grow exponentially with education levels. A log-linear specification of the human capital model is expected to work quite well even at the disaggregated sectoral level. That different coefficients are obtained implies differing rates of return to education by sector.

The next step is to control for education-income effects by age. The distribution of workers (males and females) by both age groups and education levels is given in table 6-5. One interesting feature is immediately apparent. The higher the education level, the higher the age at which income peaks. This is graphed in Figure 6-1C, which shows the human capital model to be clearly relevant for Bogotá; the standard specification of the logarithm of income with education, experience, and (experience)^2 is likely to suffice. Interestingly, the higher education-age-income profile in figure 6-1C is quite similar to the sector 8 age-income profile in figure 6-1A. The primary-education profile is similar to that of sector 2. The other sectors correspond roughly to the secondary-education profile. (The earnings distribution of workers by age and education by sector is tabulated in table 6A-3.)

The similarities between the sectoral and education-level profiles are not, of course, accidental. Of all workers in sector 2, about 60 percent are educated only up to the primary level. Of all workers in section 8, about 45 percent have higher education. These constitute the extremes of the spectrum. Sets of sectoral age-income profiles for each education level are graphed in figure 6-2, which applies to all workers. Some of the regularities are lost because female workers are included, but enough remain to warrant retaining the hypothesis that returns to schooling vary systematically by sector. Note that

Table 6-5. Distribution and Earnings of Workers in Bogotá by Age and Education, 1978

| | Education | | | | | | | | | |
| | None | | Primary | | Secondary | | Higher | | All | |
Age group	Earnings	Percent	Earnings	Percent	Earnings	Percent	Earnings	Percent	Earnings	Percent
12–14	0.40	1.1	0.68	2.0	0.49	0.4	n.a.	n.a.	0.53	1.0
15–24	1.00	5.0	1.00	29.0	1.00	38.2	1.00	20.0	1.00	30.2
	(2,553)		(3,376)		(4,080)		(7,966)		(4,197)	
25–34	1.20	13.9	1.30	24.8	1.78	31.2	2.18	44.5	2.04	30.0
35–44	1.15	29.0	1.43	23.2	2.40	16.9	3.21	19.8	2.26	20.4
45–54	1.13	27.0	1.38	13.4	2.73	9.7	3.52	11.3	2.38	12.1
55–64	1.18	18.3	1.56	5.8	3.40	2.9	4.06	3.1	2.35	4.7
65 +	0.91	5.8	1.33	1.9	2.11	0.8	5.16	1.2	1.81	1.5
All age groups	1.13	100.0	1.26	100.0	1.72	100.0	2.37	100.0	1.81	100.0

n.a. Not applicable.

Note: All earnings are expressed as multiples of earnings of workers in the 15–24 age group. Figures in parentheses are mean monthly earnings in current Colombian pesos for this age group. Percentages may not add to 100 because of rounding.

Source: 1978 World Bank–DANE Household Survey.

Figure 6-2. *Earnings Profile of Bogotá by Age and Education,*
Selected Sectors, 1978

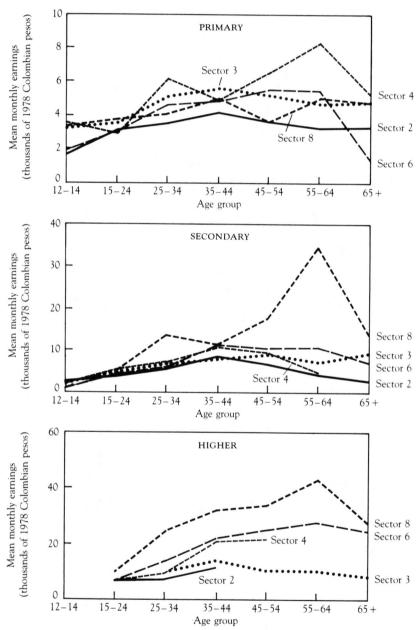

Source: Table 6A-3.

the differences in magnitude between the sectors increase with the level of education.

Is it reasonable to suppose that within a city the location of residence *causes* different rates of return to education? This hypothesis clearly needs to be tested systematically, but a few conjectures may be offered here. Starting from the premise that location can stand as a proxy for other unmeasured variables, one could say with some justification that the quality of schooling available in a city differs by location (this, of course, is a familiar phenomenon within U.S. cities)—and quality is a factor that the years of schooling variable cannot capture. Parents' education and income are likely to determine household location in the first place and then to affect the children's schooling by virtue of location. Well-to-do parents living in "upper-class" neighborhoods may also expose their children to experiences not available to parents and children in poorer areas—and these experiences may have a positive effect on the children's subsequent employment and earnings patterns. Location in a low-income neighborhood can also mean that a person's network of contacts will only be suitable for finding a low-income job.[7] Moreover, the fact that lower-income neighborhoods have rather flat age-earnings profiles may have a dampening demonstration effect on residents' expectations and aspirations. The idea that this might have a cumulative effect on earnings leads to a "discouraged earner" hypothesis analogous to the discouraged worker hypothesis for nonparticipators. Another significant factor is that location of residence is also a proxy for social class, which probably has a significant effect on earnings.

The larger question is whether this pattern is peculiar to Bogotá or whether it exists in other cities as well. Clearly, all cities have their poor and rich neighborhoods, but the point is, are they clustered in other cities as they are in Bogotá? The clustering found in Bogotá probably exacerbates the noneducational disadvantages facing individuals born to poor parents. Is there much spatial mobility, or can cross-sectional data be generalized over time? Only cross-sectional data have been examined here, so it is difficult to draw any conclusions about patterns over time. The question is whether potential earnings (or permanent income) are affected by location in different parts of the city rather than simply by current earnings. Questions such as this can only be answered with the aid of panel data, which are not yet available in Colombia.

---

7. McGregor (1977) makes a similar point in an investigation of variations in the duration of unemployment in Glasgow, which he found to be higher in poor neighborhoods after controlling for all other standard variables (age, education, sex, and so on).

Profile of Workers by Occupation

Table 6-6 shows the distribution of workers by occupation for Bogotá as a whole in 1973 and 1978. The distributions are broadly similar but some variations are discernible. The 1978 sample has a far greater proportion of professional and technical workers and rather more administrators and managers, but it is consistent with the 1977 sample (as reported in Mohan 1980). Overall mean income surpassed 400 percent of its 1973 level, and inflation between the two years was about 250–300 percent. In part, this trend probably reflects better coverage of labor incomes in our survey, but it is also due to the higher proportion of people in better-paying occupations. At the same time, reported mean earnings in these well-paid categories have not increased by as much as they have in other occupations. This pattern is consistent with the observed rising level of education of the labor force as a whole, and the consequent expansion of the supply of better-educated people. Indeed the greatest increases in mean earnings are reported for some of the lowest-paid occupations, such as production, construction, and transport work.

Maids constitute about one-fifth of all female workers; thus Bogotá appears to have about 100,000 female domestic servants (one to every five or six households, on the average). Their income is reported to have been significantly higher in 1978 than in 1973 (about two-and-a-half times higher in real terms). This increase is due mainly to improved coverage of the group's income in kind, which was characteristically neglected in the 1973 census. Although there were far fewer production supervisors in 1978 than in 1973, the incomes of those covered roughly doubled in real terms. The proportion of construction workers also decreased, possibly as a result of a real fall in the proportion in this category since 1973, when there was a building boom. (Construction workers were one of the main categories of the underemployed in 1977.)

Only about one-quarter of all workers are categorized as production workers and they are among the lowest-paid groups; the only categories with significantly lower earnings are construction workers and domestic servants (among women, even maids are better paid than production workers). Sales workers earn almost one-and-a-half times as much as production workers. Thus measures to promote small-scale industry might, paradoxically, increase poverty rather than alleviate it! The problem is more one of low productivity than lack of jobs. The coefficient of variation is high for service jobs in comparison with that for production and construction workers. Thus there *are* a large number of poor production workers, but some of the poor are also service workers. Women's incomes amount to 40 percent or more of male incomes, depending on occupation.

When the distribution of workers by occupation was examined at the comuna level, some distinct patterns emerged. Table 6A-4 gives the occupational distribution of all workers by sector for 1978.[8] Occupations are distributed by location essentially in the order of their mean incomes. Table 6A-5 summarizes the information in table 6A-4 by presenting "indexes of concentration" by occupation; the index numbers reflect the proportion of workers in a given occupation who live in a particular sector relative to the proportion of all workers living in the sector.[9] If all occupations were distributed uniformly across the city, all indexes would be 100; the boldface figures refer to cases in which the index is 120 or greater.

The most striking concentrations of workers by occupation are shown in map 6-1 (p. 156). Production, construction, and transport workers (all poorly paid groups) are overrepresented in both sectors 2 and 6, and service and sales workers are also overrepresented in sector 2. In sector 3, clerks and typists as well as production and transport workers are overrepresented. Sectors 4 and 5 constitute the industrial corridor. Production supervisors are overrepresented in both these sectors. Salespeople are also overrepresented in sector 4. Sectors 7 and 8 differ considerably from the others in that professionals, administrators, and their servants ("maids" in the classification used here) are concentrated here. The center (sector 1) specializes in the residences of sales and service workers, as might be expected. Interestingly, most construction workers live at the periphery, but much of the construction work is presumably carried out in the center and the affluent north. Information on the location of employment helps to make sense of the residential location pattern. Most of the city's large manufacturing plant is in fact located in the industrial corridor (sectors 4 and 5), whereas a large proportion of retail and service employment is to be found in the central comunas (31 and 81).

Having shown that the residence of workers is concentrated by occupation in particular sectors, I can compare the characteristics of workers in each occupation across sectors, since all occupations are represented in each sector. Figure 6-3 (p. 157) illustrates the mean incomes of each occupation by sector. Sector 7 has been omitted since it is similar to sector 8, and sectors 4, 5, and 1 are omitted because they are mixed in character. Again, the pattern is clear; the ranking of sectors by income persists even when controlled for occupation. Occupations are arranged in descending order by incomes to highlight the finding that people in the same occupation earn different incomes according to their sector of residence. This picture further reinforces

8. Similar and consistent computations for 1973 and 1977 are given in Mohan (1980). The distribution for 1978 was not significantly different from these two years.

9. Thus, in 1973, for example, 39.5 percent of construction workers lived in sector 1, but only 29.1 percent of all workers lived there. The index is therefore $39.5 \times 100/29.1 = 136$. Hoover and Vernon (1959, p. 284) called this "the index of occupational specialization."

Table 6-6. *Distribution and Earnings of Workers in Bogotá by Occupation, 1973 and 1978*
(mean monthly earnings in current Colombian pesos)

Occupation (ILO code)	1973					
	Male		Female		All (percent)	Earnings ratio (female/male)
	Earnings	Percent	Earnings	Percent		
Professional and technical (1–19)	6,090 (1.18)	8.3	2,740 (1.68)	8.0	8.2	0.45
Administrative and managerial (20–29)	9,412 (0.98)	2.1	3,692 (1.03)	0.5	1.6	0.32
Clerks and typists (30–39)	2,136 (1.42)	10.3	1,760 (1.24)	17.4	12.7	0.82
Sales managers and proprietors (40–41)	3,338 (1.92)	7.8	1,736 (2.55)	3.8	6.5	0.52
Other sales (42–49)	2,059 (2.00)	8.6	743 (0.98)	7.9	8.4	0.36
Service, excluding maids (50–53; 55–59)	1,416 (2.5)	7.1	807 (2.37)	14.0	9.4	0.57
Maids (54)	537 (0.90)	0.5	364 (1.64)	30.4	10.6	0.68
Agriculture (60–69)	2,698 (3.02)	1.9	3,032 (2.24)	0.2	1.3	1.13
Production supervisors (70)	1,325 (1.29)	5.1	851 (0.68)	3.5	4.6	0.64
Production workers (71–94, 96, 97)	1,279 (1.15)	27.2	810 (1.71)	14.1	22.7	0.63
Construction (95)	968 (1.29)	10.8	487 (0.83)	0.1	7.2	0.50
Transport (95)	1,369 (0.77)	8.3	1,408 (0.82)	0.0	5.5	1.01
Other	701 (0.73)	2.1	597 (0.70)	0.0	1.4	0.85
All occupations	2,166 (1.95)	100.0	1,043 (2.13)	100.0	100.0	0.48
Number of workers (thousands)	436		223		659	
Number of workers responding	37,455		17,456		53,911	
No information (percent)	12.0		12.4			

Note: Coefficients of variation in parentheses. Percentages may not add to 100 because of rounding.

Occupation (ILO code)	1978					
	Male		Female		All (percent)	Earnings ratio (female/ male)
	Earnings	Percent	Earnings	Percent		
Professional and technical (1–19)	20,600 (0.82)	12.4	12,501 (1.32)	11.1	11.9	0.61
Administrative and managerial (20–29)	28,049 (0.08)	4.2	14,093 (032)	0.3	2.7	0.50
Clerks and typists (30–39)	7,622 (0.77)	11.2	6,153 (0.60)	19.2	14.2	0.81
Sales managers and proprietors (40–41)	11,797 (1.17)	7.8	4,759 (1.24)	6.3	7.2	0.40
Other sales (42–49)	8,733 (1.19)	9.4	3,513 (0.05)	7.5	8.7	0.40
Service, excluding maids (50–53; 55–59)	4,877 (1.11)	8.6	3,302 (0.95)	17.9	12.2	0.68
Maids (54)	1,486 (0.38)	0.1	3,301 (1.02)	19.9	7.7	2.22
Agriculture (60–69)	19,228 (1.00)	0.8	3,224 (0.23)	1.0	0.3	0.17
Production supervisors (70)	8,408 (0.55)	1.0	3,447 (0.35)	0.5	0.8	0.51
Production workers (71–94, 96, 97)	4,894 (0.71)	27.5	3,134 (0.63)	14.9	22.7	0.65
Construction (95)	3,944 (0.63)	8.7	2,009 (0.20)	0.2	5.4	0.66
Transport (95)	5,795 (0.63)	7.4	6,169 (0.35)	0.2	4.6	1.06
Other	6,243 (0.79)	1.1	4,472 (0.62)	0.3	0.8	0.72
All occupations	9,153 (1.26)	100.0	1,070 (1.42)	100.0	100.0	0.55
Number of workers (thousands)	732		454		1,186	
Number of workers responding	3,078		1,914		4,992	

Sources: 1973 population census sample; and 1978 World Bank–DANE Household Survey.

Map 6-1. *Bogotá: Distribution of Occupations by Sector*

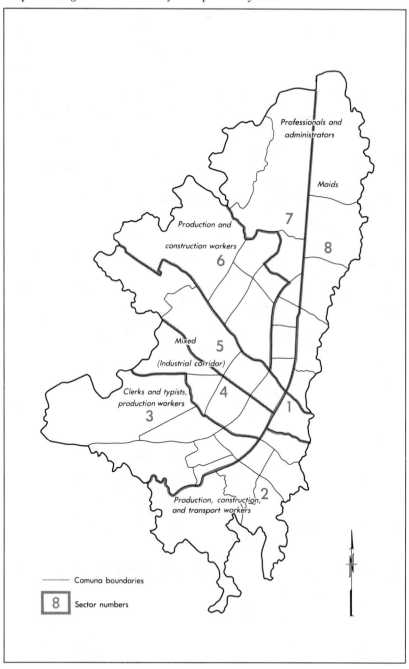

Figure 6-3. *Profile of Occupation and Income, Bogotá Males, 1977*

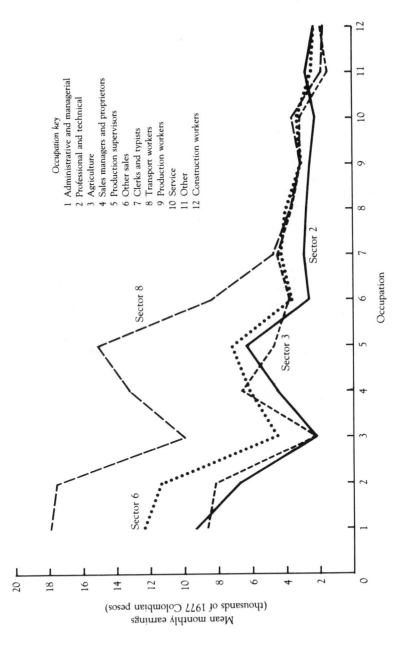

the evidence presented earlier that points to income segregation by sector, along with other associated characteristics.

As might be expected, poor workers are concentrated in blue-collar occupations; around 70–75 percent of all poor male workers are blue-collar workers (classified as *obreros* as distinguished from *empleados* in Spanish), as are about 65–70 percent of all female workers. In the overall distribution, only about 55–57 percent of male and female workers fall in that category. About 65–70 percent of all poor workers can be classified as production and service workers (excluding maids); this group also includes male construction and transport workers, and female sales workers. Somewhat surprisingly, maids make up only about 20 percent of all poor female workers; they appear to be better off than their counterparts who work in service and manufacturing jobs. If the minimum wage is used as a yardstick, the main occupations in which males receive less than the minimum wage are sales and construction. Among women, only a very small percentage of maids are paid below minimum wage rates—and some of these work only part-time. (For more details on occupational characteristics of poor workers, see Mohan and Hartline 1984.)

In summary, people in particular occupations are more likely to be poor; furthermore, the poor (including the less well paid in "better" occupations) tend to cluster in specific sectors. The better-paid occupations are clustered in the northern sectors of the city, but the ordering of location of residence essentially depends on income, rather than on occupation.

Profile of Workers by Industry of Activity

The distribution of workers by industry of activity is consistent with the occupational distribution, but it provides further information on their characteristics. Table 6-7 presents the distribution of employment and mean incomes by activity for both 1973 and 1978. The 1978 distribution, which is consistent with other household surveys in different years, is probably more accurate than the census-based 1973 distribution. Manufacturing turns out to have been overrepresented in the 1973 census; a large proportion of respondents—who were apparently concentrated in the trade and service activities, which are characteristically more difficult to classify accurately — gave no answer to the relevant question.[10]

10. DANE publications for the 1973 census report a distribution that is quite different from the one presented here and more consistent with household surveys. Inquiries at DANE revealed that they imputed industry of activity to the nonrespondents, utilizing occupation and other information, where available.

Predictably, women predominate in domestic service and retail trade—these two categories account for almost half of all female employment. In manufacturing, a large proportion of women work in the textiles and footwear category. They are also present in large numbers in "public instruction" (that is, teaching). These four categories together account for 70 percent of all female employment. Among the males, about 27 percent were in various manufacturing categories, 12 percent in construction, and 17 percent in commerce. Within the manufacturing sector, there is no bunching of males in particular industries, as there is in textiles and footwear for women. Incomes are in the expected order—low in manufacturing and construction, and high in financial establishments, public administration, wholesale trades, and teaching (all of which are white-collar activities).

The spatial distribution of workers by industry of activity in 1978 is presented in table 6A-6. (Indexes of concentration similar to those for occupation were constructed for 1973 and 1977 and presented in Mohan 1980.) The disaggregation of manufacturing in table 6A-6 offers some interesting information about geographical concentrations of workers by individual industries. Manufacturing workers as a whole are concentrated in sectors 2, 3, and 4, but table 6A-6 provides evidence of further specialization within manufacturing. Workers in the industrial chemicals and metal industries, for example, along with those in paper and printing, tend to be overrepresented in sectors 4, 5, and 6. A glance at table 6-7 reveals that these are the kinds of manufacturing activities in which earnings are relatively high; hence the concentration in sectors 4, 5, and 6 rather than in 2, where the poor are concentrated. Sector 4 specializes in commerce and also in textiles and footwear. If it is not merely a sampling artifact, the data for sector 6 reveal an increasing concentration of manufacturing workers in 1978 relative to 1973 (see Mohan 1980). Construction workers are also heavily represented in sector 6. With large manufacturing moving outward along the industrial corridor of sectors 4 and 5, a movement of manufacturing workers to sector 6 would not be surprising. As expected, white-collar workers employed in financial establishments, wholesale trade, public instruction, and public administration are concentrated in sectors 7 and 8, along with their domestic servants. I have ignored mining and agriculture since they form a negligible proportion of the Bogotá labor force.

As might be expected from the earlier results based on occupational data, manufacturing and construction are the industries most likely to have poor male workers. Within manufacturing, lumber and wood products and mineral production appear to have unusually high proportions of poor workers. Among tertiary activities, retail trades, transport and communications, and personal and domestic services stand out as activities employing a large proportion of poor people (see Mohan and Hartline 1984). Among the females, poor

Table 6-7. *Distribution and Earnings of Workers in Bogotá by Activity, 1973 and 1978*
(mean monthly earnings in current Colombian pesos)

	1973					
	Male		Female		All	Earnings ratio
Activity (ILO code)	Earnings	Percent	Earnings	Percent	(percent)	(female/male)
Agriculture (10–19)	4,029 (2.4)	2.4	2,459 (2.13)	0.5	1.7	0.61
Mining (20–29)	4,016 (1.59)	0.7	4,014 (0.77)	0.1	0.5	1.00
Food products, beverages, and tobacco (31)	1,782 (1.64)	5.8	918 (1.17)	4.0	5.2	0.52
Textiles and footwear (32)	1,726 (2.03)	8.1	920 (1.76)	15.3	10.7	0.54
Lumber and wood (33)	1,334 (1.42)	4.4	840 (1.20)	0.5	5.0	0.63
Paper, printing, and publishing (34)	2,220 (1.30)	2.7	1,043 (0.72)	1.8	2.4	0.47
Mineral products (36)	1,622 (1.85)	1.8	852 (1.11)	0.7	1.4	0.53
Industrial chemicals and petroleum (35)	3,199 (1.40)	3.2	1,305 (2.87)	3.4	3.3	0.41
Metal industry (37, 38)	1,509 (1.49)	8.5	1,274 (2.11)	2.2	6.3	0.67
Other industry (30, 39)	2,147 (1.85)	4.9	1,123 (3.41)	3.4	4.4	0.52
Utilities (40–49)	2,963 (0.97)	1.1	1,886 (1.76)	0.3	0.8	0.74
Construction (50–59)	1,268 (1.95)	17.9	1,632 (1.50)	0.7	11.7	1.28
Wholesale trade (61)	3,889 (1.87)	2.2	2,185 (2.95)	1.5	2.0	0.56
Retail trade (62)	2,578 (2.01)	8.1	1,087 (4.08)	6.6	7.5	0.42
Other commerce (60, 63)	4,320 (2.09)	4.3	1,195 (2.27)	4.5	4.4	0.28
Transport and communication (70–79)	2,631 (1.59)	5.4	2,166 (0.59)	1.3	3.9	0.82
Financial establishments (80–89)	5,034 (1.33)	4.8	2,307 (0.90)	3.7	4.4	0.41
Public administration and social services (96–99)	3,649 (1.36)	5.6	2,195 (.072)	3.9	5.0	0.60
Public instruction (93)	5,524 (1.18)	4.0	2,309 (1.79)	9.4	5.9	0.42
Domestic and personal service (95)	1,468 (1.54)	4.2	385 (1.22)	36.4	15.7	0.26
All activities	2,515 (1.92)	100.0	1,063 (1.92)	100.0	100.0	0.42
Number of workers (thousands)	291		162		454	
Number of workers responding	24,335		11,987		36,352	
No information (percent)	41		36		39	

Note: Coefficient of variation in parentheses. Percentages may not add to 100 because of rounding.

Activity (ILO code)	1978					
	Male		Female		All	Earnings ratio
	Earnings	Percent	Earnings	Percent	(percent)	(female/male)
Agriculture (10–19)	19,218 (0.94)	0.9	3,354 (0.26)	1.2	1.0	0.17
Mining (20–29)	37,737 (0.63)	0.3	8,156 (0.33)	0.6	0.4	0.22
Food products, beverages, and tobacco (31)	7,624 (1.70)	3.5	11,679 (0.62)	2.3	3.1	0.61
Textiles and footwear (32)	6,337 (1.07)	4.8	3,168 (0.75)	8.9	6.4	0.50
Lumber and wood (33)	4,718 (0.25)	2.9	5,021 (0.30)	0.2	1.9	1.06
Paper, printing, and publishing (34)	9,233 (1.84)	2.0	6,664 (0.63)	1.6	1.9	0.72
Mineral products (36)	7,085 (1.07)	1.6	3,318 (0.74)	0.5	1.2	0.47
Industrial chemicals and petroleum (35)	13,662 (1.23)	2.7	5,354 (0.85)	3.1	2.9	0.39
Metal industry (37, 38)	8,406 (1.10)	7.5	6,334 (2.23)	2.4	5.5	0.75
Other industry (30, 39)	3,488 (0.64)	0.6	3,132 (0.50)	1.3	0.9	0.90
Utilities (40–49)	5,359 (0.79)	0.8	7,181 (0.51)	0.2	0.5	0.93
Construction (50–59)	5,276 (1.27)	11.3	7,986 (0.95)	1.0	7.4	1.33
Wholesale trade (61)	19,532 (0.84)	1.9	11,979 (0.89)	1.1	1.6	0.61
Retail trade (62)	7,527 (1.19)	18.8	1,145 (0.98)	17.8	18.4	0.53
Other commerce (60, 63)	5,197 (1.01)	2.1	3,200 (0.70)	5.5	3.4	0.62
Transport and communication (70–79)	8,439 (0.90)	8.4	6,939 (0.42)	1.8	5.9	0.82
Financial establishments (80–89)	15,187 (1.18)	9.6	7,884 (0.77)	6.1	8.3	0.52
Public administration and social services (96–99)	11,578 (0.99)	8.6	11,462 (1.91)	5.6	7.5	0.39
Public instruction (93)	14,475 (0.09)	5.2	7,067 (0.62)	12.3	7.9	0.43
Domestic and personal service (95)	4,392 (1.36)	6.6	3,226 (1.16)	26.4	14.2	0.61
All activities	9,156 (1.26)	100.0	5,064 (1.42)	100.0	100.0	0.55
Number of workers (thousands)	728		452		1,170	
Number of workers responding	3,063		1,904		1,967	
No information (percent)	0.5		0.5		0.5	

Sources: 1973 population census sample; and 1978 World Bank–DANE Household Survey.

women are disproportionately employed in textiles and shoes, in the lumber and wood industries, and in printing and publishing. As with males, poor female workers are also overly represented in retail trades. Again, personal and domestic services do not account for a disproportionate number of poor women.

The Distribution of Workers by Residence and Workplace

When the distribution of workers in Bogotá is analyzed by sector of residence, the characteristics of workers in each sector differ systematically from those in other sectors, whatever dimension is being considered. Table 6-8 presents sector-by-sector data on mean earnings and proportions of male and female workers for 1978. The pattern is similar to that for households; the income ranking of sectors remains unchanged when based on workers' earnings rather than household incomes. The unexpectedly large proportion of female workers with low mean incomes in sectors 7 and 8 (the rich northern sectors) is accounted for by the presence of a large number of female domestic servants working in rich households in those sectors. Note, too, that the mean earnings of women are only about half those of men in Bogotá. The particularly low female-male earnings ratio for sector 8 is again explained by the presence of female domestic servants. There are fewer women than men in better-paid occupations, particularly in the administrative and managerial categories (see table 6-6).

Table 6-8. *Distribution and Earnings of Workers in Bogotá by Sector, 1978*
(mean monthly earnings in current Colombian pesos)

Sector	Male		Female		Earnings ratio (female/male)
	Earnings	Percent	Earnings	Percent	
1	5,108	3.1	5,055	1.4	0.99
2	4,598	20.8	2,905	16.2	0.63
3	6,411	25.1	4,341	20.7	0.68
4	8,760	6.9	4,703	5.8	0.54
5	8,443	6.1	4,748	6.7	0.56
6	8,074	17.9	5,030	17.5	0.62
7	11,455	9.1	5,005	11.7	0.44
8	25,771	10.9	7,879	19.9	0.31
All sectors	9,153	100.0	5,067	100.0	0.55

Note: Percentages may not add to 100 because of rounding.
Source: 1978 World Bank–DANE Household Survey.

The DANE surveys do not record workers' places of work, so they tell us nothing about the spatial match of residence and workplace. However, the 1972 Bogotá Urban Development Phase II Household Survey and the World Bank–DANE Household Survey did include questions about workplaces, and tabulations can therefore be made according to the City Study zonification scheme. The spatial distribution of workers by residence in the Bogotá Urban Development Phase II Household Survey of 1972 is consistent with the 1973 census, and with the 1977 and 1978 surveys. We can therefore consider its results comparable with those of the sources being used in the rest of this book.

Consider now the residential and employment distributions of workers in 1972 and 1978 by rings and sectors (table 6-9). Here Bogotá emerges as a relatively centralized city with as much as 15–25 percent of all its employment in the central business district. In comparison, a typical large city in the United States has about 10–15 percent of all its employment located in the center (Bronitsky and others 1975). In New York, for example, which is one of the more centralized cities in the United States, about 15 percent of the city's total employment is in the central business district. The employment density in Bogotá's central business district is about 400–500 jobs per hectare, compared with 890 in New York and 630 in Chicago—cities that are renowned for their skyscrapers. Thus although Bogotá has a higher proportion of employment in the central business district than New York or Chicago, it is not quite as congested as they are.

According to the distribution of employment by rings (table 6-9), the density of employment falls rapidly as one moves to the outer rings. Indeed, an exponentially declining employment density function fits the ring data surprisingly well. The function estimated was the standard density function

$$E_x = E_o \exp\,(-ax)$$

where E_o and a are the estimated coefficients, 'a' is the gradient, and E_o the hypothetical (estimated) density at the center. E_x is the employment density at distance x. When Mills (1972) estimated density functions for eighteen U.S. cities, he found that they had been flattening over a long period of time. His most recent estimates, for the year 1963 (which are converted from miles to kilometers here for comparability), have an average gradient of 0.26 for manufacturing, 0.27 for retailing, 0.33 for services, and 0.35 for retailing. Here the estimates are 0.241 for 1972 and 0.204 for 1978 for employment as a whole.

The Bogotá gradients are surprisingly lower than Mills's estimates for the eighteen U.S. cities. Thus it appears that employment in Bogotá is more decentralized than it was in U.S. cities in 1963, even though Bogotá's central business district has a higher proportion of employment than U.S. cities.

Table 6-9. *Distribution of Workers in Bogotá by Residence and Workplace, 1972 and 1978*

| | | Workers (percent) | | | | Density (number per hectare) | | | |
| | | 1972[a] | | 1978[b] | | Workers living | | Jobs | |
City division	Area	Living	Working	Living	Working	1972	1978	1972	1978
Ring									
1	398	1.7	25.7	2.4	14.5	37	73	507	420
2	1,357	10.9	15.0	9.7	18.3	70	85	87	155
3	2,575	13.1	16.3	13.3	17.0	44	61	50	76
4	5,960	34.5	20.7	26.0	21.2	50	52	27	41
5	14,330	37.6	20.4	43.0	25.5	23	36	11	20
6	5,804	2.2	1.8	5.5	3.6	3	11	2	7
All rings	30,423	100.0	100.0	100.0	100.0	28	39	26	38
Sector									
1	398	1.7	25.7	2.4	14.5	37	73	507	420
2	4,357	18.3	7.6	19.1	8.5	36	52	14	22
3	5,313	25.1	13.4	23.4	13.4	41	52	20	29
4	1,914	9.5	9.3	6.5	9.2	43	40	38	55
5	3,065	7.1	10.9	6.3	12.6	20	24	28	47
6	5,673	16.3	9.8	17.8	12.4	25	37	14	25
7	5,065	13.3	9.9	10.1	10.2	23	24	15	23
8	4,638	8.8	13.4	14.3	19.0	10	37	23	47
All sectors	30,423	100.0	100.0	100.0	100.0	28	39	26	38
Number in sample (thousands)		877	786	1,185	1,150				

Note: The workers' residence and workplace totals do not match because of missing information for workplaces. Percentages may not add to 100 because of rounding.

a. Based on Pachon (1979), table 5. Workers by residence from Phase II (1972), Survey Household File, and by work zone from Phase II Person File.

b. 1978 World Bank–DANE Household Study.

Two explanations are possible: first, the two-point estimation procedure followed by Mills may have produced biased estimates; and, second, his sample may have contained relatively smaller cities (Philadelphia being the largest), which characteristically have steeper density gradients. (The density gradient for employment in Cali is calculated to be 0.481.)

The density of workers by residence across Bogotá is much more even than the density by employment, and a "crater" can be observed at the center.

Furthermore, the number of workers in the outer rings exceed jobs, so that considerable inward commuting appears to take place.

According to the distributions by sector (table 6-9), apart from the central business district, jobs are concentrated in sectors 4 and 5—Le Corbusier's industrial corridor. Moreover, there is a net deficit of jobs in the poor sectors (2 and 3) and a net excess in the rich sectors (7 and 8).

Table 6-10 provides a more detailed picture of the commuting patterns in Bogotá. The proportion of people living and working in the same ring (note the numbers along the diagonal in table 6-10) falls as one moves away from the center. Since 1972, however, the proportion of people commuting to the central business district (ring 1) from other rings has declined considerably (for the 1972 patterns, see Pachon 1979). In 1972 about 20–30 percent of workers traveled to the central business district from every ring. Now a larger proportion are found to travel to ring 2. As is evident from table 6-9, a

Table 6-10. *Distribution of Workers in Bogotá by Zone of Origin and Destination, 1978*
(percent)

Residence zone	Work zone								Total
	Ring 1	Ring 2	Ring 3	Ring 4	Ring 5	Ring 6			Total
Ring									
1	71.0	16.7	5.7	4.7	1.9	0.0			100.0
2	20.6	54.6	10.0	8.4	5.6	0.8			100.0
3	11.3	19.1	50.1	9.7	7.9	2.0			100.0
4	14.9	15.5	12.9	44.5	11.3	0.8			100.0
5	11.2	12.6	11.8	15.1	47.4	1.8			100.0
6	10.2	9.1	13.3	17.0	9.5	40.9			100.0
All rings	14.5	18.3	17.0	21.2	25.5	3.6			100.0
	Sector 1	Sector 2	Sector 3	Sector 4	Sector 5	Sector 6	Sector 7	Sector 8	
Sector									
1	71.0	0.0	1.3	12.0	3.8	4.1	2.5	5.3	100.0
2	15.5	35.5	7.6	7.6	10.0	4.5	6.3	12.5	100.0
3	12.5	2.0	42.6	9.6	13.9	4.8	4.4	10.1	100.0
4	12.0	2.0	7.6	42.1	14.8	6.3	3.9	11.2	100.0
5	16.5	4.5	7.5	9.2	43.8	7.8	2.4	8.4	100.0
6	12.0	2.4	4.0	5.7	8.8	44.0	8.7	14.5	100.0
7	12.0	2.2	1.7	3.2	9.5	8.9	48.0	14.4	100.0
8	12.0	0.8	1.6	4.2	8.4	5.0	7.0	61.1	100.0
All sectors	14.5	8.5	13.4	9.2	12.6	12.4	10.2	19.0	100.0

Note: Percentages may not add to 100 because of rounding.
Source: 1978 World Bank–DANE Household Survey.

considerable densification of employment has taken place in ring 2, as it has correspondingly in sectors 6, 7, and 8—all the northern sectors (the densification is therefore essentially in the intersection of ring 2 and sectors 6, 7, and 8). As mentioned in chapter 3 and as is evident from the higher proportion of employment in sector 8 and ring 2, the central business district has expanded northward.

The general picture is even more interesting when viewed by sectors. About 25 percent of workers from each sector worked in the central business district in 1972, but by 1978 the figure was only about 12–15 percent from each sector, the movement away being mainly to sector 8, along with the movement of the central business district. As can be seen from the sector diagonal in table 6-10, commuting increases almost as average income decreases by sector. Thus, although about 65 percent commute out from sector 2, less than 40 percent do so from sector 8, and about half from sector 7. Note that a very small proportion of people commute into sectors 2 and 3—the poorest sectors—whereas sector 8 receives a significant proportion from every other sector. Thus there is a net flow of workers from the poorer to the richer sectors.

The Informal Sector

This section provides information for Bogotá on four labor market variables that are often used to determine the existence or extent of so-called informal sector employment. Size of firm is the most important classificatory variable used here, but, as the following paragraphs indicate, it is difficult to assemble reliable data for such a classification. Subsequently, I examine the distribution of workers according to their primary and secondary status, the number of hours worked, and their status as migrants or natives of the city. Although many informal sector workers are thought to have uncertain or irregular employment patterns, the data examined here cover only a single reference week, so offer no clue as to uncertainty of employment; nonetheless, uncertainty should be reflected in the proportion of those who work for only a few hours.

Distribution of Workers between Small and Large Establishments

As pointed out by Mazumdar (1976a), the formal sector is often identified with the "enumerated" sector, and consequently the informal sector is defined as the residual obtained by deducting employment in the enumerated sector from the total employment figure provided by a population census. This is a hazardous exercise at best, as can be shown by comparing alternative results for Bogotá with regard to employment in large and small firms.

Consider, for example, the distribution of employment for 1970, 1972, and 1978 (table 6-11). The numbers for 1970 are derived using the residual method and those for 1972 and 1978 are based on responses to a question on size of workplace that was included in the relevant household surveys. For 1970, the distribution of all workers by industry code is taken from the national household survey of that year, as are the figures for the total number of workers. The proportion of workers in large firms (those employing more than five workers) is the number of workers enumerated in the 1970 economic census in each industry as a fraction of the implied total number from the household survey. The distribution of all workers among industries seems reliable, since it is striking that the proportions are constant over the different surveys. As many as 50 percent of all workers in manufacturing apparently worked in small firms in 1970. The food and fabricated metals industries appear to be dominated by large firms, while all the others have about 50 percent or fewer workers in large firms. According to the 1972 data, however, the proportion of workers in large manufacturing firms is about 60 percent; the comparable figure for 1978 is about 70 percent. The latter figure should be more reliable because it is from a much larger sample.

Thus data sets for three years in the same decade give significantly different results for the split between large firms and small firms in Bogotá. The proportions reported for the three years at the two-digit level are even less comparable. It is not unreasonable to assume that the 1970 figures for large firms are on the low side because the economic census was not likely to have had 100 percent coverage of large firms. Hence at least 50 percent of manufacturing employment must be in large firms. It is difficult to speculate any further since the 1972 and 1978 estimates are so far apart. If these surveys suffered from the kind of sampling problems conjectured for the 1977 survey (see Mohan 1980), it would not be surprising to find employment in large firms overrepresented. Furthermore, even if employment in small manufacturing is, at most, 50 percent of all manufacturing, it constitutes only 10 percent of the total labor force (in fact, it is more likely to be around 8 percent).[11]

Although the 1970, 1972, and 1978 data sets give sharply contrasting results, there was a wide measure of agreement between the 1975 survey analyzed in Mohan (1980) and the 1978 World Bank–DANE Household Survey. On this basis, it seems safe to suppose that the proportion of workers

11. In examining social security data for the City Study, Kyu Sik Lee found that in 1977 about 210,000 manufacturing workers worked in firms having more than five employees and were covered by social security. The 1977 survey reveals that total manufacturing employment was about 290,000. Thus, even if we assume that all firms employing more than five employees were represented in the social security records (an unreasonable assumption), less than 30 percent of manufacturing workers would be in small firms.

Table 6-11. Distribution of Workers in Bogotá by Size of Establishment, 1970–78

SIC code	Industry	1970 Percent of SIC category Small	Large	Percent of all industry	Number of workers	1972 Percent of SIC category Small	Large	Percent of all industry	Number of workers	1978 Percent of SIC category Small	Large	Percent of all industry	Number of workers
31	Food	24.6	75.4	2.4	19,540	25.0	75.0	3.6	34,830	30.3	69.7	3.1	36,242
32	Textile, leather	65.4	34.6	7.1	57,430	62.1	37.7	7.0	67,650	44.3	55.7	6.4	45,423
33	Lumber, wood	76.0	24.0	2.3	18,400	78.4	21.6	2.2	21,420	49.8	50.2	1.9	22,000
35	Chemicals, petroleum	45.0	55.0	2.7	21,520	7.9	92.1	2.7	26,440	18.2	86.3	1.2	13,663
36	Clay, glass	63.1	36.9	1.1	8,710	34.6	65.4	1.1	10,900	13.3	86.7	2.8	37,678
37	Metals	57.2	42.8	1.1	8,870	11.1	88.9	0.8	7,530	22.4	42.6	0.2	2,355
38	Fabricated metals	23.6	76.4	3.7	30,160	26.4	73.6	3.1	30,200	17.2	87.8	5.3	62,902
	Total manufacturing	50.3	49.7	22.5	175,250	41.2	58.8	22.5	217,980	30.0	40.0	22.6	268,516
	Commerce												
61	Wholesale	22.3	77.7	2.4	19,310	39.3	60.7	1.2	11,770	17.7	82.3	1.6	18,943
62	Retail	74.0	26.0	15.4	123,400	65.2	34.8	16.8	161,640	66.2	35.8	18.3	211,804
63	Restaurants, hotels	55.8	44.2	3.2	25,590	53.0	47.0	2.9	27,700	50.3	45.7	3.4	41,208
	Total commerce	72.1	27.9	21.0	168,900	62.0	38.0	20.9	201,110	60.6	39.4	23.3	276,065
	Services												
71	Transport	98.6	1.4	4.8	39,250	47.0	53.0	5.2	49,990	52.6	47.4	4.8	50,855
83	Real estate	90.5	9.5	2.5	20,250	56.7	43.3	3.2	31,070	81.3	48.7	4.6	54,052
93	Social services	100.0	0.0[a]	9.5	76,520	17.6	82.4[a]	9.4	90,710	15.4	81.7	7.8	99,081
95	Personal services	95.2	4.8	16.7	134,660	55.6	44.4	15.0	144,845	87.2	12.8	14.1	167,052
	Total services	96.7	3.3	33.5	270,680	54.3	45.7	32.9	316,615	58.5	41.5	31.3	371,090
	Other			23.5	108,907			23.7	229,285	25.1	74.3	22.8	269,917
	Total			100.0	803,900	47.9	52.1	100.0	964,990	45.1	54.3	100.0	1,185,538

Note: "Small" refers to firms employing fewer than five employees, and "large" refers to firms employing more than five. Columns may not add to totals because some subcategories are excluded.

a. For 1972, social services includes government employees who fall in the large category. They were not covered by the 1970 economic census; hence 0.0 percent for large establishments in 1970.

Sources: 1970 economic census; 1970 DANE Household Survey EH2; 1972 DANE Household Survey EH6FT; and 1978 World Bank–DANE Household Survey EH21. Total number of workers in 1970 is from the Household Survey Distribution. Total number of workers in large firms is from the 1970 economic census of industry, commerce, and services covering all firms employing more than five employees. The number of workers in small firms is then calculated as a residual.

who are employed in manufacturing firms of five people or less is about one-third of the total labor force in manufacturing. Consequently, efforts to raise employment in small-scale industry can, at best, expect to make a difference of only 1 or 2 percentage points in total employment (an increase of 12–25 percent in small industry). In areas with open unemployment rates of 6–9 percent, such a strategy would make only a marginal difference.

In commerce, about 60–70 percent of all employment is in small firms in all three years. Predictably, a large proportion of wholesale trade is in large firms, but it is surprising that as much as half of all restaurant and hotel employment is in small establishments. The pattern in services in 1972 is quite consistent with that in 1978 (except for personal services), but the coverage of the economic census appears to have been poor for the services segment of the labor market. Only 30 percent of employment in services is reported in large establishments for 1975, and about 45 percent is reported for 1972. Employment not covered in any of the above categories amounts to about 20 percent. For both 1972 and 1975, total employment in small firms amounted to 45–50 percent of all employment—although, as demonstrated above, major discrepancies exist among the subcategories.

To sum up, there are pitfalls in any effort to deduce the extent of the informal or formal sector on the basis of statistical data on firm size. Policies based on such calculations can consequently be seriously misdirected. Finally, even if orders of magnitude can be obtained by comparing sources, as has been done here, there is little or no possibility of deducing time trends.

Distribution of Primary and Secondary Workers

When the distribution of primary and secondary earners and of male and female workers is examined according to income (Mohan 1980), the results tend to resemble another supposed characteristic of the informal sector—namely, that it consists of a disproportionately large percentage of secondary earners and women. The patterns for males and females are quite distinct. About 70 percent of all male workers, but only about 14 percent of women workers, are primary earners. Among the males, secondary earners are predominantly in the bottom half of the labor income distribution; as many as 50 percent of males in the bottom decile are secondary earners, whereas only 12 percent of the top decile are secondary earners. Sixty-five percent of all heads of households are in the top half of the male income distribution. Mohan finds the picture for females somewhat more complicated. About 62 percent of all women workers fall in the bottom half of the income distribution, and the proportion of primary earners first falls and then rises by decile. This distribution implies that many women workers must have a rather flat age-earnings profile. It seems likely that many of the female heads of households in the lower deciles are unskilled and uneducated women entering the labor force at a late age, possibly as widows, that is, when participation in the labor force is a matter of necessity rather than choice.

In summary, about 70 percent of all workers falling in the bottom 30 percent of the worker income distribution are male secondary earners or women. This finding matches the characteristics commonly attributed to the "informal sector," if this title is merely applied to the poorer section of the labor force.

Distribution of Workers according to Hours Worked

The informal sector is sometimes also characterized as offering opportunities for sporadic participation in the labor force, or irregular working hours. Participation rates are discussed in chapter 7; here I consider the distribution of workers according to weekly hours worked. As table 6-12 shows, about 70 percent of all workers put in what might be termed "regular hours" (40–60 hours a week). About 20–25 percent work excessive hours—more than 60 hours a week—and only about 10 percent work less than 40 hours. Males who work less than 30 hours are proportionately divided between the top 70 (3.5 percent) and bottom 30 percent (3 percent). Almost 25 percent of all males who work less than 30 hours a week are classified as professional or technical workers. Construction and production workers predominate among the other occupational categories with short working weeks.

Thus the "underemployed" in Bogotá (those who work less than 30 hours a week) consist of two distinct groups: relatively well-off professionals and technical workers who probably voluntarily limit their working hours, and poor construction and production workers who are indeed underemployed. This observation is borne out by analysis of the categories of workers who say that they would like more work. Almost 50 percent of all male workers who would like more work are production or construction workers. Only one-quarter of this group work less than 30 hours, however. This suggests that the underemployed have different characteristics, depending on the definition used. If the underemployed are defined on the basis of the few hours worked, then they are not necessarily poor or involuntarily unemployed. If instead the definition comprises all those who say that they would like more work, most of these individuals (about 70–75 percent) are already working for more than 40 hours a week—and many of them may not in practice be able to work more, even if their poverty makes them in principle anxious to do so. Another point worth noting is that the roughly 10 percent of workers with the most excessive hours (70 or more a week) earn less than the overall mean. This group consists mainly of sales workers, managers, and service employees.

Table 6-12. *Distribution of Workers in Bogotá by Number of Hours Worked Weekly, 1977 and 1978*

Hours worked weekly	Male				Female			
	Percent		Earnings[a]		Percent		Earnings[a]	
	1977	1978	1977	1978	1977	1978	1977	1978
0–14	0.5	0.8	1.59	0.74	0.5	0.8	0.37	0.73
15–29	3.8	3.1	0.83	1.13	6.8	4.8	0.80	1.06
30–39	5.1	4.1	0.83	0.97	6.5	5.3	0.75	1.10
40–49	60.1	51.8	1.02	1.00	50.9	49.3	1.15	1.14
50–59	12.8	14.0	1.07	1.08	11.3	12.6	0.96	0.71
60–69	9.0	10.1	1.08	1.15	13.1	9.2	0.87	1.22
70–98	8.7	15.2	0.92	0.83	11.1	17.0	0.80	0.71
No information	—	0.9	—	0.73	—	1.0	—	0.67
All categories	100.0	100.0	1.00	1.00	100.0	100.0	1.00	1.00
Mean monthly earnings (pesos)			5,404	9,153			2,823	5,067
Total number of workers (thousands)			732				454	

— Not applicable.
a. Expressed as multiples of mean monthly earnings of all workers in current Colombian pesos.
Sources: 1977 Household Survey EH15; and 1978 World Bank–DANE Household Survey.

Mohan and Hartline (1984) investigated the hours worked by poor workers in some detail and found that the poor are overrepresented among male workers who work long hours. About 20 percent of poor male workers work more than 60 hours a week while only 15 percent of all male workers work such hours. Sales workers, construction workers, and transport workers who are poor appear to work particularly long hours. Only professional and technical workers who are poor seem to work relatively short hours; among the poor, only about 8 percent work less than 40 hours, whereas about 55–60 percent work the "normal" 40-hour week. Note also that sales and transport workers work the longest hours in general. The story is somewhat different for female workers. Although it is again sales workers (along with maids) who work very long hours, those working less than "normal" hours seem to consist disproportionately of poor women. Therefore, many poor women working part-time may indeed like more work but cannot find it—or cannot in practice work longer hours because of responsibilities at home.

The pattern of weekly hours worked is thus quite complex. In general, males do not seem to lack work: there is little open underemployment. If anything, the poor are overworked in low-productivity occupations—although it may be that sales workers are actually underemployed, that is, idle for a substantial part of their apparently long working hours. But this group constitutes only about 25 percent of all poor workers, whereas almost half of the poor males working long hours are transport or construction workers (who are not likely to be idle during much of their working day). Among the women, however, a substantial proportion of workers seem to be either genuinely underemployed (that is, willing and able to work more hours) or unable to work "normal" hours. These findings suggest that poverty will not be alleviated simply by expanding employment opportunities. In the case of males, opportunities for higher-productivity employment are needed; this may also mean providing training programs for the least skilled and over-worked. For the females, what seems to be needed is a combination of more employment opportunities and day care programs for children, so that mothers can participate more effectively in income-producing activities.

Migrant Status

Conventional wisdom has it that migrants are disproportionately poor, work in the informal sector, and live either in inner-city slums when they first arrive or in shantytowns (that is, favelas or barrios) at the periphery later. These conjectures are not borne out in Bogotá. Table 6-13 shows the distribution of migrants and nonmigrants. Female migrants are significantly poorer but they are dominated by the large proportion of domestic servants that form part of that category. Male migrants earned marginally (4–5 percent) less than nonmigrants in 1973 and 1978, but 1977 data (see Mohan 1980) show them earning more. It is not clear that migrants are systematically and significantly poorer than natives—and, in fact, the proportion of migrants among the bottom 30 percent is the same as nonmigrants, that is, 30 percent. Jaramillo's (1978) careful analysis of the characteristics of migrants from the 1973 national census sample showed that migrants earn more than nonmigrants for all income categories; that migrants of long standing earn more than nonmigrants; that migrants born in large cities earn more than migrants born in small towns, who in turn earn more than natives; and that migrants earn more than nonmigrants at all education levels.

Table 6-14 reports the distribution of workers in Bogotá according to their length of residence in the city. The data for 1977 (not reported here) and 1978 show a strongly U-shaped pattern. The 1978 data show the newest migrants earning more than those in residence 6–10 years, while those in residence 21 or more years earn the most (and more, indeed, than nonmigrants). The 1973 data differ somewhat, in that migrants in residence 3–5 years earn the least, but the U-shaped pattern persists.[12] It may be coincidental that migrants in residence 3–5 years in 1973 were in the 6–10 year

12. These data refer only to workers; hence all children under 12 years of age are excluded. Thus native-born individuals who could have been included in the categories covering 1–10 years do not appear.

Table 6-13. *Distribution of Workers in Bogotá according to Migrant Status,*
1973 and 1978
(mean monthly earnings in current Colombian pesos)

| | 1973 | | | 1978 | | |
Status	Male	Female	All	Male	Female	All
Migrant[a]						
Percent	74.0	77.3	75.1	66.3	68.3	67.1
Earnings	2,107	927	1,695	9,038	4,769	7,374
Nonmigrant						
Percent	26.0	22.7	24.9	33.7	31.7	32.9
Earnings	2,291	1,349	1,999	9,380	5,710	8,026
All						
Percent	100.0	100.0	100.0	100.0	100.0	100.0
Earnings	2,155	1,023	1,770	9,153	5,067	7,589

a. Migrant is defined as one who was born outside Bogotá.
Sources: 1973 population census sample; and 1978 World Bank–DANE Household Survey.

category in 1978—and in each case constituted the group that earned the least. The relatively small percentages for new migrants in 1978 compared with 1973 may reflect a slowing trend in migration.

The spatial distribution of migrant and nonmigrant workers by location of residence in rings and sectors is shown in tables 6A-7 and 6A-8. The distributions also take into account sex and length of residence. The distribution of male migrant workers for each ring is not very different from the overall distribution except for the preponderance of fresh migrants in ring 1. Since this ring (the central business district) accounts for only about 3 percent of the total population, this preponderance represents only a small portion of the total number of fresh migrants. However, fresh single migrants seem likely to gravitate to the center of the city for residence and presumably employment. With this exception, migrants are distributed throughout the city in much the same way as everyone else.

The sectoral distribution in table 6A-8 is consistent with the findings for rings. For males, nonmigrants as well as recent migrants are relatively strongly represented in the rich sector 8, as are recent female migrants. Otherwise, as for the rings, the distribution of workers by length of residence in each sector is similar to that of the city as a whole. Note that the poorest sector (sector 2) has relatively few recent female migrants, counterbalancing the picture for the rich sectors 7 and 8—where the large proportion of newly migrating females reflects their employment as domestic servants of the rich. The overrepresentation of this group in ring 3 is probably explained by the fact that a substantial part of the rich sector 8 falls in ring 3.

Table 6-14. *Distribution of Workers in Bogotá by Length of Residence,*
1973 and 1978
(mean monthly earnings in current Colombian pesos)

Years resident		1973			1978		
		Male	Female	Total	Male	Female	Total
Migrant							
Less than 1	Percent	7.0	9.0	7.7	5.4	8.5	6.6
	Earnings	1,811	575	1,319	8,588	3,629	6,140
1–2	Percent	8.0	9.3	8.4	4.0	7.2	5.2
	Earnings	1,716	612	1,305	8,895	5,143	6,930
3–5	Percent	11.4	12.7	11.9	6.3	7.7	6.8
	Earnings	1,657	770	1,335	8,619	3,862	6,564
6–10	Percent	14.7	15.0	14.8	12.7	11.9	12.4
	Earnings	1,813	994	1,531	7,826	4,196	6,492
11–20	Percent	20.0	19.6	19.9	21.5	19.0	20.5
	Earnings	2,146	1,066	1,785	8,733	4,560	7,251
21–99	Percent	12.8	11.6	12.4	16.4	14.0	15.4
	Earnings	3,197	1,303	2,593	10,732	6,546	9,285
Nonmigrant	Percent	26.0	22.7	24.9	33.7	31.7	32.9
	Earnings	2,291	1,348	1,999	9,380	5,710	8,026
All	Percent	100.0	100.0	100.0	100.0	100.0	100.0
	Earnings	2,155	1,023	1,771	9,153	5,067	7,589

Note: Percentages may not add to 100 because of rounding.
Sources: 1973 population census sample; and 1978 World Bank–DANE Household Survey.

Summary

This chapter has laid the groundwork for a systematic investigation of the
urban labor market. In describing the general characteristics of the labor
force, I have shown that factors widely considered to be the determinants of
labor income also play a significant role in Bogotá, but that the variables
have an interesting spatial dimension.

Spatially, Bogotá is strongly segmented by levels of household income.
Moreover, as noted in chapter 4, it shows little sign of changing in this
respect. The message that emerges strikingly from the cross-tabulations is
that workers' earnings appear to vary systematically according to their place
of residence; thus, people of similar age and education have different earnings
according to where they live. In line with this apparent spatial segmentation
by income, residential locations also seem to be geographically differentiated
within broad occupational groupings; the relatively unskilled live in specific
(poorer) areas, and the professionals are concentrated in another geograph-

ically distinct (and distant) segment. That cities have rich and poor neighborhoods, or that people from similar occupations tend to cluster together,
are in themselves not surprising findings. What *is* surprising in Bogotá is the
extent of spatial segmentation by level of income and its possible implications
for the working of the labor market. For example, job opportunities are few
in sectors 2 and 3, where almost half the city and its poor live; consequently
many commute out from these areas to work, but few come in. Is this pattern
evident in other cities? Are most cities with high degrees of income inequality
also strongly spatially segregated? Is there feedback from residential location
to income opportunities in the labor market?

Income variation appears to be related not only to variation in investments
in human capital but also to a worker's occupational category and location
of residence. Of course, these variables cannot be considered strictly causal
in and of themselves. Nevertheless, careful analysis of these and other classifications relevant to urban labor markets and income distribution tends to
bring to light clusters of correlates that could be used in setting policy. If it
is true that when a person is born and raised in a poor sector of the city he
or she is doomed, because of that fact, to attend a low-quality school, to
have only limited aspirations, to develop a poor network of contacts, and is
consequently assured of a low and flat age-income profile—it is of little
relevance or comfort to him or her to say that the human capital model
works, that the market is not segmented, and therefore that no policy in-
terventions are required. When the alleviation of urban poverty is indeed a
goal of policy, the existence of such spatial segregation and resulting economic
deprivation points to direct policy actions, which upgrade social capital in
deprived locations and provide good schools and health centers in these
deprived neighborhoods.

This chapter has also examined some labor market characteristics that are
often used to attest to the existence of "informal sector" employment. It has
looked at the balance between large and small firms in the Bogotá labor
market; the distribution by income of male and female primary and secondary
workers; the distribution of worker characteristics according to weekly hours
worked; and the income and residential location of migrants to and natives
of Bogotá. However, no evidence of a distinct informal sector in the Bogotá
labor market has been found. In particular, there is no evidence that migrant
workers earn less than nonmigrants or that they congregate in specific areas
of the city—or in particular occupations or activities.

These results contradict the popular idea that large numbers of poor migrants tend to stream into cities seeking or finding jobs in particular industries
or under distinctive terms and conditions of employment. That more migrants
are poor than rich in Bogotá is a reflection of the distribution of income in
the receiving city and the country as a whole. There is little evidence that

migrants are disadvantaged in the labor market there or that they are disproportionately represented in activities commonly held to be characteristic of the "informal sector." As noted earlier, production workers, who are normally regarded as being well-paid "formal sector" employees, are among the lowest paid, and that if any kind of employment is protected, it might be some parts of the service sector. These findings suggest that the informal sector as conventionally defined is not a helpful analytical construct. The question of segmentation in the labor market is investigated more systematically in chapter 9; first, however, some attention should be given to labor force participation (chapter 7) and the determinants of labor earnings in Bogotá and Cali (chapter 8).

Table 6A-1. *Mean Monthly Earnings of Workers in Bogotá by Age Group and Sector, 1978*
(current Colombian pesos)

| | Age group | | | | | | | |
Sector	12–14	15–24	25–34	35–44	45–54	55–64	65–98	Total
1	0	4,735	6,449	5,901	4,461	3,003	3,838	5,097
2	1,345	3,279	4,551	5,155	3,458	3,110	2,944	4,046
3	2,768	4,192	6,335	6,874	6,286	4,996	5,915	5,708
4	3,163	4,769	7,276	10,162	9,071	7,456	5,486	7,369
5	2,393	4,487	6,691	10,578	9,712	10,619	5,217	1,962
6	1,628	3,881	9,935	9,561	9,027	7,798	6,940	6,924
7	1,810	4,335	8,382	12,605	12,422	12,936	6,052	8,603
8	3,410	5,635	19,346	18,076	21,600	26,750	16,175	16,285
All sectors	2,204	4,197	8,565	9,497	9,983	9,861	7,607	7,598
Percentage in age group	1.0	30.2	30.0	20.5	12.1	4.7	1.5	100.0

Source: 1978 World Bank–DANE Household Survey.

Table 6A-2. *Distribution of Workers in Bogotá by Education Level and Sector, 1978*
(mean monthly earnings in current Colombian pesos)

Sector		Education				
		None	Primary	Secondary	Higher	Total
1[a]	Percent	5.8	46.8	35.6	11.8	100.0
	Earnings	2,977	3,123	5,699	12,167	5,097
2	Percent	6.5	58.9	32.1	2.4	100.0
	Earnings	2,577	3,451	5,108	8,385	4,046
3	Percent	3.5	44.1	43.3	9.2	100.0
	Earnings	3,034	4,828	5,967	9,744	5,708
4	Percent	2.3	37.5	45.3	14.9	100.0
	Earnings	3,342	5,288	7,582	12,572	7,369
5	Percent	3.9	42.2	41.2	12.8	100.0
	Earnings	4,158	4,644	7,210	14,527	6,942
6	Percent	2.3	38.8	46.4	12.5	100.0
	Earnings	2,975	4,584	6,588	16,172	6,924
7	Percent	3.5	35.4	35.3	25.8	100.0
	Earnings	2,124	3,715	8,236	16,668	8,603
8	Percent	1.7	26.9	26.7	44.7	100.0
	Earnings	3,237	4,217	12,488	26,311	16,285
All sectors	Percent	3.6	42.1	38.4	15.9	100.0
	Earnings	2,880	4,239	7,030	18,868	7,589

Note: Percentage may not add to 100 because of rounding.
a. Central business district.
Source: 1978 World Bank–DANE Household Survey.

Table 6A-3. *Age-Education Profile of Workers in Bogotá by Sector, 1978*
(mean monthly earnings in 1978 Colombian pesos)

Sector and education	Age group							
	12–14	*15–24*	*25–34*	*35–44*	*45–54*	*55–64*	*65–98*	*Total*
No education								
1	n.a.	n.a.	n.a.	n.a.	4,343	2,340	n.a.	2,977
2	1,299	3,000	2,039	2,415	3,032	3,510	2,320	2,577
3	800	3,540	4,101	3,270	2,747	2,167	860	3,434
4	n.a.	1,709	n.a.	5,240	2,082	n.a.	6,000	3,342
5	n.a.	n.a.	n.a.	3,199	3,276	10,908	n.a.	4,158
6	n.a.	2,320	2,512	3,888	2,721	3,599	2,474	2,925
7	n.a.	1,900	2,000	2,543	1,387	2,243	1,898	2,124
8	n.a.	2,000	2,946	3,692	3,125	3,701	n.a.	3,237
Primary education								
1	n.a.	2,855	3,741	3,303	2,653	2,741	3,838	3,123
2	1,673	3,091	3,507	4,188	3,588	3,206	3,280	3,451
3	3,233	3,544	5,101	5,600	5,166	4,661	4,830	4,828
4	3,534	2,907	6,184	4,887	6,555	8,291	5,250	5,288
5	2,393	4,581	3,888	4,679	3,853	5,381	5,217	4,647
6	1,931	3,144	4,628	4,830	5,537	5,442	1,220	4,584
7	1,810	3,096	3,470	4,225	3,030	4,911	6,828	3,715
8	3,410	3,788	4,091	4,977	3,598	4,966	4,737	4,217
Secondary education								
1	n.a.	4,452	5,649	7,148	6,361	6,067	n.a.	5,699
2	2,944	3,531	5,996	8,479	6,209	3,764	2,534	5,108
3	2,528	4,207	6,432	7,788	8,463	7,095	9,173	5,967
4	1,732	5,274	7,116	10,840	9,868	4,776	n.a.	7,582
5	n.a.	4,050	7,088	10,450	12,810	16,438	n.a.	7,210
6	1,161	3,778	5,971	11,525	10,217	10,265	6,935	6,588
7	n.a.	4,380	6,915	10,862	14,529	20,199	7,943	8,236
8	n.a.	4,695	13,819	11,452	17,684	34,465	13,307	12,488
Higher education								
1	n.a.	15,250	11,431	10,833	10,788	n.a.	n.a.	12,167
2	n.a.	6,787	7,309	11,788	n.a.	n.a.	n.a.	8,385
3	n.a.	6,678	9,980	14,231	10,639	10,625	8,667	9,744
4	n.a.	7,150	9,552	21,161	22,009	n.a.	n.a.	12,572
5	n.a.	5,778	11,273	36,116	38,293	5,000	n.a.	14,527
6	n.a.	6,907	14,024	22,148	25,433	28,082	25,000	16,172
7	n.a.	7,601	13,972	25,520	18,619	20,824	n.a.	16,668
8	n.a.	10,131	24,737	32,454	34,302	43,457	28,598	26,311

n.a. Not available.
Source: 1978 World Bank–DANE Household Survey.

Table 6A-4. *Distribution of Workers in Bogotá by Occupation and Sector, 1978*
(percent)

Occupation	Sector								Total	Percentage in Bogotá
	1	2	3	4	5	6	7	8		
Professional and technical	3.2	4.6	16.6	6.0	3.9	16.8	**15.2**	33.7	100.0	11.9
Administrative and managerial	0.0	2.3	10.6	1.7	3.7	15.5	10.3	**56.1**	100.0	2.9
Clerks and typists	2.4	13.2	**26.0**	8.3	3.0	20.0	11.4	9.7	100.0	14.2
Sales managers and proprietors	2.0	20.9	18.6	**11.7**	5.0	17.4	9.3	15.2	100.0	7.2
Other sales	1.3	**24.3**	27.1	8.3	5.5	16.5	8.1	8.3	100.0	8.7
Service (excluding maids)	**8.6**	**29.3**	21.2	3.4	7.3	17.9	6.1	6.2	100.0	12.2
Maids	2.0	1.2	3.5	7.3	7.7	5.3	**13.1**	**23.2**	100.0	7.7
Agriculture	0.0	9.3	14.6	5.6	**21.6**	8.1	**21.6**	**19.2**	100.0	0.9
Production supervisors	0.0	10.3	**48.8**	**12.2**	8.1	11.4	7.0	2.3	100.0	0.8
Production workers	1.0	24.3	**31.4**	6.2	6.2	13.2	7.4	3.7	100.0	27.7
Construction	0.0	**39.4**	19.9	3.2	4.9	17.9	13.7	1.0	100.0	5.4
Transport	2.8	20.9	**27.4**	7.6	6.6	23.4	4.5	6.8	100.0	4.6
Other	3.9	24.8	**41.2**	7.3	4.0	14.0	1.3	3.0	100.0	0.8
All occupations	2.4	19.1	23.4	6.5	6.3	17.8	10.1	14.4	100.0	100.0

Note: For occupational classifications see table 6-6. Figures in boldface imply concentration of those occupations in the sector. Percentages may not add to 100 because of rounding.

Source: 1978 World Bank–DANE Household Survey.

Table 6A-5. *Concentration of Workers in Bogotá by Occupation and Sector, 1978*
(index of concentration)

Occupation	Sector							
	1	2	3	4	5	6	7	8
Professional and technical	133	24	71	92	62	94	**150**	**234**
Administrative and managerial	0	12	45	26	59	87	102	**390**
Clerks and typists	100	69	111	**128**	**143**	112	113	67
Sales managers and proprietors	83	109	79	**180**	79	98	92	106
Other sales	54	**130**	116	**128**	87	93	80	58
Service (excluding maids)	**358**	**153**	91	52	116	101	60	43
Maids	83	6	15	112	**122**	30	**130**	**101**
Agricultural	0	49	62	86	**343**	46	**214**	**133**
Production supervisors	0	54	**208**	**188**	129	64	69	16
Production workers	42	**130**	**134**	95	98	108	73	26
Construction	0	**206**	85	49	78	101	136	7
Transport	117	109	117	117	105	**131**	45	47
Other	162	130	176	112	63	79	17	21
All occupations	100	100	100	100	100	100	100	100
Percentage of workers	2.4	19.1	23.4	6.5	6.3	17.8	10.1	14.4

Note: The index of concentration, w_{ij}, is the concentration of occupation i in sector j where

$$w_{ij} = \frac{\text{Proportion of all workers with occupations } i \text{ who live in sector } j}{\text{Proportion of all workers in sector } j}.$$

For occupation classification, see table 6-6. Figures in boldface imply concentration of those occupations in the sector.

Source: Table 6A-4.

Table 6A-6. *Distribution of Workers in Bogotá by Activity and Sector, 1978*
(percent)

Activity	Sector 1	2	3	4	5	6	7	8	Total	Percentage in Bogotá
Agriculture	3.2	8.0	13.2	4.9	23.7	9.9	17.2	19.9	100.0	1.0
Mining	2.0	11.0	3.7	0.0	4.0	17.2	0.0	64.2	100.0	0.4
Food products, beverages, and tobacco	0.5	25.8	36.0	6.8	3.6	13.2	7.0	7.2	100.0	3.1
Textiles and footwear	1.0	26.1	37.3	5.2	6.9	16.9	7.0	4.6	100.0	6.4
Lumber and wood	1.7	20.4	32.3	0.0	4.7	33.5	6.3	1.1	100.0	1.9
Paper, printing, and publishing	1.7	18.1	31.6	7.1	2.6	16.1	7.4	15.5	100.0	1.9
Mineral products	0.0	36.1	29.5	4.2	11.5	6.0	12.8	0.0	100.0	1.2
Industrial chemicals, petroleum	1.1	15.0	27.1	6.1	7.3	24.4	6.3	12.8	100.0	2.9
Metal industry	1.1	13.6	36.4	7.9	12.6	15.6	5.7	7.1	100.0	5.5
Other industry	0.0	33.6	11.8	10.3	3.5	34.4	3.0	3.5	100.0	0.9
Utilities	3.0	13.9	23.2	13.0	2.5	18.7	3.1	2.7	100.0	0.5
Construction	0.0	33.7	20.2	3.8	4.7	18.3	13.9	5.4	100.0	7.4
Wholesale trade	0.0	6.0	11.0	7.8	3.7	17.3	21.7	32.6	100.0	1.6
Retail trade	1.6	23.7	24.8	9.4	6.4	18.7	8.2	7.3	100.0	18.4
Other commerce	8.5	38.5	18.7	3.9	11.5	15.0	1.2	2.7	100.0	3.4
Transportation, communications	3.1	17.4	27.4	8.8	5.2	19.2	7.1	11.8	100.0	5.9
Financial establishments	8.6	10.4	17.1	8.2	4.4	14.3	12.0	25.0	100.0	8.3
Public administration, social services	5.2	15.6	21.0	3.9	7.4	16.8	12.4	19.8	100.0	7.5
Public instruction	2.1	5.8	20.3	5.4	5.3	23.8	14.7	22.8	100.0	7.9
Personal and domestic services	0.9	14.4	16.8	5.6	4.9	15.0	14.3	27.5	100.0	14.2
No information	6.6	13.0	26.8	8.1	3.5	26.3	0.0	10.8	100.0	—
All activities	2.4	13.1	23.4	6.5	6.3	17.7	10.1	14.4	100.0	100.0

Note: For activity classifications see table 6-7. Percentages may not add to 100 because of rounding.

Source: 1978 World Bank–DANE Household Survey.

Table 6A-7. *Distribution of Workers in Bogotá by Length of Residence in Ring, 1978*
(percent)

Sex and ring	Migrants' years of residence						Non-migrants	Total	Percentage in ring
	0ᵃ	1–2	3–5	6–10	11–20	21–99			
Male									
1	17.1	7.3	8.6	12.9	21.7	19.6	12.9	100.0	3.1
2	5.9	3.8	7.6	14.0	13.4	17.6	37.7	100.0	9.4
3	5.5	2.8	6.6	7.5	23.1	16.0	38.5	100.0	11.2
4	4.2	4.8	4.7	15.5	21.5	16.7	32.4	100.0	26.1
5	5.0	3.8	6.6	12.3	22.9	16.3	33.0	100.0	45.0
6	7.6	3.5	6.8	10.9	19.3	12.6	39.4	100.0	5.3
All males	5.4	4.0	6.3	12.7	21.5	16.4	33.7	100.0	100.0
Female									
1	3.9	17.8	0.0	15.7	5.7	36.7	20.2	100.0	1.4
2	5.2	12.6	8.5	10.6	9.4	22.9	30.8	100.0	10.3
3	14.8	3.8	7.8	8.0	15.1	15.9	34.6	100.0	16.7
4	8.8	10.8	6.8	11.5	21.7	11.3	29.1	100.0	25.9
5	6.3	4.5	8.2	14.4	21.6	12.3	32.6	100.0	40.0
6	11.3	7.2	8.1	8.6	21.1	10.5	33.2	100.0	5.8
All females	8.5	7.2	7.7	11.9	19.0	14.0	31.7	100.0	100.0

Note: Percentages may not add to 100 because of rounding.
a. Less than one year.
Source: 1978 World Bank–DANE Household Survey.

Table 6A-8. *Distribution of Workers in Bogotá by Length of Residence in Sector, 1978*

Sex and sector	Migrants' years of residence						Non-migrants	Total	Percentage in sector
	0[a]	1–2	3–5	6–10	11–20	21–99			
Male									
1	17.1	7.3	8.6	12.9	21.7	19.6	12.9	100.0	3.1
2	3.0	4.3	6.3	14.4	25.8	11.4	34.7	100.0	20.8
3	3.8	4.2	6.9	14.2	23.7	15.3	31.7	100.0	25.1
4	5.3	2.8	7.2	11.8	19.4	21.7	31.8	100.0	6.9
5	11.4	4.6	10.6	13.1	17.2	14.6	28.4	100.0	6.1
6	4.9	3.4	3.2	11.9	23.1	18.9	34.6	100.0	17.9
7	5.5	4.9	3.7	11.5	15.7	20.6	38.1	100.0	9.1
8	7.9	3.1	8.2	8.8	13.7	17.2	41.1	100.0	10.9
All males	5.4	4.0	6.3	12.7	21.5	16.4	33.7	100.0	100.0
Female									
1	3.9	17.8	0.0	15.7	5.7	36.7	20.2	100.0	1.4
2	5.3	5.9	5.6	12.3	27.6	15.2	28.2	100.0	16.2
3	5.4	5.5	8.3	13.0	21.0	12.9	33.9	100.0	20.7
4	12.8	5.4	9.4	12.4	14.9	13.8	31.3	100.0	5.8
5	10.6	7.4	12.5	12.1	16.3	9.7	31.4	100.0	6.7
6	4.7	3.7	7.1	13.2	21.7	14.5	35.0	100.0	17.5
7	7.9	10.7	9.2	13.0	17.0	12.1	33.0	100.0	11.7
8	16.6	10.7	6.7	8.1	13.8	14.5	29.6	100.0	19.9
All females	8.5	7.2	7.7	11.9	19.0	14.0	31.7	100.0	100.0

Note: Percentages may not add to 100 because of rounding.

a. Less than one year.

Source: 1978 World Bank–DANE Household Survey.

7

The Determinants of Labor Force Participation

Among the chajnges that have taken place in Colombia over the past 30 years or so, two are particularly important: education has expanded dramatically and employment has risen considerably. It will be recalled from table 2-8 that between the early 1950s and the 1970s, the growth rate of employment was slower than that of the working-age population, and thus unemployment increased; however, the massive expansion of education partly offset the adverse consequences of this imbalance by keeping people in school longer. As the expansion in education began to slow down, the booming 1970s presented new employment opportunities, and the rate of unemployment fell over most of the decade (Berry 1975a,b, 1978). Labor force participation increased between 1973 and 1978 when employment rose at an astounding 6.2 percent a year. The expansion of female participation in the late 1970s (see table 2-9) consisted largely of housewives going out to work. Educational opportunities for women also grew (though starting from a lower level). But the most notable change of the decade was the jump in the proportion of women who were actually employed by the latter part of the 1970s.

Measured rates of rural unemployment have always been low in Colombia, but the growth of urban employment in the late 1970s is a novel phenomenon for developing countries and deserves systematic study. Subsequent events have reversed some of these trends, but it is still possible to hope that the observed reverses are essentially cyclical in nature. The analysis of labor force participation in this chapter is based on the DANE–World Bank household survey conducted in 1978, an unusually good year for the Colombian economy. Some of the results reported here (low unemployment, tight labor market conditions, high participation) may thus reflect a cyclical upswing.

Male and female participation rates in Bogotá by age groups from 1964 to 1978 (table 7-1) are particularly interesting. For the males, the expansion in education, which mainly affected participation rates in the 15–24 age group, had more or less come to an end by the mid-1970s; participation rates

184

Table 7-1. *Bogotá Participation Rates by Age Group, 1964–78*

Age group	1964	1973	1975	1977	1978
Male					
15–24	66.7	61.2	55.2	50.6	52.2
25–34	94.9	92.8	94.3	94.3	92.7
35–44	97.2	93.7	96.2	96.2	96.0
45–54	94.4	88.2	91.9	94.9	87.3
55–64	81.8	68.8	73.8	72.0	68.9
65+	41.6	36.5	42.1	33.7	37.5
All males	75.1	70.2	66.9	65.9	65.4
Female					
15–19	40.4 ⎱	36.2	36.8	38.8	37.5
20–24	47.5 ⎰				
25–34	37.4	37.0	42.2	46.1	45.1
35–44	34.0	34.4	33.9	41.2	37.9
45–54	27.3	26.9	26.3	31.0	35.6
55–64	18.0	17.2	14.6	17.5	19.6
65+	9.3	13.9	6.7	7.2	6.6
All females	33.5	30.7	30.7	33.8	33.4

Sources: 1964 and 1973 population censuses; and 1975, 1977, and 1978 DANE Household Surveys.

among the prime working-age group (25–54) were broadly constant, between 92 and 97 percent,[1] and participation among the elderly declined. The long-term fall in the overall rate mainly reflects the expansion in education together with earlier withdrawal of the old from the labor market; the rate appears to have stabilized at around 65 percent in the late 1970s.

The data for women are quite different. As with the men, participation rates fell between 1964 and 1973, but then began to increase. It is difficult to comment on the extremely high rates for 1964 without specific knowledge about that year's census. Nonetheless, increasing participation in nonhousehold employment by the young apparently kept the rate high in spite of the expansion in education. The prime working-age group (25–54) clearly increased its participation, particularly in the late 1970s, after a possible decline earlier. As with the men, participation fell somewhat among old women.

These data support Urrutia's (1985) conjectures on participation. Drawing mainly on information from Cali, he argued that higher labor force participation among poor women was largely responsible for the income gains of the poor. Table 7-2 illustrates this point with data on male and female

---

1. The 1978 figure for the 45–54 age group is substantially lower and is difficult to understand.

Table 7-2. *Bogotá Participation Rates by Income Group, 1975–78*
(percentage in labor force above age 15)

Income group (classified by HINCAP)	1975	1977	1978
Male			
Bottom 30 percent	59.2	53.7	57.6
Top 70 percent	70.0	70.2	68.2
All males	66.9	65.9	65.4
Female			
Bottom 30 percent	17.1	21.2	33.8
Top 70 percent	36.0	38.6	33.2
All females	30.7	33.8	33.4

Sources: DANE Household Surveys EH8E, EH15, and EH21.

participation rates by income groups classified by household income per capita. The male rates remain broadly constant over the period, but there is a dramatic increase in the participation of poor women in 1977 and 1978.

Table 7-3 gives participation rates by education levels. The increase in the female rates is mainly accounted for by higher participation among women with primary education. The weight of women with higher education is small (only about 9 percent overall), but about half of them work. A further breakdown of participation among the poorest 30 percent of households in June 1977 and December 1978 shows that the rate for poor women with primary education rose from about 22 percent to more than 40 percent over these two years.

Clearly, economic expansion accompanied by a tightening in the labor market of the kind experienced in Colombia in the late 1970s makes an increase in participation rates likely. Since participation of prime-age males is usually close to 100 percent anyway, additional participation is likely to take place among groups that have not traditionally participated extensively in the labor market, that is, women and young and old men. The cross-tabulations on education suggest that increasing levels of education also tend to push up the rates of labor force participation. Women who have higher education are more likely to work once their schooling is completed than their less-educated counterparts.

The most significant change to have occurred in the labor markets of developed countries since World War II has been a secularly rising rate of female labor force participation—a fact that has attracted considerable analytical attention (see Greenhalgh 1980; Smith 1980). The phenomenon is usually explained by the hypothesis that participation can be expected to increase when the expected market wage is greater than the perceived op-

Table 7-3. *Bogotá Participation Rates by Education, 1973–78*
(percentage of persons in labor force above age 15)

Education	1973	1975	1977	1978
Male				
None	69.4	64.3	63.2	60.2
Primary	74.3	74.6	71.8	73.0
Secondary	63.7	58.3	58.5	57.3
Higher	71.7	72.0	72.5	70.6
Total	70.2	67.1	65.9	65.4
Female				
None	30.0	27.9	34.0	31.3
Primary	30.2	32.3	36.2	35.5
Secondary	31.1	26.7	29.0	27.9
Higher	42.5	48.6	49.4	53.0
Total	30.7	30.8	33.8	33.4

Sources: 1973 population census; and 1975, 1977, and 1978 DANE Household Surveys EH8E, EH15, and EH21.

portunity cost of alternative activities (Mincer 1962). In the case of married women, this alternative is the perceived return from nonmarket or household work. As the economy expands, as the stock of educated women grows, and as more women acquire higher education, market work-opportunity costs increase much faster than the returns from household work, and the result is higher female participation. This is an important issue for the fast-growing newly industrializing countries, from both the supply and the demand side of the labor market. From the supply side, as educational opportunities expand, more and more women can be expected to want to enter the labor market. Policies for educational expansion need to take this phenomenon into account with respect to both the quality and content of education supplied. Similarly, from the demand side, economic expansion could be affected by constraints in the availability of labor once the traditional inflow from the countryside slows down. Another important consequence of higher female participation—its positive effect on income distribution—has already been noted.

This chapter, focusing on the determinants of labor force participation, must be seen in the context of the wider study of the effect of rapid city growth on labor market structure—and in the context of economywide concerns. It should be noted at the outset that the spatial factors highlighted in chapter 6 have not turned out to be significant determinants of labor force participation, although, as will be shown later, they *are* important determinants of earnings.

Since almost all prime-age men always participate in the labor force, an investigation of their decision to participate will tell us little. Business cycle fluctuations usually affect unemployment rates much more than participation rates among this group. This chapter is therefore principally concerned with the participation decision of women and other groups largely composed of secondary workers (for example, young men). The next section lays out the theoretical framework for the estimation exercise; the derivation of the behavioral model is supplied in appendix 7B.

Estimating Labor Supply: Theoretical Considerations

Labor supply analysis is a relatively new field of economic research that has been expanding since the early 1960s. This is one branch of economics in which theoretical and empirical work have progressed hand in hand. As new kinds of data have become available, theory has moved in new directions; at the same time, theoretical developments have been closely linked with new estimation techniques. An excellent and extensive review is available in Killingsworth (1983), so that only the points relevant to this discussion need to be outlined here.

To a large extent, the explosion of research on labor supply has been stimulated by observed dramatic increases in labor force participation among women in western countries since World War II. There had been little prior interest in this phenomenon since the labor force participation (LFP) of prime-age men has historically varied only slightly around the 100 percent mark in urban labor markets. Economists' interest in prime-age men had had much more to do with cyclical changes in the labor market associated with changes in the unemployment rate.

The LFP of secondary workers in general (not just among women) has been affected by a variety of factors in recent years. For example, the expansion of education has typically reduced the LFP of young men and young women, while the provision of better social security has reduced the LFP of old men and women. Some forces have also been working in the opposite direction, however: improvements in life expectancy and general health levels have tended to increase the LFP of older people; lower fertility, the availability of home appliances, and other developments that have reduced the number of hours that women must spend at home have tended to increase the LFP of women at all age levels; the acquisition of higher education has led to increased LFP among women aged 25 or older. Evidently, explaining changes in LFP is not a simple matter. Nevertheless, ad hoc approaches over the years have gradually led to a unified theoretical framework.

In earlier work, inferences about the determinants of LFP had to be drawn from the variance in participation rates between and within different sex and age groups in different cities and regions and over different periods of time (for an exhaustive work of this kind, see Bowen and Finegan's 1969 study based on data for the United States). Thus the average participation rate of a group was typically taken as the dependent variable to be explained. In this approach, the average participation rate for the group is said to represent the probability of participation of each individual. It also means that the participation decision of the individual, as revealed by the group average, is divorced from his or her position in the household. It was the focus on the LFP of married women that forced analysts to examine labor supply in the context of household behavior patterns and priorities (see Cain 1960; Mincer 1962; Becker 1965; Ashenfelter and Heckman 1974; and Cogan 1980b). At the same time, the increased availability of household-level data made it feasible in practice (as well as desirable in principle) to examine individual participation decisions within the household context.

The theory behind labor force participation analysis is derived from the traditional utility maximization framework. Although the theory is relatively straightforward and available in other sources (for example, Heckman 1974; Nakamura, Nakamura, and Cullen 1979; and Killingsworth 1983), it is briefly outlined in appendix 7B because it is closely related to the estimation technique used here. As reviewed in Killingsworth (1983), labor supply can be estimated in a bewildering number of ways. Consequently, several different techniques have been used in this study in order to test for the robustness of the estimates and the need for more sophisticated methods.

Estimation Technique

As derived in appendix 7B, the basic labor market equations are equations (7B-17), (7B-18), and (7B-29):

$$w_i^* = \alpha_0 + \alpha_1 h_i + \alpha_2 y_i + \alpha_3 A_i + \alpha_4 Z_i + u_i.$$

For convenience we can write $Z_i^* = (1, y_i, A_i, Z_i)$.
Then

(7-1)
$$w_i^* = \alpha_1 h_i + Z_i^* \alpha + u_i$$
$$w_i = \beta_0 + \beta_1 S_i + \beta_2 E_i + \beta_3 X_i + e_i.$$

As above, we can write $X_i^* = (1, S_i, E_i, X_i)$.
Then

(7-2)
$$w_i = X_i^* \beta + e_i$$

and

(7-3)
$$P_i = f(w_i - w_i^*)_{h_i=0}$$
$$= f(X_i^* \beta - Z_i^* \alpha + e_i - u_i)$$

where

$$w_i^* = \text{shadow price of the individual's time}$$
$$w_i = \text{market wage rate}$$
$$P_i = 1 \text{ when } h_i > 0$$
$$= 0 \text{ when } h_i = 0$$

h_i = the number of hours of market work

y_i = the household labor income

A_i = household nonlabor income, that is, return from assets

$\mathbf{Z_i}$ = a vector of other individual and household characteristics arrived at through earlier decisions

S_i = years of schooling

E_i = years of market experience

$\mathbf{X_i}$ = a vector of other individual characteristics relevant to the wage offered for market work

u_i and e_i = random disturbances: u_i is $\sim N(0, \sigma_1)$, e_i is $\sim N(0, \sigma_2)$, and they may be correlated with each other.

From (7-1) the labor supply equation can be derived,

$$(7\text{-}4) \qquad h_i = \frac{1}{\alpha_1} \{w_i^* - (\alpha_0 + \alpha_2 y_i + \alpha_3 A_i + \alpha_4 \mathbf{Z_i} + u_i)\}.$$

There are five basic problems in estimating (7-2), (7-3), and (7-4):

1. *Censored dependent variable.* The labor supply equation (7-4) and the participation equation (7-3) both have dependent variables that are censored since h_i is observed only when $h_i > 0$ and P_i is a binary variable.

2. *Censored sample.* In the cases of equation (7-2) for w_i and equation (7-4) for h_i (if estimated for workers only), the sample itself is censored since it is composed of workers only and not the whole population. As shown in appendix 7B, u_i and e_i are correlated with each other and are truncated as well.

3. *Selectivity bias.* Again in equations (7-2) and (7-4), the available sample of workers results from systematic decisionmaking in the past (the decision on schooling, age at marriage, number of children, and so on). The sample is therefore subject to selectivity bias. Naturally, this is more important for groups in which the levels of participation are low, that is, groups composed of different types of secondary workers; it is not important for prime-age men, almost all of whom work.

4. *Errors in measurement.* The most serious problems arise with respect to

hours of work and wages. Annual or monthly income is the sum of the product of hours and wages and bonus payments, and so on. Thus, invariably, the "true" wage has to be calculated by dividing some index of total labor income by the number of hours worked. Moreover, income is notoriously subject to reporting error.

5. *Costs of entry into the labor market.* The derivation of the labor supply function has characterized the function to be continuous in the positive quadrant. This assumes zero costs of entry, whereas in practice there are considerable search costs. Hours of work are also not entirely flexible, so that the decision to work can depend on the minimum feasible hours of work.

The different estimations take these problems into account in varying degrees. The following paragraphs outline the four methods that have been used.

Method I: Reduced-Form Estimation

Method I is a one-stage procedure that is used to estimate (7-3) and (7-4) in reduced form. Since the whole sample is used, problems 2 and 3 do not arise. Problem 4 is also muted since w_i is not used. Problem 1 is solved by using tobit to estimate (7-4) and probit or logit for equation (7-3). The main drawback of this procedure is that the coefficients derived in this way are difficult to interpret since the supply and demand sides are mixed up. Moreover, interesting elasticities (for example, the own-wage elasticity of labor supply), have to be calculated indirectly, with the result that selectivity bias is introduced here. This procedure also ignores the differences between workers and nonworkers with respect to their decisionmaking.[2] Thus method I can be written as

$$(7\text{-}4a) \qquad h_i = \frac{1}{\alpha_1} (\mathbf{X}_i^* \beta - \mathbf{Z}_i^* \alpha + e_i - u_i) \qquad\qquad i = 1 \ldots n$$

$$(7\text{-}3a) \qquad P_i = f(\mathbf{X}_i^* \beta - \mathbf{Z}_i^* \alpha + e_i - u_i) \qquad\qquad i = 1 \ldots n$$

Method IA. Ordinary least squares (OLS)
Method IB. Tobit for equation (7-4a) and probit or logit for equation (7-3a)

If (7-3a) is linearized, the coefficients from equations (7-4a) and (7-3a) should differ by only a factor of proportionality.

---

2. Heckman (1974) formed a likelihood function of workers and nonworkers and then solved the resulting simultaneous equation system by full-information maximum-likelihood procedures. This is also a one-stage method, but too costly to implement.

Method II: Two-Stage Procedure

The first stage of method II is to estimate w_i by equation (7-2) over a sample of workers and then to use $\hat{w}_i$ as an instrumental variable to estimate equations (7-3) and (7-4) over the whole sample. The assumption here is that sample selectivity bias does not exist and that the wage estimated from the market demand equation for workers applies equally well to nonworkers. Both of these can be estimated by OLS, admitting problem 1, or by logit or probit for equation (7-3) and tobit for equation (7-4). Thus method II can be written as

(7-2b) $w_i = X_i^* \beta + e_i$ $i = 1 \ldots m$

(7-4b) $h_i = \dfrac{1}{\alpha_1} \{\hat{w}_i - (Z_i^* \alpha + u_i)\}$ $i = 1 \ldots n$

(7-3b) $P_i = f\{\hat{w}_i - (Z_i^* \alpha + u_i)\}$ $i = 1 \ldots n$

where there are m workers and $n - m$ nonworkers.
    Method IIA. OLS for all equations
    Method IIB. OLS for equation (7-2b), probit or logit for equation (7-3b), and tobit for equation (7-4b)

Method III: Three-Stage Procedure

The first stage of method III is to estimate P (reduced form) by probit to calculate the probability of selection as a worker and thereby to account for sample selectivity bias in equations (7-2) and (7-4). The second stage is to estimate equation (7-2) admitting selectivity bias by the inclusion of

$$\lambda_i = \frac{\phi(I_i)}{\Phi(I_i)}$$

as an explanatory variable (see appendix 7B). The third stage is to estimate equation (7-4) by using $\hat{w}_i$ (corrected for selectivity bias) and λ_i as explanatory variables. Here equation (7-3) is estimated over the whole sample and equations (7-3) and (7-4) over workers only. Equation (7-3) is estimated by probit and equations (7-2) and (7-3) by OLS. Here problem 1 is taken care of in equation (7-3) and does not arise in equation (7-4) since the sample itself is censored, but selectivity bias (problem 3) is taken into account. Thus method III can be written as

(7-3c) $P_i = f(X_i^* \beta - Z_i^* \alpha + e_i - u_i)$ Probit $i = 1 \ldots n$

(7-2c) $w_i = X_i^* \beta + \beta_k \lambda_i + V_{i2}$ OLS $i = 1 \ldots m$

$$(7\text{-}4c) \quad h_i = \frac{1}{\alpha_1} (\hat{w}_i - \mathbf{Z}_i^* \alpha + \alpha_k \lambda_i - V_{i1}) \qquad \text{OLS} \qquad i = 1 \ldots m$$

Method IV: Three-Stage Procedure

Method IV is the same as method II except that (7-4) is estimated over the whole sample by tobit. The assumption is that $\hat{w}_i$, having taken into account sample selectivity bias, is a good predictor of potential market earnings for nonworkers as well. Thus method IV can be written as

$$(7\text{-}3d) \quad P_i = f(\mathbf{X}_i^* \beta - \mathbf{Z}_i^* \alpha + e_i - u_i) \qquad \text{Probit} \qquad i = 1 \ldots n$$

$$(7\text{-}2d) \quad w_i = \mathbf{X}_i^* \beta + \beta_k \lambda_i + V_{i2} \qquad \text{OLS} \qquad i = 1 \ldots m$$

$$(7\text{-}4d) \quad h_i = \frac{1}{\alpha_1} \{\hat{w}_i - (\mathbf{Z}_i^* \alpha + u_i)\} \qquad \text{Tobit} \qquad i = 1 \ldots n$$

No comments have been made above concerning problems 4 and 5. The reason for using $\hat{w}_i$ as opposed to observed w_i (for workers) is to eliminate measurement error and transitory variations in earnings. Measurement error in h_i remains. The variations in experience due to costs of entry are taken into account, in part, by including family nonlabor income and total family labor income in equation (7-4) as explanatory variables. Presumably, people with high family income are better able to search. That the supply-of-labor function is not continuous is suggested in our data by the fact that, of those who work, very few work less than fifteen hours a week.

It is useful at this point to summarize what has been derived so far. The individual labor supply schedule has been derived in appendix 7B from the optimization of the *household* utility function, but the subsequent discussion has been based on the *individual*; the household has been overlooked to some extent. It should be noted that, with regard to derivation, the main result of the household optimization is that family labor income and nonlabor income are arguments in the supply function. Second, $\mathbf{Z}$ contains family characteristics that have been achieved by earlier household decisions. These characteristics essentially include variables that affect the opportunity cost of the individual's time—such as number of children present, size of house, and the like. Since the discussion so far has also been "system-free" or "culture-free," the implication is that, at this level of generality, the specification of the labor supply function is equally valid for developing and developed countries. It is in the specification of the two vectors, $\mathbf{Z}$ on the labor supply side and $\mathbf{X}$ on the market demand side, that the differences between different situations can be brought in. Similarly, the discussion so far has not distinguished between male and female labor supply functions. Again, at this level of generality, it is argued that the framework is a unified one and that the differences between men and women would be in the specifications of Z and X, to the extent that different kinds of variables affect the opportunity cost of time and of market demand for men and women. The optimization made here has been a static one, with no dynamic elements to capture life cycle effects.

Life Cycle Effects

In principle, a dynamic household utility function could be optimized to obtain a lifetime labor supply function, as has been done for women by Lehrer and Nerlove (1980, 1982a, b). Here, as in most other studies, the life cycle effects are captured by dividing the sample into groups at different stages of the life cycle. Two key results from Lehrer and Nerlove are worth noting. First, a woman may supply labor to the market at a given time even if her shadow price of time is higher than the market wage at that time, if this results in an increase in her lifetime earnings that is more than compensating over her life cycle. Second, husband's (or other family) income has a bigger effect on the wife's labor supply after the arrival of children than before. The first result means that at all stages of their life cycle we should observe higher participation of women who expect higher incomes later; for example, women with higher education can reasonably expect an increasing age-earnings profile and should therefore have higher participation rates immediately after the completion of schooling. This is clearly true in the sample. But this result also implies that a lower return to education should be observed for women. Although these results are not directly captured by the procedures used in this study, the findings are quite consistent with them; the knowledge of these results helps to interpret the coefficients estimated here and to delineate the variables that should be included in Z.

The different groups used in this study are:

Group	Age
Young men (YM)	15–24
Prime-age men (PM)	25–54
Old men (OM)	55+
Young women (YF)	15–24
Married women with husband present (MF)	All ages
All prime-age women other than MF (UF)	25–54
Old women (OF)	55+

Although estimations were made for all the categories for the sake of completeness, the group of greatest interest is that of married women, followed by UF, YM, and YF—since these are the main secondary-worker groups whose participation varies with economic conditions. As noted earlier, prime-age men are of little interest since almost all of them work, and we do not have enough information on OM and OF to derive any results of interest. For the old people, it would be useful to have better information on social security provisions or other living arrangements in lieu of social security. In the case of old women, the working sample is often too small for good estimation. Hence, although estimations were made for these two groups, the results have not been reported here.

Final Empirical Specification and Variables Used

The estimation equations for each group have a common structure. The vectors Z_i and X_i in equations (7-4) and (7-2) can be divided into subvectors Z_{ji} and X_{ki} for convenience. Hence

$$h_i = \frac{1}{\alpha_1} \{ w_i^* - (\alpha_0 + \alpha_2 y_i + \alpha_3 A_i + \alpha_4 Z_{1i}$$

$$+ \alpha_5 Z_{2i} + \alpha_6 Z_{3i} + \alpha_7 Z_{4i} + u_i) \}$$

(7-5)
$$= \delta_0 + \delta_1^* w_i + \delta_2 y_i + \delta_3 A_i + \delta_4 Z_{1i}$$

$$+ \delta_5 Z_{2i} + \delta_6 Z_{3i} + \delta_7 Z_{4i} + u_i$$

and

$$(7\text{-}6) \quad w_i = \beta_0 + \beta_1 S_i + \beta_2 E_i + \beta_3 X_{1i} + \beta_4 X_{2i} + \beta_5 X_{3i} + e_i$$

where Z_{1i} = quality of leisure variables

Z_{2i} = life cycle variables

Z_{3i} = background variables

Z_{4i} = home activity variables

X_{1i} = region of origin

X_{2i} = location of residence

X_{3i} = characteristic of employment.

The earnings function—equation (7-6)—is investigated in detail later and is therefore not discussed at this point. The only concern here is the magnitude of selectivity bias and the use of equation (7-6) in predicting $\hat{w}_i$ for use in equation (7-5). Moreover, since x_{3i}, the characteristics of employment, are available by definition for workers only, they are not used in these estimations. (A detailed description of the variables used for the estimations is given in appendix 7C.)

The Data

All the estimations are based on data from the 1978 World Bank–DANE household survey conducted in Bogotá in December 1978. As reported in chapter 4, the survey sampled about 3,000 households in Bogotá, and the quality of the data is considered good, since it covered more than 90 percent of labor income. Earnings questions were asked of each individual in the household, along with questions on their work status and place of work; details on the survey are available in appendixes A–D at the end of the book. The main group excluded for present purposes is that of live-in domestic servants, who are almost all female. The reason for their exclusion is that they are listed with the households for whom they work and there is therefore no background information on their own families. A small number of other workers also had to be excluded because of lack of information on their hours of work.

Estimates of the Determinants of Labor Supply

This section reports the empirical results obtained from the different methods outlined in the preceding section. The objective is to obtain robust parameter estimates for labor supply in Bogotá and also to make judgments on the estimation strategy used. It is cumbersome to report the results of all four models seriatem; moreover, the methods overlap, and part of the purpose is to compare results. Therefore, all the results for the participation equation (7-3) are reported first, followed by all the results for the hours worked equation (7-4).

The Labor Force Participation Decision: Comparing OLS and Probit Estimates

There are essentially two participation equations: equations (7-3a) and (7-3b), since equations (7-3c) and (7-3d) are identical to (7-3a). Tables 7-4 and 7-5 report the parameter estimates, along with the means of each variable used. The first two estimates reported are of the reduced form equation (OLS and probit A), corresponding to methods IA and IB, respectively, and the third equation includes estimated own wage as determinant and corresponds to method II (see appendix 7A for estimation of the wage equation). As already explained, the OLS estimates are biased because the dependent variable is censored, and is in fact a dichotomous variable. It is useful, however, to see the magnitude and direction of the bias.

For each group, the probit coefficients are larger in absolute magnitude than the OLS coefficients in almost all cases. The effect is clearer when the coefficient is significant, and in each of these cases the t statistic is higher for the probit coefficient. This is as one might expect, but note that the OLS coefficients are all of the right sign and of a similar order of magnitude. Chi-square statistics with the appropriate degrees of freedom are reported in the tables. The chi-square statistics exceed the critical value of χ^2 0.995 for all the regressions. Thus the null hypothesis that all slope parameters are equal to zero is rejected.

The probit coefficients reported are transformed since the probit model is

$$P(I_i) = \frac{1}{\sqrt{2\pi}} \int_\infty^I e^{-t^2/2} \, dt \qquad\qquad i = 1 \ldots n$$

where $P(I_i)$ is the probability that a person participates and

$$I_i = \frac{X_i'\beta - Z_i'\alpha}{\sigma_3}$$

(see appendix 7B for derivation).

Hence the probit coefficients β and α are not comparable to OLS coefficients and are difficult to interpret intuitively. However, our interest is in the marginal effect of each variable on participation, that is, in $\partial E(P)/\partial x_{ij}$, which is analogous to OLS coefficients. It can be shown that

(7-7)
$$\frac{\partial E(P)}{\partial x_{ij}} = \phi(I_i) \cdot \beta_j$$

evaluated at (I_i), where $\phi(I_i)$ is the standard normal distribution function. At the mean, $\Phi(I_i)$, the cumulative normal distribution, is merely the proportion of people participating, hence $\phi(I_i)$ can also be found at the mean. The coefficients reported are those given by equation (7-7) evaluated at the mean. The linear approximation suggested by Amemiya (1981) for the constant term is $\phi(I_i)\beta_1 + 0.5$ (see tables 7-4 and 7-5).

The approximate similarity of the OLS and probit coefficients is then only at the mean, where the OLS coefficients are downward biased in absolute terms. The slopes become quite different the further away one is from the mean.

Young Men and Young Women

A comparison of the results for young men and young women indicates that the mean values of the independent variables for the two groups are quite similar. In particular, both groups have mean schooling of just over eight years, the men having a marginally higher mean. The findings reported here show that the deepening of education in Colombia in recent years has

Table 7-4. *Participation Decision for Young Men and Women*
(dichotomous dependent variable)

Variable	Young men				Young women			
	Mean	OLS	Probit A[a]	Probit B[a]	Mean	OLS	Probit A[a]	Probit B[a]
CONSTANT	—	-2.769 (3.29)	—	—	—	-1.839	—	—
AGE	19.26	+0.304 (3.42)	0.376 (4.25)	0.412 (4.67)	19.35	0.169 (2.03)	0.349 (5.02)	0.347 (5.02)
AGESQ	379.16	-0.006 (2.46)	-0.007 (2.94)	-0.007 (2.93)	382.86	-0.003 (1.20)	-0.007 (3.93)	-0.007 (3.92)
YRSEDU	8.24	-0.045 (7.69)	-0.064 (10.87)	—	8.11	-0.008 (1.39)	-0.008 (1.99)	—
OFLY	11.95	-0.001 (0.81)	-0.002 (1.27)	-0.002 (1.48)	11.89	-0.001 (1.13)	-0.002 (1.93)	-0.002 (2.09)
FNLY	2.11	-0.012 (3.48)	-0.023 (5.29)	-0.024 (5.58)	1.78	-0.007 (1.95)	-0.009 (2.94)	-0.010 (3.19)
HHHEAD	0.116	0.129 (1.79)	0.472 (4.22)	0.499 (4.50)	0.023	0.156 (1.51)	0.128 (1.74)	0.137 (1.87)
MIG3	0.121	0.069 (1.40)	0.105 (2.20)	0.112 (2.40)	0.134	-0.033 (0.73)	-0.033 (0.96)	-0.031 (0.93)
SECT1	0.015	-0.054 (0.40)	-0.148 (1.12)	—	0.011	-0.126 (0.84)	-0.227 (1.47)	—
SECT3	0.278	-0.055 (1.15)	-0.093 (1.96)	—	0.283	-0.014 (0.30)	-0.027 (0.79)	—
SECT4	0.082	-0.119 (1.76)	-0.172 (2.60)	—	0.078	-0.060 (0.91)	-0.077 (1.50)	—
SECT5	0.072	-0.066 (0.95)	-0.124 (1.79)	—	0.066	0.039 (0.55)	0.042 (0.82)	—

198

	(1)	(2)	(3)	(4)	(5)	(6)	(7)	(8)
SECT6	0.194	−0.095 (1.80)	−0.134 (2.62)	—	0.211	−0.001 (0.02)	−0.010 (0.27)	—
SECT7	0.119	−0.054 (0.89)	−0.081 (1.37)	—	0.111	−0.008 (0.13)	−0.017 (0.38)	—
SECT8	0.058	−0.139 (1.70)	−0.237 (2.84)	—	0.068	−0.029 (0.38)	−0.035 (0.63)	—
CHIL6	—	—	—	—	0.474	−0.069 (3.07)	−0.078 (4.49)	−0.076 (4.39)
CHIL612	—	—	—	—	0.515	−0.005 (0.25)	−0.006 (0.40)	−0.005 (0.35)
MREL	—	—	—	—	0.352	0.048 (1.43)	0.052 (2.12)	0.055 (2.24)
MARRIED	0.108	0.062 (0.85)	0.278 (2.70)	0.254 (2.48)	0.263	−0.188 (4.32)	−0.188 (5.94)	−0.185 (5.88)
OWNYHAT[b]	2.964	—	—	−0.663 (11.97)	3.050	—	—	−0.062 (1.79)
R^2	0.391	0.393	0.385			0.177	0.176	0.172
Log likelihood		−727.4	−738.9				−904.4	−909.1
χ^2 statistic	1,044	820	797				355	345
Number of observations		1,641	1,641	1,641		1,830	1,830	1,830
Mean of dependent variable $\Phi(I_t)$	0.502				0.278			
$\phi(I_t)$		0.3989	0.3989	0.3989		0.3352	0.3352	0.3352

— Not applicable.

Note: t statistics in parentheses.

a. The coefficients reported for the probit estimations are transformed coefficients to give the marginal effect of each variable on P; that is, $\partial P/\partial x_{ij} = \phi(I_t)\,\beta_j$, where $\phi(I_t)$ is the standard normal distribution evaluated at the mean of P, and β_j is the probit coefficient. t statistics reported are of the probit coefficients themselves.

b. OWNYHAT is estimated ln of expected own hourly wage (see table 7A-1).

Source: My estimates from 1978 World Bank–DANE survey.

Table 7-5. *Participation Decision for Prime-Age Unmarried and Married Women*
(dichotomous dependent variable)

Variable	Prime-age unmarried women				Married women			
	Mean	OLS	Probit A[a]	Probit B[a]	Mean	OLS	Probit A[a]	Probit B[a]
CONSTANT	—	0.412 (0.74)	0.475	0.345	—	−0.190 (1.22)	−0.377	−0.518
AGE	36.8	0.025 (0.82)	0.022 (0.96)	0.016 (0.71)	35.54	0.024 (3.15)	0.037 (5.61)	0.027 (4.07)
AGESQ	1,436.9	−0.0005 (1.27)	−0.0004 (1.63)	−0.0004 (1.30)	1,394.4	−0.0003 (3.53)	−0.0003 (5.92)	−0.0003 (4.57)
YRSEDU	6.85	0.013 (1.90)	0.014 (2.84)	—	6.38	0.028 (5.84)	0.031 (8.77)	—
OFLY	8.17	−0.002 (0.90)	−0.002 (1.39)	−0.002 (1.23)	11.06	−0.004 (3.26)	−0.004 (4.13)	−0.004 (4.11)
FNLY	2.23	−0.003 (0.55)	−0.003 (0.95)	−0.002 (0.77)	1.43	−0.005 (1.66)	−0.007 (2.34)	−0.007 (2.53)
HHHEAD	0.51	0.191 (2.97)	0.221 (4.58)	0.223 (4.71)	—			—
MIG3	0.07	−0.161 (1.57)	−0.171 (2.31)	−0.150 (2.05)	0.088	0.082 (1.60)	−0.092 (2.40)	−0.097 (2.57)
FREUNI	—	—	—	—	0.101	0.053 (1.07)	0.049 (1.41)	0.040 (1.19)
HUSBLU	—	—	—	—	0.211	0.001 (0.03)	−0.004 (0.16)	−0.021 (0.83)
SECT1	0.010	0.046 (0.18)	0.151 (0.61)	—	0.012	0.050 (0.38)	0.039 (0.43)	—
SECT3	0.275	−0.064 (0.85)	−0.066 (1.19)	—	0.295	−0.027 (0.64)	−0.027 (0.87)	—
SECT4	0.066	−0.136 (1.18)	−0.159 (1.95)	—	0.074	0.003 (0.05)	0.014 (1.31)	—
SECT5	0.067	−0.012 (0.11)	−0.008 (0.09)	—	0.061	−0.084 (1.25)	−0.103 (2.02)	—

SECT6	0.195	-0.078 (0.94)	-0.085 (1.42)	—	0.195	0.005 (0.11)	0.013 (0.39)	—
SECT7	0.121	0.043 (0.45)	0.060 (0.83)	—	0.108	0.023 (0.41)	0.022 (0.55)	—
SECT8	0.070	0.038 (0.30)	0.055 (0.59)	—	0.068	-0.029 (0.40)	-0.011 (0.21)	—
CHIL6	—	—	—	—	0.781	-0.046 (2.56)	-0.053 (4.05)	-0.053 (4.09)
CHIL612	—	—	—	—	0.710	-0.013 (0.84)	-0.017 (1.47)	-0.020 (1.77)
MREL	—	—	—	—	0.293	0.112 (3.38)	0.126 (5.34)	0.125 (5.35)
NROOMS	—	—	—	—	3.394	-0.009 (1.54)	-0.024 (3.38)	-0.021 (2.97)
WIDOW	0.441	-0.079 (1.26)	-0.094 (2.00)	-0.096 (2.07)	—	—	—	—
OWNYHAT[b]	2.748	—	—	+0.096 (3.03)	3.120	—	—	0.175 (7.73)
R^2		0.131	0.128	0.114		0.089	0.093	0.080
Log likelihood			-387.17	-392.93			-1,180.5	-1,195.9
χ^2 statistic			96	85			213	182
Number of observations	701		701	701	2,169	2,169	2,169	2,169
Mean of dependent variable					0.280			
$\Phi(\bar{I})$	0.688							
$\phi(\bar{I})$			0.3538	0.3538			0.3372	0.3372

— Not applicable.

Note: t statistics in parentheses.

a. The coefficients reported for the probit estimations are transformed coefficients to give the marginal effect of each variable on P; that is, $\partial Pp/\partial x_{ij} = \phi(\bar{I})\beta_j$, where $\phi(\bar{I})$ is the standard normal distribution evaluated at the mean of P, and β_j is the probit coefficient. t statistics reported are of the probit coefficients themselves.

b. OWNYHAT is estimated ln of expected own hourly wage (see table 7A-1).

Source: My estimates from 1978 World Bank–DANE survey.

been almost as important for men as for women and that the women have now almost caught up.

EDUCATION. One would expect education to be a negative influence on participation among those in the 15–24 age group, since many group members would still be in school. Indeed, those in the labor force are almost bound to comprise the early entrants with relatively less schooling than nonworkers in the same age group. This effect is quite pronounced for the men but only barely so for the women, despite the fact that about one-half of the men and only about one-quarter of the women are participating.

FAMILY INCOME AND ASSETS. The coefficient of other family labor income (OFLY) measures the cross-substitution effect and that of family nonlabor income (FNLY) the pure income effect. Both have coefficients in the predicted direction—that is, negative—but have different magnitudes and significance for men and women. As might be expected, the cross-substitution effect is stronger for women, and the pure income effect is stronger for men. Again, this suggests that women are secondary workers. Predictably, men from wealthier families are more apt to stay in school longer.

LIFE CYCLE EFFECTS. Life cycle effects are observable for both young men and women, but in different directions. In the case of men, the responsibilities of marriage and duties as head of household have a strongly positive effect on the probability of participation, as might be expected. Women experience the opposite effect; marriage would seem to take them out of the labor force. In this age group, only about 11 percent of the men are married, in contrast to about 26 percent of the women. The coefficients of age are quite similar and in the right direction (positive) for both groups.

HOME ACTIVITY. These variables are relevant for the women only and their coefficients are all in the expected direction. The presence of small children inhibits labor force participation whereas the presence of a maid or adult relative in the household encourages it.

BACKGROUND. As will be seen in the discussion of the determinants of earnings in chapter 8, background has quite significant effects on labor earnings. One of the proxies used for background here is location of residence. The normalizing sector is sector 2, the poorest part of the city. The fact that all the remaining sectors have a negative sign for both men and women, implies that the poor are more likely to leave school and participate early. Note, however, that none of the coefficients for women are significant. These results do *not* imply that the poor are disadvantaged with respect to participation. They reinforce the earlier result that people from wealthier families tend to stay in school longer and are thus less likely to participate at an early age. The other "background" variable tested is whether a person is a recent migrant. For men, the coefficient is significant and positive; thus it appears that, ceteris paribus, young migrant men are more likely than their native counterparts to be in the labor force. Again, this is as might be expected, since it is reasonable to assume that recent young male migrants have come to the city in search of jobs. The coefficient is not significant for women; a large proportion of young women workers are live-in domestic servants, and many of them are recent migrants—but this category of workers has been excluded from the present sample.

OWN WAGE. The second probit estimation (probit B) includes an estimated value of expected hourly wage (see appendix 7A for the estimation). The key determinants of wage are education and experience, and location of residence is used as a background proxy. This estimation was designed in part to obtain a direct estimate of own-wage elasticity of participation, and in part to distinguish education as a quality-of-leisure variable from its contribution to expected earnings. It was found, however, that education and estimated own wage were too collinear and so education was dropped from the equation. Standard theory predicts a positive association between labor force participation and expected wage: the higher the expected wage, the more likely a person is to participate in the labor force. In these samples of young men and women, the main alternative is to invest in education for higher future earnings: hence labor force participation is found to be negatively associated with higher expected earnings. The effect is much more pronounced for young men than for women.

The coefficients of the other variables that are common to probit A and probit B are very similar, and confidence in their magnitudes is therefore reinforced.

In summary, these estimates indicate that the participation of young women in the labor force is dictated much more by life cycle and home activity considerations than by labor market career aspirations, despite a considerable deepening of the education system and almost equal investment in education by men and women. Many more women than men marry early; once they start having children, they generally cannot enter the labor market. Predictably, the presence of household help in the shape of a domestic servant or a live-in adult relative is a key to possible participation. The estimations indicate that women still enter the labor market mainly as secondary workers. For young men, the estimations give largely expected results. Investment in education for later higher earnings takes precedence over current labor force participation. It is clear that family wealth helps here; the negative coefficients for the richer residential locations support this conclusion. Life cycle considerations are also evident, in that married young men and heads of household are more likely to participate—but there may be some self-selection here.

Prime-Age Unmarried and Married Women

Table 7-5 reports the results on labor force participation for prime-age unmarried (UF) and married (MF) women. (The MF group includes all married women, whatever their age, whereas the UF group consists of unmarried women aged 25–54.) These results are of great interest since they pertain to women in similar age groups who differ mainly in their marital status. Unmarried women include widowed, divorced, and separated women. Married women include only those currently living with husbands.

The two groups have quite similar characteristics, except that the UF are somewhat bettjer educated (average YRSEDU = 6.85) than the MF (average YRSEDU = 6.38). Paradoxically, however, the UF have lower average expected earnings. The UF also have higher family nonlabor income (FNLY) but (naturally) lower other family labor income (OFLY). Their relatively high FNLY is explained in part by the fact that about 44 percent of the UF are widows who may be expected to have nonlabor income from bequests, insurance, and transfers. The participation rate of the UF (0.69) is more than twice that of the MF (0.28).

The striking result for the UF is that most of the coefficients are not significant. Clearly, these women appear to have little choice but to work as breadwinners for their families. Higher education and higher expected earnings do, however, have a small but significant positive effect, as might be expected.

FAMILY INCOME AND ASSETS. As might be expected, other family labor and nonlabor income reduce the probability that a married woman will be working. The cross-substitution effect of other family labor income (mainly the earnings of husbands) is quite significant in magnitude and more important than nonlabor income. The negative pure income effect is quite small. Surprisingly, despite the higher mean value of FNLY for UF, it does not have a significant effect on their participation—the conclusion that the majority of UF have to work is therefore reinforced.

LIFE CYCLE EFFECTS. Life cycle effects are quite important for the UF in terms of household headship and widowhood as mentioned earlier. For married women, age is an important factor. Older married women are more likely to work, presumably after their childbearing years are over; the probability of their participating in the labor force increases up to age 61, according to these estimates. About 10 percent of the married women in the sample live in *union libre*, that is, they are not legally married but live with a man. The hypothesis was that these women would be more likely to participate than married women to the extent that their status involved a greater state of uncertainty. This idea seems to be only partly confirmed: the coefficient is positive but not statistically significant. The result implies that, for the majority of women in this category, the nonlegality of their "marriage" is not important with respect to stability and that they behave more or less as if they were married. Contrary to expectations that necessity would force widows to work, the results suggest that among the UF group they are less likely to participate in the labor force than others—although they could, of course, still be more likely to work ceteris paribus than married women. It is likely that a widow would be inexperienced or frightened or have children to care for and perhaps be able to live on bequests.[3]

HOME ACTIVITY. These variables are relevant for the married women only. The presence of children below the age of six inhibits the participation of married women significantly, whereas the presence of older children is not important in the participation decision. The effect of young children on the probability of participation is of the same order of magnitude as it was for young women. The presence of a domestic servant or adult relative (MREL) makes participation much more likely; indeed, the magnitude of the effect just about neutralizes the negative effect of a young child. The positive effect of domestic help is much stronger for married women than for young women. For the latter, the young child will generally be their first, but the married women sample also includes siblings who were born later; the result for domestic help suggests that it is more likely to be substituted for the mother's care in the case of second and subsequent children. Another variable, NROOMS (the number of rooms in the house), was used as a proxy for the volume of housework—an activity that could compete with labor force participation in the case of married women. The coefficient has the expected negative sign, but this could also mean that the variable serves as a proxy for wealth.

BACKGROUND. As in the case of the young women, location of residence, used as a proxy for background, does not have a significant effect on the decision of married women or prime-age unmarried women to participate in the labor force. Again, there is little evidence of spatial disadvantage with regard to labor force participation. Unlike the men, however, recent migrants

3. I am grateful to Peter Bocock for articulating these implications of my results.

in both the UF and MF groups are less likely to participate. This implies that few women migrants move in search of jobs; most of them probably come as nonworking spouses.

OWN WAGE. Unlike the results for the young men and women, a higher expected wage does increase the probability that married and prime-age unmarried women will work. That the effect is more pronounced for the MF group than for the UF group reflects the fact that married women generally have greater freedom of choice about whether or not to work.

In the case of both UF and MF, as for young men and women, the estimates in probit B are quite similar to those in probit A for variables that are common to the two equations.

In summary, the estimates for prime-age unmarried women show them behaving much more like primary workers, whereas married women behave much more like secondary workers. The married women's propensity to participate is affected much more by higher levels of schooling and expected earnings; at the same time, it is inhibited by the presence of small children and other home activities. These result indicate that a tightening of the labor market should increase the participation of married women, as was the case in Colombia in the late 1970s. Higher average levels of education among women will also lead to higher participation—or at least greater availability for participation. Similarly, the availability of child care facilities undoubtedly facilitates participation, although the results for young women indicate that this feature has its limitations; it seems likely that women will still opt out of the labor force to look after the first child, but that the availability of child care could hasten their return to participation.

The Total Supply of Labor: Hours Worked in the Labor Market

INTERPRETING COEFFICIENTS.   This section gives estimates for the full labor supply function, taken as a continuous function from zero hours worked to the maximum number of hours recorded. Appendix 7B gives the derivation of two different methods of estimating these functions. The first is Heckman's procedure, which utilizes information from the reduced-form participation equation (method I) to derive estimates of selectivity bias ($\hat{\lambda}_i$). These calculations are then used to estimate (1) the wage function corrected for selectivity bias and (2) the hours supplied by workers, again corrected for selectivity bias. This is method III. The second method is a direct tobit estimation of the censored dependent variable of hours supplied in the market. This itself is done in two ways: first using the reduced-form hours equation (method IB) and second with estimated wages from method III. This is method IV. The two tobit estimations correspond to probit A and probit B.

The last section in appendix 7B explains the interpretations of different coefficients. For the sake of convenience, all the tobit coefficients reported here correspond to the marginal effect of each independent variable y_j on the expected value locus of hours supplied, that is, $\partial E(h_i)/\partial y_j$ evaluated at the mean. The tobit coefficients are therefore "scaled down" by $\Phi(I_i)$ evaluated at the mean (which is merely the proportion of people working the sample). The OLS coefficients from Heckman are reported directly.

THE TOBIT AND HECKMAN ESTIMATES. Tables 7-6 to 7-9 give the estimates for methods I, III, and IV as explained above for young men, young women, and prime-age unmarried and married women, respectively. The tobit coefficients are as scaled above.

Overall, the results of the tobit estimates are similar in direction to the probit results and are therefore not discussed in detail. The tobit coefficient estimates (suitably transformed) are of a similar order of magnitude (evaluated at the mean) and in the same direction as the OLS coefficients. In general, the tobit coefficients give a higher slope than the OLS coefficients and have a higher level of significance. Further, the tobit coefficients from the reduced form equation (method IB) are similar in magnitude to the structural equation with estimated wage as a determinant (method IV).

In contrast to these generally satisfactory results, the coefficients in the Heckman procedure (method III) are quite different from those obtained in the tobit analysis. As shown in appendix 7B, the Heckman coefficients should in principle be identical to the tobit coefficient, that is, δ_j. In fact, the tables present estimates of $\Phi(I_i)\,\delta_j$ for the tobit regressions, whereas the Heckman coefficients given are δ_j. Almost all the Heckman coefficients are small in magnitude and not significantly different from zero in statistical terms. One reason for this outcome is that, in these samples, weekly hours do not vary much among the people who work. The standard deviation in the number of hours worked is in the range of 0.25 to 0.37 in all the samples. Moreover, for those who do work, the mean is relatively high: between 44 and 47 hours in each group. This suggests that there are some costs of entry into the labor market. It seems that if a person decides to work, he or she is faced with a decision to work a substantial number of hours or not at all. For married women, moreover, the decision to participate often involves the additional decision to use child care services. A married woman is therefore likely to participate only if work hours and wages are substantial enough to offset these costs; in other words, her reservation wage is high. If these speculations are correct, the Heckman procedure is inappropriate for this problem in the absence of adequate corrections for costs of entry (some of these problems are addressed in Heckman 1980 and Cogan 1980a). The correction for sample selectivity is not "enough" to generate the "true" labor supply schedule.

Another unusual feature in this sample is responsible for some of these

(Text continues p. 216.)

Table 7-6. *Supply of Labor Schedule: Young Men*
(dependent variable: weekly hours of work)

Variable	Mean	Method I (reduced form)		Method IV (estimated wage)	Method III (Heckman: worker only)	
		OLS	Tobit[a]	Tobit[a]	OLS	Mean
CONSTANT	—	-140.7	-194.1	-176.8	96.64	—
		(5.23)	(6.92)	(6.33)	(2.44)	
AGE	19.26	15.95	19.17	20.64	-2.30	20.61
		(5.63)	(6.56)	(6.95)	(0.59)	
AGESQ	379.2	-0.308	-0.394	-0.397	0.06	431.4
		(4.20)	(5.30)	(5.30)	(0.66)	
YRSEDU	8.24	-2.72	-2.039	—	—	—
		(4.68)	(11.06)			
OFLY	11.95	-0.057	-0.121	-0.129	-0.093	9.22
		(1.39)	(2.63)	(2.85)	(1.67)	
FNLY	2.11	-0.560	-0.983	-1.03	-0.285	1.02
		(5.24)	(6.50)	(7.01)	(1.31)	
HHHEAD	0.116	7.91	3.94	4.63	-0.177	0.227
		(3.44)	(1.55)	(1.87)	(0.09)	
MIG3	0.121	4.45	4.16	4.46	1.445	0.154
		(2.84)	(2.86)	(3.17)	(1.04)	
SECT1	0.015	-5.01	03.25	—	—	—
		(1.17)	(0.92)			
SECT3	0.278	-3.05	-2.55	—	—	—
		(2.00)	(1.74)			
SECT4	0.082	-5.83	-5.21	—	—	—
		(2.69)	(2.47)			
SECT5	0.072	-3.95	-3.41	—	—	—
		(1.77)	(1.52)			

SECT6	0.194	−4.93	−4.29	—	—	—
		(2.94)	(2.66)			
SECT7	0.119	−3.50	−2.43	—	—	—
		(1.80)	(1.33)			
SECT8	0.058	−6.86	−7.66	—	—	—
		(2.63)	(2.75)			
MARRIED	0.108	4.31	2.54	1.88	0.849	0.210
		(1.84)	(1.02)	(0.74)	(0.49)	
OWNYHAT[b]	—	—	—	−21.70	−8.12	2.894
				(12.08)	(3.10)	
SIGMA	—	—	17.00	17.16	—	—
			(28.31)	(28.69)		
LAMBDA	—	—	—	—	−4.33	0.724
					(1.78)	
R^2	0.402				0.113	
Log likelihood			−4,548.2	−4,558.9		
Number of observations	1,641	1,641	1,641	1,641	823	
Mean of dependent variable	23.97	23.97	23.97	23.97	47.74	
$\Phi(l_i)$			0.504	0.504		
Θ^c			0.37	0.37		

— Not applicable.

Note: t statistics in parentheses.

a. The tobit coefficients reported are transformed to make them comparable to OLS estimates. The coefficients reported are $\partial E(h)/\partial x_i = \Phi(l_i)\beta_j$ (see text). t statistics reported are of original tobit coefficients.

b. OWNYHAT is log of estimated expected hourly wage.

c. See text, equation (7-8).

Source: My estimates from 1978 World Bank–DANE survey.

Table 7-7. *Supply of Labor Schedule: Young Women*
(dependent variable: weekly hours of work)

Variable	Mean	Method I (reduced form)		Method IV (estimated wage)	Method III (Heckman: worker only)	
		OLS	Tobit[a]	Tobit[a]	OLS	Mean
CONSTANT	—	97.35 (3.92)	-189.2 (6.88)	-183.2 (6.70)	140.9 (1.17)	—
AGE	19.35	9.62 (3.71)	16.45 (5.92)	16.50 (5.92)	-4.52 (0.46)	20.91
AGESQ	382.9	-0.164 (2.47)	-0.336 (4.84)	-0.334 (4.82)	0.105 (0.51)	443.0
YRSEDU	8.11	-0.984 (5.47)	-0.537 (3.27)	—	—	—
OFLY	11.89	-0.056 (1.44)	-0.072 (1.79)	-0.074 (1.86)	0.089 (1.16)	10.84
FNLY	1.78	-0.362 (3.35)	-0.444 (3.38)	-0.470 (3.61)	-0.466 (1.46)	1.42
HHHEAD	0.02	8.27 (2.57)	3.93 (1.49)	4.24 (1.61)	-0.081 (0.02)	0.049
MIG3	0.134	-0.060 (0.04)	-0.659 (0.49)	-0.554 (0.41)	4.92 (2.16)	0.118
SECT1	0.011	-5.89 (1.26)	-10.47 (1.69)	—	—	—
SECT3	0.283	-0.88 (0.60)	-1.57 (1.13)	—	—	—
SECT4	0.078	-2.30 (1.11)	-2.71 (1.34)	—	—	—
SECT5	0.066	1.34 (0.61)	1.43 (0.71)	—	—	—
SECT6	0.212	0.26 (0.17)	-0.61 (0.41)	—	—	—

	(1)	(2)	(3)	(4)	(5)	(6)
SECT7	0.112	−1.45 (0.77)	−1.30 (0.73)	—	—	—
SECT8	0.068	−0.20 (0.08)	−0.97 (0.44)	—	—	—
CHIL6	0.474	−3.70 (5.28)	−3.45 (4.88)	−3.36 (4.75)	−1.61 (0.80)	0.385
CHIL612	0.515	−0.25 (0.42)	−0.10 (0.18)	−0.091 (0.16)	0.44 (0.46)	0.403
MREL	0.352	2.16 (2.08)	2.09 (2.15)	2.19 (2.25)	−1.38 (0.73)	0.397
MARRIED	0.263	−9.84 (7.23)	−7.45 (5.90)	−7.37 (5.84)	0.141 (0.03)	0.263
OWNYHAT[b]	3.05	—	—	−4.23 (3.10)	−13.28 (5.12)	2.87
SIGMA	—	—	774.8 (14.63)	783.4 (14.61)	—	—
LAMBDA	—	—	—	—	−6.68 (0.71)	1.36
R^2					0.193	
Log likelihood			−3,307.4	−3,313.1		
Number of observations	1,830	1,830	1,830	1,830	509	
Mean of dependent variable	12.78	12.78	12.78	12.78	45.83	
$\Phi(I_i)$			0.281	0.281		
Θ^c			0.26	0.26		

— Not applicable.

Note: t statistics in parentheses.

a. The tobit coefficients reported are transformed to make them comparable to OLS estimates. The coefficients reported are $\partial E(h_i)/\partial x_j = \Phi(I_i)\beta$, (see text). t statistics reported are of original tobit coefficients.

b. OWNYHAT is log of estimated expected hourly wage.

c. See text, equation (7-8).

Source: See table 7-6.

211

Table 7-8. *Supply of Labor Schedule: Prime-Age Single Women*
(dependent variable: weekly hours of work)

Variable	Mean	Method I (reduced form)		Method IV (estimated wage)	Method III (Heckman: worker only)	
		OLS	Tobit[a]	Tobit[a]	OLS	Mean
CONSTANT	—	32.19	11.23	10.56	62.75	—
		(1.57)	(0.55)	(0.51)	(2.79)	
AGE	36.77	0.776	1.11	1.03	0.192	35.32
		(0.70)	(1.01)	(0.95)	(0.18)	
AGESQ	1,436.9	-0.020	-0.025	-0.023	-0.008	1,321.4
		(1.44)	(1.80)	(1.71)	(0.52)	
YRSEDU	6.85	-2.217	0.028	—	—	—
		(0.90)	(0.11)			
OFLY	8.17	-0.108	-0.114	-0.107	-0.024	7.71
		(1.28)	(1.39)	(1.31)	(0.27)	
FNLY	2.23	-0.195	-0.163	-1.151	-0.148	2.12
		(1.13)	(0.93)	(0.90)	(0.94)	
HHHEAD	0.505	10.35	10.52	10.85	3.27	0.531
		(4.43)	(4.60)	(4.79)	(0.88)	
MIG3	0.066	-4.08	-6.27	-5.89	3.33	0.052
		(1.09)	(1.72)	(1.64)	(0.76)	
SECT1	0.010	11.50	8.47	—	—	—
		(1.20)	(0.77)			
SECT3	0.275	-1.60	-2.29	—	—	—
		(0.58)	(0.85)			
SECT4	0.066	-5.00	-5.54	—	—	—
		(1.19)	(1.46)			
SECT5	0.067	2.49	1.78	—	—	—
		(0.60)	(0.47)			

	(1)	(2)	(3)	(4)	(5)	(6)
SECT6	0.195	-1.67 (0.56)	-2.54 (0.87)	—	—	—
SECT7	0.121	2.39 (0.69)	2.39 (0.60)	—	—	—
SECT8	0.070	-1.66 (0.37)	-0.56 (0.11)	—	—	—
WIDOW	0.441	-2.39 (1.04)	-3.10 (1.39)	-3.50 (0.15)	0.514 (0.21)	0.405
OWNYHAT[b]	2.75	—	—	-0.255 (1.59)	-6.91 (3.57)	3.01
SIGMA	—	—	22.69 (24.46)	22.80 (24.39)	—	—
LAMBDA	—	—	—	8.47 (1.15)	—	0.717
R^2		0.108			0.126	
Log likelihood			-2,576.7	-2,580.0		
Number of observations		701	701	701	482	
Mean of dependent variable		31.79	31.79	31.79	46.17	
$\Phi(l_i)$			0.690	0.690		
Θ^c			0.48	0.48		

— Not applicable.

Note: t statistics in parentheses.

a. The tobit coefficients reported are transformed to make them comparable to OLS estimates. The coefficients reported are $\partial E(h_i)/\partial x_i = \Phi(l_i)\beta_i$ (see text). t statistics reported are of original tobit coefficients.

b. OWNYHAT is log of estimated expected hourly wage.

c. See text, equation (7-8).

Source: See table 7-6.

Table 7-9. *Supply of Labor Schedule: Married Women*
(dependent variable: weekly hours of work)

Variable	Mean	Method I (reduced form)		Method IV (estimated wage)[a]	Method III (Heckman: worker only)	
		OLS	Tobit[a]	Tobit[a]	OLS	Mean
CONSTANT	—	-2.84 (0.56)	-36.43 (6.26)	-41.87 (6.44)	28.02 (0.90)	—
AGE	35.54	1.01 (3.99)	1.68 (5.95)	1.30 (4.91)	0.888 (1.05)	34.08
AGESQ	1,394.4	-0.014 (4.66)	-0.023 (6.54)	-0.019 (5.64)	-0.013 (1.16)	1,252.5
YRSEDU	6.38	0.798 (5.14)	1.105 (5.58)	—	—	—
OFLY	11.06	-0.187 (4.22)	-0.186 (4.11)	-0.179 (4.00)	-0.104 (0.85)	10.65
FNLY	1.43	-0.278 (2.62)	-0.342 (2.49)	-0.358 (2.64)	-0.458 (1.45)	1.11
MIG3	0.088	-2.58 (1.54)	-3.55 (2.09)	-3.82 (2.26)	2.82 (0.67)	0.066
FREUNI	0.101	1.38 (0.86)	1.53 (0.99)	1.30 (0.84)	-2.69 (0.83)	0.105
HUSBLU	0.211	-0.91 (0.76)	-0.668 (0.58)	-1.31 (1.15)	-3.93 (1.56)	0.189
SECT1	0.012	0.873 (0.20)	1.00 (0.26)	—	—	—
SECT3	0.295	-0.486 (0.35)	-0.734 (0.54)	—	—	—
SECT4	0.074	1.45 (0.71)	1.46 (0.76)	—	—	—
SECT5	0.061	-3.88 (1.76)	-4.52 (1.96)	—	—	—
SECT6	0.195	-0.84 (0.54)	0.204 (0.14)	—	—	—

SECT7	0.108	0.770	0.947	—	—
		(0.41)	(0.51)		
SECT8	0.068	-0.639	0.174	—	—
		(0.27)	(0.08)		
CHL6	0.781	-2.73	-2.68	-2.70	-3.64	0.714
		(4.58)	(4.29)	(4.32)	(2.33)	
CHL612	0.710	-0.426	-0.69	-0.82	0.465	0.673
		(0.82)	(1.41)	(1.66)	(0.42)	
MREL	0.293	4.88	5.40	5.42	4.08	0.373
		(4.47)	(4.59)	(4.60)	(1.31)	
NROOMS	3.39	-0.448	-1.13	-0.976	-1.05	3.36
		(2.43)	(3.36)	(2.99)	(1.33)	
OWNYHAT[b]	3.12	—	—	6.34	-2.45	2.88
				(5.08)	(0.62)	
SIGMA	—	—	16.36	16.47	—	—
			(16.86)	(16.71)		
LAMBDA	—	—	—	—	11.56	1.47
					(1.33)	
R^2	0.057				0.115	
Log likelihood			-4,082.7	-4,094.6		
Number of observations	2,169	2,169	2,169	2,169	608	
Mean of dependent variable	12.64	12.64	12.64	12.64	44.91	
$\Phi(l_i)$			0.285	0.285		
Θ[c]			0.26	0.26		

— Not applicable.

Note: t statistics (in parentheses).

a. The tobit coefficients reported are transformed to make them comparable to OLS estimates. The coefficients reported are $\partial E(h_i)/\partial x_i = \Phi(l_i)\beta_j$ (see text). t statistics reported are of original tobit coefficients.

b. OWNYHAT is log of estimated expected hourly wage.

c. See text, equation (7-8).

Source: My estimates from 1978 World Bank–DANE survey.

215

unexpected results. Among those who work, hourly earnings fall monotonically with increases in weekly hours worked. This is opposite to the expected
upward sloping supply curve and looks more like a demand curve. This result
suggests, once again, that the more important decision is the participation
decision: once that decision is made, the majority of women either have
little choice in the hours of work or have a low opportunity cost for an
additional hour of work such that their supply essentially responds to demand.
This behavior is akin to a situation of unlimited labor supply. It is consistent
with the observation of a particular increase in the participation of poor
women in the lean years of the late 1970s in urban Colombia.

Bourguignon and others (1985) recently suggested that some of these unusual problems are caused by segmentation of the labor market between the
self-employed and salaried workers. This conclusion was prompted by the
significant differences they found between means of wages of self-employed
and salaried workers among married women. In running simple regressions
of weekly hours of work with log hourly earnings rates, they found sharp
differences in behavior: for wage earners, the curve is convex and decreasing
over the range of most actual wage rates, whereas for the self-employed there
is no significant statistical relationship. Further analysis of the City Study
sample does not suggest such significant differences between wage earners
and the self-employed. First, if the distribution of hourly earnings is decomposed (by the method utilized in chapters 4 and 9), the intergroup contribution of the salaried and self-employed married and unmarried working
women to total inequality is very small—less than 5 percent of the total.
Thus the large difference between means is misleading as an indicator of
segmentation. Second, if a similar decomposition is carried out for the distribution of hours worked by salaried and self-employed women, there is again
little difference in the two distributions; that is, the intergroup contribution
to the distribution of hours worked is low. Third, a negative relationship
between hours worked and the log of hourly wage is observed for the salaried
and self-employed groups. The existence of segmentation in the Bogotá labor
market is therefore unlikely to account for this anomaly.

There is yet another problem here. The dependent variable used in this
study is weekly hours of work in a reference week as reported in the survey.
Much debate in the literature centers around the correct dependent variable
to use in a labor supply study. It is often suggested that annual hours, taking
vacation time and other weeks not worked into account, represent a better
measure than weekly hours. It is probably true that the use of this measure
would at least inject greater variance in the hours variable. In view of all
these problems, the specification of the model for using the Heckman procedure is simply inappropriate here.

As appendix 7B shows (equations 7B-37 to 7B-39), the tobit coefficients can be used to obtain three types of information:

1. The marginal effect of each explanatory variable on the latent tobit index. This is the estimated coefficient δ.

2. The marginal effect on the observed hours supplied. This is $\Phi(I_i)\delta_j$, evaluated at I_i. In a study of hours supplied, this is the marginal effect of interest, that is, the effect of an explanatory variable on actual hours supplied.

3. The proportion of the effect that is due to variation in the hours supplied given that a person is participating. This is given by:

(7-8) $$\theta = \left\{1 - I_i \frac{\phi(I_i)}{\Phi(I_i)} - \frac{\phi(I_i)^2}{\Phi(I_i)^2}\right\}$$

and $(1 - \theta)$ would be the effect on the probability of the person participating. The value of θ is noted in the tables in each case. In principle, the probit coefficients should be equivalent to $(1 - \theta)$ of the tobit coefficients.

Comparison of Estimates across Models

Table 7-10 gives the elasticities of participation and labor supply for each of the methods estimated. Elasticities are given for only a few key variables: OWNYHAT (expected own wage), OFLY (other family labor income), FNLY (family nonlabor income), YRSEDU (years or schooling), CHIL6 (number of children less than six, for women). The elasticity for OWNYHAT measures the gross uncompensated income elasticity; that for OFLY measures the cross-substitution effect of (mainly) spouse's income, and that for FNLY measures the pure income effect. The elasticity with respect to education is important when education is continuing to deepen, as is the case in Colombia. Finally, the elasticity with respect to the presence of young children suggests to what extent the availability of child care facilities might encourage married women to work.

Young Men and Young Women

The own-wage elasticity of participation as well as labor supply is highly negative for young men and women. The negative effect is much greater for young men. In both cases, it seems that the poorer workers tend to have longer hours; the Heckman elasticities are significant and negative in both cases. The probit and tobit characteristics are roughly comparable for men. For women, the participation elasticity is not statistically significant. These

Table 7-10. *Elasticities of Participation and of Labor Supply*

	Participation			Work hours			
				Method I		Method IV	Method III (Workers only)
Variable	OLS	Probit A	Probit B	OLS	Tobit[a]	Tobit[a]	OLS
Young men							
OWNYHAT[b]	—	−0.828[c]	−1.321	—	−0.552[c]	−0.905	−0.170
OFLY	−0.024*	−0.048*	−0.048*	−0.028*	−0.060	−0.064	−0.018*
FNLY	−0.050	−0.097	−0.101	−0.049	−0.087	−0.091	−0.006*
YRSEDU	−0.739	−1.051	—	−0.936	−0.701	—	—
Young women							
OWNYHAT[b]	—	−0.208[c]	−0.223*	—	−0.304[c]	−0.331	−0.290
OFLY	−0.043*	−0.086	−0.086	−0.052*	−0.067*	−0.069*	0.021*
FNLY	−0.045	−0.058	−0.064	−0.050	−0.062	−0.065	−0.015*
YRSEDU	−0.233*	−0.233	—	−0.625	−0.341	—	—
CHIL6	−0.118	−0.133	−0.129	−0.137	−0.128	−0.125	−0.014*
Prime-age unmarried women							
OWNYHAT[b]	—	0.155[c]	0.140	—	−0.007[c]	0.008*	−0.150
OFLY	−0.024*	−0.024*	−0.024*	−0.028*	−0.029*	−0.028*	−0.004*
FNLY	−0.010*	−0.010*	−0.007*	−0.014*	−0.011*	−0.011*	−0.007*
YRSEDU	0.129	0.139	—	−0.047*	−0.006*		
Married women							
OWNYHAT[b]	—	0.772[c]	0.624	—	0.610[c]	0.501	−0.055*
OFLY	−0.158	−0.158	−0.158	−0.164	−0.163	−0.157	−0.025*
FNLY	−0.025	−0.036	−0.036	−0.031	−0.039	−0.040	−0.011*
YRSEDU	0.637	0.705	—	0.402	0.557	—	—
CHIL6	−0.128	−0.148	−0.148	−0.168	−0.165	−0.167	−0.058

— Not applicable.

Note: All elasticities calculated at the mean. The elasticities marked with an asterisk are derived from coefficients *not* significant at the 5 percent level.

a. All tobit elasticities are for the expected value locus (not for the tobit index).

b. All elasticities for OWNYHAT are with respect to estimated expected hourly wage.

c. Calculated through the coefficient on education in the participation or hours equation and that in the wage equation.

Source: My estimates from 1978 World Bank–DANE survey.

results are plausible, in that young men and women expecting a higher income are likely to delay participation, but they are at odds with most estimates in the United States, where own-wage elasticity is invariably positive. (Bear in mind, however, that it is difficult to compare results from different studies because of differing model formulations and definitions of variables.) Jen's (1983) study of urban female labor force participation in Brazil found the elasticity for young women (daughters) to be about 0.2. When further dis-aggregated into the 15–19 and 20–24 age groups, the elasticities were about −1.0 and 0.1, respectively. These findings are consistent with my results. Moreover, Jen's income variable was a monthly income measure, which tends to inflate the wage elasticities if there is a positive association between hours worked and wage.

Estimates of cross-substitution elasticity with respect to other family income are generally not significant for these groups. This is somewhat surprising since family nonlabor income elasticities are significantly negative and are between −0.05 and −0.1 for both groups. These figures are quite consistent with most estimates in other studies.

As might be expected from the OWNYHAT elasticity estimates, the education elasticities are significantly negative (much more so for the men), and for the same reasons.

For young women, the presence of young children strongly inhibits labor force participation. The magnitudes of the tobit and probit elasticities are very similar. It would seem that the presence of children is important in the decision about whether or not to participate, but that it has little effect on hours supplied once the decision to work is made.

Prime-Age Unmarried (UF) and Married Women (MF)

For both these groups, the participation elasticities with respect to own expected wage and education are positive. For UF, the estimate is about 0.14–0.15 whereas for MF the estimate is about 0.6–0.7. These results are quite consistent with other studies although, as documented by Killingsworth (1983), there is still no general agreement on their magnitude. Elasticities as high as 4 to 5 have been calculated by Heckman (1980), but most estimates are in the range of 0.5–2.0 (for example, Layard, Barton, and Zabalza 1980 for the United Kingdom; Schultz 1980 for the United States; Jen 1983 for Brazil; see Killingsworth 1983 for a full survey). In both cases, the Heckman elasticities are negative and the tobit elasticities are lower than the probit ones, implying that people earning lower wages are apt to work longer hours. This has been documented for Bogotá workers in chapter 5. As might be expected, this effect is much stronger for the UF. Many of them must work out of necessity (about 40 percent are widows); they could well have to work long hours at low wages because of low prior investment in education. Jen (1983) reports similar participation elasticities for wives (0.9) and female household heads (0.2) in urban Brazil. The positive participation elasticities are consistent with, and indeed explain, the increased female participation in Bogotá during the late 1970s documented earlier in the chapter.

As might be expected, the elasticities for both OFLY and FNLY are not significant for UF. Both are significantly negative for MF but, unlike the results for young men and women, OFLY (mainly spouse's income) is much more important than FNLY. The magnitude of the elasticity with respect to OFLY for MF is about -0.15 to -0.16, and that for FNLY is about -0.03 to -0.04. The latter are quite consistent with Schultz's (1980) estimates for the United States, although he reports a much higher elasticity for spouse's income (about -1.0) than was found here.

The participation elasticity with respect to CHIL6 for MF is quite comparable (about -0.15) to that for YF. In addition, in this case, the tobit elasticities are greater in magnitude: married women with small children who do work tend to work fewer hours.

Once again, the Heckman elasticities are generally not statistically significant.

Urban Labor Supply: Conclusions

The tightening of the labor market in the late 1970s in Colombia has offered an interesting opportunity for investigating the determinants of changes in urban labor supply in a situation of relatively rapid economic growth.

Supply of Labor in Bogotá

The estimates show that the main component of the labor force that can be expected to expand rapidly with rising real wages is married women. Until the expansion of education is complete, the number of young people—both men and women—entering the labor force at early ages will continue to fall. The same forces that induce greater participation of married women slow down the entry of young women into the labor force (and vice versa). Rising real wages are associated with increases in marginal returns to human capital, which are in turn related to overall increases in productivity. The apparent increase in marginal returns to human capital is really an increase in the average endowment of human capital. In fact, as is shown in subsequent chapters, increases in the stock of human capital in Colombia have tended to reduce the returns to education over time. This is consistent with increasing average real wages if the average stock of human capital is increasing. This seems to have been the case in Colombia in the 1970s, and was reflected in higher labor force participation among prime-age women. At the same time, women have been catching up rapidly when it comes to average educational attainment; the estimates show a marked negative association between the probability of participation and expected wages for young men and women alike. Clearly, achieving high education levels has become important for women.

The elasticity estimates for labor force participation were found to be quite robust across different estimation methods and can therefore be relied on. Married women seem the most wage-responsive group, followed by prime-age unmarried women. The element of necessity in the participation of unmarried women—especially those who are household heads—makes them less responsive to wage increases. Estimates for prime-age men have not been reported here; since almost all of these men are in the labor force anyway, their participation is not wage responsive. The results for young men and women suggest that as these cohorts grow older, we can expect much higher levels of desired labor force participation.

When the results for females are coupled with the association of LFP and fertility, the future growth of female LFP can be comprehended. The presence of young children was found to be a key inhibitor of the participation of married women. As fertility continues to decline in Colombia, there will be fewer married women of prime age with young children. One can therefore expect the combined effect of higher educational attainment and lower fertility to work itself out during the 1980s, and to lead to marked increases in the desire of women to join the labor force. One can also expect a higher demand for child care services. Both of these issues are important for policy in the coming decades.

The results for the hours-of-work decision are less robust than those for participation. The fact that the poor work longer hours in Bogotá suggests that there is little or no elasticity of labor supply with respect to wages. Indeed, the labor supply curve seems to be backward bending, once the decision to participate has been made. Thus little choice appears to be available to poor women: they need income for survival and are willing to work long hours at any available job. This is consistent with the observation that there was a major increase in participation among poor women in the relatively tight urban labor markets of the late 1970s. It is possible, however, that somewhat different results might have been obtained had the measure of labor supply been something other than weekly work hours.

Migrants do not appear to have the disadvantages with regard to participation that are often claimed in the literature. Other chapters show that migrants are paid no less than nonmigrants; if anything, they are marginally better off. Indeed, a more detailed examination of the evidence shows that migrants have, ceteris paribus, higher participation than others. It must therefore be concluded that migrants are no less able to find work nor liable to earn less than others once they have found a job.

The calculations of earnings functions reported in chapter 8 indicate that the location of a worker's residence is a good proxy for ability and background, in that workers who live in richer neighborhoods appear to earn significantly more than otherwise equivalent individuals from poorer neighborhoods. No such pattern of locational disadvantage emerges from this chapter's analysis of labor force participation. In fact, the probability of participation among equivalent individuals is marginally higher for those from poor neighborhoods than for those from better-off neighborhoods—arguably because the poor simply have to work.

Econometric Considerations

Considerable attention has been given to econometric considerations in this chapter's estimation of participation and hours worked. I am not aware of other similar work on developing countries, except for that of Jen (1983)—and even her study did not include estimation of hours worked. Findings are therefore hard to compare, although Jen's results for urban Brazil seem quite similar to those reported here. As household-level data become more readily available in developing countries, we can expect an outpouring of this kind of work in the future. It is therefore important to ensure that biased estimates do not lead to false conclusions.

A number of studies have used OLS for participation. My results suggest that OLS is a good first approximation: since the direction of bias is known (OLS tends to understate the effect of different variables on labor force participation), a reasonable understanding of the participation decision can be achieved by merely doing OLS estimates. However, there is no question that the estimates are seriously biased. The probit estimates were found to be quite robust and are therefore recommended as the best available. The hours of work estimates from the tobit analysis suffered from the lack of variance in the hours of work of those who do work; little more information was gained than from the probit estimates. Given the significant extra costs and difficulties of tobit estimation, the results were probably not worth the time devoted to them. Tobit analysis would be more useful if the data contained more variance in the hours of work.

The Heckman method was not very useful for this study, although the wage estimates corrected for selectivity bias were somewhat different from the uncorrected ones. The estimation of hours worked suffered from the lack of variation mentioned above, with the result that the Heckman procedure was inappropriate (it is of limited use anyway, if a tobit algorithm is easily available). This underlines the need to specify the model carefully and to tailor the estimation accordingly. Furthermore, more work needs to be done on female labor supply in developing countries.

The choice of variables was found to be important. For example, many of my early estimations were based on monthly earnings rather than hourly wages, because the former were the primary survey data and had been used for much of the work on earnings functions. But monthly income is a product of monthly hours and hourly wages, and the results obtained can be quite misleading. If, for example, labor force participation is positively associated with expected wage, then the own-earnings participation elasticity will be highly overstated; this was found to be the case and was corrected. Any results obtained from a typical census when only monthly earnings are available should therefore be treated with caution. The problem about the choice of labor supply variable has already been discussed; it is probably true that a measure of annual labor supply is better than weekly hours, and more likely to have greater variance.

Appendix 7A. Wage Function Estimates

Table 7A-1 gives the estimated wage functions for each of the four groups under consideration. These estimates are corrected for sample selection bias as set up in method III (see the text).

There is only mild evidence of sample selection bias in these samples since the coefficients of LAMBDA are not statistically significant. The last row in the table gives the schooling (YRSEDU) coefficient if the regressions are run without LAMBDA. Since these are higher than the corrected regression in all cases, it appears that the women with higher education who do in fact work are those with a higher propensity to work—and therefore that the returns to schooling are exaggerated. The difference is least among prime-age unmarried women, that is, those with the least choice in their decision to work or not to work, as noted in the text of chapter 7.

The experience variable in the equations is not very appropriate. There was no direct survey information on the number of years spent working by women. Hence, the usual (age − schooling − 6) approximation was made. This naturally takes no account of the time taken out by women for childbearing. The low experience coefficients provide evidence of this problem. As Heckman (1980) has shown, women's experience is particularly susceptible to sample selectivity bias, but this cannot be shown in this estimation.

Appendix 7B. Derivation of the Labor Supply Function and Estimation Strategy

Assume that each individual decides on his work-leisure choice so that the utility of the whole household is optimized.[4] If there are n individuals

---

4. This is not universally accepted. For example, Shields (1980) has suggested that in many African countries, both husband and wife provide independently for their material needs and therefore optimize individual utility functions.

Table 7A-1. *Wage Functions Corrected for Selectivity Bias*
(dependent variable: ln of hourly wage from method III)

Variable	Young men	Young women	Prime-age unmarried women	Married women
CONSTANT	1.29	1.70	1.56	1.64
	(4.03)	(3.96)	(5.40)	(3.69)
YRSEDU	0.154	0.138	0.131	0.143
	(10.63)	(6.65)	(9.89)	(8.46)
EXPER	0.057	0.046	0.026	0.033
	(1.51)	(1.20)	(1.41)	(2.24)
EXPSQ	−0.0004	−0.001	−0.0006	−0.0005
	(0.22)	(0.57)	(1.72)	(1.82)
SECT1	0.560	−0.068	−0.681	−0.031
	(2.94)	(0.13)	(1.73)	(0.09)
SECT3	0.168	0.070	0.015	0.196
	(2.49)	(0.71)	(0.12)	(1.44)
SECT4	−0.044	−0.070	0.054	−0.249
	(0.39)	(0.46)	(0.28)	(1.34)
SECT5	0.014	0.128	0.285	0.222
	(0.14)	(0.94)	(1.55)	(0.95)
SECT6	0.100	−0.065	0.276	0.290
	(1.25)	(0.63)	(2.01)	(2.02)
SECT7	0.164	0.179	0.101	0.167
	(1.84)	(1.45)	(0.66)	(0.99)
SECT8	0.320	0.260	0.592	0.548
	(1.85)	(1.68)	(3.13)	(2.57)
LAMBDA	−0.105	−0.191	0.273	−0.272
	(1.15)	(1.73)	(1.29)	(1.43)
R^2	0.260	0.311	0.385	0.330
Number of observations	823	509	482	608
Mean of dependent variable	2.89	2.87	3.01	2.88
YRSEDU[a]	0.164	0.162	0.133	0.158

Note: t statistics in parentheses.
a. Not corrected for sample selectivity bias.
Source: My estimates from 1978 World Bank–DANE survey.

in the household, the utility function U may be written as

$$(7B\text{-}1) \qquad\qquad U(l_1, l_2, \ldots, l_n; x, \mathbf{Z})$$

where $l_1, l_2, \ldots l_n$ is the time devoted to leisure by each family member i, x is the Hicksian composite good consumed by the household,[5] and $\mathbf{Z}$ is a

5. This assumes that relative prices of goods do not change over the optimization procedure.

vector of other characteristics of the household arrived at through earlier decisions.

The household maximizes U subject to the budget constraint

(7B-2)
$$px = \sum_{i=1}^{n} h_i w_i + A$$

and

(7B-3)
$$0 \leqslant l_i \leqslant T \qquad i = 1, \ldots n$$

where h_i is hours worked in the market by individual i, for hourly market wage w_i, p is the price level, and A is the nonlabor income of the household.

Equation (7B-3) states that leisure time is nonnegative and is, moreover, bounded by the total time available T. It can be rewritten as

(7B-4)
$$l_i + h_i = T \qquad i = 1, \ldots n$$

where h_i can be interpreted as a slack variable in a programming context and $h_i \geqslant 0$.

Thus the household maximizes U subject to (7B-2), (7B-3), and (7B-4). Assuming the usual conditions on U—that is, U is a twice differentiable quasiconcave function and has positive first partial derivatives for all its arguments—the Lagrangian may be written as

(7B-5)
$$L = U(l_1, l_2, \ldots l_n; x; Z) + \lambda \left\{ \sum_{i=1}^{n} h_i w_i + A - px \right\}$$
$$+ \sum_{i=1}^{n} \gamma_i (T - l_i - h_i).$$

Now, for simplicity, assume that individual 1 is optimizing l_1 given all other $l_j, j = 2, \ldots n$. We can then interpret $l_2 \ldots l_n$ to be included in Z, that is, decisions taken prior to the problem of individual 1.

Now, the Kuhn Tucker conditions are

(7B-6)
$$\frac{\partial L}{\partial x} = U_x - \lambda p = 0$$

(7B-7)
$$\frac{\partial L}{\partial l_1} = U_{l_1} - \gamma_1 \leqslant 0$$

(7B-8)
$$l_1 \frac{\partial L}{\partial l_1} = l_1 (U_{l_1} - \gamma_1) = 0$$

(7B-9)
$$(l_1 \geqslant 0)$$

(7B-2)
$$\frac{\partial L}{\partial \lambda} = 0$$

(7B-4)
$$\frac{\partial L}{\partial \gamma_1} = 0$$

(7B-10)
$$\frac{\partial L}{\partial h_1} = -\gamma_1 + \lambda w_1 \leq 0$$

(7B-11)
$$h_1 \frac{\partial L}{\partial h_1} = (-\gamma_1 + \lambda w_1)h_1 = 0$$

$$(h_1 \geq 0).$$

We have five unknowns (λ, γ_1, h_1, l_1, x) and five equations, and given the conditions on U, the system of equations can be solved for these unknowns in terms of p, w_1, A, and Z. Our objective is to derive the labor supply function. From (7B-6):

$$\lambda = \frac{U_x}{p}$$

and when $l_1 > 0$, from (7B-7) and (7B-8)

$$\frac{\partial L}{\partial l_1} = U_{l_1} - \gamma_1 = 0$$

or $\gamma_1 = U_{l_1}$, that is, the marginal utility from leisure. When $h_i > 0$, from (7B-10) and (7B-11),

$$\gamma_1 = \lambda w_1$$

or

$$U_{l_1} = \lambda w_1$$

or

$$U_{l_1} = \frac{U_x}{p} \cdot w_1$$

that is,

(7B-12)
$$w_1 = \frac{U_{l_1}}{(U_x/p)} = \frac{MU_{l_1}}{MU_x} \quad \text{when } h_1 > 0.$$

Equation (7B-12) shows that when $h_1 > 0$, that is, when a person works, the market wage is equal to the marginal rate of substitution between leisure and other goods, in other words, the shadow price of the individual's time.

However, if $h_1 = 0$, from (7B-10) and (7B-11),

$$\gamma_1 - \lambda w_1 > 0$$

$$\frac{U_{l_1}}{U_x/p} - w_1 > 0.$$

We can write the first term as w_1^*, the shadow price of the individual's time, then

(7B-13) $w_1^* - w_1 > 0$ if $h = 0$

where

(7B-14) $w_1^* = \dfrac{U_{l_1}}{(U_x|p)}$

Equations (7B-12), (7B-13), and (7B-14) determine the labor supply schedule and, incidentally, also suggest the estimation procedure.

Equation (7B-14) holds for both $h = 0$ and $h > 0$ and can be written as

(7B-15)
$$w_1^* = f(l_1, x; \mathbf{Z}; p)$$
$$= f(h_1, \Sigma w_i h_i + A; p; \mathbf{Z}).$$

This is the result of the household's optimization process. If f exists and is continuous, the labor supply function for h_1 also exists in terms of w_1^* and the other variables.

The demand-side function for the market wage rate w_1 is well known and is generally expressed in terms of education (S), experience (E), and other background variables $(\mathbf{X})$. That is,

(7B-16) $w_1^* = g(S, E; \mathbf{X})$

but w_1 is only observed if $h > 0$.

The problem now is to estimate these functions econometrically.

Estimation Strategy

For estimation purposes, (7B-15) and (7B-16) can be rewritten as linear functions along with a stochastic disturbance term. For convenience, the individual identifier (within the household) subscripts are now omitted for h and w.
Hence,

(7B-17) $w_i^* = \alpha_0 + \alpha_1 h_i + \alpha_2 y_i + \alpha_3 A_i + \alpha_4 \mathbf{Z}_i + u_i$

(7B-18) $w_i = \beta_0 + \beta_1 S_i + \beta_2 E_i + \beta_3 \mathbf{X}_i + e_i$

where

$$E(u_i) = 0, \quad E(u_i^2) = \sigma_1^2, \; E(u_i u_j) = 0$$
$$i \neq j$$

$$E(e_i) = 0, \quad E(e_i^2) = \sigma_2^2, \; E(e_i e_j) = 0$$
$$i \neq j$$

Assume that e_i, u_i are jointly normally distributed, and may be correlated; that is, $E(u_i e_i) = \rho\sigma_1\sigma_2$ where ρ is the correlation coefficient between e_i and u_i.

For convenience, rewrite (7B-17) as

$$(7B-19) \qquad\qquad w_i^* = \alpha_1 h_i + \mathbf{Z}_i^* \alpha + u_i$$

and (7B-18) as

$$(7B-20) \qquad\qquad w_i = \mathbf{X}_i^* \beta + e_i.$$

Now the problems in estimating (7B-19) and (7B-20) are that w_i^* is unobservable, and h_i and w_i are observed only when $h_i > 0$.

In a population sample, we have two groups of people: those who are currently in the labor force and for whom h_i and w_i are observed; and others who are not, and for whom h_i and w_i are not observed. However, $\mathbf{X}_i^*$ and $\mathbf{Z}_i^*$ are available for all.

From conditions (7B-12) and (7B-13), $h_i = 0$ if

$$w_i^* - w_i > 0.$$

That is, $\Pr(h_i = 0) = \Pr\{(w_i^* - w_i)_{h_i=0} > 0\}$ whose complement is

$$\Pr(h_i > 0) = \Pr\{(w_i - w_i^*)_{h_i=0} > 0\}.$$

At $h_i = 0$,

$$w_i^* = \mathbf{Z}_i^* \alpha + u_i$$

and hence,

$$(7B-21) \qquad \Pr(h_i > 0) = \Pr[\{(\mathbf{X}_i^* \beta - \mathbf{Z}_i^* \alpha) - (u_i - e_i)\} > 0]$$

$$= \Pr\{(\mathbf{X}_i^* \beta - \mathbf{Z}_i^* \alpha) > (u_i - e_i)\}.$$

For $h_i > 0$, market wage w_i is observed, from (7B-20),

$$(7B-22) \quad E(w_i|h_i > 0) = \mathbf{X}_i^* \beta + E(e_i|h_i > 0)$$

$$= \mathbf{X}_i^* \beta + E\{e_i|\mathbf{X}_i^* \beta - \mathbf{Z}_i^* \alpha) > (u_i - e_i)\}$$

Hence e_i is truncated and the conditional expectation of $e_i \neq 0$. Similarly, from (7B-19), for $h_i > 0$, $w_i^* = w_i$ and hence,

$$h_i = \frac{1}{\alpha_1} (\mathbf{X}_i^{\cdot} \beta - \mathbf{Z}_i^* \alpha + e_i - u_i)$$

and

$$(7B-23) \quad E(h_i|h_i > 0) = \frac{1}{\alpha_1} (\mathbf{X}_i^* \beta - \mathbf{Z}_i^* \alpha) + \frac{1}{\alpha_1} E\{(e_i - u_i)|h_i > 0\}$$

$$= \frac{1}{\alpha_1}(\mathbf{X}_i^*\beta - \mathbf{Z}_i^*\alpha) + \frac{1}{\alpha_1}E\{(e_i - u_i)|(\mathbf{X}_i^*\beta - \mathbf{Z}_i^*\alpha) > (u_i - e_i)\}$$

$$= \frac{1}{\alpha_1}(\mathbf{X}_i^*\beta - \mathbf{Z}_i^*\alpha) + \frac{1}{\alpha_1}E\{(e_i - u_i)|(e_i - u_i) > \mathbf{X}^*\beta - \mathbf{Z}_i^*\alpha)\}.$$

Again it is clear that the conditional expectation of the disturbance term is not zero.

However, both (7B-22) and (7B-23) can be estimated if estimators for $E(e_i|.)$ and $E(e_i - u_i|.)$ can be utilized as right-hand side variables. Now, u_i is $\sim N(0, \sigma_1^2)$ and e_i is $\sim N(0, \sigma_2^2)$. Hence

$$e_i - u_i \text{ is } \sim N(0, \sigma_1^2 + \sigma_2^2 - 2\sigma_1\sigma_2)$$

$$\sim N(0, \sigma_3^2).$$

Then, using the standard result for a truncated normal distribution (see, for example, Maddala 1983, appendix),

(7B-24) $$E\{(e_i - u_i)|h_i > 0\} = \frac{\sigma_3^2}{\sigma_3}\frac{\phi_i(I_i)}{1 - \Phi(I_i)}$$

where $\phi(I)$ and $\Phi(I)$ are the standard normal density and cumulative distribution function, respectively, and

$$I_i = \frac{\mathbf{X}_i^*\beta - \mathbf{Z}_i^*\alpha}{\sigma_3}.$$

Similarly,

$$E(e_i|h_i > 0) = \frac{\sigma_{13}}{\sigma_3} \cdot \frac{\phi(I_i)}{1 - \Phi(I_i)}$$

where $\sigma_{13} = \text{cov}(e_i, e_i - u_i)$.

That is,

$$E(e_i|h_i > 0) = \frac{\sigma_1^2 - \rho\sigma_1\sigma_2}{\sigma_3} \cdot \frac{\phi(I_i)}{1 - \Phi(I_i)}$$

write

$$\lambda_i = \frac{\phi(I)}{1 - \Phi(I)}.$$

Then

(7B-26) $$h_i = \frac{1}{\alpha_1}(\mathbf{X}_i^*\beta - \mathbf{Z}_i^*\alpha + \sigma_3\lambda_i + V_{i1})$$

and

(7B-27) $$w_i = \mathbf{X}_i^*\beta + \frac{\sigma_{13}}{\sigma_3}\lambda_i - V_{i2}$$

where
$$E(V_{i1}|h_i > 0) = 0$$

and

$$E(V_{i2}|h_i > 0) = 0.$$

Now, if estimates of λ are available, then (7B-27) and (7B-28) can be estimated from data on workers only.

Now, return to (7B-22):

$$\Pr(h_i > 0) = \Pr\{\sigma_3 I_i > (u_i - e_i)\}$$

$$\Pr(h_i = 0) = \Pr\left\{I_i < \frac{u_i - e_i}{\sigma_3}\right\} = \Phi(-I_i)$$

and

$$\Pr(h_i > 0) = \Pr\left\{I_i > \frac{u_i - e_i}{\sigma_3}\right\} = \Phi(I_i).$$

The likelihood function for the participation decision is then

(7B-28)
$$L = \prod_{i=1}^{m} \Phi(I_i) \prod_{i=m+1}^{n} \Phi(-I_i).$$

Maximum likelihood techniques yield the probit estimates for the participation decision and hence the values of λ_i that can be used in (7B-26) and (7B-27).

The full estimation model is then

(7B-29) $\quad P(I_i) = \dfrac{1}{\pi\sqrt{2}} \displaystyle\int_{-\infty}^{I} e^{-t^2/2} dt$ $\qquad\qquad\qquad i = 1 \ldots n$

where $\quad I_i = (\mathbf{X}_i^* \boldsymbol\beta - \mathbf{Z}_i^* \boldsymbol\alpha)/\sigma_3$

(7B-27) $\quad w_i = \mathbf{X}_i^* \boldsymbol\beta + \dfrac{\sigma_{13}}{\sigma_3} \hat\lambda_i + V_{i2}$ $\qquad\qquad i = 1 \ldots m$

and

(7B-26) $\quad h_i = \dfrac{1}{\alpha_1} (\mathbf{X}_i^* \boldsymbol\beta - \mathbf{Z}_i^* \boldsymbol\alpha + \sigma_3 \lambda_i + V_{i1})$ $\qquad i = 1 \ldots m$

in a sample of n people of whom m are in the labor force.

The procedure of (7B-29), (7B-27), and (7B-26) describes the Heckman procedure (Heckman 1978), which is essentially a two-step procedure to estimate an equation in which the left-hand variable, in this case h_i, is censored and is only observable for positive values. An alternative procedure is to estimate a censored regression model (that is, a tobit model) directly.

The Tobit Procedure

The tobit procedure merely extends the likelihood function of (7B-28) utilizing the information on observations of $h_i > 0$. For the observations h_i that are zero,

(7B-30) $\qquad\qquad \Pr(h_i = 0) = \Phi(-I_i) \qquad$ (as above).

For the observations h_i greater than zero,

$$\Pr(h_i > 0) \cdot f(h_i | h_i > 0) = \Phi(I_i) \cdot \frac{\dfrac{1}{\sigma_3}\phi(I_i)}{\Phi(I_i)} = \frac{1}{\sigma_3}\phi(I_i).$$

The likelihood function is therefore

(7B-31) $\qquad\qquad L = \prod_{i=1}^{m} \frac{1}{\sigma_3}\phi(I_i) \prod_{i=m+1}^{n} \Phi(-I_i).$

Maximum likelihood techniques then yield direct estimates of β, α, and σ_3 from (7B-31).

Interpreting Tobit Coefficients

To interpret the coefficients derived from the tobit technique[6] and to see their relationship with the OLS and Heckman procedures, it is useful to rewrite the model as follows:

(7B-32) $\qquad h_i = \dfrac{1}{\alpha_1}(\mathbf{X}_i^*\beta - \mathbf{Z}_i^*\alpha + e_i - u_i)$ when RHS > 0

$\qquad\qquad h_i = 0$ otherwise.

To simplify notation, rewrite (7B-32)

(7B-33) $\qquad\qquad\qquad h_i^* = Y_i\delta + u_i^*$

where

$$Y_i = (\mathbf{X}_i^*, \mathbf{Z}_i^*)$$

$$\delta = \left(\frac{\beta}{\alpha_i}, \frac{\alpha}{\alpha_1}\right)$$

$$u_i^* = \frac{1}{\alpha_1}(e_i - u_i) \sim N(0, \sigma_3^2).$$

6. See Maddala (1983), chap. 6, for more detailed discussion, and McDonald and Moffitt (1980) for interpretation of tobit coefficients.

We can now write

$$h_i = h_i^* \quad \text{when} \quad h_i^* > 0$$

$$h_i = 0 \text{ otherwise.}$$

h_i^* is a latent variable observable only when positive. Now, since $E(u_i^*) = 0$,

(7B-34) $E(h_i^*) = Y_i\delta.$

$E(h_i^*|h_i^* > 0 = E(h_i|h_i > 0)$ is the same as equation (7B-27). Hence

(7B-35) $E(h_i^*|h_i^* > 0) = Y_i\delta + \sigma_3\lambda_i.$

Equation (7B-34) gives the expected value of h_i^*, that is, the latent unrestricted variable. The tobit coefficients that are obtained are δ.

Equation (7B-35) gives the expected value of h_i given that h_i is positive. Thus the coefficients given by Heckman's procedure are also in principle δ if $\hat{\lambda}_i$ is a good estimator of λ_i in that procedure.

What we now need is the expected value of h_i, that is, the mean of all observed values of h_i, both positive and zero.

$$E(h_i) = \text{Pr}(h_i > 0) \cdot E(h_i|h_i > 0) + \text{Pr}(h_i = 0) E(h_i|h_i = 0)$$

$$= \Phi(I_i)(Y_i\delta + \sigma_3\lambda_i) + \Phi(-I_i) \cdot 0$$

$$= \Phi(I_i)(Y_i\delta + \sigma_3\lambda_i)$$

(7B-36) $[= \Phi(I_i) \cdot E(h_i|h_i > 0)].$

The expected value of all observations is then merely the expected valuje conditional upon being above the limit multiplied by the probability of being above the limit. Equation (7B-36) gives the expected value locus of labor supply.

Corresponding to each of these three expected values are their derivatives with respect to each y_j (in Y_i):

(7B-37)   from (7B-34) $\dfrac{\partial E(h_i^*)}{\delta y_j} = \delta_j$

(7B-38)   from (7B-36) $\dfrac{\partial E(h_i)}{\partial y_j} = \Phi(I_i) \cdot \delta_j$

(7B-39)   from (7B-35) $\dfrac{\partial E(h_i^*|h_i^* > 0)}{\partial y_j} = \delta_j[1 - I_i\lambda_i - \lambda_i^2]$

where $\lambda_i = \phi(I_i)/\Phi(I_i)$ as before.

Then δ_j is the slope of the fitted tobit line relating the tobit index or latent variable h_i^* to the y_i.

Since hours of work cannot in principle be negative, this is not the slope of interest in a study of labor supply. The slope that is sought here is the second one

$$\frac{\partial E(h_i)}{\partial y_j} = \Phi(I_i) \cdot \delta_j$$

the slope of the expected value locus. At the mean, $\Phi(I_i)$ is merely the proportion of observations that are positive.

Equation (7B-39) gives the fraction of total effect of y_j on h_i due to variation above the limit. Thus $(1 - I_i\lambda_i - \lambda_i^2)$ gives the portion of response of h_i given that it is positive. If $\Phi(I_i)$ is known, $\Phi(I_i)$ and I_j can be calculated and hence λ_i.

OLS coefficients are analogous to $\partial E(h_i)/\partial y_j$ and are therefore to be compared with $\Phi(I_i) \cdot \delta_j$. This makes intuitive sense as the marginal effect of y_j on h_i and is therefore the estimate reported in all tobit tables.

As mentioned earlier, the Heckman coefficients estimated in (7B-26) correspond to δ_j. If, however, the derived estimates of $\hat{\lambda}_i$ are not "good" estimates, the Heckman coefficients may correspond to (7B-39), since the OLS regression is done on workers only and the variance in h_i is only due to effects above the limit, that is, zero hours.

Appendix 7C. Definition of Variables

This appendix gives detailed information on the variables used in estimating the determinants of labor force participation in chapter 7.

1. y_i, *household labor income*. This has been redefined to refer to other family labor income (OFLY). This has been done to purge it of w_i, the individual's own contribution to y_i. OFLY: Total monthly labor income of all other household members (in thousands of pesos). The coefficient of OFLY is expected to be negative, if leisure is taken as a normal good.

2. A_i, *family nonlabor income* (FNLY). Monthly nonlabor income of the household (thousands of pesos). This variable includes interest and dividend earnings, rental income, pensions, gifts, and other transfers.

3. Z_{1i}, *quality-of-leisure variables*. Only one variable has been used here, YRSEDU (the number of years of education). It is expected that education pushes up the value of a person's time since he or she can use leisure

time more productively. Hence it should have a negative effect on labor supply (purged of its effect of increasing expected market wages).

4. Z_{2i}, *life cycle variables*

AGE	= years
AGESQ	= $(age)^2$, $(years)^2$
MARRIED	= 1 if currently married, 0 otherwise
WIDOW	= 1 if widowed (and not remarried), 0 otherwise
HHHEAD	= 1 if individual is identified as the head of household, 0 otherwise
FREUNI	= 1 if individual is living with a spouse but not formally married, 0 otherwise.

These variables are included to account for life cycle effects. The last four variables measure some sense of "need to work." It would be expected that being married or being a household head would increase the responsibility of the individual, thus making it important that they work. Naturally, these variables are of more importance for young men and women. FREUNI may capture the lack of security for women, if the lack of formal marriage implies lack of a permanent commitment. It may be expected to increase their labor supply. Being a widow among currently unmarried women may increase the tendency to work, out of sheer necessity.

5. Z_{3i}, *background variables*

| MIG3 | = 1 if the individual is a recent migrant and has been in Bogotá for less than 3 years, 0 otherwise |
| HUSBLU | = 1 if the head of the individual's household is a blue-collar worker, 0 otherwise. |

It may be expected that a lower value is placed on the leisure time of recent migrants and hence they are more likely to participate and work longer hours. The variable HUSBLU could capture some social background effects. If it is expected that blue-collar workers are more socially conservative, their presence would have a negative effect on the labor supply of women.

6. Z_{4i}, *home activity variables*

CHIL6	= the number of children in the household under 6
CHIL612	= the number of children in the household between 6 and 12 years of age
MREL	= 1 if there is a maid or adult relative in the household, 0 otherwise
NROOMS	= the number of rooms in the house.

These variables are expected to capture the opportunity cost of women's time in terms of the degree of home activity. The signs of their expected effects are the obvious ones. The data can only identify the presence of children in the household and their relationship to the household head. Hence the children are not *necessarily* those of the women in question. It has been assumed that (1) in almost all cases of married women (with husband present), they would be their children; and (2) for other women, the presence of young children in the household raises the demand for household work, even if the children are not theirs.

Table 7C-1 gives the specification of equation (7-5) used in the labor supply equations.

The variables used in equation (7-6) are

1. S_i, YRSEDU

2. E_i, work experience (years)
   EXPER $=$ age $-$ YRSEDU -6
   EXPSQ $=$ $(\text{EXPER})^2$

The data do not give a direct measure of experience, except for a measure of the number of years spent by a worker in the same firm or in the same occupation. As will be shown later, the indirect measure performs better

Table 7C-1. *Specification of Labor Supply Equations*

Variable	Young men	Prime-age men	Young women	Married women	Prime-age unmarried women
OFLY	x	x	x	x	x
ONLY	x	x	x	x	x
Z_{1i}					
YRSEDU	x	x	x	x	x
Z_{2i}					
AGE	x	x	x	x	x
AGESO	x	x	x	x	x
MARRIED	x		x		
FREUNI				x	
WIDOW					x
HHHEAD	x	x	x		x
Z_{3i}					
MIG3	x	x	x	x	x
HUSBLU				x	
Z_{4i}					
CHIL6			x	x	
CHIL612			x	x	
MREL			x	x	
NROOMS				x	

than limited direct measures. This is therefore regarded as an accurate enough measure for men. It is clearly inadequate for married women who may have interrupted their careers. Experiments in constructing a better measure by using the number of children to impute number of years interrupted did not succeed either. Thus this inadequate measure has been used for women as well.

3. X_{1i}, region of origin

There are a set of dummy variables designed to account for the origin of the individual:

DCITY   = 1 if migrant was born in the three next largest cities,[7] 0 otherwise

DBOG   = 1 if the individual was born in Bogotá or migrated before the age of 10, 0 otherwise

DTOWN = 1 if migrant was born in town with more than 100,000 people,[8] 0 otherwise

DURB   = 1 if migrant was born in other urban place, 0 otherwise.

The excluded category is migrants from rural areas. (This set of variables has been used in some estimations only but not reported here.)

4. X_{2i}, location of residence

Chapter 8 shows that the current location of a worker's residence in the city was a good proxy for other background variables such as quality of schooling, ability, and the like. (See map 3-1 for the sector and ring divisions of Bogotá.) The location of residence of each worker can be classified according to which sector he or she lives in. The residential sectors are controlled for by a set of seven dummy variables, with sector 2 (the poorest sector located in the south of the city) acting as the reference sector. The seven dummy variables are: RSECT1, RSECT3, RSECT4, RSECT5, RSECT6, RSECT7, and RSECT8. Each takes the value 1 if the worker lives in that sector, 0 otherwise.

The specifications of equation (7-6) are the same for all the groups, so all the variables are used for estimating the earnings function for each.

Where reduced form estimation is done, all the variables specified are used as appropriate for each group.

---

7. Medellín, Cali, and Barranquilla.

8. Bucaramanga, Cartagena, Cúcuta, Manizales, Pereira, Ibague, Armenia, Palmira, Pasto, Buenaventura, Neiva, and Santa Marta.

Dependent Variables

There are three dependent variables:

1. $P_i = 1$ if the person is in the labor force or not, 0 otherwise

A person is in the labor force if he or she is 15 years old or more, and is defined as working or unemployed during the week before the survey (live-in domestic servants have been excluded from the sample).

2. h_i = the number of weekly working hours as reported by the workers

3. w_i = log of hourly wage.

Workers were asked the periodicity of their wage payments along with the unit wage. They were also asked a second question designed to elicit the same information: their total labor earnings in the previous month. The monthly earnings are the derived monthly earnings for employees who report the periodicity of wage payment and unit wage. For others, they are the monthly earnings reported for the previous month. The hourly wage variable is constructed from the monthly earnings and hours of work information.

8

The Determinants of Labor Earnings

The discussion now turns to the missing link between labor force participation, on the one hand, and poverty and the maldistribution of labor incomes, on the other—that is, the factors that determine labor earnings.

With the development of the human capital model of labor earnings by
Schultz (1961), Becker (1964), and Mincer (1974), much research in the
1960s and 1970s became caught up in the attempt to estimate the returns
to education in the United States. More recently, work on the development
of earnings functions among the less developed countries has also become a
minor industry.[1] As in earlier chapters, the analysis here represents both a
consolidation of the extensive work that has already been conducted on
Colombia,[2] and an expansion of previous knowledge. The discussion is again
based on City Study analyses of a number of different micro data sets for
different years during the 1970s.

In this chapter I attempt to establish systematic patterns for the determinants of labor earnings through the use of earnings functions. In so doing,
I throw some light on the returns to schooling distinguished by different
levels of education achieved, a task that has not previously been attempted
in as direct a fashion as it is here. Furthermore, I examine workers' regions
of origin and location of residence as proxies for background characteristics
not otherwise measured directly.

I have paid considerable attention to the question of segmentation in the
labor market to complement the work already done by Fields (1980b). Segmentation is still a lively issue in discussions of urban labor markets in
developing countries, despite the murkiness (as demonstrated by Fields) of
the concept itself. It is perhaps more appropriate to talk of the "protected

1. For literature reviews, see Psacharopoulos (1973), Berry (1980a), and Fields (1980a). See
particularly Mazumdar (1981) and Anand (1983)—both exhaustive works on Malaysia.
2. For summaries of work on Colombia, see Bourguignon (1983), Fields (1978), Berry and
Soligo (1980), and Ribe (1979).

sector" as that portion of the labor market where entry is restricted and returns are higher. Various formulations of the problem are attempted here. (Segmentation is discussed further in chapter 9.)

A special feature of the present analysis is that all estimations have been done for women as well as for men (although all are not reported here). Whereas estimates of the returns to education abound for male workers, few are available for women. I have tried to fill this gap despite the greater hazards associated with interpreting female earnings functions (see chapter 10 for further details). My general approach has been to use the conventional earnings function (with a few extra wrinkles) as a device to explore the heterogeneity of the urban labor market. My view is as eclectic as that of Anand (1983): although the earnings function grew out of the human capital framework, it is in fact consistent with other theories of earnings such as "screening," "job competition," and "segmentation." It is difficult to find tests that can distinguish between these different models. Nonetheless, the estimation of earnings functions for different groups is helpful for summarizing labor market information and for identifying statistical regularities that, at a minimum, hint at the determinants of earnings.

Theoretical Background

A full-fledged investigation of the determinants of earnings in an urban labor market would ideally involve the articulation of a model of labor supply, earnings, consumption, and education investments akin to the models developed by Heckman (1976) and Ben-Porath (1967). Such a model would determine the education level chosen by an individual (or for an individual by his or her parents); it would test hypotheses about household behavior that determines labor and leisure choices for household members; and it would clarify the determinants of earnings in the light of these prior choices. Such a merger of the human capital, labor supply, and household economics literature would give a rounded understanding of the operation of the urban labor market. Although chapter 7 examines the decision to participate in the labor force, this study does not attempt a comprehensive investigation of the kind suggested above. Rather, a more "labor-intensive" approach is adopted to probe life cycle and other effects on labor earnings. The data are stratified in various ways to suggest results that would otherwise be obtained from a structural model.

The basic human capital model may be expressed as follows (Griliches 1977):

(8-1) $$Y = P_h \cdot H \cdot e^u$$

(8-2) $H = e^S \cdot e^v$

(8-3) $y = \ln Y = \ln P_h + S + u + v$

where Y is labor earnings, H is the unobserved quantity of human capital, P_h is the market rental price of a unit of human capital (which may vary over time and space), and u represents other influences on wages.

Equation (8-2) is a production function for human capital using schooling (S) as input; ability, efficiency, health, and nutrition are denoted by v. Substituting equation (8-2) in equation (8-1) yields equation (8-3), which is the traditional earnings function and is the basic formulation used here.

Much debate centers around the content of the u and v variables. Since they are usually difficult to measure; an equation such as (8-3) is often estimated with only measures of schooling, S, or, at best, with imperfect measures of u and v. This is of great relevance here, since various features of a person's background are seen as influencing his or her ability to translate schooling into human capital, which then determines labor earnings streams. How accurate, then, are estimates of returns to schooling? How great is the error when measures of ability and other influences are excluded? Can these influences be proxied by measures of a person's background? In what follows, I discuss these issues in relation to the existing literature before turning to the empirical investigations made for this study.

One of the principal criticisms of studies that have attempted to use the traditional human capital earnings function to estimate the returns to education is that they tend to omit a measure of "ability." Not only do well-known biases arise when variables are omitted in a least-squares estimation, but, in this case, the effect of interaction of the omitted variable with the level of schooling achieved is also overlooked. Some attempts have been made to include direct measures of ability (usually based on IQ tests), notably in the United States (see, for example, Griliches and Mason 1972). A common procedure is to include ability (or IQ) as an instrumental variable in a simultaneous equation framework. Ability itself is then explained by family background variables, sometimes along with schooling. To complete the circle, the level of schooling achieved is determined by ability as well as background variables. It is argued, therefore, that in a reduced-form earnings function of an equation such as (8-3), u and v should at least contain measures of ability as well as background variables.

Another criticism concerns measurement of the schooling variable. There are two aspects to this problem. In the formulation of the model in equations (8-1) to (8-3), the stock of human capital, conventionally measured as a function of the years of schooling, is used as the relevant determinant of earnings. In an attempt to account for variations in the intensity of schooling,

Leibowitz (1976) has noted that individuals vary in how intensively they conduct their schooling; some people pursue their education full-time whereas others hold part-time jobs as well. She argues that these variations depend on the person's ability as well as on his or her background. Furthermore, Welch (1966) and Summers and Wolfe (1977) tried to measure differences in the quality of schooling and showed that five years of education in one school are not equivalent to five years in another.

Thus two types of problems have to be resolved in measuring the schooling variable. First, the input itself must be measured (as affected by the intensity of schooling), and second, the efficiency with which this input is transformed into human capital must be measured. Summers and Wolfe (1977) suggest that students of high ability are less affected by the quality of schooling than their less able counterparts. In other words, the value added of high-quality schooling is relatively higher for less able students than for more able ones. As for the intensity of schooling, the ability and background variables (which influence choice of school) are the determining factors (Hause 1972).

Hoffman (1979) and Willis and Rosen (1979) address another type of problem that biases the results estimated from an earnings function—that of "positive sorting." When individuals are classified into two types—type A representing college graduates and type B representing high school graduates—it is found that type B individuals would have done less well than type A's with similar backgrounds had they also decided to go to college. More important, type A's would have done less well than type B's with similar backgrounds had the type A's not gone to college. The implication of these findings is that by and large people sort themselves out according to their aptitudes, background, and resulting aspirations. Most who do not go to college would not be able to justify foregoing earnings in order to do so, because the increase in their future earnings would not compensate for the opportunity cost involved. Accordingly, estimated returns to education are said to be biased upward because of this positive sorting. Hoffman discussed a different kind of sorting problem. He argued that, because of past experience with discrimination, blacks have lower expectations and consequently it is rational for them to underinvest in education. Again, the implication is that a person's background and ability affect his or her choices about appropriate education level as well as aspirations—which ultimately affect life cycle earnings.

Many of these problems have been examined in the light of panel cross-sectional data from the United States that trace the life histories of certain cohorts of workers. These data sets include information on the employment records of individuals, and on variables such as intelligence test scores and quality of schools attended. Thus it is possible to measure and correct some of the aforementioned biases. Among those who have had access to such data sets are Griliches (1977), Leibowitz (1976), Calvo and Wallisz (1979), Hoffman (1979), Schiller (1977), Nickell (1979), and others.

In a lucid review of econometric problems associated with estimating earnings functions, Griliches (1977) focuses on the bias caused by the omission of ability. He demonstrates convincingly that the results of sophisticated models that use schooling and ability as instrumental variables in a simultaneous equation framework seldom differ much from estimations of simple earnings functions that include schooling and experience as variables. Griliches (1977, p. 18) concludes that

> (i) Treating the problem asymmetrically and including direct measures of "ability" in the earnings functions indicates a relatively small direct contribution of "ability" to the explanation of the observed dispersion in expected and actual earnings. The implied upward bias in the estimated schooling coefficient is about 0.01. (ii) Allowing for errors in measurement in such ability measures does little to change these conclusions except increase the estimated bias by about 0.005 or so. But (iii) when schooling is treated symmetrically with ability measures, allowing it, too, to be subject to errors of measurement and to be correlated to the disturbance in the earnings function, the conclusions are reversed. The implied net bias is either nil or negative. In addition, (iv) a more detailed examination of data on brothers indicates that if we identify "ability" with the thing that is measured (albeit imperfectly) by test scores, and if we accept the underlying genetic model which postulates that such a variable has a family components of variance structure, then the "unobservable" that fits these requirements seems to have little to do with earnings beyond its indirect effect via schooling.

Griliches thinks it is unlikely that the coefficients of education derived from simple earnings functions would be biased by more than 5 to 10 percent. The amount of information contained in any data set is limited, and the more variables that are entered into an equation to protect against biases, the more serious the measurement problem becomes.

All the aforementioned observations have bearing on this study because one of the phenomena that it tries to explain is the apparent existence of systematic differences between people living in different parts of Bogotá. As has been shown, when Bogotá is divided into eight pie slices or sectors, the rich are found to live predominantly in the northern sector and the poor in southern areas, with various gradations between the two. Associated variations exist in the occupational and industrial distributions in different sectors. According to the descriptive data, people of similar human capital endowment appear to earn different wages according to where they live. In addition, with the rapid growth of the city, workers' backgrounds have come to vary widely in terms of their places of origin. It is possible that these differences affect their ability.

The data sets used in the City Study are rich but lack panel data. Moreover, they include no direct ability, family background, or schooling quality variables. In view of the problems that arise when these variables are omitted from earnings functions, it may be helpful to use family background and status in the reduced form as proxies for ability and school quality. The only background variables that are available in this study are the location of current and previous residence and place of birth.

This study utilizes two of these sets in particular. First, in view of the distinctive characteristics observed for different parts of the city, the sector of residence is regarded as a good proxy for background. This is somewhat risky because of high intraurban mobility (Hamer 1981); thus current residence may not necessarily indicate where the worker lived during his or her formative years. The same data, however, show that the majority of household movements are lateral ones within close distances and within sectors, and thus current location of residence can be used as a proxy for family background and schooling quality. Second, since the birthplace is available, the background of migrants can be controlled for. I define all people born in Bogotá and all others who arrived in Bogotá before the age of ten as natives of Bogotá, and divide the remaining people into four sets according to their origin: cities with 1 million people or more (Cali, Barranquilla, Medellín), towns with more than 100,000 people, other urban, and rural areas. The hypothesis is that schooling quality and intensity of schooling might vary positively with city size, as might the aspirations of the individual. In concurrence with Griliches, however, these background variables are not expected to affect the estimated schooling coefficients much, or to add significantly to the explanatory power of simple earnings functions.

With regard to location of residence, causation is generally thought to work in the opposite direction; that is to say, the incomes of wealthy people induce them to live in wealthy neighborhoods and the poor in poor neighborhoods. This line of causation is not being challenged here; as mentioned in chapter 6, however, it is being suggested that there might be feedback effects of the type hypothesized above that need to be taken into account.

Interpreting the Earnings Function

The derivation of the earnings function from human capital theory has been explained in detail by Mincer (1970, 1974) so that only a brief derivation is offered here. The exposition follows Rosen (1977).

Assume that earnings (y) are simply a function of schooling (years of education, S, and ability, A),

(8-4) $$Y = f(S; A).$$

Assume that schooling is a full-time activity and individuals earn zero labor incomes while in school. Then the present value at birth of all future incomes is

(8-5)
$$V(S) = \int_{S}^{N} Y(S; A)e^{-rt}dt$$

$$= Y(S; A) \frac{1}{r} (e^{-rS} - e^{-rN})$$

where r is the rate of discount expressing people's rate of time preference and N is the age at retirement.

S may be chosen so as to maximize $V(S)$; that is, when

(8-6) $$V'(S) = 0$$

or

(8-7) $$\{1 - e^{-r(N-S)}\} \frac{Y'}{Y} = r.$$

An individual would then invest in schooling until the internal rate of return equals the interest rate. Now, if N is large, equation (8-5) can be simplified to

(8-8) $$V(S) = Y \cdot \frac{1}{r} e^{-rS}.$$

Hence

(8-9) $$\ln Y = \ln(rV) + rS.$$

The maximum point of V is given by the point of tangency between equation (8-4), which is parameterized by A, and equation (8-9), parameterized by V. To the extent that A and r vary between individuals, the point of tangency will occur at different values of y and S. The implication is that if earnings functions are estimated for people with different ability levels, the estimated r will be the common value of r. If the estimation is for people with similar abilities, equation (8-4) is identified. If information is available for both A and r, the model of equations (8-4) to (8-9) is recursive and exactly identified and summarized by the following three equations:

(8-10) $$Y = F(S; A)$$

(8-11) $$S = G(r, A)$$

(8-12) $$r = F(S, A)$$

Equation (8-10) is the earnings function normally used; by implication, it involves assumptions about (8-11) and (8-12) if they are not explicitly specified. The earlier discussion on the biases likely to arise in the estimation of (8-10) essentially involved the relationship between S and A and the difficulties caused by not including A in (8-10).

These considerations have to be connected with the demand side of the labor market to arrive at a better interpretation of the earnings functions. One interpretation begins with the assumption that labor can be measured in terms of homogeneous efficiency units and that the labor market, if it is competitive, equilibrates returns to these efficiency units. Then, if all workers were alike, they would have the same schooling, and consequently, no variance in earnings would be observed. The implication is that any variance in earnings is solely due to differences in the initial stock of ability A or in differences in individuals' access to financial markets. Inequality is then due to inequalities in A and r and not in S.

The second interpretation comes from Mincer (1970, 1974). Here the assumption is that if different levels of schooling impart different types of skills and ability to conduct different work activities that are only imperfectly substitutible, then people with more years of schooling earn more in later years to compensate for earnings foregone in earlier years. According to this interpretation, if A and r are equal for everyone (and N is large),

$$(8\text{-}13) \qquad V(S) = Y(S) \frac{e^{-rS}}{r} = V_0 \quad \text{for } all \ S$$

and the present value of income streams are equalized by everyone. Equation (8-13) may be written as

$$(8\text{-}14) \qquad Y(S) = E_0 e^{rS}$$

where

$$(8\text{-}15) \qquad E_0 = V_0 r.$$

This is the fundamental earnings function:

$$(8\text{-}16) \qquad \ln Y = E_0 + rS$$

justifying the semilog specification normally used. Although everyone's wealth would be the same, earnings would be different in particular years. Estimated r should then merely reflect the prevailing real rate of interest.

The second interpretation is an extreme view in that people do have ability differences, they do have different financial market constraints, and markets are not completely perfect. An estimate of r that differs from the prevailing market interest rates can then be said to be a measure of how far removed the labor market is from long-term equilibrium (in this sense). In view of the argument associated with equation (8-7), estimated r is also interpreted as the internal rate of return to schooling,[3] given the assumptions that schooling was pursued full time, that the marginal cost of schooling was only the earnings foregone, and that after completion of schooling the earnings profile is flat for a long period of time. To the extent that these assumptions do not hold, estimated r is only an approximation of the internal rate of return.

The above discussion suggests that it is appropriate to use earnings functions in order to delineate segmented markets if these are believed to exist. If returns to schooling are strongly associated with prevailing interest rates, estimated r for different groups of people can reflect the different financial markets they face, as between blacks and whites, rural and urban people, and people in different countries or cities. Similarly, shift variables controlling for areas of origin or family background as proxies for ability are justified on theoretical grounds. The equality of estimated coefficients for different samples can be interpreted as the absence of segmentation.

Model Specification and Variables Used

Thus far, the theory behind earnings functions has been given with emphasis on the effects of schooling on earnings. The other important component of human capital theory, on-the-job training, has not been addressed specifically, since it is a straightforward extension of the schooling variable, except that experience is acquired on the job. The equations estimated in this study are then of the form:

(8-17) $Y = f$ (schooling; experience; region of origin, current location of residence; characteristics of employment).

The region of origin and current location of residence act as proxies for ability differences (if they themselves are related systematically to these background variables) and for differences in access to financial markets. Furthermore, if ability and the quality of schooling as well as its length are correlated, these would provide greater justification for regarding these background variables as reasonable proxies. The characteristics of employment have been included as shift variables that try to measure imperfections on the demand side of the market—that is, they try to detect the existence of a protected sector.

The equation estimated is

(8-18) $\ln Y = X_1\beta_1 + X_1\beta_2 + X_3\beta_3 + X_3\beta_4 + X_5\beta_5 + \varepsilon$

where X_1 = education variables, X_2 = experience variables, X_3 = region

---

3. In an efficient market this should, according to the arguments above, be the same as the rate of interest.

of origin shift variables, X_4 = location of residence shift variables, X_5 = characteristics of employment, and ε is the error term with the normal assumptions associated with ordinary least squares estimation.

A complete list of variables X_1 to X_5 is given in the appendix 8A, which also explains their characteristics. In addition, table 8A-1 gives the mean values of the whole sample for all variables used in estimations for 1978. Table 8A-2 gives the correlation matrix for 1978.

All the observations in the regressions have been weighted according to the procedure described in appendix A at the back of the book.

The Returns to Education

There has been considerable controversy over the interpretation of returns to education as measured by differences in earnings. The extensive work in the field has been summarized by Psacharopoulos (1980), and detailed work on micro data sets has been conducted in recent years by Anand (1983) and Mazumdar (1981) for Malaysia, Bourguignon (1978, 1983) and Fields and Schultz (1980) for Colombia, Chiswick (1976, 1977) for Thailand, and a host of others for the United States and the United Kingdom.

Psacharopoulos distinguishes between directly calculated rates of return and those derived from earnings functions. Table 8-1 summarizes his results for private returns to an additional year of schooling by level as well as the returns for education overall. The estimates for earnings functions are all lower than the direct estimates. All estimates for developed countries are lower than those for developing countries. This is partly because the variance in years of schooling in developed countries is substantially less than that in

Table 8-1. *Private Returns to Education by Country Group*
(percent)

Country group	Direct methods			Earnings function
	Primary	Secondary	Higher	All levels
Developing				
Africa	29	22	32	13.4
Asia	32	17	19	12.8
Latin America	24	20	23	18.2
Average	29	19	24	14.4
Intermediate	20	17	17	9.2
Advanced	n.a.	14	12	7.7

n.a. Not available owing to absence of control group of illiterates.
Source: Psacharopoulos (1980), tables 2 and 4.

developing countries; hence the quality of schooling becomes more important, as do the returns from on-the-job training and experience. The reason for the higher direct estimates is that they do not account for returns to on-the-job training; consequently, all increases in earnings that occur with age are attributed to educational factors. As was explained earlier, the earnings functions method calculates returns while keeping years of experience constant. Thus, despite their limitations, the earnings functions estimates may be regarded as better.

Psacharopoulos also reports that social returns are lower than private returns, especially in the case of higher education because of high public expenditures per student in this sector. At the same time, as Meerman (1971) has documented for Malaysia, private costs also appear to increase with education level. Out-of-pocket (tuition) costs are usually much higher for higher education (and often not accounted for in rates of return calculations), as is the government subsidy per student. Thus, correctly calculated private rates of return for higher education may not be as different from the social rates as is sometimes suggested. The results reported in this study should be viewed in this context.

The Returns to Education in Bogotá and Cali, 1978

Earnings functions were estimated for all individuals who reported any labor income. The samples included employees as well as those who were self-employed or owners.[4] This section presents the main results for returns to education based on 1978 data. Later sections discuss other variables and results from data for other years, as well as results from various stratification schemes. Tables 8-2 and 8-3 present the main results for this chapter. Earnings functions are developed incrementally, adding the X_1, X_2, X_3, X_4, and X_5 sets of variables in steps in order to test for the stability of coefficients and to obtain indications of possible biases.

As the tabulations show, most of the overall variance in earnings is explained by the traditional education and experience variables. There is an increment of only about 7 percent in the explained variance of the logarithm of earnings after all the additional variables are used—though all are significant at the 5 percent level.

Table 8-2 reports the regressions for male workers using the conventional years of schooling variable, YRSEDU. The region-of-origin variables do not affect the education coefficient significantly, but the residential sector var-

---

4. Estimations were also done separating employees from the self-employed and owners. See chapter 9. Income from capital assets is not included in the earnings variable used.

Table 8-2. *Determinants of Earnings of Male Workers in Bogotá, 1978*

	Regression			
Variable	1	2	3	4
YRSEDU	0.147	0.144	0.124	0.119
	(52.7)	(49.8)	(38.7)	(36.5)
EXPER	0.068	0.067	0.064	0.063
	(23.3)	(22.1)	(21.5)	(21.1)
EXPS	−0.0009	−0.0009	−0.0009	−0.0009
	(17.2)	(16.6)	(16.5)	(16.1)
DBOG	—	0.113	0.099	0.108
		(3.4)	(3.1)	(3.4)
DCITY	—	0.151	0.167	0.178
		(1.9)	(2.2)	(2.4)
DTOWN	—	0.227	0.189	0.186
		(4.0)	(3.4)	(3.4)
DURB	—	0.100	0.084	0.079
		(2.9)	(2.5)	(2.4)
RSECT1	—	—	0.003	−0.014
			(0.04)	(0.2)
RSECT3	—	—	0.130	0.115
			(3.9)	(3.5)
RSECT4	—	—	0.219	0.212
			(4.4)	(4.3)
RSECT5	—	—	0.184	0.159
			(3.6)	(3.1)
RSECT6	—	—	0.096	0.089
			(2.6)	(2.4)
RSECT7	—	—	0.163	0.169
			(3.6)	(3.6)
RSECT8	—	—	0.618	0.612
			(13.0)	(12.9)
UNION	—	—	—	0.063
				(3.1)
SOCSEC	—	—	—	0.071
				(2.6)
CONTRACT	—	—	—	0.046
				(1.6)
CONST	6.72	6.66	6.72	6.69
R^2	0.486	0.490	0.519	0.525
Number of observations	3,014	3,014	3,014	3,014

— Not applicable.

Note: t statistics in parentheses. Dependent variable: mean of log monthly earnings = 8.70.
Source: My estimates from 1978 World Bank–DANE survey.

iables do (the influence of these variables on labor earnings is discussed later in the chapter). The coefficient is reduced by about 20 percent from 0.147 to 0.119, the main cause being that the residential sector 8 dummy is somewhat correlated with years of education (the simple correlation coefficient being about 0.4; see table 8A-2).

As explained in the appendix to this chapter, two types of education variables were used. The first, as reported in table 8-2, was the usual total years of education variable (YRSEDU). The second is a set of variables (DUMP to POSTED in table 8-3) that attempt to measure the return to different levels of schooling: the coefficients of PRIMED, SECED, HIGHED, and POSTED measure the returns to an additional year of primary, secondary, higher, and post-

Table 8-3. *Determinants of Earnings in Bogotá by Education Level, 1978*

Variable	Regression					
	1	2	3	4	5	6
DUMP	0.085	0.072	0.056	0.055	0.022	0.023
	(1.5)	(1.2)	(1.0)	(1.0)	(0.4)	(0.4)
DUMS	0.299	0.290	0.266	0.258	0.226	0.227
	(4.2)	(4.1)	(3.8)	(3.9)	(3.5)	(3.5)
DUMH	0.627	0.616	0.558	0.573	0.526	0.515
	(4.1)	(4.1)	(3.8)	(3.9)	(3.5)	(3.5)
PRIMED	0.075	0.073	0.071	0.068	0.071	0.071
	(3.7)	(3.7)	(3.6)	(3.5)	(3.5)	(3.5)
SECED	0.095	0.091	0.083	0.078	0.073	0.073
	(10.1)	(9.6)	(8.9)	(8.4)	(7.5)	(7.5)
HIGHED	0.131	0.131	0.106	0.099	0.099	0.103
	(4.5)	(4.5)	(3.7)	(3.5)	(3.4)	(3.5)
POSTED	0.136	0.133	0.100	0.097	0.110	0.097
	(3.1)	(3.1)	(2.3)	(2.3)	(2.4)	(2.2)
EXPER	0.064	0.064	0.063	0.062	0.063	0.063
	(21.9)	(21.8)	(21.3)	(20.8)	(20.4)	(20.4)
EXPSQ	−0.0009	−0.0009	−0.0009	−0.0009	−0.0009	−0.0009
	(16.8)	(16.9)	(16.7)	(16.2)	(15.8)	(15.8)
DBOG	—	0.144	0.129	0.138	0.120	0.122
		(4.4)	(4.0)	(4.3)	(3.6)	(3.7)
DCITY	—	0.182	0.192	0.204	0.180	0.193
		(2.4)	(2.5)	(2.7)	(2.4)	(2.5)
DTOWN	—	0.249	0.211	0.208	0.162	0.169
		(4.5)	(3.9)	(3.9)	(2.9)	(3.0)
DURB	—	0.116	0.100	0.095	0.077	0.082
		(3.4)	(3.0)	(2.9)	(2.2)	(2.4)
RSECT1	—	—	0.006	−0.012	0.023	0.013
			(0.1)	(0.2)	(0.2)	(0.1)

Table 8-3 (continued)

Variable	Regression					
	1	2	3	4	5	6
RSECT3	—	—	0.145	0.129	0.210	0.196
			(4.4)	(4.0)	(5.7)	(5.6)
RSECT4	—	—	0.234	0.228	0.223	0.221
			(4.8)	(4.7)	(4.5)	(4.4)
RSECT5	—	—	0.207	0.183	0.255	0.247
			(4.1)	(3.6)	(4.9)	(4.7)
RSECT6	—	—	0.105	0.098	0.207	0.206
			(2.9)	(2.7)	(5.1)	(5.1)
RSECT7	—	—	0.143	0.145	0.243	0.243
			(3.1)	(3.2)	(5.0)	(5.0)
RSECT8	—	—	0.534	0.526	0.601	0.593
			(11.1)	(10.9)	(12.1)	(11.9)
UNION	—	—	—	0.065	0.054	0.034
				(3.2)	(2.6)	(1.6)
SOCSEC	—	—	—	0.079	0.089	0.052
				(2.9)	(3.2)	(1.7)
CONTRACT	—	—	—	0.041	0.049	0.029
				(1.7)	(2.0)	(1.1)
LOGFSIZE	—	—	—	—	—	0.023
						(3.3)
DIST	—	—	—	—	−0.025	−0.025
					(6.4)	(6.4)
DTRAIN	—	—	—	—	—	0.011
						(0.3)
CONST	7.08	6.97	6.93	6.90	7.05	7.02
R^2	0.505	0.509	0.530	0.536	0.536	0.538
Number of observations	3,014	3,014	3,014	3,014	2,819	2,819

— Not applicable.
Note: t statistics in parentheses.
Source: See table 8-2.

graduate education, respectively. They are all continuous variables measuring the number of years in school at the respective levels.

The dummy variables DUMP, DUMS, and DUMH measure the "certification bonus." It is often argued that the returns to education measured by conventional earnings functions ignore the use of educational levels as screening devices—on the hypothesis that employers are more interested in certification and credentials than in such intrinsic gains from schooling as might be reflected in workers' skills. The present analysis therefore used these dummy variables in an attempt to distinguish the validity of the screening hypothesis from the "genuine" returns to schooling.[5] It is hypothesized that each additional year of education has a return consisting of additional marginal earnings, but that there is also a value to certification: a completed level of education—primary, secondary, or higher—brings a bonus over and above the marginal return to each year of schooling. The coefficients of DUMP, DUMS, and DUMH then measure the percentage increase in earnings solely due to certification $\partial \log Y / \partial DUM$. PRIMED, SECED, HIGHED, and POSTED are more like the conventional YRSEDU, and the interpretation of their coefficients is similar to that for the rate of return to education.[6] The two methods give somewhat comparable results, but the splined method clearly implies a higher rate of return to higher education. Thus predicted incomes for college graduates are lower and those for others are higher when the YRSEDU variable is used rather than the splined method.

---

5. Smith and Welch (1977) also used a splined education variable but did not include the certification dummy variables.

6. To clarify the structure of this splined variable, the predicted income from regression 1 in both tables 8-2 and 8-3 is given below for two types of individuals:

Aged 40 years, graduated from college, one year of postgraduate education

$$DUMP = 0, \ DUMS = 0, \ DUMH = 1$$
$$PRIMED = 5, \ jSECED = 6, \ HIGHED = 4, \ POSTED = 1$$
$$YRSEDU = 16$$
$$EXPER = 18.$$

From regression 1, table 8-2,
$$\ln Y = 0.147 \ (16) + 0.068 \ (18) - 0.0009 \ (18) \ 2 + 6.72$$
$$= 10.04$$
$$Y = 22,123.$$

From regression 1, table 8-3,
$$\ln Y = 0.085 \ (0) + 0.299 \ (0) + 0.627 \ (1)$$
$$+ \ 0.075 \ (5) + 0.059 \ (6) + 0.131 \ (4)$$
$$+ \ 0.136 \ (1) + 0.064 \ (18) - 0.0009 \ (18) \ 2$$
$$+ \ 7.08$$
$$= 10.17$$
$$Y = 26,170.$$

Aged 40 years, graduated from high school, one year of college

$$DUMP = 0, \ DUMS = 1, \ DUMH = 0.$$
$$PRIMED = 5, \ SECED = 6, \ HIGHED = 1, \ POSTED = 0$$
$$YRSEDU = 12$$
$$EXPER = 22.$$

The result shown in table 8-2 (that is, that returns to higher education are greater than those to secondary education, which themselves are greater than the returns to primary education) is rather surprising in view of the clear pattern implying the opposite in table 8-1. Other estimates for Colombia (see Bourguignon 1983 and Fields and Schultz 1980) are consistent with these results, however, and thus give confidence to the splined specification. Moreover, as reported by Mazumdar (1981), results from Mexico and Kenya as well as from his own work on Malaysia are also consistent with these findings. High returns to secondary education are found in each case. Mazumdar also attempted to distinguish between the returns to different levels of education, although his specification was different from the one used here. Table 8-3 shows that the estimated certification bonus for completion of primary education is about 2–8 percent, but is not statistically significant, whereas the additional bonus for high school graduation is about 20 percent (DUMS – DUMP) and that for college graduation is about 25 percent (DUMH – DUMS – DUMP); the latter two estimates are both significant. These are quite plausible numbers and comparable with Mazumdar's results for Malaysia. From Mazumdar's work, it is difficult to distinguish between the return to an additional year of schooling and that due to certification. However, an approximation would be between 20–35 percent for secondary certification and 10–20 percent for primary certification. I have not seen any comparable estimates for other developing countries or for the United States, so it is difficult to be confident about these magnitudes.

When the education estimates in regressions 1 to 5 in table 8-3 are compared, the change in coefficients is not statistically significant (given the comparatively lower t value) though each falls when the residential location variables are added, as was the case with YRSEDU. The largest change occurs in the higher-education coefficients and thus reflects a correlation with RSECT8. The fact that the smallest change is in the PRIMED coefficient implies that

---

From regression 1, table 8-2,

$$\ln Y = 0.147 \, (12) + 0.068 \, (22) - 0.0009 \, (22) \, 2 + 6.72$$
$$= 9.54$$
$$Y = 13{,}905.$$

From regression 1, table 8-3,

$$\ln Y = 0.085 \, (0) + 0.299 \, (1) + 0.627 \, (0)$$
$$+ \, 0.075 \, (5) + 0.095 \, (6) + 0.131 \, (1) + 0.136 \, (0)$$
$$+ \, 0.064 \, (22) - 0.0009 \, (22) \, 2 + 7.08$$
$$= 9.43$$
$$Y = 12{,}456.$$

less-educated people are geographically dispersed throughout the city. Once again the addition of all the variables increases the level of explanation (R^2) by only about 7 percent as compared with regression 1; this result is similar to that obtained in table 8-2. The best regression in table 8-3 is regression 5; all the coefficients are significant at the 5 percent level except for DUMP. Note that in both tables 8-3 and 8-4 for Cali, the simple earnings function explains about 50 percent of the log variance of earnings—a rather high proportion for such a simple formulation.

These results are consistent with the conclusions reached by Griliches (1977) on the magnitude and nature of biases in the estimated coefficients of education in earnings functions. First, the addition of background variables adds little to the level of explanation. Second, if the background variables used here are indeed good proxies for schooling quality and ability, they may correct for overestimates of the return to schooling, but their correlation with schooling may be causing opposite biases of comparable magnitudes. If Griliches is correct in claiming that the biases are of the order of 5–10 percent, these results would be quite consistent with his findings. That having been said, the fact that all the additional variables are significant suggests that their addition is defensible.

The certification variables are of interest in that they provide some direct evidence that education is used as a screening device. It is not surprising that the DUMP coefficient is not significant, since completion of primary schooling is not associated with a degree or document, as is completion of secondary and higher education. The main point about these estimates is the high return to higher education, a result consistent with the high observed indices of inequality in Colombia. (The regressions in tables 8-2 and 8-3 were estimated for female workers as well, but are reported in chapter 10.)

Table 8A-3 reports estimates equivalent to regression 5 using the three different measures of earnings (hourly wage rates and monthly and annual earnings). It is not obvious which is the correct measure, but the evidence in table 8A-3 indicates that the choice is not very important, at least for male workers, since none of the estimated coefficients change significantly. The education coefficients do increase somewhat for the hourly wage equation except for POSTED; thus hours of work appear to be negatively correlated with the level of education. If that is the case, it may be argued that the value of leisure time may also have increased as a result of increased schooling. It would then be defensible to assert that the HWAGE estimates are better estimates of the return to schooling. The fact that the certification coefficients register increases for YRLYINC imply that school completers have more stable jobs, that is, work more months in a year. Note, too, the increase in the UNION coefficient for the HWAGE equation (although the change is not sta-

Table 8-4. *Determinants of Earnings of Male Workers in Cali, 1978*

Variable	Regression using education by level			Regression using YRSEDU
	1	*2*	*3*	*4*
DUMP	−0.134	−0.148	−0.140	—
DUMS	−0.117	−0.156	−0.181	—
DUMH	0.165	0.121	0.100	—
PRIMED	0.099*	0.100*	0.094*	—
SECED	0.165*	0.152*	0.147*	—
HIGHED	0.197*	0.154*	0.152*	—
POSTED	−0.361*	−0.312*	−0.294*	0.120*[a]
EXPER	0.081*	0.078*	0.076*	0.074*
EXPSQ	−0.0012*	−0.0012*	−0.0011*	−0.0010*
DCALI	0.086	0.062	0.063	0.054
DCITY	0.024	−0.043	−0.010	0.071
DTOWN	0.119	0.099	0.117	0.064
DURB	0.077	0.068	0.068	0.096
RSECT1	—	−0.341	−0.304	−0.159
RSECT2	—	0.520*	0.504*	0.508
RSECT3	—	0.042	0.034	0.047
RSECT4	—	−0.030	−0.034	−0.007
RSECT6	—	0.206*	0.199*	0.209*
RSECT7	—	0.440*	0.447*	0.597*
UNION	—	—	0.125*	0.131*
SOCSEC	—	—	0.035	0.036
CONTRACT	—	—	0.016	0.027
DIST	−0.018	−0.009	−0.011	−0.004
CONST	6.91	6.91	6.93	6.67
R^2	0.417	0.439	0.443	0.469
Number of observations	946	946	946	946
Mean of log monthly earnings	8.54	8.54	8.54	8.54

— Not applicable.
Note: Regression coefficients marked with asterisks are significant at the 5 percent level.
a. Coefficient of YRSEDU.
Source: See table 8-2.

tistically significant). It suggests that union membership has a greater effect on hourly wages but that union members can also work fewer hours, a quite plausible result.

Comparable estimates were made for Cali and are given in table 8-4. (The mean values for the variables in Cali are given in appendix table 8A-4.) The *t* statistics have been omitted for convenience. The results are somewhat different from those for Bogotá. Although regression 4 in table 8-2 shows that the average return to education in Cali is almost identical to that in Bogotá, the proportion of log variance of earnings explained is less than that for Bogotá and the splined education specification does less well than the conventional specification. None of the certification variables are statistically significant, and the coefficients of PRIMED, SECED, and HIGHED are all higher than for Bogotá, although the differences are not statistically significant. POSTED has a significantly negative coefficient. The means of DUMS and DUMH—that is, the proportion of high school and college graduates in the labor force—are much lower in Cali than in Bogotá. These may be characterized as "city-size effects"; the smaller city simply lacks enough demand for highly educated persons. It may be the case that the more able Cali postgraduates migrate to Bogotá (or abroad), leaving only the less able ones— and that these people cannot get jobs commensurate with their qualifications; this would explain the negative coefficient of POSTED. Once again, the addition of the location of residence variables causes the greatest change in the HIGHED coefficients, because of the correlation between the rich sectors (2 and 6) and higher education.

Changes over Time

Bourguignon (1983) collected the results from various studies and added his own estimates to obtain a profile of the returns to education in Bogotá from the mid-1960s to the mid-1970s. This chapter adds estimates for 1973, 1975, 1977, and 1978 to his series to obtain a somewhat longer-term picture. The additional results are fully consistent with his work and only serve to reinforce his conclusions.

Table 8-5 gives results for selected years from Bourguignon along with the new estimates. The coefficient for YRSEDU has clearly continued to fall. The results in table 8-5 are slightly misleading, however, because the reported regressions for 1973–78 include the background and residential location variables, which lower the YRSEDU coefficient, as noted above.

The general picture does not change, however, if comparisons are made between equivalently specified regressions with only YRSEDU, EXPER, and

Table 8-5. *Earnings Functions for Male Workers in Bogotá, 1965–78*

Variable	Schultz[a] 1965	Bourguignon[a] 1971	1974	City Study 1973	1975	1977	1978
YRSEDU	0.173 (13.4)	0.167 (38.9)	1.151 (59.2)	0.171 (167.1)	0.147 (51.4)	0.136 (47.4)	0.124 (38.7)
EXPER	0.121 (8.8)	0.078 (17.6)	0.068 (25.8)	0.078 (79.8)	0.057 (21.9)	0.062 (22.3)	0.064 (21.5)
EXPSQ	−0.0018 (7.3)	−0.0011 (12.6)	−0.0009 (19.3)	−0.0010 (59.4)	−0.0008 (16.7)	−0.009 (16.9)	−0.0009 (16.5)
DBOG	—	—	—	0.036 (4.6)	−0.049 (2.1)	−0.019 (0.8)	0.099 (3.1)
DCITY	—	—	—	0.113 (4.2)	—	—	0.167 (2.2)
DTOWN	—	—	—	0.086 (5.3)	—	—	0.189 (3.4)
DURB	—	—	—	—	—	—	0.086 (2.5)
RSECT1	—	—	—	−0.054 (2.8)	0.193 (2.2)	0.047 (0.6)	0.003 (0.04)
RSECT3	—	—	—	0.094 (8.7)	−0.010 (0.3)	0.077 (2.3)	0.130 (3.9)
RSECT4	—	—	—	0.145 (10.4)	0.065 (1.5)	0.216 (4.9)	0.219 (4.4)
RSECT5	—	—	—	0.093 (6.1)	0.167 (3.4)	0.186 (3.8)	0.184 (3.6)
RSECT6	—	—	—	0.120 (10.1)	0.051 (1.5)	0.124 (3.5)	0.096 (2.6)
RSECT7	—	—	—	0.218 (16.4)	0.177 (4.2)	0.176 (4.4)	0.163 (3.6)
RSECT8	—	—	—	0.366 (22.2)	0.241 (5.1)	0.396 (7.9)	0.618 (13.0)
CONST	4.8	5.08	5.88	5.03	5.89	6.25	6.72
R^2	0.881[b]	0.629	0.508	0.492	0.456	0.495	0.519
Number of observations	722	1,016	3,640	37,311	3,999	3,289	3,014
Mean of log monthly earnings					7.72	8.18	8.70

— Not applicable.

Note: t statistics in parentheses.

a. From Bourguignon (1983).

b. Regression run on 47 aggregate age-education groups: hence the high R^2.

Source: 1973 population census sample; and 1975 and 1977 DANE Household Surveys EH8E and EH15. See appendix A at the back of the book for details.

EXPSQ variables. The relevant coefficients on YRSEDU are then[7]

1965	1971	1973	1974	1975	1977	1978
0.173	0.167	0.176	0.151	0.154	0.144	0.144

Table 8-6 shows the comparable results for the splined education variable along with Bourguignon's calculation for the rate of return to different levels of education. The two sets of estimates are not directly comparable for two reasons. First, Bourguignon's results were obtained by running regressions using only dummy variables for those who completed primary, secondary, and higher education along with age dummy variables. The reported coefficients are the estimated education dummy coefficients divided by the appropriate number of years in each schooling category (Bourguignon 1983 used 5 years for primary, 10 years for secondary, and 16 years for higher education). Second, given the structure of the splined variable used here, it is difficult to decide how the certification bonuses should be apportioned to each education level. It is clear that the correct interpretation of the PRIMED, SECED, and HIGHED coefficients is the marginal return to each additional year of schooling at that level, and that this is in some sense the "correct" rate-of-return estimate. But since the certification variables imply an increase in earnings due to the completion of each level, it can be argued that the marginal return estimates underestimate the "gross" return derived from each level of education. According to my specification, the strict interpretation is that the certification bonus should only be added as a return to the last year of the level concerned and not to the preceding years. Whatever the correct interpretation, however, the broad findings are clear.

The estimated returns to each level of education have been falling over time. In contrast to many other countries, the private returns to each year of higher education in Colombia seem to be greater than those for primary education. The returns to secondary education are higher in some years and not in others. In 1978, however, the returns to primary education are consistently lower than secondary education; in turn, these returns are lower than those to higher education in all the regressions estimated. One reason for this result may be that private direct (tuition) costs are neglected in the calculations. Jallade (1974) reports the percentage enrollment in public and private schools in Colombia for each income level. The overall proportions showing the percentage in each category are as follows:

	Public	Private	Total
Primary	72.5	27.5	100
Secondary	49	51	100
Higher	55	45	100

7. Coefficients for 1965, 1971, and 1974 are from Bourguignon (1983); the others are my estimates from log earnings = $\beta_0 + \beta_1$YRSEDU + β_2EXPER + β_1EXPSQ + ϵ.

He also shows, as might be expected, that the proportions enrolled in private schools rise with income. Thus earnings functions estimates for the private return to secondary and higher education probably overstate the actual returns. Accounting for public subsidies to all levels of education, particularly to higher education, would lower the social rates of return even further. The high proportion of private secondary and higher-level schooling in Colombia might then account for the atypically large rates of return to these levels of education.

Table 8-6. *Estimating Returns to Different Levels of Education for Male Workers in Bogotá, 1973–78*

Variable	Schultz 1965[a]	Bourguignon 1971[b]	1974[c]	City Study 1973	1975	1977	1978
DUMP	—	—	—	0.063 (4.5)	0.087 (1.7)	0.038 (0.7)	0.056 (1.0)
DUMS	—	—	—	0.140 (5.3)	0.131 (1.7)	0.038 (0.4)	0.266 (3.2)
DUMH	—	—	—	0.262 (4.8)	0.570 (3.7)	0.254 (1.8)	0.558 (3.8)
PRIMED	0.126 (3.7)	0.069 (6.2)	0.062 (11.1)	0.116 (25.9)	0.073 (4.1)	0.089 (4.8)	0.071 (3.6)
SECED	0.130 (7.9)	0.082 (14.7)	0.088 (25.6)	0.172 (55.4)	0.141 (15.8)	0.132 (15.0)	0.083 (8.9)
HIGHED	0.123 (9.2)	0.117 (25.0)	0.109 (41.8)	0.157 (5.2)	0.074 (2.4)	0.096 (3.5)	0.106 (3.7)
POSTED	—	—	—	0.162 (8.4)	0.122 (2.5)	0.138 (3.4)	0.100 (2.3)
EXPER	—	—	—	0.078 (80.2)	0.057 (21.4)	0.062 (22.4)	0.063 (21.3)
EXPSQ	—	—	—	0.0009 (60.6)	−0.0011 (16.9)	−0.0008 (17.3)	−0.0009 (16.7)
DBOG	—	—	—	0.041 (5.2)	−0.043 (1.8)	−0.017 (0.7)	0.129 (4.0)
DCITY	—	—	—	0.115 (4.4)	—	—	0.192 (2.5)
DTOWN	—	—	—	0.086 (5.4)	—	—	0.211 (3.9)
DURB	—	—	—	—	—	0.100 (3.0)	—
RSECT1	—	—	—	−0.054 (2.4)	0.131 (1.5)	−0.048 (0.5)	0.006 (0.1)
RSECT3	—	—	—	0.103 (9.5)	0.045 (1.3)	0.146 (4.3)	0.145 (4.4)

(Table continues on the following page.)

Table 8-6 (continued)

Variable	Schultz 1965[a]	Bourguignon 1971[b]	1974[c]	City Study 1973	1975	1977	1978
RSECT4	—	—	—	0.152	0.081	0.225	0.234
				(11.0)	(1.9)	(5.1)	(4.8)
RSECT5	—	—	—	0.095	0.202	0.254	0.207
				(6.2)	(4.1)	(5.1)	(4.1)
RSECT6	—	—	—	0.122	0.137	0.241	0.105
				(10.4)	(3.5)	(6.1)	(2.9)
RSECT7	—	—	—	0.207	0.251	0.260	0.143
				(15.7)	(5.6)	(6.1)	(3.1)
RSECT8	—	—	—	0.336	0.306	0.500	0.534
				(20.2)	(5.7)	(9.2)	(11.1)
CONST	3.30	1.58	6.36	5.20	6.4	6.55	6.93
R^2	0.881	0.577	0.497	0.497	0.465	0.502	0.530
Number of observations	722	1,016	3,640	37,311	3,950	3,289	3,014
Mean of log monthly earnings					7.72	8.18	8.70

— Not applicable.

Note: t statistics in parentheses. Mean values of all variables for 1973–78 are reported in chapter 9, appendix.

a. Regression run on 47 aggregate-age education groups. Dependent variable is log weekly earnings.

b. The dependent variable in this regression is log hourly wage.

c. The dependent variable is log monthly earnings. Regressions 1 to 3 also had age cohort dummies not reported here.

Source: See table 8-5.

Bourguignon has attributed the falling returns to education over time to the increasing relative supply of educated workers at each level. Table 8A-1 gives the mean values of all variables used for the 1973 to 1978 regressions. The change in the stock of workers at each education level is reflected in the DUMP, DUMS, and DUMH means. The percentage of the male work force at each level has changed as follows:

	Less than primary	Primary	Secondary	Higher	Total
1973	33	52	9	6	100
1975	26	53	12	9	100
1977	20	52	16	12	100
1978	22	50	15	13	100

Note that these percentages are for the completion of each level. It is interesting to note that the proportion of all secondary school leavers who then
complete college has been increasing over time. If these trends continue, it
can be predicted with some confidence that the private returns to higher
education will continue to decline in Colombia. Given the large proportion
of private schools, it is likely that this decline will continue until the rates
of return become comparable to those for other investments.

Age Cohort Effects

Separate regressions were run for individual age cohorts (15–24, 25–34,
35–44, 45–54, 55–64, and 65 +) to test for differential effects in the returns
to education. Table 8A-5, which reports the results from these regressions,
yields an inverse U-shaped pattern. If the small sample of those over 65 is
excluded, the YRSEDU coefficient increases up to the 35–44 group and then
declines. This pattern would be consistent with the combined effects of two
conflicting processes. The average years of schooling for each age group were
as follows:

	15–24	*25–34*	*35–44*	*45–54*	*55–64*
Mean years of schooling	7.5	8.6	7.5	7.3	6.9

Thus each successive age cohort has a higher mean level of schooling (the
data for the youngest age group, 15–24, are biased because many of the most
qualified members of the cohort will not yet have entered the labor force).
As with the declining returns to education over time, increasing supplies of
educated manpower at each successive age cohort would lower the returns
to schooling over its lifetime. There should then be a narrowing down of the
differences in age-income profiles between groups with different education
levels (chapter 6 documented the large divergences between the groups with
primary, secondary, and higher education). At the same time, as workers get
older the education-specific value added to productivity or skill declines.
Individual-specific skills (not quantifiable by years of experience alone), the
exigencies of luck, on-the-job training, and other such factors all become
more important as determinants of earnings than education. One would then
expect differences in levels of education to explain less of the variance in
earnings and the YRSEDU coefficient to be correspondingly lower for older
workers. The first process is important in explaining differences in the returns
to education in lifetime earnings of individuals and the second in explaining
differences observed in cross sections.

The particular pattern shown in table 8A-5 would appear to be consistent
with these observations. The relatively low coefficient of YRSEDU for the

youngest cohort may be explained by the biased selection of workers noted above, as evidenced by the lower mean of YRSEDU with respect to the next cohort. The higher coefficient for the 35–44 cohort with respect to the 25–34 cohort may be a result of the former group's higher mean level of education, and the subsequent pattern of declining returns with age would be the result of the second factor mentioned above. As education levels for different cohorts converge, the education coefficient should decline monotonically with age in a cross-sectional sample. The returns to education for each cohort should be the same, however, when calculated from lifetime earnings. The lifetime returns will then vary only when the size of each cohort is different, as shown by Welch (1979) for the postwar baby boom cohort in the United States.

The Returns to Experience

The basic human capital formulation of the earnings function explains the increase in earnings with age in terms of on-the-job human capital investment through learning by doing. This is said to be as important an investment in human capital as education—perhaps becoming a more important determinant of earnings as age increases.

If measuring educational investment by years of schooling seems difficult, measuring on-the-job training is even harder. The very nature of the concept makes it impossible to separate the "training" aspect from the "productive" aspect of any work situation. Further, the intensity and quality of such training are as difficult to measure as that of education. There are few direct measures (Lazear 1976).

This study follows the normal practice of using (AGE − YRSEDU − 6) as the relevant proxy for experience—the assumption being that the individual completes full-time formal schooling and starts full-time work soon thereafter. As is conventional, both EXPER and EXPSQ (EXPER^2) are used.

The data provide three other variables that can be used as proxies for on-the-job training. The first is the response to a question that asks the worker how long he or she has worked in his or her current occupation (YRSOCCUP). This variable would be a good proxy for EXPER if it is hypothesized that only occupation-specific work is useful for increasing a worker's productivity. A second potentially helpful variable is the number of years the worker has been working in the same firm (YRSFIRM), on the hypothesis that only firm-specific experience is relevant for job performance. The coefficient for this variable could indicate the importance of the internal labor market in a firm. Doeringer and Piore (1971) have suggested that firms reward longevity, loyalty, and firm-specific experience much more than general work experience gained outside. As a result, internal labor markets are formed within firms to the detriment of interfirm mobility. The implication of such behavior on the demand side is that otherwise equivalent workers may have very different labor earnings, depending on the firm they work in and their work history within the firm: the labor market can then be said to be segmented in this fashion. A comparison of the coefficients of EXPER, YRSOCCUP, and YRSFIRM can therefore give some indication of which is the more appropriate proxy for on-the-job training.

Workers were also asked if they had received specific employer-paid or sponsored training while they were working. This included vocational training that might have been provided by the government or SENA (Servicio Nacional de Aprendizaje, a government-sponsored agency for promoting technical training in Colombia), but with the concurrence of the employer. This variable could only be introduced as a dummy DTRAIN on whether or not training was received. It should have a strongly positive coefficient if vocational training is indeed a significant determinant of earnings.

Refer back to Tables 8-2 and 8-3, which reported the basic earnings functions estimated for 1978. The coefficients of EXPER and EXPSQ are remarkably stable through the addition of all the background and other variables in successive stages. Furthermore, these coefficients do not change even when the education variable is splined in table 8-3. Unlike the education coefficients, the EXPER coefficients do not appear to be affected by the addition of the residential location variable. The gains through years of experience are then not correlated with location of residence.

Now

$$\ln Y = X_1\beta_1 + X_2\beta_2 + X_3\beta_3 + X_4\beta_4 + X_5\beta_5 + \varepsilon$$

$$X_1 = (1; \text{YRSEDU}) \text{ or } (1; \text{DUMP, DUMS, etc.})$$

$$X_2 = (\text{EXPER, EXPSQ})$$

and

$$\beta_1 = (b_0, b_1)$$

$$\beta_2 = (b_2, b_3)$$

are the respective coefficients with b_0 being the constant term.

Now

$$\frac{\partial \ln Y}{\partial \text{ EXPER}} = b_2 + 2b_3(\text{EXPER})$$

but

$$\text{EXPER} = \text{AGE} - \text{YRSEDU} - 6, \text{ hence } = \frac{\partial \ln Y}{\partial \text{ AGE}} = \frac{\partial \ln Y}{\partial \text{ EXPER}}$$

and

$$\frac{\partial \ln Y}{\partial \text{ AGE}} = b_2 + 2b_3(\text{AGE} - \text{YRSEDU} - 6).$$

For maximum earnings,

$$\frac{\partial \ln Y}{\partial \text{ AGE}} = 0$$

that is,

$$\text{AGE} = -\frac{b_2}{2b_3} + \text{YRSEDU} + 6.$$

From tables 8-3 and 8-4,

$$\hat{b}_2 = 0.064$$

$$\hat{b}_3 = -0.0009.$$

Hence maximum earnings for workers who have completed primary, secondary, and higher education are estimated to occur at the ages of 46, 52, and 57, respectively.[8] The marginal contribution to earnings of a year of additional experience $\partial \ln Y/\partial$ EXPER, is 4.6, 2.8, and 1.0 percent at 10-, 20-, and 30-year levels of experience. (The percentage increases for Cali are 5.7, 3.3, and 0.9.)

Tables 8-5 and 8-6 confirm the stability of the EXPER coefficients over time, in that coefficients for years in the 1970s do not differ significantly, except in the case of 1973.

Table 8-7 reports the regressions estimated using the YRSOCCUP and YRSFIRM variables in lieu of EXPER as proxies for on-the-job training. For purposes of comparison, the regression using EXPER is also reported. The mean values of the three variables and the relevant estimated coefficients are all highly significant statistically:

	EXPER	YRSOCCUP	YRSFIRM
Mean (years)	20.4	8.5	5.6
b_2	0.063	0.040	0.044
b_3	-0.0009	-0.0006	-0.0008

8. From table 8-4, for Cali $b_2 = 0.080$, $b_3 = -0.0012$. Hence maximum earnings occur at similar ages in Cali and Bogotá: at 45, 51, and 56 years.

First, note that the mean values of the occupation-specific and firm-specific experience variables are substantially less than the traditional experience variable. This implies that there is considerable mobility of workers between jobs or firms as well as between occupations, and that occupation- and firm-specific experience is not valued especially highly. The maximum earnings with respect to YRSOCCUP and YRSFIRM occur after 33 years and 28 years, respectively. The marginal contribution of an additional year of occupation-specific and firm-specific experience is only 2.8 percent after 10 years, which is much less than the estimated contribution of the EXPER variable. There is thus little evidence that occupation-specific experience or the operation of internal labor markets in the firm offers significantly higher advantages than general work experience.

According to the changes in other coefficients between regressions 1 and 3 in table 8-7, they are by and large quite stable, except in two instances: both DUMH and HIGHED decline as does DBOG; thus highly educated workers and Bogotá natives seem more likely to have the same occupations and jobs for longer periods of time. This is not surprising; it seems quite plausible that the longer one invests in formal education the more specialized one becomes and that such specialization brings returns.

Regression 4 in table 8-7 reports the addition of DTRAIN to the determinants of earnings. Since the coefficient is small and not significant, at least measured in this way, job- or firm-specific training appears to have little effect on earnings. This conclusion is surprising; it may be that DTRAIN is simply not a good measure of job-specific training, or that it is correlated with an ability or experience variable—that is, more able and experienced workers are more likely to be given training.

This whole set of results is rather surprising, since it is often argued that earnings variations for otherwise equivalent workers are by and large the product of the protected nature of the internal labor market within firms (a hypothesis associated primarily with Doeringer and Piore 1971 from their work in U.S. labor markets). The hypothesis has been extended to urban labor markets in developing countries to help explain the segmented labor markets that are said to exist there. The suggestion is that firms in the protected sector pay their employees more than otherwise equivalent workers, and the longer these employees remain with the firm, the greater the divergence between their earnings and those of other workers. It is also suggested that, for efficient functioning in a particular firm, an employee needs a lot of firm-specific information and training that is not useful to other firms, and that this fact deters mobility. To the extent that a protected sector exists, workers within that sector would be loath to leave their firms and would continue, in some sense justifiably, to earn increments to their incomes. The results from Bogotá and Cali indicate that these hypotheses are not borne

Table 8-7. *Earnings Functions for Male Workers in Bogotá Using Different Experience Variables*

	Regression			
Variable	EXPER 1	YRSOCCUP 2	YRSFIRM 3	EXPER 4
DUMP	0.022	−0.003	−0.019	0.025
	(0.4)	(0.0)	(0.3)	(0.4)
DUMS	0.226	0.230	0.220	0.227
	(2.6)	(2.6)	(2.5)	(2.7)
DUMH	0.526	0.717	0.670	0.525
	(3.5)	(4.7)	(4.3)	(3.5)
PRIMED	0.071	0.068	0.065	0.071
	(3.5)	(3.3)	(3.2)	(3.5)
SECED	0.073	0.047	0.042	0.073
	(7.5)	(4.9)	(4.3)	(7.5)
HIGHED	0.099	0.042	0.41	0.103
	(3.4)	(1.4)	(1.4)	(3.3)
POSTED	0.110	0.066	0.107	0.097
	(2.4)	(1.5)	(2.4)	(2.2)
EXPER	0.063	0.040	0.044	0.063
	(20.4)	(13.0)	(11.9)	(20.4)
EXPSQ	−0.0009	−0.0006	−0.0008	−0.0009
	(15.8)	(8.1)	(6.2)	(15.8)
DBOG	0.120	−0.048	−0.041	0.122
	(3.6)	(1.4)	(1.3)	(3.7)
DCITY	0.180	0.133	0.089	0.193
	(2.4)	(1.7)	(1.1)	(2.5)
DTOWN	0.162	0.144	0.143	0.169
	(2.9)	(2.6)	(2.5)	(3.0)
DURB	0.077	0.043	0.042	0.082
	(2.2)	(1.2)	(1.2)	(2.4)
RSECT1	0.023	0.057	0.059	0.013
	(0.2)	(0.6)	(0.6)	(0.1)
RSECT3	0.201	0.191	0.183	0.196
	(5.7)	(5.3)	(5.1)	(5.6)
RSECT4	0.223	0.252	0.244	0.221
	(4.5)	(4.9)	(4.8)	(4.4)
RSECT5	0.255	0.258	0.245	0.247
	(4.9)	(4.8)	(4.6)	(4.7)
RSECT6	0.207	0.195	0.215	0.206
	(5.1)	(4.7)	(5.2)	(5.1)
RSECT7	0.243	0.230	0.245	0.243
	(5.0)	(4.6)	(4.9)	(5.0)
RSECT8	0.601	0.627	0.647	0.593
	(12.1)	(12.3)	(12.7)	(11.9)
UNION	0.054	0.086	0.051	0.034
	(2.6)	(4.1)	(2.4)	(1.6)

	Regression			
Variable	EXPER 1	YRSOCCUP 2	YRSFIRM 3	EXPER 4
SOCSEC	0.089 (3.2)	0.126 (4.4)	0.099 (3.5)	0.052 (1.7)
CONTRACT	0.049 (2.0)	0.039 (1.5)	0.032 (1.3)	0.029 (1.1)
FSIZE	—	—	—	−0.023 (3.3)
DIST	−0.025 (6.4)	−0.023 (5.8)	−0.022 (5.7)	−0.025 (6.4)
DTRAIN	—	—	—	0.011 (0.3)
CONST	7.05	7.73	7.84	7.02
R^2	0.536	0.502	0.500	0.538
Number of observations	2,819	2,927	2,929	2,819
Mean (EXPER)	20.4	6.52	5.60	20.4

— Not applicable.

Note: t statistics in parentheses. Dependent variable: mean of log monthly earnings = 8.70.
Source: See table 8-2.

out for the cities' labor markets as a whole. The results for better-educated workers, however, are consistent with these arguments. The explanation for the low returns to firm-specific and occupation-specific experience may lie in the overall low skill level of the labor force, which is thus not very amenable to acquiring nontransferable skills. At the same time, the fact that better-educated workers do exhibit somewhat higher returns to firm- and occupation-specific experience implies returns to specialization.

Workers' Regions of Origin

The rationale for including certain kinds of indicators of workers' backgrounds in explaining the variance in labor earnings was discussed earlier in the chapter. The underlying hypothesis is that the region of origin of a person affects the kind of schooling he or she receives. In the literature on the United States, for example, the common practice is to suppose that schooling was relatively poor in the South or in non-SMSA (that is, Standard Metro-

268 DETERMINANTS OF LABOR EARNINGS

politan Statistical Areas, a name used by the U.S. Bureau of the Census to refer to urban agglomerations). Dummy variables controlling for these factors are usually significantly negative.

The region-of-origin variables used here (DBOG, DCITY, DTOWN, DURB) represent a plausible starting point. Schools in larger cities, especially in developing countries, are likely to have higher-quality teachers and facilities. Thus the inclusion of variables for the size of settlement of origin is in part designed to correct for bias in the education variables. In addition to the quality-of-schooling argument, it is reasonable to believe that people who grow up in metropolitan areas are exposed to more varied influences and a wider variety of information than those growing up in smaller settlements. By extension, it would be reasonable to suppose that the smaller the town of origin of the worker, the more disadvantaged he or she would be in a large metropolitan area. Moreover, it is often suggested that migrants compete at a disadvantage with natives in urban labor markets, because natives are more likely to be "street wise," to have a range of local contacts, and to be familiar with local sources of information.

A different view of migrants is now beginning to gain wide acceptance, however. Helena Ribe (1979, 1980) has probably expounded this view best:

The analysis of income profiles reported in this paper gives a favorable picture of the relative income position of migrants with respect to natives at destination. Most migrants have larger incomes than comparable natives and their relative income advantage increases with time after migration. It had been expected that migrants would initially be at a relative economic disadvantage because of their lack of location specific experience. However, comparisons of predicted incomes for migrants and natives indicate that most migrants have larger incomes even immediately after moving. The analysis indicates that in urban locations the relative income advantage of migrants does not seem to be explained by their observed characteristics. Education or total post schooling experience alone would give migrants no advantage with respect to comparable natives. Thus, migrants' higher incomes must be accounted for by their unobserved productivity-related characteristics. This finding is consistent with a characteristic of migration as a process which draws especially capable and motivated people away from their origins. (Ribe 1980, p. 24.)

She did, however, find that migrants from larger cities tend to do better than those from smaller towns, who in turn tend to do better than their rural counterparts. As an explanator of earnings, location-specific experience after arrival in the large city was positive and statistically significant.

Although Ribe's specifications are more careful than mine, the region-of-origin variables used here are designed to perform much the same function.

The descriptive information in chapter 6 on migrants' earnings largely corroborated her findings. In the specification of the dummy variables, migrants from rural areas are taken as the reference group. The coefficients of the variables then measure the percentage "premium" earned by others over the rural migrants, with all other characteristics being the same. DBOG is the dummy for Bogotá natives (including migrants who arrived there before the age of 10); DCITY is for migrants from other large cities—Cali, Medellín, Barranquilla—with populations of a million or more; DTOWN is for migrants from cities with over 100,000 population (in the 1973 census); and DURB is for migrants from all other towns.

Refer once again to tables 8-2 and 8-3, and note that the addition of the region variables does not affect the education coefficients for either the YRSEDU specification or the splined specification. Therefore the first of the hypotheses above does not seem to be borne out by the data. All the region dummy coefficients are positive and statistically significant at the 5 percent level (see tables 8-2 and 8-3).

| | | Education specification | |
	Percentage in Bogotá	YRSEDU	Splined (DUMP, DUMS, DUMH)
DBOG	46	0.10 to 0.11	0.12 to 0.14
DCITY	3	0.15 to 0.18	0.18 to 0.20
DTOWN	6	0.19 to 0.23	0.16 to 0.25
DURB	26	0.08 to 0.10	0.08 to 0.12

Given that the t statistics are all between about 2 and 4, these coefficients must be considered stable between the differently specified regressions. Recall that the Bogotá natives (DBOG) also include all those who immigrated to Bogotá before the age of 10. The comparison is with migrants from rural areas. These results indicate that the immigrants from larger towns and cities (with populations in the range of 100,000 to 1 million people) are better off (all other characteristics being equal) than the Bogotá natives, who are similar to immigrants from the fourth and smallest of the settlement-of-origin categories used here (represented in the specification by DURB). All seem to be about 10–20 percent better off than the rural immigrants. These results are essentially consistent with those of Ribe and lend support to her suggestion that migrants are often better off than natives, but that migrants from larger towns are the best off. According to the results for Cali in table 8-4, however, none of these coefficients are statistically significant in Cali; therefore, migrants and natives must be regarded as essentially similar.

Another cut at the same issue was taken by estimating earnings functions separately for each group. The results from these regressions are reported in table 8A-6. The first point to note is that there is little to distinguish between the returns to education for the Bogotá natives and migrants from the other three urban categories. Rural migrants do get significantly lower returns, presumably because of the quality of schooling and other negative influences mentioned above. In summary, there is little difference between all the urban folk but the rural folk are clearly somewhat behind. The least log variance in earnings explained is for the rural migrants, because of the lower variance in their education levels. Within-city locational differences are somewhat different for each group; these are discussed in the next section.

Another point to note is that membership in a union seems to make a significantly positive contribution only to migrants from rural and smaller urban areas; furthermore, returns to education are significantly lower for female migrants from rural and smaller urban areas than for Bogotá natives. The union effect for the rural and small-town migrants is of special interest since it is the first indication that some kind of protected sector exists in which successful entrants are clearly better off than "outsiders."

Thus the data lead one to conclude that the education of rural migrants is of inferior quality relative to that of their urban counterparts (or that their ability is lower). There is little to distinguish between the returns to education to urban migrants and natives. It seems that one way for rural and small-town migrants to improve their lot is to gain union membership.

Current Location of Residence

The inclusion of the location-of-current-residence variables (RSECT1 to RSECT8) is perhaps the most controversial aspect of the estimation of earnings functions in this study and therefore needs more explanation than the brief rationale given earlier.

Earlier chapters have amply documented the systematic differences that exist between different parts of the city of Bogotá. Somewhat similar patterns are found in Cali. The rich live mainly in certain parts of the two cities, and other parts are particularly poor; the remaining areas are relatively heterogeneous. It will be recalled that Bogotá runs from north to south along a high mountain boundary to the east and has a semicircular western extension. The rich residential area of the city lies in the north, extending from almost the center of the city to its northern tip—sector 8 in map 3-1. The diametrically opposite area in the south (sector 2) is the poorest part of the city. The ranking of the radial sectors or pie slices of the city by average household income per capita is 2, 3, 6, 4, 5, 7, 8 in ascending order; that is, income increases as one rotates from south to north, except in sector 6. There are virtually no rich people in the extreme south, but there are some poor people in almost every part of the city.

Most large cities in the world have discrete rich and poor neighborhoods. As mentioned earlier, people choose residential locations according to what they can afford, where they work, and their preferences regarding local a-menities and other neighborhood characteristics. Normally income helps to determine residential location. Furthermore, people sort themselves out according to ethnic origin, and to some extent according to occupational and class status (which, of course, is correlated with income).

The issue to be examined here is whether there also exists a feedback mechanism that to some extent reverses the direction of causation, such that the location of a person's residence affects his or her earnings potential. The implications of the inclusion of the location variables in earnings functions is that it does. An ideal analytical framework would combine residential location theory with the determinants of earnings in a simultaneous equation framework. The location of residence would then become endogenous. Such a framework is difficult to establish because residential location theory is not developed enough to interrelate household location decisions with the characteristics of the labor market. A necessary part of such a link would be the elaboration of a within-household decisionmaking model in which labor force participation decisions would be made simultaneously with location decisions. The discussion quickly leads one to the kind of comprehensive model referred to earlier, with residential location thrown in for good measure! The state of the art is simply not advanced enough to enable us to estimate such a model with the data normally available. One is then left with the kind of reduced-form earnings functions approach adopted here, under which some-what indirect evidence is examined to probe the underlying causation process.

As mentioned above, every city has its rich and poor neighborhoods, but what is striking in Bogotá is the relatively systematic nature of income gra-dation. Hoyt (1939, 1966) documented the structure of American cities by income and the movement of rich and poor neighborhoods over time. Amato (1968) did the same for Bogotá. Hoyt's idea was essentially that the rich initially happen to live in one part of town. As the town expands into a city and then into a metropolitan area, and as incomes increase, the rich pro-gressively demand new and larger houses. The new rich neighborhoods then are built adjacent to the old ones so that the rich end up expanding in one or a few particular directions—usually the more desirable ones environmen-tally—and the poor fill up the interstices. This story describes the central city decay common in American cities and the flight of the rich further and further away from the center. Although many American cities conform to this pattern, more recent urban economic theory has emphasized the ring structure of cities. (See Mohan 1979, chap. 2, for a summary of this vast literature.) The tradeoff between transportation costs and the income-elastic desire for greater space results in the rich locating in relatively large houses further away from the city center with progressively poorer people locating nearer the center. The most recent work on this issue appears to reach conclusions nearer Hoyt's (although stated differently) than the prevailing urban economic model (Wheaton 1977). Amato's (1968) work documented the movement of Bogotá's elite in the late nineteenth and early twentieth centuries from the northern part of the city center to neighborhoods further and further north in what is here called sector 8.

If the above representation of city development is accurate, it is possible to suggest some feedback effects of residential location on potential earnings. Parts of the city that have always had high-income residents would seem likely to have better-quality schools than poorer areas. They would also have a higher demand for goods and services so that businesses would be more likely to become established in locations convenient to these areas. (See Lee 1985 for details on the location of service employment and its strong relationship with household income used as a proxy for demand intensity.) This is indeed the case in Bogotá, where the rich sectors have more employment than resident labor whereas the poor sectors have net employment deficits. Chapter 6 gave some information on the pattern of interaction between residential and work location. People from the poorest sectors commute extensively to other areas (and may therefore be termed spatially disadvantaged). When specific parts of a city are identifiably rich and poor, a person's address can indicate his or her background. The advantages of a "good" business address or a residential address have long been recognized, but the reverse has attracted less discussion. One possible consequence is that people's addresses may be used by employers as a screening mechanism and a gauge of a job applicant's likely characteristics—reliability, family background, and so on—much as the names of schools are used as screening devices. The more income-segregated a city, the more such screening is likely to be used.

There are at least three reasons why residential-location variables could turn out to have a significant effect on earnings. First, in the human capital tradition, it may be argued that where one lives acts as a proxy for otherwise unmeasured variables such as ability, schooling quality, and the like. Second, also in the human capital tradition, it may be suggested that residential location is a proxy for other productivity characteristics of workers who are themselves correlated with place of residence (class, status, aspirations, attitudes, contacts, etc.).[9] Third, location information may be used as a screening device, with the implication that people from poorer areas are being discriminated against and that the labor market is in this sense segmented.

---

9. McGregor (1977) examines a low-income public housing project in Glasgow and finds rates and duration of unemployment for youths from poor neighborhoods to be significantly higher than expected.

Two location variables have been used in tables 8-2 and 8-3 to estimate basic earnings functions. First are the dummies for each residential sector with sector 2, the poorest, used as the comparator base; second is DIST, the distance from the city center. Given that employment is relatively centralized in Bogotá, the hypothesis is that people living at the periphery are disadvantaged with respect to access. The coefficients are as follows:

Sector	Coefficient	Sector	Coefficient
1	—	6	0.09 to 0.20
3	0.12 to 0.20	7	0.14 to 0.24
4	0.22	8	0.53 to 0.62
5	0.16 to 0.26		

The coefficients are quite stable over different regressions except when DIST is added in regression 5 (table 8-3). They are not significantly different between sectors 3 to 7, all being between about 0.15 and 0.2. The addition of DIST puts them all around 0.2. Sector 8 is obviously different, with coefficients of about 0.6. Note that these coefficients measure the deviation in log income from sector 2 means, with all other variables held constant. Thus people living in sectors 3 to 7 receive about 20 percent more in earnings— and workers living in sector 8 receive 50–60 percent more than otherwise equivalent workers in sector 2. The center of the city (sector 1) is too heterogeneous for residence there to have a measurable differential impact on earning.

The location-of-residence variables do not add appreciably to the R^2 or variance of log income explained by the estimated equations. All the coefficients (except for sector 1) are significantly positive. On the basis of these results, it would appear that people living in sector 8 earn substantially more than those of otherwise equivalent characteristics except that they live in all other sectors, and that people in sector 2 earn significantly less than otherwise equivalent people living elsewhere. Note that about 20 percent of Bogotá's population lives in sector 2 and about 10 percent in the rich sector 8.

Chapter 6 indicated that migrants are not overrepresented in any area of the city and that as a group, they do not differ significantly from natives. Further, the region of origin has been controlled for as described in section 8-5. Thus, it is reasonable to assume that the above results are not due to any distortions on this account. Moreover, the estimated coefficients of the residential sector dummies are not significantly different in the two types of schooling specifications. Regression 5 in table 8-3 controls for distance from the city center; interestingly, almost all the coefficients increase and become more statistically significant. DIST itself receives a significantly negative coefficient of −0.025; that is, workers' incomes fall (other things being equal) on the average by 2.5 percent per kilometer from the city center. Thus adjusting for distance further accentuates the differences in earnings between otherwise equivalent workers with different locations of residence.

In order to investigate the residential location effect further, I estimated earnings functions separately for workers in each sector; the results are reported in table 8A-7. The coefficients on YRSEDU are as follows:

Sector	Coefficient	Sector	Coefficient
1	0.095	5	0.111
2	0.081	6	0.114
3	0.086	7	0.137
4	0.104	8	0.163

The figures show a remarkably consistent pattern of increase as one moves clockwise from sector 2 to sector 8. The differences are not statistically significant between sectors 2 and 3, and between sectors 4, 5, and 6, but the overall pattern is clear. The low coefficient of sector 2 may be partly due to truncation bias, since there are few high-income people in that sector. The UNION coefficient is significant only for sectors 2 and 6, both of which have large proportions of blue-collar workers. The log-variance is of much lower magnitude in the sectors with low YRSEDU coefficients.

A further test was performed by estimating the same earnings function separately for the top and bottom halves of the workers' income distribution. Such a procedure suffers from the obvious econometric problems arising from truncation of the dependent variable (see Gary Fields 1980b for a brief exposition of truncation bias). The R^2 for the bottom half is only about 0.09. The results for the top half are not very different from the overall results. But none of the sector coefficients are significant for the low-income sample. Despite the truncation problem, if the location of residence matters, it is apparently only for the better-paid and better-educated workers. Incidentally, these results also suggest that truncation bias is not too severe in the sector regressions of table 8A-7.

Before any conclusions can be drawn from this evidence, the extent of mobility between different types of neighborhoods needs to be examined. As Hamer (1980) has demonstrated, there is considerable intracity mobility in Bogotá: about 20 percent of all households move every year, a figure quite similar to the percentage for the United States. However, Hamer shows that most of the movement takes place within sectors or to adjacent ones. It is difficult to decide what constitutes upward mobility since there are few norms for comparison. This is important: if it is relatively easy for households to move up the neighborhood ladder and buy into whatever neighborhood effects that exist, there may be somewhat less reason to worry about the negative effects on earnings potential of location of residence.

It has been difficult to resolve this issue even with the existence of mobility data; only a limited experiment could be done with the available information. An attempt was made to purge the effects of different kinds of movers by dividing people into three categories: those who had not moved between dwellings in the past ten years, those who have moved upward (DUP), and those who had moved downward (DDOWN) in terms of new neighborhoods (see exact definitions in the appendix to this chapter). Using the stationary workers as the comparator group, I added dummy variables DUP and DDOWN to regression 5 of table 8-3. There were no significant changes in the original coefficients, but DDOWN was significantly positive while DUP was positive but not statistically significant:

	Coefficient	t statistic
DUP	0.045	1.48
DDOWN	0.103	3.03
$R^2 = 0.545$		

R^2 increased from 0.536 to 0.545. Thus people who move down from higher-income to lower-income locations appear to retain some higher-income characteristics. This result tends to undermine the screening or segmentation hypothesis and to support that of the background effect of residential location.

What can be concluded from all these quantitative results? First, these location variables do little in the way of explaining earnings based on the traditional human capital variables. However, the magnitudes of their effects are quantitatively as well as statistically significant. Some of this is undoubtedly due to positive sorting. Workers who do well tend to move to higher-income locations: thus only the less successful of otherwise equivalent workers are left behind in low-income neighborhoods. The lower coefficients on YRSEDU in the separate sector regressions are close to the PRIMED coefficients for the whole sample, again suggesting that part of the explanation is simply that apparently disadvantaged sectors contain only or mainly the relatively uneducated and poor workers. The truncated regressions indicate that the location effect is more relevant for the better educated. This is consistent with the screening hypothesis as well as the supposition concerning quality of education. People from poorer areas who do achieve higher education levels probably do suffer from lower schooling quality, but they may also be discriminated against on account of negative labeling. This is in the nature of a vicious cycle, in that negative labeling is probably statistically appropriate but militates against the brighter individual and is therefore self-propagative. The evidence from U.S. studies mentioned earlier suggests that school quality does matter, particularly to the more disadvantaged students. It may be concluded that high spatial income segregation in Bogotá does contribute negatively to the earnings potential of workers from disadvantaged areas of the city, with the background and quality of education effect probably hav-ing more impact than the segmentation or labeling effect. The results may then be self-propagating and therefore still more important for the next generation.[10]

Summary

The traditional variables—years of schooling and of work experience—were found to account for almost half of the log variance of labor earnings. The addition of the two "background" variables—region of origin and the location of current residence—adds little to the level of statistical explanation of the variance of earnings, though the variables do have statistically sig-nificant effects. If the background variables are interpreted as proxies for schooling quality and ability, then the results are quite consistent with studies in the United States, which conclude that the omission of ability and back-ground variables from earnings functions does not cause biases of large mag-nitude.

The education variable was also specified somewhat differently earlier in the chapter in an attempt to estimate the marginal returns to each distinct level of education (primary, secondary, higher, postgraduate), and to measure the "certification bonus" received on completing each level of education. In contrast to most other studies, the results presented here suggest that the returns to higher education are greater than those to secondary education, which in turn are higher than those to primary schooling. The results also appear to indicate that education acts as a screening device, and that people receive a 20–25 percent premium for graduating from high school and from college.

The availability of data sets from different years made it possible to estimate changes in the same earnings function over time. A declining trend was observed in the returns to education on the whole, as well as to each level—a finding that is consistent with other estimates for Colombia. In observing different average private rates of return for different levels of schooling, it should be noted that the proportion of private education increases with level of education as well as income. Thus, if tuition costs were accounted for, the observed differentials in rates of return to higher and lower levels of schooling would probably diminish.

Returns to schooling vary with age; workers in their early middle age receive

10. Pachon (1979) gives evidence for the fact that most children go to school within walking distance from home. It is therefore justifiable to assume that location of residence largely determines the school that a child attends.

higher returns than their younger and older counterparts. The increasing stock of workers with a higher education may account for the lower rate of return to schooling among younger workers: for older workers, it may be that education is a less important determinant of earnings than other factors such as experience and pure luck.

Overall, the simple specification of earnings functions based on human capital does explain well the variance in labor earnings in Bogotá and Cali, and the fact that adding other variables has little effect on the education coefficient gives confidence in the results for rates of return to schooling; consistent estimates are obtained for different years as well as different levels of education. With regard to the work experience variable, the returns to each additional year of experience turn out to be substantially lower than those for years of schooling. In contrast to conventional hypotheses, years of firm-specific and occupation-specific experience do not appear to be more useful than the simple total of years of work experience as a whole.

As for the influence of a male worker's background on his earnings, two types of background variables were considered: the region of origin of the individual (with respect to the settlement where he was born), and the location of his current residence within the city. The first hypothesis examined was that the quality of schooling would differ according to the size of the individual's settlement of origin. The inclusion of these variables did not affect the estimates of the return to schooling: those estimates are therefore not biased by the exclusion of such variables. It was found that most migrants were no worse off than natives, although both natives and migrants from other towns and cities did seem to earn 10–20 percent more than rural migrants, with immigrants from large cities being the best off. Rates of return to education are essentially similar for natives and immigrants from urban areas, but rural migrants do receive significantly lower returns. One interesting feature of these estimations is that union membership seems to be especially beneficial to migrants from rural areas.

Income levels are generally regarded as a principal determinant of residential location. Rich people generally live in rich neighborhoods, and the poor in poor ones; as the latter become better off, they may move to better areas. The results from the estimation of these earnings functions suggest, however, that there might be income feedback effects as well, and that these may reverse the causal chain in the sense that the location of an individual's residence might affect his or her potential earnings. These effects have been interpreted in several ways. As with the region-of-origin variables, the location of residence acts as a proxy for schooling quality and ability. Even if the individual has not lived all his or her life in the current location, mobility data indicate that he or she is likely to have lived in similar neighborhoods previously. Hence neighborhoods also act as a proxy for class and status, and perhaps for other unmeasured productivity characteristics such as initiative or the will to succeed. Finally, in a city as segregated by income as Bogotá, it is also possible that a person's address can be used as a screening or labeling device by employers.

Whatever the explanation, differences according to location of a worker's residence do indeed turn out to be statistically significant in Bogotá and Cali. Workers with otherwise equivalent characteristics apparently earn more or less according to where they live, with those in the rich northern part of the city earning about 50–60 percent more than their counterparts in the poor south, and those in the rest of the city earning about 20 percent above the mean for the poorest areas. Stratifying the sample by location of residence and estimating the returns to education add further credence to the hypothesized neighborhood effect. Although the differences are not statistically significant, the rates of return to schooling follow closely the gradation of neighborhoods. Furthermore, spatial segmentation seems to affect better-educated individuals particularly strongly; the neighborhood differentials are less important for blue-collar workers.

In summary, it turns out that earnings functions based on traditional human capital work well in explaining the variance of labor incomes in Bogotá, but that workers' regions of origin and location of current residence also play a part in determining their potential earnings. The exact nature of the chain of causation operating here needs further investigation. In particular, it would be worth exploring whether cities with higher levels of spatial segregation by income exacerbate these locational or neighborhood effects.

Appendix. Variables Used in Estimating Earnings

This appendix describes the variables used in estimating the earnings functions discussed in chapter 8. Tables 8A-1 to 8A-7 provide detailed data to supplement the tables in the body of the text.

Education Variables (X_1)

Two sets of education variables were used: the first was the usual number of years of schooling completed. In order to estimate the differential rates of return to different levels of schooling as well as to test for the value of credentials, the number of years of schooling was spliced into the following seven variables.

DUMP = 1 if 5 years of primary schooling are completed but secondary not completed, 0 otherwise

DUMS   = 1 if 6 additional years of secondary education are completed but higher education not completed, 0 otherwise

DUMH   = 1 if 4 additional years of higher education are completed, 0 otherwise

PRIMED = Number of years of primary schooling completed. If schooling is greater than primary, PRIMED = 5

SECED   = Number of years of secondary schooling completed. If schooling is greater than secondary, SECED = 6

HIGHED = Number of years of higher education completed. If more than 4 years completed, HIGHED = 4

POSTED = Number of years of postgraduate education completed.

Experience Variables (X_2)

A number of proxies for the on-the-job component of human capital were attempted. The first was the traditional variable,

$$\text{EXPER} = \text{Age} - \text{YRSEDU} - 6 \text{ (years)}$$

and

$$\text{EXPSQ} = (\text{EXPER})^2 \text{ (years)}^2$$

jwhich was used in most regressions.

The two other experience variables were available in the data. The respondents were asked how long they had been in their current occupation and how long they had been working in the same firm. The other two sets of experience variables are therefore

YRSOCCUP   = years spent in current occupation

YRSOCCUPSQ = (years in current occupation)^2

YRSFIRM   = years spent in current firm

YRSFIRMSQ   = $(\text{YRSFIRM})^2$

One other firm-specific variable was available. People were asked if they had received formal job training while working. A dummy variable is therefore used.

DTRAIN = 1 if formal training was received while working, 0 otherwise.

Origin Variables (X_3)

These are a set of dummy variables designed to control for the origin of the individual. The data record every individual's place of birth. Since the aim is to control for the quality of schooling, environment, and so on, Bogotá is regarded as the origin of everyone who migrated there before the age of 10 plus all those who were born there. The dummy variables are

DBOG = 1 if the individual was born in Bogotá or migrated there before age 10, 0 otherwise

DCITY = 1 if migrant was born in the three next largest cities of Colombia, each of about 1 million population,[11] 0 otherwise

DTOWN = 1 if migrant was born in a town with more than 100,000 people according to the 1973 census,[12] 0 otherwise

DURB = 1 if migrant was born in other urban settlements.

The excluded category is that of migrants from rural areas.

Location of Residence (X_{4a})

The location of residence has been controlled in two ways (see maps 3-1 and 3-2 for the division of Bogotá and Cali into radial sectors and rings). The location of residence of each worker is classified according to which sector he lives in and is controlled for by a set of seven dummy variables with sector 2 (the poorest sector located in the south) acting as the reference sector. The seven dummy variables are RSECT1, RSECT3, RSECT4, RSECT5, RSECT6, RSECT7, and RSECT8. Each takes the value 1 if the worker lives in that sector, 0 otherwise.

DIST is a measure of the distance of residence from the city center (sector 1 and ring 1) measured in kilometers from centroid of city center to centroid of worker's barrio (see appendix A to this book).

Mobility Variables (X_{4b})

Information on the location of former residence was also available. Movers were classified as "upwardly" mobile people and "downwardly" mobile people. The ranking of sectors is 2, 3, 6, 4, 5, 7, 8 in ascending order of mean household income per capita, with sector 1 being small and rather heterogeneous. Movers were defined as those who moved within the previous ten years. Mobility was therefore characterized by the following two dummy variables:

DUP   = 1 for people who moved into a sector with higher average income than their previous sector of residence and all whose last move was from outside Bogotá.

11. Cali, Medellín, and Barranquilla.

12. Bucaramanga, Cartagena, Cúcuta, Manizales, Pereira, Ibague, Armenia, Plamira, Pasto, Buenaventura, Neiva, and Santa Marta.

DDOWN = 1 for people who moved from relatively high-income sectors to low-income ones.

The reference was nonmovers, defined as those who had not moved in the past ten years or those who had moved within their own sector.

Employment Variables (X_5)

Four variables were used as proxies of characteristics of what is usually called the protected sector or formal sector:

UNION   = 1 if a union exists in the worker's workplace, 0 otherwise
CONTRACT = 1 if the worker has a written employment contract
FSIZE   = Number of workers in place of work
LOGFSIZE = ln (FSIZE).

Dependent Variables (y)

Three dependent variables for earnings were used. The main one was monthly earnings. Workers were asked about the periodicity of their wage payments along with the unit wage.[13] A second question was asked to elicit the same information: their total labor earnings in the previous month.[14] Information was also available on weekly hours usually worked and the number of months worked in the previous twelve months. The three income variables used are:

Log monthly earnings (1978 Colombian pesos)

$$\text{Log HWAGE} = \ln \frac{\text{monthly earnings}}{4 \times \text{weekly hours}}$$

$$\text{Log YRLYINC} = \ln \frac{\text{monthly earning} \times \text{number of months worked}}{1{,}000}.$$

13. Throughout the earnings functions estimation, workers have been defined as those individuals who reported working to be their major activity during the week preceding the interview or who worked more than fifteen hours per week. Maids have also been included.

14. The monthly earnings variable used is the derived monthly earnings for employees who report the periodicity of wage payment and unit wage. For others, it is the monthly earnings reported for the previous month.

Table 8A-1. *Mean Values of Variables, Bogotá, 1978*

	Male		Female	
Variable[a]	Mean	Standard deviation[b]	Mean	Standard deviation
YRSEDU (years)	7.75	4.45	7.10	4.44
DUMP	0.50	—	0.44	—
DUMS	0.15	—	0.17	—
DUMH	0.13	—	0.10	—
PRIMED (years)	4.48	1.15	4.19	1.47
SECED (years)	2.51	2.59	2.36	2.58
HIGHED (years)	0.61	1.39	0.49	1.25
POSTED (years)	0.14	0.45	0.06	0.29
EXPER (years)	20.49	13.36	17.62	12.92
EXPSQ	598.10	708.99	477.58	649.25
YRSOCCUP (years)	8.52	9.57	6.02	6.98
YRSOCCUPSQ	164.15	364.34	84.90	212.30
YRSFIRM (years)	5.60	7.54	3.83	5.43
YRSFIRMSQ	88.16	229.92	44.19	127.99
DBOG	0.459	—	0.439	—
DCITY	0.025	—	0.015	—
DTOWN	0.058	—	0.060	—
DURB	0.262	—	0.264	—
Rural[c]	0.196	—	0.222	—
RSECT1	0.018	—	0.014	—
RSECT2[c]	0.205	—	0.154	—
RSECT3	0.250	—	0.207	—

Variable[a]	Male		Female	
	Mean	Standard deviation[b]	Mean	Standard deviation
RSECT4	0.072	—	0.058	—
RSECT5	0.063	—	0.067	—
RSECT6	0.185	—	0.177	—
RSECT7	0.094	—	0.117	—
RSECT8	0.113	—	0.200	—
DIST (kilometers)	7.35	3.50	7.15	3.46
DUP	0.37	—	0.40	—
DDOWN	0.14	—	0.13	—
Stationary[c]	0.49	—	0.47	—
UNION	0.24	—	0.18	—
SOCSEC	0.53	—	0.50	—
CONTRACT	0.45	—	0.45	—
Log monthly earnings	8.70	0.89	8.20	0.78
Log HWAGE	3.42	0.95	2.95	0.91
Log YRLYINC/1,000	4.15	1.00	3.57	1.01

— Not applicable.

a. See chapter 8, appendix, for explanation of variable names.

b. Standard deviation not given for dummy variables.

c. The comparative base for the set of dummy variables.

Source: 1978 World Bank–DANE Household Survey.

Table 8A-2. *Matrix of Correlation Coefficients for Male Workers in Bogotá*

Variable	LOGINC	EXPER	EXPSQ	DBOG	DCITY	DTOWN	DURB
LOGINC	1.00000	0.02119	−0.02501	−0.02279	0.06119	0.09794	0.08603
EXPER	0.02119	1.00000	0.95499	−0.33322	−0.01143	−0.00853	0.16413
EXPSQ	−0.02501	0.95499	1.00000	−0.27283	−0.01571	−0.02655	0.14165
DBOG	−0.02279	−0.33322	−0.27283	1.00000	−0.14989	−0.22045	−0.55157
DCITY	0.06119	−0.01143	−0.01571	−0.14989	1.00000	−0.03895	−0.09746
DTOWN	0.09794	−0.00853	−0.02655	−0.22045	−0.03895	1.00000	−0.14334
DURB	0.08603	0.16413	0.14165	−0.55157	−0.09746	−0.14334	1.00000
DUMP	−0.25439	−0.03065	−0.04993	0.04879	−0.02345	−0.01782	−0.01662
DUMS	0.16677	−0.16187	−0.12577	0.07190	0.05632	0.03656	−0.01105
DUMH	0.55477	−0.18451	−0.16474	0.02948	0.03670	0.04887	0.05401
PRIMED	0.26060	−0.36748	−0.36003	0.16106	0.03397	0.05132	−0.00877
SECED	0.51958	−0.37371	−0.32095	0.14307	0.08448	0.07619	0.00719
HIGHED	0.57211	−0.22117	−0.19012	0.04534	0.03489	0.05864	0.04529
POSTED	0.47981	−0.14393	−0.13130	0.01619	0.02699	0.04693	0.05722
RSECT1	−0.00698	0.00543	0.01565	−0.05085	0.05776	0.09592	0.01067
RSECT3	−0.08174	0.00640	0.00091	−0.01813	−0.01186	−0.00267	−0.03809
RSECT4	0.04088	0.00882	−0.00126	−0.02924	−0.03170	0.04694	0.01516
RSECT5	−0.01585	−0.01876	−0.02021	−0.03436	−0.03063	0.01078	0.00606
RSECT6	−0.02673	0.04345	0.03657	−0.02150	0.03446	−0.01542	0.03332
RSECT7	0.05300	−0.03164	−0.01632	0.02362	−0.02205	−0.02229	0.04894
RSECT8	0.42183	−0.05254	−0.04160	0.04475	0.02619	0.04501	0.03479
UNION	0.18114	−0.01088	−0.03298	−0.06201	−0.00780	0.04124	0.07747
SOCSEC	0.22217	−0.08903	−0.09729	−0.04938	0.02720	0.04327	0.04761
CONTRACT	0.15245	−0.15458	−0.15413	−0.00839	−0.00183	0.03102	0.03373
DIST	−0.15087	0.04293	0.02778	−0.02140	−0.01026	−0.06912	−0.00250
DTRAIN	0.12823	−0.10534	−0.10972	0.02549	−0.03197	0.07223	0.00975
FSIZE	0.12089	−0.00187	−0.02004	−0.06592	−0.03297	0.00435	0.08332
LOGFSIZE	0.21155	−0.13051	−0.14093	−0.00645	−0.02030	0.01215	0.01986

DUMP	DUMS	DUMH	PRIMED	SECED	HIGHED	POSTED	Variable
−0.25439	0.16677	0.55477	0.26060	0.51958	0.57211	0.47981	LOGINC
−0.03065	−0.16187	−0.18451	−0.36748	−0.37371	−0.22117	−0.14393	EXPER
−0.04993	−0.12577	−0.16474	−0.36003	−0.32095	−0.19012	−0.13130	EXPSQ
0.04879	0.07190	0.02948	0.16106	0.14307	0.04534	0.01619	DBOG
−0.02345	0.05632	0.03670	0.03397	0.08448	0.03489	0.02699	DCITY
−0.01782	0.03656	0.04887	0.05132	0.07619	0.05864	0.04693	DTOWN
−0.01662	−0.01105	0.05401	−0.00877	0.00719	0.04529	0.05722	DURB
1.00000	−0.42473	−0.38510	0.46553	−0.34092	−0.43950	−0.31373	DUMP
−0.42473	1.00000	−0.15916	0.19240	0.57584	0.00118	−0.12966	DUMS
−0.38510	−0.15916	1.00000	0.17445	0.52211	0.94499	0.81468	DUMH
0.46553	0.19240	0.17445	1.00000	0.43891	0.19909	0.14212	PRIMED
−0.34092	0.57584	0.52211	0.43891	1.00000	0.59586	0.42535	SECED
−0.43950	0.00118	0.94499	0.19909	0.59586	1.00000	0.76986	HIGHED
−0.31373	−0.12966	0.81468	0.14212	0.42535	0.76986	1.00000	POSTED
0.02499	0.01558	−0.00993	0.02430	0.02717	−0.01098	−0.01051	RSECT1
0.06958	−0.00961	−0.13497	−0.03099	−0.08338	−0.13618	−0.12489	RSECT3
0.00510	0.05404	−0.02207	0.03652	0.03838	−0.01111	−0.02107	RSECT4
0.06563	0.00523	−0.06198	0.02001	−0.01966	−0.05088	−0.04983	RSECT5
0.04819	0.01274	−0.03775	0.04077	−0.00416	−0.03931	−0.04169	RSECT6
−0.07774	0.06129	0.10253	0.03429	0.11170	0.10466	0.09323	RSECT7
−0.20958	0.02452	0.45600	0.11561	0.31675	0.46202	0.40991	RSECT8
−0.07324	0.09400	0.09233	0.06250	0.15247	0.12729	0.07412	UNION
−0.05290	0.12653	0.14482	0.15104	0.24297	0.16272	0.12612	SOCSEC
−0.04129	0.10853	0.11818	0.13412	0.18982	0.12525	0.09522	CONTRACT
0.04349	−0.07155	−0.11154	−0.09059	−0.15736	−0.11905	−0.07691	DIST
−0.02561	0.10461	0.07632	0.10901	0.15665	0.08181	0.06912	DTRAIN
−0.02120	−0.01410	0.12078	0.06211	0.08215	0.11369	0.17735	FSIZE
−0.06495	0.08297	0.14839	0.11550	0.19305	0.15761	0.16189	LOGFSIZE

(Table continues on following page.)

Table 8A-2 (continued)

Variable	RSECT1	RSECT3	RSECT4	RSECT5	RSECT6	RSECT7	RSECT8
LOGINC	−0.00698	−0.08174	0.04088	−0.01585	−0.02673	0.05300	0.42183
EXPER	0.00543	0.00640	0.00882	−0.01876	0.04345	−0.03164	−0.05254
EXPSQ	0.01565	0.00091	−0.00126	−0.02021	0.03657	−0.01632	−0.04160
DBOG	−0.05085	−0.01813	−0.02924	−0.03436	−0.02150	0.02362	0.04475
DCITY	0.05776	−0.01186	−0.03170	−0.03063	0.03446	−0.02205	0.02619
DTOWN	0.09592	−0.00267	0.04694	0.01078	−0.01542	−0.02229	0.04501
DURB	0.01067	−0.03809	0.01516	0.00606	0.03332	0.04894	0.03479
DUMP	0.02499	0.06958	0.00510	0.06563	0.04819	−0.07774	−0.20958
DUMS	0.01558	−0.00961	0.05404	0.00523	0.01274	0.06129	0.02452
DUMH	−0.00993	−0.13497	−0.02207	−0.06198	−0.03775	0.10253	0.45600
PRIMED	0.02430	−0.03099	0.03652	0.02001	0.04077	0.03429	0.11561
SECED	0.02717	−0.08338	0.03838	−0.01966	−0.00416	0.11170	0.31675
HIGHED	−0.01098	−0.13618	−0.01111	−0.05088	−0.03931	0.10466	0.46202
POSTED	−0.01051	−0.12489	−0.02107	−0.04983	−0.04169	0.09323	0.40991
RSECT1	1.00000	−0.07743	−0.03745	−0.03563	−0.06375	−0.04312	−0.04662
RSECT3	−0.07743	1.00000	−0.15953	−0.15179	−0.27157	−0.18368	−0.19857
RSECT4	−0.03745	−0.15953	1.00000	−0.07342	−0.13135	−0.08884	−0.09604
RSECT5	−0.03563	−0.15179	−0.07342	1.00000	−0.12498	−0.08453	−0.09138
RSECT6	−0.06375	−0.27157	−0.13135	−0.12498	1.00000	−0.15123	−0.16349
RSECT7	−0.04312	−0.18368	−0.08884	−0.08453	−0.15123	1.00000	−0.11058
RSECT8	−0.04662	−0.19857	−0.09604	−0.09138	−0.16349	−0.11058	1.00000
UNION	−0.03734	0.04329	0.03353	−0.00277	−0.01641	−0.00578	0.08528
SOCSEC	−0.04655	0.01942	−0.00814	0.06607	0.01013	−0.01405	0.08429
CONTRACT	−0.04445	0.02613	0.00231	0.07771	−0.00898	−0.01839	0.04263
DIST	−0.24389	0.07752	−0.16957	0.05958	0.30937	0.15536	−0.08673
DTRAIN	0.00777	0.01029	0.01066	0.02569	−0.03201	0.01751	0.08158
FSIZE	−0.00743	0.01504	0.01664	0.00373	−0.01205	−0.02612	0.10565
LOGFSIZE	−0.02972	0.04374	−0.00027	0.06583	−0.02568	−0.02341	0.10310

Source: 1978 World Bank–DANE Household Survey.

UNION	SOCSEC	CONTRACT	DIST	DTRAIN	FSIZE	LOGFSIZE	Variable
0.18114	0.22217	0.15245	−0.15087	0.12823	0.12089	0.21155	LOGINC
−0.01088	−0.08903	−0.15458	0.04293	−0.10534	−0.00187	−0.13051	EXPER
−0.03298	−0.09729	−0.15413	0.02778	−0.10972	−0.02004	−0.14093	EXPSQ
−0.06201	−0.04938	−0.00839	−0.02140	0.02549	−0.06592	−0.00645	DBOG
−0.00780	0.02720	−0.00183	−0.01026	−0.03197	−0.03297	−0.02030	DCITY
0.04124	0.04327	0.03102	−0.06912	0.07223	0.00435	0.01215	DTOWN
0.07747	0.04761	0.03373	−0.00250	0.00975	0.08332	0.01986	DURB
−0.07324	−0.05290	−0.04129	0.04349	−0.02561	−0.02120	−0.06495	DUMP
0.09400	0.12653	0.10853	−0.07155	0.10461	−0.01410	0.08297	DUMS
0.09233	0.14482	0.11818	−0.11154	0.07632	0.12078	0.14839	DUMH
0.06250	0.15104	0.13412	−0.09059	0.10901	0.06211	0.11550	PRIMED
0.15247	0.24297	0.18982	−0.15736	0.15665	0.08215	0.19305	SECED
0.12729	0.16272	0.12525	−0.11905	0.08181	0.11369	0.15761	HIGHED
0.07412	0.12612	0.09522	−0.07691	0.06912	0.17735	0.16189	POSTED
−0.03734	−0.04655	−0.04445	−0.24389	0.00777	−0.00743	−0.02972	RSECT1
0.04329	0.01942	0.02613	0.07752	0.01029	0.01504	0.04374	RSECT3
0.03353	−0.00814	0.00231	−0.16957	0.01066	0.01664	−0.00027	RSECT4
−0.00277	0.06607	0.07771	0.05958	0.02569	0.00373	0.06583	RSECT5
−0.01641	0.01013	−0.00898	0.30937	−0.03201	−0.01205	−0.02568	RSECT6
−0.00578	−0.01405	−0.01839	0.15536	0.01751	−0.02612	−0.02341	RSECT7
0.08528	0.08429	0.04263	−0.08673	0.08158	0.10565	0.10310	RSECT8
1.00000	0.27598	0.21295	−0.01121	0.19133	0.22858	0.37953	UNION
0.27598	1.00000	0.53882	0.02309	0.29983	0.21470	0.55353	SOCSEC
0.21295	0.53882	1.00000	0.03551	0.23670	0.13999	0.47585	CONTRACT
−0.01121	0.02309	0.03551	1.00000	−0.02744	−0.02149	0.02599	DIST
0.19133	0.29983	0.23670	−0.02744	1.00000	0.22458	0.32682	DTRAIN
0.22858	0.21470	0.13999	−0.02149	0.22458	1.00000	0.59782	FSIZE
0.37953	0.55353	0.47585	0.02599	0.32682	0.59782	1.00000	LOGFSIZE

Table 8A-3. *Earnings Functions for Male Workers in Bogotá*
Using Different Income Variables, 1978

Variable	Log monthly earnings	Log HWAGE[a]	Log YRLYINC[b]
DUMP	0.011	0.022	0.034
	(0.4)	(0.4)	(0.5)
DUMS	0.226	0.235	0.281
	(2.6)	(2.7)	(2.8)
DUMH	0.526	0.624	0.693
	(3.5)	(3.9)	(4.0)
PRIMED	0.071	0.090	0.067
	(3.5)	(4.1)	(2.9)
SECED	0.073	0.086	0.067
	(7.5)	(8.4)	(6.8)
HIGHED	0.099	0.109	0.075
	(3.4)	(3.5)	(2.6)
POSTED	0.110	0.026	0.085
	(2.4)	(0.6)	(2.2)
EXPER	0.063	0.055	0.083
	(20.4)	(16.7)	(23.3)
EXPSQ	−0.0009	−0.0008	−0.00012
	(15.8)	(2.4)	(18.0)
DBOG	0.120	0.161	0.103
	(3.6)	(4.6)	(2.7)
DCITY	0.180	0.191	0.182
	(2.4)	(2.3)	(2.1)
DTOWN	0.162	0.171	0.092
	(2.9)	(2.9)	(1.4)
DURB	0.077	0.125	0.076
	(2.2)	(3.4)	(1.9)
RSECT1	0.023	0.131	−0.092
	(0.2)	(1.3)	(0.9)
RSECT3	0.201	0.225	0.236
	(5.7)	(6.0)	(5.8)
RSECT4	0.223	0.163	0.260
	(4.5)	(3.1)	(4.5)

Variable	Log monthly earnings	Log HWAGE[a]	Log YRLYINC[b]
RSECT5	0.255	0.273	0.277
	(4.9)	(4.9)	(4.5)
RSECT6	0.207	0.245	0.190
	(5.1)	(5.7)	(4.1)
RSECT7	0.243	0.282	0.292
	(5.0)	(5.4)	(5.2)
RSECT8	0.601	0.584	0.593
	(12.1)	(11.0)	(10.3)
UNION	0.054	0.081	0.066
	(2.6)	(3.6)	(2.8)
SOCSEC	0.089	0.067	0.137
	(3.2)	(2.2)	(4.1)
CONTRACT	0.049	0.044	0.083
	(2.0)	(1.7)	(3.0)
DIST	−0.025	−0.025	−0.031
	(6.4)	(6.1)	(7.0)
CONST	7.05	1.69	2.26
R^2	0.536	0.533	0.513
Number of observations	2,819	2,928	2,921
Mean dependent variable	8.70	3.42	4.15

Note: t statistics in parentheses.

a. $\text{HWAGE} = \dfrac{\text{monthly earnings}}{4 \times \text{weekly hours}}$.

b. $\text{YRLYINC} = \dfrac{\text{monthly earnings} \times \text{months worked}}{1,000}$.

Table 8A-4. *Mean Values of Variables for Female Workers
in Bogotá, 1973–78, and Cali, 1978*

	Bogotá				Cali
Variable	1973	1975	1977	1978	1978
YRSEDU	5.64	6.46	6.56	7.10	—
DUMP	0.47	0.48	0.48	0.44	0.51
DUMS	0.09	0.11	0.16	0.17	0.09
DUMH	0.04	0.07	0.06	0.10	0.04
PRIMED	3.87	4.12	4.15	4.19	3.98
SECED	1.52	1.90	2.05	2.36	1.58
HIGHED	0.23	0.36	0.32	0.49	0.19
POSTED	0.18	0.085	0.043	0.06	0.024
EXPER	17.72	17.03	17.60	17.62	18.37
EXPSQ	465.37	433.92	467.74	477.58	459.15
DBOG (DCALI)	0.36	0.32	0.33	0.44	0.42
DCITY	0.01	—	—	0.015	0.014
DTOWN	0.05	—	—	0.06	0.078
RSECT1	0.029	0.017	0.028	0.014	0.010
RSECT2	0.145	—	—	0.154	0.099
RSECT3	0.210	0.240	0.220	0.207	0.170
RSECT4	0.086	0.098	0.070	0.058	0.120
RSECT5	0.080	0.074	0.064	0.067	0.363
RSECT6	0.180	0.190	0.170	0.177	0.150
RSECT7	0.160	0.120	0.180	0.117	0.188
RSECT8	0.110	0.120	0.130	0.200	—
DIST	6.88	7.11	6.98	7.15	—
Log of monthly earnings	6.63	7.37	7.73	8.20	—

— Not applicable.

Sources: 1973 population census; 1975, 1977 DANE household surveys EH8E and EH15; and 1978 World Bank–DANE Household Survey EH21.

Table 8A-5. *Earnings Functions for Male Workers in Bogotá by Age Group, 1978*

Variable	Age group					
	15–24	*25–34*	*35–44*	*45–54*	*55–64*	*65 +*
YRSEDU	0.103*	0.118*	0.126*	0.105*	0.085*	0.134*
EXPER	0.069*	0.137	−0.063	0.109	0.078	0.132
EXPSQ	−0.0006	−0.0010	0.0016*	−0.0016	−0.0010	−0.0011
DBOG	0.118	0.132*	0.304*	−0.007	−0.030	−0.024
DCITY	0.403*	0.344*	0.206	−0.263	0.140	n.a.
DTOWN	0.736*	0.143	0.109	0.062	−0.363	−2.295
DURB	0.143	0.078	0.168*	−0.013	−0.007	−0.191
RSECT1	0.188	0.053	−0.167	0.138	n.a.	0.131
RSECT3	0.163*	0.282*	0.108	0.366*	0.108	0.268
RSECT4	0.089	0.307*	0.139	0.213	0.555*	1.090
RSECT5	0.144	0.198*	0.250*	0.510*	1.24*	0.179
RSECT6	0.103	0.230*	0.240*	0.363*	0.446*	0.078
RSECT7	0.154*	0.291*	0.272*	0.598*	0.491*	0.785
RSECT8	0.287*	0.769*	0.228*	1.172*	1.504*	0.803
UNION	0.022	−0.0003	0.092*	0.274*	0.428*	0.009
SOCSEC	0.064	0.177*	0.166*	−0.129	0.095	−0.048
CONTRACT	0.055	0.037	−0.070	−0.0002	−0.029	−0.300
DIST	−0.015*	−0.027*	−0.026*	−0.037*	−0.027	−0.036
CONST	6.80	7.03	8.22	6.15	6.54	3.75
R^2	0.318	0.553	0.479	0.559	0.616	0.359
Number of observations	786	936	694	393	168	60
Mean of log monthly earnings	8.22	8.80	8.92	8.97	8.88	8.48
YRSEDU (female)[a]	0.077[a]	0.062[a]	8.898	0.017	−0.040	0.516[a]

n.a. Not available.

Note: Regression coefficients marked with asterisks are significant at the 5 percent level.

a. Coefficients for female workers from similar regressions.

Source: My estimates from 1978 World Bank–DANE Household Survey.

Table 8A-6. *Earnings Functions for Male Workers in Bogotá by Region of Origin, 1978*

Variable	Bogotá	City	Town	Urban	Rural
YRSEDU	0.122*	0.138*	0.105*	0.116*	0.092*
EXPER	0.073*	0.029	0.055*	0.064*	0.059*
EXPSQ	−0.0010*	−0.0003	−0.0010	−0.0009*	−0.0007*
RSECT1	0.107	0.153	−0.238	0.265	−0.270
RSECT3	0.136*	−0.839	−0.192	−0.250*	0.300*
RSECT4	0.190*	0.0890	0.288	0.233*	0.203
RSECT5	0.308*	−0.793	0.253	0.145	0.304*
RSECT6	0.197*	0.136	0.639*	0.165*	0.201*
RSECT7	0.246*	0.045	0.548*	0.316*	0.354*
RSECT8	0.621*	0.796*	0.965*	0.762*	0.034
UNION	−0.0002	−0.033	−0.034	0.074*	0.170*
SOCSEC	0.078*	−0.226	0.003	0.122*	0.081
CONTRACT	0.072*	0.515*	0.149	−0.026	0.099
DIST	−0.017*	−0.0004	−0.058*	−0.021*	−0.036
CONST	6.26	7.13	7.41	6.87	6.98
R^2	0.595	0.599	0.560	0.553	0.240
Number of observations	1,393	77	176	796	595
Mean of log monthly earnings	8.69	9.00	9.09	8.82	8.41
YRSEDU (female)[a]	0.091*	0.093*	0.062*	0.057*	0.051*

Note: Region of origin according to place of birth. Bogotá also includes all residents there since age 10. City includes cities of about 1 million (Cali, Medellín, and Barranquilla). Town includes all towns with population greater than 100,000. Urban includes all other urban. Regression coefficients marked with asterisks are significant at the 5 percent level.

a. Coefficients for female workers from similar regressions.

Source: See table 8A-5.

Table 8A-7. *Earnings Functions for Male Workers in Bogotá by Sector of Residence, 1978*

Variable	Sector							
	1	2	3	4	5	6	7	8
YRSEDU	0.095*	0.081*	0.086*	0.104*	0.111*	0.114*	0.137*	0.163*
EXPER	0.040*	0.052*	0.059*	0.072*	0.086*	0.075*	0.060*	0.053*
EXPSQ	-0.0006*	-0.0008*	-0.0009*	-0.0010*	-0.0012*	-0.0011*	-0.0007*	-0.005*
DBOG	0.586*	0.054	-0.023	0.180	0.265*	0.250*	0.115	0.639*
DCITY	0.562*	0.156	-0.018	1.089*	-0.809	0.369*	0.057	0.926*
DTOWN	0.449*	0.156	-0.101	0.231	0.053	0.420*	0.224	0.856*
DURB	0.450*	0.052	0.047	0.152	-0.121	0.085	0.101	0.679*
UNION	0.186	0.188*	0.035	-0.017	0.219	0.151*	0.113	0.004
SOCSEC	-0.091	0.130*	0.008	0.026	-0.116	0.150*	0.223*	0.105
CONTRACT	0.187	0.034	0.080	0.005	0.007	0.067	-0.136	0.215*
DIST	-1.75	-0.027	-0.037*	0.024	-0.034	-0.036	-0.007	-0.035
CONST	8.55	7.20	7.53	6.75	7.03	6.89	6.66	6.34
R²	0.527	0.269	0.297	0.277	0.423	0.451	0.605	0.519
Number of observations	53	628	759	217	192	561	284	343
Mean of log monthly earnings	8.67	8.24	8.55	8.80	8.64	8.65	8.88	9.78
YRSEDU (female)[a]	0.096*	0.046*	0.038*	0.068*	0.066*	0.091*	0.063*	-0.100*

Note: Regression coefficients marked with asterisks are significant at the 5 percent level.

a. Coefficients for female workers from similar regressions.

Source: See table 8A-5.

9

How Segmented Is the Bogotá Labor Market?

Many of the analysts working on labor markets are motivated by a desire to understand the determinants of inequality. They want to know why the distribution of earnings is more unequal in some countries than in others. Part of the explanation may be found in the factors underlying the U-shaped Kuznets curve, which suggests that inequality rises as a country first develops and declines as income rises further. But considerable differences in inequality are observed even between countries at similar levels of development. Since income arises from the ownership of physical and human capital, the explanation of income distribution must lie in the distribution of this ownership. Moreover, the distribution of the ownership of physical assets clearly depends much more on the nature of a society's political system than does the distribution of human capital. The analysis of labor markets obviously concentrates on the latter distribution, and the issue of labor market segmentation arises essentially as a result of the perception that the observed distribution of labor earnings is somehow more unequal than what seems to be warranted by the distribution of human capital. As pointed out by Fields (1980b), notions of labor market segmentation have a long intellectual history, perhaps starting with J. S. Mill. If it is hypothesized that imperfections in the labor market cause otherwise similar people to have different levels of earnings, then the task for analysis is to measure the "similarity" and differences in earnngs after this similarity has been accounting for.

Some of the confusion in the discussion of labor market segmentation arises from the relationship that may exist between what might be termed the human capital market and the physical capital market. To the extent that acquisition of human capital is related to the initial distribution of assets and income, the resulting human capital distribution will also be uneven—and this situation will be perpetuated indefinitely unless there is deliberate policy intervention. The traditional intervention used to break the link between the distribution of physical assets and human capital has by and large been the provision of free education to all, or of tuition fees linked to means tests. Whatever the reasons for the unequal distribution of human capital, the labor market should not be considered segmented as long as the market for the resulting distribution works. Segmentation should then be shown to exist when otherwise similar people are observed to obtain different earnings. Furthermore, the group that earns higher or lower incomes should be identifiable and, as Fields (1980b) has suggested, the mechanism by which these groups become separated or protected should be identified.

There has been considerable progress over the years in the discussion of segmentation (see Cain 1976). Early arguments were based merely on observed heterogeneity in the labor market, and differences in the mean earnings of different groups were taken as evidence of segmentation. Now much of the work on the subject is devoted to identifying differences after accounting for similarities between human capital variables—which is the approach used in this study. One criticism of this approach is that it involves an econometric identification problem. If there is a protected sector that, for whatever reasons, pays relatively high wages, its selection criteria are likely to be such that the educated will be found in these better-paid jobs—even if the jobs do not actually require high education or skills. An earnings function approach would then attribute these higher earnings to human capital variables rather than to segmentation. But this problem will arise only if the supply of people with higher education equals the demand for jobs in the protected sector. Otherwise, even if the protected sector places individuals with higher skills and education in jobs that do not require them, there will be others with similar qualifications who are outside the protected sector and earning less. Thus the earnings function approach can always be used to identify the protected sector differential *unless* there is a *coincidental* clearing of the market.

This chapter uses the earnings functions developed in chapter 8 to probe these issues in the Bogotá and Cali labor markets. Although there is some evidence of the existence of some "mildly protected" sectors, the data point overwhelmingly to a surprisingly well-functioning labor market in Bogotá and Cali. As shown earlier, returns to education have been declining in these cities as the deepening of human capital stock has taken place over time. The influence of background on earnings was also investigated; differences in earnings arising from such influences are often included in a discussion of segmentation but have not been included here because they essentially belong to a discussion of the relationship between capital markets and labor markets. That relationship is itself important for understanding the nature of labor markets and the existence of inequality, and for formulating policies aimed at income redistribution.

The Protected Sector

The question of segmentation can be posed in terms of the presence of a protected sector—often called the formal sector in analyses of urban labor markets in developing countries—in which some workers earn more than otherwise similar workers because of the existence of various kinds of restrictive practices. Restriction can take the form of a government-imposed minimum wage, which has the effect of limiting employment and keeping wages in the "legal" or formal sector higher than elsewhere. Similar effects can be produced by officially legislated social security payments that employers may be required to make. On the supply side, the existence of unions in some industries or firms can serve to restrict supply and cause wages to be kept higher than in nonunion firms. A common view is that these characteristics are highly correlated and exist mainly in larger firms, many of which are owned by foreign enterprises. Size of firm is then used as the indicator separating the formal from the informal sector. All of government is usually assigned to the formal sector, as are all workers with higher education (see Mazumdar 1976a for a succinct review of work on the informal sector).

The central purpose of any analysis of segmentation is to identify intervening or segmenting variables that restrict mobility within the labor market and can thus help to explain the observed variance in earnings between people who would otherwise be regarded as equivalent. What follows is an effort to test whether four commonly used segmenting variables can help to identify a protected sector in Bogotá's labor market, and therefore help to explain observed variations in earnings. The first variable used is the presence of a UNION in the workplace. The fact that a union exists is considered sufficient to have an effect on earnings, regardless of a worker's membership in it. The second variable tested, SOCSEC, represents a worker's membership in any kind of social security scheme. This variable is used as a proxy for both the "formal" characteristics of a firm and the "minimum wage" type of effect alluded to above. One problem in using this variable is that if social security contributions are mandated for employees in certain firms or industries, employers may regard them as compensating differentials and may pay the workers a lower cash wage. A negative coefficient on the dummy SOCSEC would then be expected. A third variable, also tested as part of the effort to capture the "formal" nature of a job, is the worker's response to a question asking whether he has a written CONTRACT in his job. The fourth variable tested is the size of firm. Since the source of this variable is a question asking the employee the number of people at his place of work, the results refer to branch size rather than to the whole enterprise. It is impossible to tell, however, how well this distinction was observed in the survey.

Consider tables 8-2 and 8-3 once again and note the performance of these variables in the explanation of earnings of male workers. Examination of the correlation matrix (see table 8A-2) reveals, surprisingly, that the four variables are not highly correlated. Moreover, when introduced separately, and step by step, the coefficient estimates do not change appreciably. The coefficients of the dummy variables (from tables 8-2 and 8-3) are as follows (t statistics are in parentheses):

	Education specification	
	YRSEDU	*With* DUMP, DUMS, DUMH
UNION	0.063	0.054
	(3.1)	(2.6)
SOCSEC	0.071	0.089
	(2.6)	(3.2)
CONTRACT	0.046	0.049
	(1.9)	(2.0)
LOGFSIZE	—	0.023
		(3.3)

Union employees seem to get about 6 percent higher earnings than comparable nonunion workers. It is possible that some kinds of jobs are more prone to unionization and that these jobs also require higher skills. The data at hand provide little information on this issue, except that unionized government employees do get a high earnings premium. The SOCSEC and CONTRACT variables are significant as well, implying the existence of some kind of formal or protected sector, but the differences are not very strong. In Cali, the UNION coefficient is the only significant variable and is about twice the size of the Bogotá estimate. About one-quarter of all workers in both Bogotá and Cali are unionized and about one-half subscribe to some form of social security. Similarly, about one-half of those in Bogotá, but only about 35 percent in Cali, say they have written contracts.

The separate age group regressions were of interest in that they implied that the UNION effect was significant only for middle-aged and older workers (age 35 +) and that SOCSEC was significant only for younger workers. In the separate region-of-origin estimates (see chapter 8), only rural migrants and those from small towns seemed to gain from union membership; union membership also appeared to be of greater importance for workers in sectors 2 and 6, where there was a relatively high concentration of blue-collar workers. Results from other stratified regressions suggest that unions are more effective in the public sector, and for production and service workers (as opposed to sales workers). Further, consistent with the finding that older workers gain more from union membership, household heads and married workers gain more than secondary workers and single workers.

The composite picture is then as follows. Union membership gives greater job stability. At early stages of a worker's life cycle, union membership appears to be unimportant and the earnings of union and nonunion workers cannot be distinguished. At later stages membership in a union appears to give definite earnings advantages, although the principle of positive sorting may also be at work here (those who became union members early may have a smoother employment history and end up earning higher incomes). The union earnings differential seems to be more important for the less-skilled rural and small-town migrants, for whom union membership may be a job-screening device. This finding gives some support to the hypothesis that migrants come to urban areas and then compete to get into a protected sector. On the whole, union membership appears to be more important where there are fewer other distinctions of labor skill or quality, and thus again seems to act as a rationing or screening device.

Two points need to be emphasized here. First, although these effects have been discussed at some length, they are not found to be as important as is often supposed. The three variables UNION, SOCSEC, and CONTRACT together contribute only about 1 percent of the total log variance explained (R^2 increases from 0.530 to 0.536). Second, UNION effects seem to be stronger than the other two formal-sector proxies. The positive coefficient of SOCSEC indicates that the contribution to social security is probably not regarded as a compensating differential and is more of an indication of the "formal" nature of an enterprise.

Regression 6 in table 8-3 adds the logarithm of firm size, LOGFSIZE (along with DTRAIN), to all the other variables in the earnings function. There is little change in R^2 but the coefficient is significantly positive (0.023). The implication is that, for every doubling of firm size (assuming the relationship holds over the whole range of the size distribution of firms), earnings increase by 2.3 percent.[1] Since an employee of a firm of 100 people would thus earn about 10–12 percent more than an employee of a firm of 5 people, there is some reason to believe that the formal sector, as distinguished by size of firm, does pay somewhat higher wages than the unorganized sector. Again, however, the differences are not large and do not point to the kind of clear dichotomy between the formal or protected sector and the rest of the economy that is sometimes hypothesized.

In summary, given the proxy variables available, there is some evidence

1. FSIZE itself was also tried, but the coefficient was found to be negligible and insignificant.

that the organized or protected sector does tend to pay its employees more than the unorganized sector, but the differences are not large enough to warrant excessive concern. Little is added to the explanation of the log variance of earnings by consideration of these variables. If segmentation exists in the Bogotá labor market, the formal-informal or organized-unorganized dichotomy is not a very useful way of capturing it.

Stratification by Nature of Employment

Another way to look for segmentation is to estimate earnings functions for different groups of workers and to test whether the returns to schooling are significantly different for the different groups. Tables 9A-1 to 9A-4 report the estimated regressions stratified by employment status, occupational status, employment in public or private sectors, and industry of activity.

The interesting feature of table 9A-1, which stratifies the sample into blue-collar and white-collar employees,[2] and owners or self-employed, is that the returns to education are not significantly different for the self-employed and white-collar employees. It is often suggested that urban labor markets in developing countries are segmented owing to the existence of a large, unorganized self-employed sector, whereas jobs in large firms are protected and pay higher wages than the rest of the market. The low coefficient of YRSEDU for blue-collar workers is partly due to truncation bias (the geometric mean of blue-collar earnings is about half of that for white-collar workers). There are few high earners and the variance of years of education is also low. The earnings function for white-collar workers explains as much as 61 percent of the log variance of earnings. A few other results are of interest:

- The residential location differentials are least for blue-collar workers and most for the self-employed.
- The union differential is most important for blue-collar workers.
- All the DIST coefficients are significantly negative and the one for the self-employed is greatest.

These observations support points made earlier. Residential location appears to matter for relatively higher-paid individuals and for the self-employed. The self-employed are probably more dependent on their location for their income; central locations are more desirable than peripheral ones;

2. For the purposes of analysis, a worker described as an obrero is classified as blue-collar and one described as an empleado is classified as white-collar. These are somewhat inexact translations from the Spanish terms, but are close enough.

and richer neighborhoods are better for business than poorer ones, presumably at least in part because demand is higher in the former.

Table 9A-2 reports estimated earnings functions for the sample stratified by type of occupation. Few conclusions can be drawn from this stratification because of econometric problems. Once again, since occupational classifications are correlated with earnings, the estimates are biased on the low side because of truncation bias. Thus administrative and managerial workers get a low coefficient of YRSEDU (all with high income as well as high levels of education), as do production workers (low incomes, low education).

Table 9A-3 shows that the earnings function performs better for government workers than for the private sector with respect to the log variance of earnings explained. As would be expected for a codified wage structure in the public sector, location of residence is not as important as it is in the private sector. Similarly, the background variables are not significant in the public sector. The returns to education are virtually equal, but again, as might be expected, experience brings somewhat higher rewards in the private sector. Union members in the public sector earn considerably more than others — almost 20 percent more — but those who subscribe to a social security scheme seem to be subject to compensating differentials and earn less. Thus the public sector wage structure conforms more to the human capital model of earnings and is perhaps more dependent on screening and certification methods, as Berry (1980b) has pointed out. The fact that the returns to education are similar indicates that the two sectors are competitive.

Table 9A-4, reports earnings function estimates for the sample stratified by industry of employment. All the industry groups have a "respectable" R^2 and the coefficients for YRSEDU are not significantly different except for transport and communication workers. I have no explanation for this, especially in view of the fact that the construction workers' YRSEDU coefficient is not low. It is interesting that the region-of-origin effects are significant mainly for this group, the most unskilled industry category. Reassuringly, the estimates for public administration and other services correspond closely with the previous public sector mates; this is the only industry category with a significant union effect.

This set of stratifications by a series of employment-related variables offers little evidence of significant segmentation in the Bogotá labor market. The self-employed and employee estimates indicate that there is relatively free entry between the two sectors: it is difficult to argue that the organized sector is protected. The estimates for occupational categories suffer from econometric problems owing to truncation bias, so little can be said about differences based on occupation except that some low-skill, low-income occupations and other high-skill, high-income ones are self-evidently correlated with different levels of educational achievement. The estimates for industry groups, as well as the one contrasting employment in the public and private sectors, reveal that returns to education are virtually equal in all industries. There is, however, a very significant union effect in the public sector — union employees appear to get a 15 – 20 percent advantage over their peers.

The last set of stratifications attempted were based on status in the family. Tables 9A-5 and 9A-6 report estimates for household heads and others, and for those who are single and married. According to Mazumdar (1979), married workers in the labor market in Bombay are paid more than equivalent single workers because of their alleged greater reliability (Griliches and Mason 1972 have also reported somewhat higher earnings for married workers). One of the characteristics of the informal sector is said to be the employment of secondary workers (nonhousehold heads). The present data indicate no significant difference in the returns to education between any of these groups. Similar observations hold for female workers as well.

The Decomposition of Labor Earnings

This section extends the analyses of income distribution and earnings functions reported thus far by undertaking a detailed decomposition of labor earnings in Bogotá. It will be recalled that when inequalities in household income and household income per capita were mapped in chapter 4, indices of inequality were calculated for different income concepts and different ranking criteria. These essentially descriptive calculations were meant to give an idea of the extent of inequality prevailing among households and individuals, but they could not offer insights into the causes of inequality. The only decompositions of inequality measures attempted were by location of residence: the results showed that spatial inequality contributed about one-quarter of total inequality in Bogotá and Cali. This would be the overall inequality prevailing in Bogotá if all income differences within geographical sectors were suppressed.

This section confirms the earlier finding that education and years of experience are the key determinant of log variance in earnings, and goes on to analyze the distribution of earnings by geographical sector and in terms of a series of widely used socioeconomic classifications (age, education, and a group of work-related categories). Because it is difficult to assess the importance of the different magnitudes of inequality obtained, the results are compared, where possible, with Anand's (1983) estimates for labor earnings for Malaysia.

The Spatial Distribution of Personal Earnings

Tables 9-1 and 9-2 present intrasectoral and intersectoral indices of inequality in labor earnings for Bogotá and Cali, respectively. In this section,

Table 9-1. *Distribution of Monthly Labor Earnings in Bogotá by Sector, 1973–78*

Sector	1973 Theil index	1973 Rank[a]	1975 Theil index	1975 Rank	1977 Theil index	1977 Rank	1978 Theil index	1978 Rank	1978 Mean[b]	1978 Rank[c]
1	0.565	6	0.392	4	0.645	8	0.228	1	0.67	2
2	0.380	2	0.363	3	0.271	1	0.268	3	0.54	1
3	0.349	1	0.281	1	0.324	2	0.259	2	0.76	3
4	0.426	3	0.306	2	0.446	4	0.355	4	1.00	6
5	0.523	5	0.462	6	0.465	6	0.415	5	0.91	4
6	0.521	4	0.430	5	0.416	3	0.423	6	0.95	5
7	0.636	7	0.487	7	0.484	7	0.486	8	1.14	7
8	0.675	8	0.549	8	0.460	5	0.449	7	2.06	8
All sectors	0.634		0.452		0.460		0.481		7,592[d]	
Between-group contribution										
Sectors (Theil index)	0.113		0.043		0.046		0.096			
Sectors (percent)	17.9		9.5		9.9		20.0			
Comunas[e] (percent)	26.4		18.0		18.4		25.9			

a. By ascending order of inequality.
b. Mean of earnings in sector as proportion of overall mean.
c. Ranking by mean earnings in sector.
d. Overall mean earnings in 1978 Colombian pesos.
e. Between-group contribution if grouped by comunas (see map 3-1).

Sources: 1973 population census; 1975 DANE Household Survey EH8E; 1977 DANE Household Survey EH15; and 1978 World Bank–DANE Household Survey EH21.

Table 9-2. *Distribution of Monthly Labor Earnings in Cali by Sector, 1973–78*

Sector	1973 Theil index	Rank[a]	1977 Theil index	Rank	1978 Theil index	Rank	Mean[b]	Rank[c]
1	0.524	4	0.312	3	0.590	7	1.36	4
2	0.628	5	0.499	6	0.480	4	2.00	7
3	0.400	2	0.284	1	0.272	2	0.85	3
4	0.337	1	0.340	4	0.255	1	0.74	1
5	0.439	3	0.308	2	0.291	3	0.77	2
6	0.760	7	0.559	7	0.500	5	1.40	5
7	0.640	6	0.372	5	0.511	6	1.58	6
All sectors	0.592		0.454		0.440		6,322[d]	
Between-group contribution								
Sectors (Theil index)	0.077		0.051		0.064			
Sectors (percent)	13.0		11.3		14.6			
Comunas[e] (percent)	21.4		21.3		23.1			

a. By ascending order of inequality.
b. Mean earnings in sector as proportion of overall mean.
c. By mean earnings in sector.
d. Overall mean earnings in 1978 Colombian pesos.
e. Between-group contribution if grouped by comunas (see map 3-2).
Sources: 1973 population census; 1975 DANE Household Survey EH8E; 1977 DANE Household Survey EH15; and 1978 World Bank–DANE Household Survey EH21.

earnings are defined as monthly earnings, and the decompositions are applied to earnings of all workers (male and female). As might be expected, the pattern is broadly similar to the distribution of household income and of HINCAP, but there are some differences. By and large, the poorer sectors of Bogotá (1, 2, and 3) have lower levels of intrasectoral inequality than the richer sectors (7 and 8). Put another way, the richer sectors do have some poor people living in them along with the rich, whereas the poorer sectors consist almost solely of poor people. There is about a 1-to-4 ratio between the mean of earnings in the poorest sector (sector 2) and in the richest (sector 8); the equivalent ratio for HINCAP is about 1 to 5. Thus spatial disparities as measured by the differences between means are less pronounced for labor earnings than for HINCAP. The intergroup contribution to the Theil index is also lower for labor earnings than for HINCAP.

Clearly, spatial income disparities in Bogotá are not caused solely by the maldistribution of labor earnings by location of residence. Earnings functions analysis (see chapter 8) has already shown that the location of residence (acting as a proxy for other unmeasured characteristics) is a significant determinant of labor earnings, but does not contribute much to the explanation of log variance, after other factors are accounted for. Tables 9A-7 and 9A-8 give the same information as does table 9-1 but use log variance as the inequality index; the spatial contribution is smaller than for the Theil index since the log variance is more sensitive to low incomes.

The fact that the intersectoral contribution to inequality is lower for labor earnings than for HINCAP indicates that dependency ratios are higher among households in poorer sectors. The spatial maldistribution of earnings is then compounded by larger families, lower participation rates, or higher unemployment rates.[3] Any of these would raise dependency ratios. Cause and effect are not easy to disentangle here: Does the presence of children inhibit poorer women from working because of child care responsibilities? Are women out of the labor force or unemployed because they can only take part-time jobs with less rigid work patterns? The spatial dimension is important in this respect. It has been demonstrated for Bogotá that since large areas in the south of the city have predominantly low-income populations, these areas have comparatively fewer jobs per resident population than the richer areas. Purchasing power in these areas is simply much lower. As a consequence, there is extensive commuting from the poorer sectors to the richer sectors, but very little in reverse. It is also true, however, that unemployment and participation rates differ little between sectors — though there are differences whose significance is difficult to assess statistically. The absence of large differences does not mean that the poor would not have higher participation rates, and therefore be better off, were spatial disparities not present. These questions cannot be answered by the evidence at hand: only suggestive inferences can be drawn.

Between 1973 and 1978 the Theil index fell from 0.38 to 0.27 in Bogotá's sector 2 and from 0.68 to 0.45 in sector 8. Thus both the poorest and richest sectors have been growing more homogeneous (and more distinct from each other) over time. Indeed, inequality fell within all sectors between 1975 and 1978, although the overall index of inequality rose. In earlier years, the Theil index had been greater for some sectors than the overall index; by 1978, intrasectoral inequality was lower in all sectors than overall inequality in the city. Cali exhibits similar trends, though the spatial disparity is somewhat less pronounced there. The ratio of mean earnings in Cali's poorest sector (4) to those in the city's richest sector (2) is less than 1 to 3; there is also clearer evidence that overall inequality has been declining in Cali.

Evidently, spatial disparities are becoming more pronounced in both cities in terms of labor earnings distributions as well as those of household income

---

3. As noted in chapter 7, however, participation rates for the poorer sectors are not different from those for other sectors.

Table 9-3. *Decomposition of Labor Earnings in Bogotá and Cali, 1978*

Variable and city	Between-group contribution (percent)		Number of groups
	Theil	Log variance	
Age			
Bogotá	11.4	8.7 ⎫	7
Cali	11.0	9.2 ⎭	
Education			
Bogotá	38.0	31.7 ⎫	4
Cali	26.6	22.4 ⎭	
Employee status			
Bogotá	8.0	7.8 ⎫	3
Cali	7.5	7.9 ⎭	
Bogotá	19.1	17.6 ⎫	6
Cali	13.4	12.6 ⎭	
Occupation			
Bogotá	40.3	32.7 ⎫	7
Cali	24.8	17.5 ⎭	
Bogotá	41.2	33.8 ⎫	13
Cali	31.1	24.5 ⎭	
Industry of activity			
Bogotá	4.6	4.4 ⎫	8
Cali	3.9	3.3 ⎭	
Bogotá	13.5	14.7 ⎫	13
Cali	11.3	12.7 ⎭	
Firm size			
Bogotá	7.5	11.6 ⎫	6
Cali	7.4	11.7 ⎭	
Sector			
Bogotá	20.0	11.9	8
Cali	14.6	6.5	7
Comunas			
Bogotá	25.9	16.7	38
Cali	23.1	12.7	25

Source: My estimates from 1978 World Bank–DANE Household Survey.

and household income per capita. If the spatial separation of income groups is considered harmful for opportunities for the poor in the future (see chapter 8 on the feedback effects of residential location on income opportunities) as well as for social cohesion in the present, then these findings are truly a cause for concern.

The next step in the analysis is to decompose the distribution of labor earnings by a series of socioeconomic classifications — age, education, employment status, occupation, industry of activity, and size of firm — and by subcategories within each classification. Table 9-3 summarizes the decomposition by the main classifications utilized. In every case, the percentage contributions to inequality of the groupings are lower for Cali than for Bogotá. As noted earlier, overall inequality is also lower in Cali. A smaller city has a somewhat less variegated or heterogeneous labor market. Occupations are perhaps less specialized at the top end. The highest financial and government functions are typically located in the political capital of a country or in its main business center; Bogotá serves as both in the case of Colombia.

Age and Education

It is somewhat surprising that age-group differences contribute only about 9 percent to total inequality in labor earnings. The implication is that age-earnings profiles are relatively flat for the majority of workers. Although age-earnings profiles are very steep for the better educated (see chapter 6), they are much less so for the less educated. Furthermore, almost half of the labor force in Bogotá still has only primary schooling or less. Moreover, as table 9-4 shows, after age 25 the overall age-earnings profile is rather flat, but inequalities *within* age groups rise consistently with age, except in the case

Table 9-4. *Distribution of Earnings by Age Group in Bogotá and Cali, 1978*

	Bogotá			Cali		
Age group	Mean earnings[a]	Theil index	Percentage in category	Mean earnings[a]	Theil index	Percentage in category
12–14	0.29	0.145	1.0	0.32	0.215	0.8
15–24	0.55	0.207	30.2	0.59	0.194	30.2
25–34	1.15	0.438	30.0	1.16	0.391	30.8
35–44	1.27	0.459	20.4	1.26	0.435	18.3
45–54	1.28	0.532	12.1	1.21	0.464	12.7
55–64	1.23	0.548	4.7	1.27	0.581	4.9
65 +	0.95	0.514	1.5	0.65	0.577	2.5
All age groups	7,600[b]	0.481	100.0	6,350[b]	0.440	100.0
Total number of workers (thousands)		1,180			350	
Intergroup percentage contribution						
Theil index		11.4			11.0	
Log variance		8.7			9.2	

Note: Here and in the following tables in this chapter percentages may not add to 100 because of rounding.

a. Mean monthly earnings of age group expressed as a multiple of the overall mean.

b. Overall mean in 1978 Colombian pesos.

Source: My estimates from 1978 World Bank–DANE Household Survey.

Table 9-5. *Distribution of Earnings by Education Group in Bogotá and Cali,*
1978

Education group	Bogotá			Cali		
	Mean earnings[a]	Theil index	Percentage in category	Mean earnings[a]	Theil index	Percentage in category
None	0.38	0.160	3.6	0.44	0.176	5.0
Primary	0.56	0.239	42.1	0.68	0.283	48.7
Secondary	0.92	0.356	38.4	1.16	0.388	37.7
Higher	2.49	0.286	15.9	2.67	0.267	7.7
All education groups	7,600[b]	0.481	100.0	6,350[b]	0.440	100.0
Total number of workers (thousands)		1,180			350	
Intergroup percentage contribution						
Theil index		38.0			26.6	
Log variance		31.7			22.4	

a. Mean monthly earnings of age group expressed as a multiple of the overall mean.
b. Overall mean in 1978 Colombian pesos.
Source: See table 9-3.

of those over 65. This is true for both Bogotá and Cali. Note that earnings
are very egalitarian for the young age group (15–24), but disparities rise with
age as those with more education increase their earnings—along with others
who are successful—while the rest have to live on almost the same earnings
for most of their lives. This is of great importance for the study of life cycle
effects on poverty. Those who have relatively flat age-earnings profiles experience decreases in per capita real household income as family formation
takes place and there are more mouths to feed. Many studies show a relatively
higher incidence of malnutrition among children at this point. Flat age-
earnings profiles could be one of the principal causes of such a phenomenon.

Differences in educational achievement account for 32–38 percent of the
overall inequality in Bogotá and about 22–27 percent in Cali (see table
9-5, which is based on four subclassifications: those with no education, any
primary, any secondary, and any higher education). According to table
9-5, a much larger proportion of Bogotá's labor force has higher education.
The capital city presumably attracts (and has jobs for) the more highly
educated. This partly accounts for the relatively higher level of inequality in
Bogotá. Furthermore, the highest level of inequality is found among the
group with secondary education. Those with higher education have more
uniformly high incomes and those with only primary education, more uniformly low incomes. Much of the unexplained variance in earnings must be

among workers with secondary schooling who have the potential for higher earnings; some make it, but many do not. Third, because of the presence of larger numbers of better-educated workers, mean earnings in Bogotá are somewhat higher than in Cali; even the mean of the group with secondary schooling is less than the overall mean. The intergroup contribution is large and attests to the importance of education in determining earnings and earnings potential.

Employment Status

Table 9-6 gives the decomposition of labor earnings according to groups of workers by employment status. Two subclassifications were attempted. The first, with only three groups, merely distinguished between all employees, owners or bosses, and the self-employed. The second subclassification broke the employee category down into blue-collar workers, white-collar workers, domestic workers, and "nonremunerated." The greatest inequality is found among the self-employed. Entrepreneurial skills, the exercise of initiative, and other unmeasured characteristics are likely to be important for this group, leading some to be quite poor and others to be very well off. The Theil index for inequality within this group is higher than the index for all workers taken together. In addition, the less-skilled groups — blue-collar workers and domestic workers — have the lowest intragroup indices.[4] The labor market for these categories must be homogeneous as well as competitive. These poorly paid groups constitute almost 30 percent of the labor force. Owners' and bosses' earnings are also distributed in a relatively egalitarian fashion; the Theil index is only about $0.34-0.35$. This is rather surprising, since one would expect there to be many small, relatively poor owners as well as rich ones. The contribution of the first classification to overall inequality is only about 10 percent, but that of the second is about 20 percent; this suggests that an expansion of categories is worth examining. Anand (1983) used four categories, the fourth being unremunerated workers, housewives, and the like. The intergroup contribution for his four categories was about 10 percent, which is comparable to these estimates.

Occupational Status

Occupational differences account for about $33-40$ percent of the inequality in earnings in Bogotá and $17-25$ percent in Cali; these figures are again similar to Anand's (1983) findings for Malaysia. The intergroup contribution does not increase much if one changes the classification from the

---

4. Ignore "unremunerated workers" as a misclassified and small category.

Table 9-6. *Distribution of Earnings by Employment Status in Bogotá and Cali, 1978*

Employment status	Bogotá			Cali		
	Mean earnings[a]	Theil index	Percentage in category	Mean earnings	Theil index	Percentage in category
Three categories						
Employee[b]	0.97	0.445	75.3	0.95	0.369	72.2
Owner or boss	2.25	0.338	5.5	2.31	0.354	4.7
Self-employed	0.76	0.516	19.3	0.85	0.574	22.8
Six categories						
Blue-collar[c]	0.57	0.169	21.6	0.74	0.242	25.8
White-collar[d]	1.25	0.429	45.7	1.18	0.387	39.1
Nonremunerated[e]	0.26	0.056	0.1	0.95	0.379	0.0
Owner or boss	2.25	0.338	5.5	2.31	0.354	4.7
Self-employed	0.76	0.516	19.3	0.85	0.574	22.8
Domestic	0.42	0.167	7.8	0.51	0.098	7.3
All categories	7,600[f]	0.481	100.0	6,350[f]	0.440	100.0
Total number of workers (thousands)		1,180			350	
Intergroup percentage contribution[g]						
Theil index		19.1			13.4	
Log variance		17.6			12.6	

a. Mean monthly earnings of employment group expressed as a multiple of the overall mean.
b. Includes obreros, empleados, nonremunerated workers, and domestic workers.
c. *Obrero*, loosely translated as blue-collar workers.
d. *Empleado*, loosely translated as white-collar workers.
e. Clearly misclassified since mean earnings, though low, are not zero.
f. 1978 Colombian pesos.
g. For six categories:
Source: See table 9-3.

one-digit level (seven categories) to a level using thirteen categories. The one-digit level is therefore adequate for disaggregating occupations. If agricultural workers are ignored, the level of inequality within occupations is substantially lower than the overall level except in the case of sales workers, as shown in table 9-7. Table 9A-9 gives analogous information for the more disaggregated classification scheme. Even when sales workers are separated into sales managers and others, the index of inequality does not decrease appreciably. There is clearly a higher variance of earnings among sales establishments and among the people who work in these establishments — a finding consistent with the high level of inequality found among the self-

Table 9-7. *Distribution of Earnings by Occupation in Bogotá and Cali, 1978*

Occupation	ILO code	Bogotá			Cali		
		Mean earnings[a]	Theil index	Percentage in category	Mean earnings[a]	Theil index	Percentage in category
Professional and technical	1–19	2.30	0.300	12.0	2.43	0.304	6.2
Administrative and managerial	20–29	3.53	0.137	2.9	3.11	0.288	2.2
Clerks and typists	30–39	0.92	0.219	14.3	1.05	0.250	12.5
Sales	40–49	1.06	0.523	16.0	1.07	0.529	16.7
Service	50–59	0.49	0.255	20.0	0.60	0.249	20.3
Agriculture	60–69	1.47	0.579	0.9	1.97	0.586	1.0
Production	70–98	0.61	0.197	33.8	0.80	0.291	41.4
All occupations	1–98	7,600[b]	0.482	100.0	6,350[b]	0.440	100.0
Total number of workers (thousands)		1,180			350		
Intergroup percentage contribution							
Theil index		40.3			24.8		
Log variance		32.7			17.5		

a. Mean monthly earnings in occupation expressed as a multiple of the overall mean.
b. 1978 Colombian pesos.
Source: See table 9-3.

employed, since many of the latter are likely to be engaged in trade. Surprisingly, the large category of production workers (35–40 percent of the labor force) is quite homogeneous, with a Theil index of only about 0.2 in Bogotá, and a somewhat higher figure in Cali. Within white-collar occupations — clerks and typists, administrators, and managers — the earnings distribution also seems to be within a relatively narrow band. Almost all the intraoccupation contributions to inequality are higher for Cali. The implication here is that, except for the sales category, one's choice of occupation is a very important predictor of potential earnings; indeed, the intergroup contribution of occupational categories to income inequality is of the same order of magnitude as that of education.

Industry of Activity

The industry-of-activity classification of workers turns out to be of relatively little interest from the viewpoint of income inequality. The one-digit level of classification yields an essentially negligible (4–5 percent) intergroup contribution to inequality (table 9-8). This is quite different from Anand's (1983) results for similar sector groupings in Malaysia, where the intergroup contribution is more like 15–20 percent. The result for Bogotá gives another clue to why so little evidence of labor segmentation has been found in the city. When manufacturing industries are disaggregated and twenty industrial categories are used, the intergroup contribution increases to 11–15 percent. Nonetheless, as shown in table 9-8, every industrial category has a rather heterogeneous composition of workers. Only the relatively small category of utilities has a low Theil index (0.2–0.25). The other two relatively homogeneous industrial categories are construction and transport and communications. Table 9A-10 gives the same information for the expanded

Table 9-8. *Distribution of Earnings by Industry of Activity in Bogotá and Cali, 1978*

Industry	SIC code	Bogotá			Cali		
		Mean earnings[a]	Theil index	Percentage in category	Mean earnings[a]	Theil index	Percentage in category
Agriculture and mining	1–29	1.77	0.474	1.4	1.62	0.669	1.4
Manufacturing	30–39	0.89	0.469	23.7	1.02	0.436	31.5
Utilities	40–49	1.14	0.214	0.5	1.45	0.249	1.0
Construction	50–59	0.72	0.394	7.3	0.78	0.281	6.2
Trade and commerce	60–69	0.92	0.514	23.4	0.89	0.476	24.2
Transport and communication	70–79	1.12	0.333	5.9	1.07	0.271	6.4
Financial	80–89	1.61	0.424	8.2	1.81	0.436	3.8
Public administration and social service	91–96	0.98	0.475	29.4	0.93	0.417	25.6
All categories	1–96	7,600[b]	0.482	100.0	6,350[b]	0.441	100.0
Total number of workers (thousands)			1,180			350	
Intergroup percentage contribution							
Theil index			4.6			3.9	
Log variance			4.4			3.3	

a. Mean monthly earnings in industry expressed as a multiple of the overall mean.
b. 1978 Colombian pesos.
Source: See table 9-3.

number of industrial categories (twenty), in which manufacturing industries have been disaggregated. As might be expected, the intragroup contributions to inequality fall and the intergroup contribution rises. The results suggest that the industrial classifications are not very helpful for studying inequality in labor earnings; by contrast, the occupational categories are quite distinct. Labor market segmentation is often asserted to exist between different industrial categories. In Bogotá and Cali, however, workers within industries appear to be so heterogeneous that intra-industry inequality is, in most cases, almost as great as overall inequality.

Size of Firm

The last decomposition attempted was by firm-size categories, since it is often suggested that the labor market is segmented in terms of this classification. As noted earlier, many have argued that a protected sector consisting of larger firms exists and that the much higher wages these firms pay account for much of the observed inequality in urban areas. Six firm-size subcategories are distinguished in table 9-9: 1, 2–5, 6–10, 11–25, 26–100, and 100 + workers. The intergroup contribution of firm size to inequality is only about 7–12 percent—a share lower than that for spatial disparities in earnings. As many as 45–50 percent of the workers in Bogotá and Cali work in firms with fewer than five people. The mean earnings of workers in single-employee establishments—presumably mostly self-employed service and trade activities—are considerably lower than in the other categories. There is not much difference between the means beyond the 10-worker size category. Moreover, inequality within each category does not vary much from the level found in the largest category (firms employing 100 or more people), for which the Theil index is about 0.34–0.38. The mean level of earning is somewhat higher for this category, however, and earnings are distributed within a relatively narrower band. But the overall evidence, which is consistent with the results from the earnings functions, is that firm size is not an important feature of the labor market in Bogotá or Cali. The mean levels are not very different between categories, the intergroup contribution of the classification is low, and intragroup contributions are not much different from the overall level of inequality.

Summary

This chapter has examined the extent of segmentation in the Bogotá labor market and sought to determine the sources of income inequality in Bogotá and Cali by decomposing labor earnings on the basis of a series of commonly

Table 9-9. *Distribution of Earnings by Firm Size in Bogotá and Cali, 1978*

Firm size (number of employees)	Bogotá			Cali		
	Mean earnings[a]	Theil index	Percentage in category	Mean earnings[a]	Theil index	Percentage in category
1	0.58	0.449	23.2	0.64	0.429	25.7
2–5	0.90	0.497	21.9	0.98	0.455	26.2
6–10	1.07	0.506	11.8	0.93	0.439	9.5
11–25	1.19	0.460	12.1	1.08	0.450	10.5
26–100	1.24	0.438	14.3	1.37	0.458	12.4
100+	1.25	0.374	16.6	1.31	0.335	15.7
All categories	7,505[b]	0.486	100.0	6,358[b]	0.459	100.0
Total number of workers (thousands)[c]		1,140			324	
Intergroup percentage contribution						
Theil index		7.5			7.4	
Log variance		11.6			11.7	

a. Mean monthly earnings of workers in firm-size category expressed as a multiple of the overall mean.

b. 1978 Colombian pesos.

c. The discrepancy between the total number of workers in this table and that in other tables is due to nonresponses for the firm-size question. Therefore, the overall mean income is also slightly different.

used socioeconomic classifications. The hypothesis tested was the familiar one that urban labor markets in developing countries are typically characterized by noncompeting or segmented sectors, and that workers in the protected or organized sector earn much more than similar workers doing similar jobs elsewhere in the labor market. The evidence, although not conclusive, suggests that on the whole the Bogotá labor market is relatively competitive and that a protected sector is not easy to identify.

The protected sector is usually identified as being more "formal" or organized. Four variables were used to proxy such characterization. Analysis of three of them—the existence of a union, a written employment contract, or social security contributions—showed that their presence raised workers' earnings by only about 3–6 percent. The fourth proxy, size of firm, raised earnings (ceteris paribus) by only about 2.5 percent for every doubling of firm size. Membership in a union seems to be more helpful to less-skilled and blue-collar workers and, interestingly, older workers (as opposed to new entrants to the labor force). The evidence also suggests that union membership might give workers greater job stability and higher earnings later in their permanent career. It was also found that unions have a greater effect on earnings in the public sector than in the private sector, and that union membership might be used as a screening device by prospective employers.

The second attempt to identify the protected sector focused on the returns to schooling for different categories of workers. There were virtually no differences between employees and the self-employed, between public and private sector workers, or between different industries; the level of explanation of the variance in earnings was better for some categories than for others, but not significantly so. Moreover, the earlier evidence on the returns to firm-specific and occupation-specific experience also indicated that mobility between jobs must be relatively easy.

The overall conclusion is that the labor market in Bogotá does not have a strong protected sector, and that its various segments appear to be competitive.

With regard to inequality parameters, spatial inequality was found to be less for labor earnings than for HINCAP — probably because of the higher dependency ratios of households in the poorer parts of the city. The spatial maldistribution of earnings is compounded by the existence of larger families, lower participation rates, and higher unemployment rates — all of which combine to produce a worse distribution of HINCAP. It was also found that inequality in earnings within geographical sectors has been falling consistently over time, whereas that between them has been rising. Thus people living in specific sectors are tending to become more homogeneous, and consequently the individual sectors are becoming more distinct from one another in terms of their inhabitants' incomes. Large areas of Bogotá — mainly in the south — are inhabited predominantly by poor people. Because of the resulting low purchasing power of the area as a whole, indigenous demand for labor is also low and there are comparatively fewer jobs per resident worker than in the richer sectors.

The other classifications with the most intergroup inequality were those for education and occupational status. Intragroup inequality was low for both those with higher and primary education. The group with secondary schooling exhibited the greatest intragroup inequality; its level was greater than the overall inequality. The fact that intergroup inequality was low for the age category classification confirms the relatively flat age-earnings profile that exists in Bogotá as a whole—which is in turn a consequence of the fact that most people still have only primary-level education or less. Naturally, since those with higher education have a relatively steep age-earnings profile, the degree of inequality increases within age groups along with age. Interestingly, inequality is very low within the 15–24 age group.

Among occupations, production workers were the most homogeneous category, whereas sales workers exhibited the most intragroup inequality. The intergroup contribution of this classification as a whole was as high as about 40 percent. It is somewhat surprising that the production-worker group exhibits low internal inequality, since one would have expected a wide variety of skill levels within the group. Significantly, neither the industry nor the size of firm classification contributes much to overall inequality. Labor market segmentation literature regularly focuses on these variables for identifying labor market segmentation, and, as was noted earlier, these categories may well contribute more to income inequality in other countries (as was found in Malaysia). To summarize, the results given here confirm that the labor market in Bogotá cannot be considered segmented when analyzed by the conventional variables of firm size or industry of activity.

These results suggest that the level of education and choice of occupation are the most important factors determining labor earnings in Bogotá and Cali. To the extent that poor education as well as low aspirations (e.g., in the choice of education) result, at least in part, from living in a poor section of the city, the increasing spatial segregation measured by increases in the index of spatial income segregation (see chapter 4) is a cause for real concern.

Another point to note is that the intergroup contribution to inequality was consistently lower for Cali than for Bogotá, as was the overall level of inequality. Being a smaller city, Cali clearly has a much less heterogeneous and variegated labor market, particularly at the highest skill levels.

Table 9A-1. *Earnings Functions for Workers in Bogotá by Type of Job, 1978*

	Male			Female			
Variable	Blue-collar	White-collar	Owner or self-employed	Blue-collar	White-collar	Owner or self-employed	Maids
YRSEDU	0.065*	0.121*	0.115*	0.008	0.088*	0.068*	0.028
EXPER	0.058*	0.058*	0.065*	0.023*	0.046*	-0.019	0.014
EXPSQ	-0.0008*	-0.0008*	0.0009*	-0.0004*	-0.0008*	0.0002	-0.0003
DBOG	0.152*	-0.007	0.136	0.071	0.062	-0.280*	-0.014
DCITY	0.331*	0.154	-0.038	-0.345	-0.117	-0.928*	0.049
DTOWN	0.116	0.148*	0.047	0.039	0.091	-0.012	-0.327
DURB	0.072	-0.036	0.147	0.045	-0.029	-0.062	0.047
RSECT1	0.188	-0.110	0.040	—	0.144	-0.630	0.387
RSECT3	0.193*	0.100*	0.313	0.080	0.115	0.154	0.359*
RSECT4	0.181*	0.156*	0.318*	0.091	0.075	0.125	0.157
RSECT5	0.091	0.178*	0.573*	0.043	0.273*	0.345	0.093
RSECT6	0.117*	0.204	0.313*	0.195*	0.172*	0.188	0.329
RSECT7	0.158*	0.257*	0.341*	0.005	0.152*	0.237	0.261
RSECT8	0.184	0.641*	0.780*	0.072	0.384*	0.869*	0.342*

UNION	0.148*	0.075*	0.034	0.049	0.207*	1.560	—
SOCSEC	0.076*	0.093*	0.226*	0.276*	0.138*	0.144	0.118
CONTRACT	0.041	0.138	—	0.125*	0.058	—	—
DIST	-0.016*	-0.027*	-0.037*	-0.005	-0.017*	-0.012	-0.004
CONST	7.10	6.88	6.86	7.39	6.98	7.66	7.47
R^2	0.327	0.610	0.414	0.299	0.438	0.218	0.016
Number of observations	822	1,286	823	238	940	334	357
Mean of log monthly earnings	8.28	8.94	8.72	8.04	8.53	7.70	7.96

— Not applicable.

Note: Coefficients marked with an asterisk are significant at the 5 percent level.

Source: My estimates from 1978 World Bank–DANE Household Survey.

Table 9A-2. *Earnings Functions for Male Workers in Bogotá by Occupation, 1978*

Variable	Professional and technical (1–19)[a]	Administrative and managerial (20–29)	Clerks and typists (30–39)	Sales (40-49)	Service (50–59)	Production (70–98)
YRSEDU	0.135*	0.035	0.082*	0.117*	0.086*	0.069*
EXPER	0.078*	0.031	0.059*	0.067*	0.034*	0.058*
EXPSQ	−0.0012*	−0.0007	−0.0008*	−0.0009*	−0.0006*	−0.0009*
DBOG	0.056	0.101	0.062	0.130	0.024	0.118*
DCITY	0.352	−0.034	0.284	−0.130	0.128	0.111
DTOWN	0.001	0.096	0.192	0.270	−0.062	0.108
DURB	−0.044	0.259	0.065	0.149	−0.098	0.077
RSECT1	0.416*	n.a.[b]	0.248	−0.312	−0.127	0.144
RSECT3	0.325*	0.497	0.162*	0.095	−0.049	0.242*
RSECT4	0.263	0.504	0.270*	0.193	−0.107	0.299*
RSECT5	0.687*	0.526	0.191	0.489*	0.023	0.167*
RSECT6	0.487*	0.368	0.269*	0.234	−0.037	0.202*
RSECT7	0.586*	0.372	0.346*	0.226	0.142	0.188*
RSECT8	0.846*	0.879*	0.594*	0.647*	−0.280	0.193*
UNION	−0.076	−0.002	0.115*	−0.040	0.274*	0.144*
SOCSEC	0.041	−0.054	−0.264*	0.185	0.050	n.a.[b]
CONTRACT	0.164*	−0.030	0.164*	0.070	0.008	0.015
DIST	−0.040	0.221	−0.032*	−0.058*	−0.013	−0.020*
CONST	6.47	8.47	7.24	6.92	7.31	7.14
R^2	0.566	0.210	0.463	0.359	0.141	0.288
Number of observations	377	124	337	488	219	1,331
Mean of log monthly earnings	9.59	10.02	8.75	8.74	8.32	8.34
YRSEDU (female)[c]	0.061*	n.a.[b]	0.086*	0.049*	0.042*	0.027

n.a. Not available.
Note: Coefficients marked with an asterisk are significant at the 5 percent level.
a. ILO code.
b. The number of observations is inadequate for estimation.
c. Coefficient for female workers from similar regressions.
Source: See table 9A-1.

Table 9A-3. *Earnings Functions for Workers in Bogotá by Type of Firm, 1978*

Variable	Male		Female	
	Government	Private	Government	Private
YRSEDU	0.113*	0.118*	0.072*	0.066*
EXPER	0.052*	0.066*	0.045*	0.017*
EXPSQ	−0.0006*	−0.0009*	−0.0009*	−0.0003*
DBOG	0.004	0.102*	0.004	−0.072
DCITY	−0.160	0.180*	−0.203	−0.265*
DTOWN	0.245*	0.137*	0.203	−0.168*
DURB	−0.009	0.085*	0.070	−0.053
RSECT1	−0.013	−0.017	0.284	0.160
RSECT3	−0.074	0.219*	−0.122	0.225*
RSECT4	0.065	0.214*	−0.140	0.160*
RSECT5	−0.087	0.284*	0.023	0.271*
RSECT6	0.119	0.202*	0.072	0.272*
RSECT7	0.233*	0.262*	0.118	0.292*
RSECT8	0.482*	0.730*	0.279*	0.528*
UNION	0.196*	0.058*	0.214*	0.113*
SOCSEC	−0.130*	0.112*	0.288*	0.206*
CONTRACT	0.143*	0.029	−0.004	0.169*
DIST	−0.021*	−0.027*	−0.024	−0.014*
CONST	7.12	6.81	7.34	7.26
R^2	0.679	0.486	0.447	0.305
Number of observations	482	2,429	300	1,562
Mean of log monthly earnings	9.14	8.60	8.84	8.09

Note: Coefficients marked with an asterisk are significant at the 5 percent level.
Source: See table 9A-1.

Table 9A-4. Earnings Functions for Male Workers in Bogotá by Industry of Employment, 1978

Variable	Manufacturing (30–39)[a]	Construction (50–59)	Trade and commerce (60–69)	Transportation and communication (70–79)	Financial establishment (80–89)	Public administration and other services (90–96)
YRSEDU	0.123	0.103*	0.111*	0.082*	0.123*	0.123*
EXPER	0.072*	0.063*	0.067*	0.040*	0.071*	0.067*
EXPSQ	-0.0010*	-0.0009*	-0.0009*	-0.0000*	-0.0011*	-0.0010*
DBOG	0.100*	0.167*	0.126	-0.113	0.041	0.096
DCITY	0.224	0.600*	-0.023	0.092	0.225	0.138
DTOWN	0.059	0.224	0.204	0.410*	0.012	0.153
DURB	0.131*	0.074	0.140	0.113	-0.104	-0.019
RSECT1	0.198	n.a.[b]	-0.214	-0.410	0.743*	0.010
RSECT3	0.255*	0.169*	0.141	0.262*	0.146	0.098
RSECT4	0.290*	0.256	0.200	0.110	0.138	0.173
RSECT5	0.244*	0.071	0.521*	0.159	0.202	-0.046
RSECT6	0.240*	0.219*	0.212	0.395*	0.204	0.119
RSECT7	0.194*	0.247*	0.259*	0.773*	0.551*	0.112
RSECT8	0.921*	0.284	0.569*	0.609*	1.027*	0.355*

UNION	0.037	0.116	-0.030	0.078	-0.053	0.168*
SOCSEC	0.094*	0.050	0.178*	0.199*	0.046	-0.012
CONTRACT	0.020	0.142*	-0.315	-0.131*	0.204*	0.066
DIST	-0.013	-0.028*	-0.049*	-0.047*	-0.036*	-0.022*
CONST	6.61	6.94	6.93	7.62	6.81	6.81
R^2	0.550	0.433	0.360	0.491	0.709	0.617
Number of observations	768	331	649	244	259	609
Mean of log monthly earnings	8.57	8.29	8.62	8.76	9.23	8.84
YRSEDU (female)c	0.085*	n.a.b	0.062*	n.a.b	0.138*	0.073*

n.a. Not available.

Note: Coefficients marked with an asterisk are significant at the 5 percent level.

a. SIC code.

b. The number of observations is inadequate for estimation.

c. Coefficients for female workers from similar regressions.

Source: See table 9A-1.

Table 9A-5. *Earnings Functions for Workers in Bogotá by Status in Household, 1978*

	Male		Female	
Variable	Household head	Other	Household head	Other
YRSEDU	0.113*	0.105*	0.067*	0.072*
EXPER	0.050*	0.062*	−0.008	0.026*
EXPSQ	−0.0007*	−0.0009*	0.0002	−0.005*
DBOG	0.096*	0.066	0.090	−0.106*
DCITY	0.134	0.213	0.005	−0.305*
DTOWN	0.123	0.146	0.098	−0.174*
DURB	0.048	0.063	0.057	−0.090*
RSECT1	−0.081	0.160	0.306	0.069
RSECT3	0.223*	0.105*	0.178	0.196*
RSECT4	0.298*	0.062	0.024	0.182*
RSECT5	0.345*	0.017	0.047	0.314*
RSECT6	0.264*	0.072	0.506*	0.218*
RSECT7	0.350*	0.113	0.118	0.314*
RSECT8	0.682*	0.662*	0.702*	0.470*
UNION	0.081*	0.0	0.224*	0.203*
SOCSEC	0.059	0.107*	0.194	0.260*
CONTRACT	0.038	0.087*	0.356*	0.069*
DIST	−0.027*	−0.017*	−0.038	−0.011*
CONST	7.08	6.91	7.50	7.18
R^2	0.511	0.469	0.485	0.380
Number of observations	2,010	922	350	1,525
Mean of log monthly earnings	8.86	8.34	8.19	8.21

Note: Coefficients marked with an asterisk are significant at the 5 percent level.
Source: See table 9A-1.

Table 9A-6. *Earnings Functions for Workers in Bogotá by Marital Status, 1978*

Variable	Male		Female	
	Single	Married[a]	Single	Married[b]
YRSEDU	0.108*	0.112*	0.074*	0.079*
EXPER	0.067*	0.052*	0.031*	0.017*
EXPSQ	−0.0012*	−0.0007*	−0.0006*	−0.0002*
DBOG	0.034	0.094*	−0.094	−0.018
DCITY	0.126	0.161	−0.241	−0.269
DTOWN	0.215*	0.111	−0.143	0.070
DURB	0.105	0.045	−0.069	−0.010
RSECT1	0.094	−0.063	0.154	0.180
RSECT3	0.118*	0.216*	0.234*	0.108
RSECT4	0.014	0.293*	0.126	0.126
RSECT5	0.027	0.323*	0.320*	0.109
RSECT6	0.038	0.271*	0.276*	0.208*
RSECT7	0.068	0.372*	0.301*	0.174
RSECT8	0.682*	0.688*	0.456*	0.505*
UNION	0.016	0.076*	0.223*	0.213*
SOCSEC	0.096*	0.059	0.139*	0.379*
CONTRACT	0.083*	0.036	0.133*	0.085*
DIST	−0.019*	−0.027*	−0.019*	−0.006
CONST	6.92	7.06	7.22	7.01
R^2	0.531	0.501	0.347	0.436
Number of observations	908	2,023	963	913
Mean of log monthly earnings	8.37	8.84	8.17	8.26

Note: Coefficients marked with an asterisk are significant at the 5 percent level.

a. Includes divorced, separated, widowed, and free union.

b. Does not include separated, widowed, and free union.

Table 9A-7. *Distribution of Labor Earnings in Bogotá by Sector, 1973–78*

	1973		1975		1977		1978	
Sector	Log variance	Rank[a]	Log variance	Rank[a]	Log variance	Rank[a]	Log variance	Rank[a]
1	0.910	6	1.773	8	1.026	8	0.403	2
2	0.577	1	0.770	3	0.454	1	0.402	1
3	0.593	2	0.674	2	0.553	2	0.462	3
4	0.707	3	0.591	1	0.661	4	0.644	4
5	0.785	5	1.187	6	0.756	5	0.609	6
6	0.725	4	0.881	4	0.595	3	0.646	5
7	1.204	7	1.057	5	0.847	6	0.866	7
8	1.911	8	1.024	7	0.938	7	1.226	8
All sectors	0.885		0.990		0.703		0.742	
Intergroup contribution								
Sectors (log variance)	n.a.		0.089		0.047		0.089	
Sectors (percent)	7.4		8.9		6.7		11.9	
Comunas (percent)	13.8		18.7		13.9		16.7	

n.a. Not available.
a. By ascending order of inequality.
Source: See table 4-2.

Table 9A-8. *Distribution of Labor Earnings in Cali by Sector, 1973–78*

	1973		1977		1978	
Sector	Log variance	Rank[a]	Log variance	Rank[a]	Log variance	Rank[a]
1	0.786	4	0.584	4	1.030	6
2	2.080	7	1.035	7	1.195	7
3	0.690	2	0.522	1	0.518	2
4	0.611	1	0.577	3	0.558	3
5	0.785	3	0.554	2	0.504	1
6	1.480	6	0.911	6	1.010	5
7	0.998	5	0.633	5	0.873	4
All sectors	0.929		0.706		0.703	
Intergroup contribution						
Sectors (log variance)	0.026		0.037		0.046	
Sectors (percent)	2.8		5.2		6.5	
Comunas (percent)	7.2		12.9		12.7	

a. By ascending order of inequality.
Sources: See table 4-2.

Table 9A-9. *Distribution of Monthly Earnings in Bogotá and Cali by Occupation (13 categories), 1978*

Occupation	ILO code	Bogotá			Cali		
		Mean earnings (1978 pesos)	Theil index	Percentage in category	Mean earnings (1978 pesos)	Theil index	Percentage in category
Professional and technical	1–19	17,512	0.300	12.0	15,454	0.304	6.2
Administrative and managerial	20–29	26,834	0.137	2.9	19,749	0.288	2.2
Clerks and typists	30–39	7,005	0.219	14.3	6,636	0.250	12.5
Sales managers	40–41	9,370	0.540	7.2	15,440	0.276	2.5
Other sales	42–49	7,004	0.482	8.8	5,305	0.492	14.2
Service workers	50–53	4,023	0.292	12.3	4,302	0.303	11.8
Maids	54	3,237	0.165	7.7	3,091	0.103	8.5
Agriculture	60–69	11,151	0.579	0.9	12,509	0.586	1.0
Production supervisors	70	7,414	0.197	0.8	8,285	0.199	1.3
Production workers	71–74	4,584	0.207	20.9	4,776	0.297	26.8
Construction workers	95	3,901	0.151	5.5	4,217	0.307	4.6
Material and equipment operators	96–97	3,592	0.102	2.0	3,811	0.181	3.0
Transport	98	5,813	0.158	4.7	6,992	0.218	5.6
All occupations	1–98	7,600	0.482	100.0	6,350	0.440	100.0
Total number of workers (thousands)		1,180			350		
Intergroup contribution Theil index			0.199			0.137	
Percent			41.2			31.1	

Source: See table 9A-1.

Table 9A-10. Distribution of Monthly Earnings in Bogotá and Cali by Industry (20 categories), 1978

Industry	SIC code	Bogotá			Cali		
		Mean earnings (1978 pesos)	Theil index	Percentage in category	Mean earnings (1978 pesos)	Theil index	Percentage in category
Agriculture	10–19	11,330	0.518	1.0	14,271	0.524	0.9
Mining	20–29	18,927	0.328	0.4	2,098	0.170	0.4
Food products, beverages, and tobacco	31	6,250	0.344	3.1	6,623	0.332	4.4
Textiles and footwear	32	4,745	0.388	6.4	4,831	0.460	12.0
Lumber and wood	33	4,877	0.296	1.9	6,465	0.351	2.4
Paper, printing, and publishing	34	8,014	0.407	1.9	10,377	0.504	2.6
Mineral products	36	6,557	0.423	1.2	6,548	0.500	1.0
Industrial chemicals	35	10,163	0.500	2.8	9,303	0.366	3.1
Metal industry	37–38	8,559	0.476	5.5	6,831	0.321	5.4
Other industry	30–39	3,244	0.163	0.9	3,437	0.148	0.6

326

Utilities	40–49	8,668	0.214	0.5	9,208	0.249	1.0
Construction	50–59	5,460	0.394	7.3	4,955	0.281	6.2
Wholesale trade	61	18,894	0.367	1.6	11,019	0.431	1.6
Retail trade	62	6,561	0.463	18.3	5,516	0.478	19.1
Other commerce	60–63	3,972	0.272	3.4	4,020	0.231	3.6
Transport and communication	70–79	8,522	0.333	5.9	6,778	0.271	6.4
Financial establishments	80–89	12,232	0.424	8.2	11,465	0.436	3.8
Public administration and social services	96–99	11,362	0.400	7.5	9,028	0.301	3.6
Public instruction	93	10,356	0.351	7.9	8,996	0.348	7.4
Domestic and personal services	95	3,760	0.287	14.1	3,598	0.284	14.6
All categories		7,694	0.482	100.0	6,322	0.441	100.0
Intergroup contribution							
Theil index			0.086			0.064	
Percent			17.8			14.4	

10

Estimating Earnings Functions for Women

In most countries of the world, the average earnings of women characteristically range from about two-thirds to one-half of the average for men. In Bogotá they are closer to one-half. The ratio becomes worse with age: young women earn almost as much as men but older women earn comparatively less and less—presumably because women are more likely than men to have their careers interrupted by marriage and childbearing. It is also possible that they are discriminated against. Women who work at later ages may also be self-selected, but the reasons for self-selection can be negative as well as positive. A good number of women who work without interruption must have a strong desire to work or good qualifications for working; indeed, those with a strong desire to work are likely to invest in human capital (in the form of education and work experience) more heavily than others. There is also self-selection of a negative kind, however: many women may be forced to work—divorcees or widows who had not planned to work, for example, may find themselves thrust into the labor market by unforeseen circumstances. A straightforward earnings function of the kind that was estimated and reported for men in the preceding chapters is therefore inappropriate for women. The coefficient of education is likely to be biased because of self-selection, and the experience variable (defined as age − years of education − 6) is incorrect for women because of their interrupted careers.

Further problems arise in estimating earnings functions for women because of some special features of female labor supply. In a good exposition of the subject, Frank (1978) focuses on the supply-side phenomena that might explain why equally qualified males and females would be paid different wages by a nondiscriminating employer. As a group, husbands possess larger stocks of human capital (education, training, experience, and the like) than women. Thus, within the household, male-chauvinist decision principles are typically in force, with the result that the husband's employment is usually given higher priority than the wife's. If both husband and wife are in the labor force, the joint search for jobs is limited geographically to a single area (town or city) for both of them. The husband's stock of human capital and hence earnings potential are usually higher and thus his job usually takes precedence over the wife's. The wife must then optimize her job choice under the constraints imposed by her husband's prior choice, and often ends up taking a job for which she may be overqualified. Her decision rule may therefore be to take the job for which her qualifications are the least in excess of requirements within the area to which she is limited. Of course, if male-chauvinist principles did not prevail, a truly joint choice might lead both husband and wife to take jobs that are suboptimal for each singly but optimal for a joint choice.

Under a supply process having the kind of essentially male-dominating decision rules sketched above women would earn less than men with identical personal characteristics. Although such a chain of reasoning has undoubted merit, it begs the question of the prior causation of the lower level of human capital stock typically found in women than in men. This presumably has to do with the expectation of lower lifetime earnings for women, an expectation that then becomes self-fulfilling.

Interruption in careers necessitated by childbearing and child care are probably more important explanations for the lower earnings of women than relative human capital endowments. These interruptions make on-the-job training investments in human capital less productive, and give employers "objective" reasons for discriminating against women. The combined effect of these "objective" reasons on supply, together with possible resulting discrimination, reduce women's expected earnings and in turn lead them to invest less in education as well.

It is difficult to correct for the experience variable without direct information on years actually spent working by women. The standard definition of this variable (AGE − YRSEDU − 6) is obviously not a good one for married women who have had children and have interrupted their careers as a result. Attempts were made to estimate the length of interruption per child born and hence to arrive at a better measure of work experience, but without much success. The results presented here are flawed because of my inability to find an adequate specification of the experience variable. Another problem is that women are much more likely to have part-time or occasional employment, but this is easier to correct for, at least in part, by using hourly wages rather than monthly earnings as the income variable. As will be seen, this makes a substantial difference to the estimate for the returns to education. Although I am not able to improve on the specification of the experience variable, it *is* possible to address the selectivity issue with the data at hand. Issues to do with selectivity and possible econometric corrections have been discussed in some detail in chapter 7. In what follows, however, I first present the results for female earnings in a form identical to those for men so as to facilitate comparisons between the two. The results obtained in chapter 7 are then discussed and compared with the more traditional earnings function presented in detail in this chapter.

The Returns to Education and Experience

Tables 10-1 and 10-2 give estimates for women using equations identical to those used for men in tables 8-2 and 8-3. The dependent variable in each of these regressions is the logarithm of monthly earnings. Several points are immediately apparent. First, the level of explanation is less than it is in the equivalent tables for men, for the reasons discussed above. The education and experience variables are both highly significant but their magnitudes are substantially lower than those for men—about 40 percent less for the returns to education and more than 50 percent less in the case of experience. The latter is to be expected because the experience variable used is likely to overstate the length of actual experience, as discussed above. To the extent that the amount of education and the length of experience are joint decision variables and are correlated, the returns to education would also be affected by the misspecification of the experience variable. The coefficient estimates are significantly affected by the addition of the protected sector variables— UNION, SOCSEC, and CONTRACT—much more so than those for men.

The results for the splined education variable are also of interest. The certification variables DUMP, DUMS, and DUMH are all statistically insignificant, as are those for PRIMED. The returns to secondary education are the most significant factor; unlike the results for the men, they are more important than returns to higher education. The returns to postgraduate education, however, are very large indeed for the women. Those who do go on to postgraduate education are more likely to work as professionals and are perhaps less prone to interrupt their careers. The SECED coefficient is the one most affected by the addition of the protected sector variables: either the women with secondary education are more likely to be union members, or union membership is the better explanation for earnings differentials. All the other coefficients are quite stable across different specifications of the earnings function.

Table 10-3 gives the estimates of identical earnings functions but uses two different measures of earnings: monthly earnings and hourly wages. The hourly wage variable is clearly the more appropriate one to use for women, even though the variance in women's hours was not very high (see chapter 7). The explanatory power of the earnings function is as high for women as

Table 10-1. *Determinants of Monthly Earnings of Female Workers in Bogotá, 1978*

Variable	Regression			
	1	2	3	4
YRSEDU	0.102	0.104	0.097	0.0.73
	(27.0)	(25..3)	(23.5)	(17.0)
EXPER	0.025	0.024	0.025	0.021
	(6.4)	(6.0)	(6.4)	(5.6)
EXPSQ	−0.0004	−0.0004	−0.0004	−0.0004
	(5.8)	(5.8)	(5.8)	(5.2)
DBOG	—	−0.045	−0.027	−0.062
	—	(1.0)	(0.6)	(1.5)
DCITY	—	−0.300	−0.209	−0.213
	—	(2.3)	(1.6)	(1.7)
DTOWN	—	0.057	0.025	−0.038
	—	(0.8)	(0.4)	(0.6)
DURB	—	−0.020	−0.033	−0.040
	—	(0.4)	(0.8)	(1.0)
RSECT1	—	—	0.170	0.244
	—	—	(1.3)	(2.0)
RSECT3	—	—	0.202	0.163
	—	—	(4.1)	(3.5)
RSECT4	—	—	0.144	0.154
	—	—	(2.0)	(2.3)
RSECT5	—	—	(0.319)	0.243
	—	—	(4.7)	(3.7)
RSECT6	—	—	0.260	0.209
	—	—	(5.1)	(4.3)
RSECT7	—	—	0.244	0.250
	—	—	(4.3)	(4.6)
RSECT8	—	—	0.425	0.495
	—	—	(8.4)	(10.2)
UNION	—	—	—	0.218
	—	—	—	(5.3)
SOCSEC	—	—	—	0.242
	—	—	—	(6.2)
CONTRACT	—	—	—	0.116
	—	—	—	(3.7)
CONST	7.26	7.27	7.08	7.10
R^2	0.306	0.306	0.331	0.391
Number of observations	1,887	1,887	1,887	1,887

— Not applicable.

Note: Dependent variable: mean of monthly earnings, 8.21; *t* statistics in parentheses.

Source: My estimates from 1978 World Bank–DANE Household Survey.

Table 10-2. *Determinants of Earnings of Female Workers in Bogotá by Education Level, 1978*

Variable	Regression					
	1	2	3	4	5	6
DUMP	−0.014	−0.010	0.040	0.040	0.052	0.046
	(0.2)	(0.1)	(0.6)	(0.6)	(0.8)	(0.7)
DUMS	0.019	0.021	0.043	0.103	0.106	0.114
	(0.2)	(0.2)	(0.4)	(1.0)	(1.0)	(1.1)
DUMH	−0.026	−0.024	−0.030	0.107	0.075	0.060
	(0.1)	(0.1)	(0.2)	(0.6)	(0.4)	(0.3)
PRIMED	0.044	0.043	0.030	0.019	0.015	0.015
	(2.1)	(2.1)	(1.5)	(1.0)	(0.7)	(0.7)
SECED	0.117	0.120	0.116	0.070	0.068	0.063
	(9.0)	(9.0)	(8.9)	(5.4)	(5.1)	(4.7)
HIGHED	0.075	0.074	0.072	0.050	0.056	0.066
	(2.0)	(1.9)	(1.9)	(1.4)	(1.5)	(1.8)
POSTED	0.427	0.431	0.403	0.381	0.377	0.348
	(6.6)	(6.6)	(6.3)	(6.2)	(6.0)	(5.5)
EXPER	0.026	0.026	0.027	0.022	0.021	0.021
	(6.7)	(6.4)	(6.7)	(5.9)	(5.5)	(5.6)
EXPSQ	−0.0005	−0.0005	−0.0005	−0.0004	−0.0004	−0.0004
	(6.5)	(6.3)	(6.5)	(5.8)	(5.6)	(5.6)
DBOG	—	−0.040	−0.032	−0.056	−0.075	−0.077
		(0.9)	(0.7)	(1.4)	(1.8)	(1.9)
DCITY	—	−0.288	−0.212	−0.191	−0.201	0.021
		(2.2)	(1.6)	(1.6)	(1.6)	(1.6)
DTOWN	—	0.067	0.028	−0.013	−0.037	−0.037
		(0.9)	(0.4)	(0.2)	(0.5)	(0.5)
DURB	—	0.003	−0.015	−0.021	−0.034	−0.033
		(0.1)	(0.4)	(0.5)	(0.8)	(0.8)
RSECT1	—	—	0.180	0.238	0.169	0.153
			(1.4)	(2.0)	(1.3)	(1.2)
RSECT3	—	—	0.211	0.176	0.205	0.203
			(4.3)	(3.8)	(4.2)	(4.2)
RSECT4	—	—	0.154	0.171	0.168	0.162
			(2.2)	(2.5)	(2.4)	(2.4)
RSECT5	—	—	0.317	0.243	0.264	0.251
			(4.7)	(3.8)	(4.0.)	(3.8)
RSECT6	—	—	0.269	0.223	0.281	0.284
			(5.3)	(4.6)	(5.2)	(5.3)
RSECT7	—	—	0.237	0.245	0.287	0.297
			(4.2)	(4.5)	(5.0)	(5.2)
RSECT8	—	—	0.399	0.461	0.486	0.497
			(7.8)	(9.4)	(9.6)	(9.8)
UNION	—	—		0.202	0.204	0.133
				(4.2)	(4.7)	(2.9)

Variable	Regression					
	1	2	3	4	5	6
SOCSEC	—	—	—	0.254 (6.6)	0.268 (6.8)	0.203 (4.8)
CONTRACT	—	—	—	0.117 (3.8)	0.102 (3.2)	0.074 (2.2)
LOGFSIZE	—	—	—	—	—	0.040 (3.8)
DIST	—	—	—	—	−0.015 (3.1)	−0.017 (3.5)
DTRAIN	—	—	—	—	—	0.067 (1.3)
CONST	7.47	7.48	7.29	7.27	7.39	7.38
R^2	0.322	0.324	0.345	0.405	0.406	0.411
Number of observations	1,887	1,887	1,887	1,887	1,807	1,807

— Not applicable.
Note: Dependent variable: mean of log monthly earnings, 8.21; t statistics in parentheses.
Source: See table 10-1.

it is for men—more than 50 percent of the log variance of women's earnings is accounted for. The certification variables are still insignificant, but the returns to SECED and HIGHED have increased significantly and are almost as high as those for men at these levels of education. The returns to experience are still much less, again understandably. When part-time workers and the irregularity of women's work patterns (not captured by the experience variable here) are taken into account, the returns to education appear to be at least as great for women as they are for men at the secondary- and higher-education levels—but not at the primary level: women with only primary education do not earn any more than those with no education. This finding is consistent with the extremely rapid expansion in women's education, which has almost equalized women's access to secondary and higher education. Moreover, it is also consistent with the fact that participation is much higher for women with higher education than for others.

Consider now the wage function estimates given in table 7A-1. Women are stratified into three groups—the young (aged 15–24), and married and single prime-age women (aged 25–54). The returns to education for these stratified groups are much higher than for women as a whole (the coefficient of YRSEDU is between 0.13 and 0.16 for these groups). Note, too, that the

Table 10-3. *Earnings Functions for Female Workers in Bogotá Using Different Income Variables, 1974*

Variable	Log of monthly earnings	Log HWAGE[a]
DUMP	0.052	0.108
	(0.8)	(1.5)
DUMS	0.106	0.162
	(1.0)	(1.5)
DUMH	0.075	0.278
	(0.4)	(1.4)
PRIMED	0.015	0.021
	(0.7)	(1.0)
SECED	0.068	0.117
	(5.1)	(8.5)
HIGHED	0.056	0.095
	(1.5)	(2.5)
POSTED	0.377	0.436
	(6.0)	(6.7)
EXPER	0.021	0.033
	(5.5)	(8.2)
EXPSQ	−0.0004	−0.0006
	(5.6)	(6.9)
DBOG	−0.075	−0.002
	(1.8)	(0.0)
DCITY	−0.201	−0.263
	(1.6)	(2.0)
DTOWN	−0.037	−0.052
	(0.5)	(0.7)
DURB	−0.034	−0.011
	(0.8)	(0.2)
RSECT1	0.169	0.189
	(1.3)	(1.4)
RSECT3	0.205	0.166
	(4.2)	(3.3)
RSECT4	0.168	0.082
	(2.4)	(1.1)
RSECT5	0.264	0.236
	(4.0)	(3.5)
RSECT6	0.281	0.271
	(5.2)	(4.9)
RSECT7	0.287	0.179
	(5.0)	(3.0)
RSECT8	0.486	0.316
	(9.6)	(6.0)
UNION	0.204	0.207
	(4.7)	(4.7)
SOCSEC	0.268	0.270
	(6.8)	(6.6)

Variable	Log of monthly earnings	Log HWAGE[a]
CONTRACT	0.102	0.121
	(3.2)	(3.6)
DIST	−0.015	−0.009
	(3.1)	(1.8)
CONST	7.39	1.75
R^2	0.406	0.525
Number of observations	1,807	1,868
Mean of dependent variable	8.21	2.95

Note: t statistics in parentheses.

a. HWAGE $= \dfrac{\text{monthly earnings}}{4 \times \text{weekly hours}}.$

returns to primary education reported above are probably explained by their returns to experience for young women are closer to those for men. There also appears to be some adverse selection of young and married women who work.

The samples used in these estimates exclude live-in domestic servants, who are included in all the other estimates reported in this chapter. The low inclusion in those samples, since many live-in domestic servants are partly educated recent migrants who do not earn much more than unskilled uneducated workers. These results suggest that earnings functions for women are quite tractable, provided that they are carefully specified in conjunction with the participation decision and that information is available on their years of actual experience in the labor market. (See table 10A-2 for comparable estimates for women in Cali; the results are largely consistent with those for Bogotá.)

This argument is bolstered by the next set of results reported here and tabulated in table 10A-3. Unlike the estimates for men, firm-specific experience for women appears to give higher returns than the traditional experience variable; this result suggests that the former is a much more accurate measure of a women's actual work experience than the latter. These returns are quite comparable in size to those for the traditional variable for young women (with presumably uninterrupted careers). It could therefore be hypothesized that, if the true work experience variable was also available for women, the returns to firm-specific experience would be no higher than they are for generalized experience in the labor market.

As mentioned earlier, an attempt was made to adjust the EXPER measure by the number of years of work lost to childbearing, but the results did not make the returns to EXPER significantly different.[1] Of the working women with children, almost 35 percent are divorced, separated, widowed, or living in free union—so that little choice is exercised in their decision—and their returns to experience are substantially lower than those for currently married women.

Frank (1978) suggested that because of the geographical constraints that married women face, their earnings would be less than those for equivalent single women. The separate regressions for single and married women given in table 9A-6 indicate that this is not true for women in Bogotá: returns to education are almost equal. The returns to experience *are* higher, but happen to be the same when compared with currently married women. The divorced or widowed women may show lower returns to experience because they have to take whatever job they can find, and probably because they have had to enter the labor market suddenly after a break—thus the EXPER variable is particularly inappropriate for them.

The time-series estimates for 1973–78 (tables 10-4 and 10A-4) reveal few surprises. The fact that the coefficient estimates are somewhat more unstable than those for males is a reflection of the relatively unsatisfactory nature of the earnings functions specification used. One surprising feature is the relatively high level of explanation ($R^2 = 0.491$) for women's earnings in the 1973 census: such an R^2 is remarkable in a cross-sectional sample of more than 18,000 observations. The explanation appears to be that many part-time workers were missed in the census, an observation supported by the female participation rates observed in different years:[2]

			Age group				
Year	12–14	15–24	25–34	35–44	45–54	55–64	65+
1973	0.09	0.36	0.37	0.34	0.27	0.17	0.14
1978	0.04	0.39	0.48	0.48	0.39	0.21	0.07

1. The standard earnings function is

$$\log Y = \beta_0 + \beta_1 \text{ YRSEDU} + \beta_2 \text{ EXPER} + \beta_3 \text{ EXPER}^2.$$

If γ years are taken out of work per child born to married women EXPER1 = EXPER − γ CHILDREN; that is,

$$\log Y = \beta_0 + \beta_1 \text{ YRSEDU} + \beta_2 (\text{EXPER} - \gamma \text{ CHILDREN}) + \beta_3 (\text{EXPER} - \gamma \text{ CHILDREN})^2.$$

Estimates were made for this specification, but γ was found to be insignificant and β_2 did not change.

2. This would be yet another reason for the undercoverage of household incomes in the 1973 census.

Table 10-4. *Earnings Functions for Female Workers in Bogotá, 1973–78*

Variable	1973	1975	1977	1978
YRSEDU	0.174	0.088	0.086	0.097
	(123.2)	(25.0)	(21.5)	(23.5)
EXPER	0.054	0.019	0.013	0.025
	(42.8)	(5.1)	(3.2)	(6.4)
EXPSQ	−0.0008	−0.0004	−0.0002	−0.0004
	(32.2)	(5.2)	(2.7)	(5.8)
DBOG	0.147	−0.051	−0.048	−0.027
	(14.2)	(1.8)	(1.5)	(0.6)
DCITY	0.295	—	—	−0.209
	(6.9)			(1.6)
DTOWN	0.169	—	—	(0.025
	(7.4)			(0.4)
DURB	—	—	—	−0.033
				(0.8)
RSECT1	0.042	0.378	0.092	0.170
	(1.4)	(3.6)	(1.0)	(1.3)
RSECT3	0.043	0.141	0.136	0.202
	(2.7)	(3.2)	(2.8)	(4.1)
RSECT4	0.093	0.131	0.206	0.144
	(4.6)	(2.4)	(3.1)	(2.0)
RSECT5	0.100	0.291	0.254	0.319
	(4.7)	(4.9)	(3.7)	(4.7)
RSECT6	0.065	0.137	0.123	0.260
	(3.8)	(3.7)	(2.4)	(5.1)
RSECT7	0.093	0.136	0.347	0.244
	(5.6)	(6.1)	(6.3)	(4.3)
RSECT8	0.136	0.407	0.474	0.425
	(7.6)	(8.0)	(8.6)	(8.4)
CONST	4.88	6.47	6.85	7.08
R^2	0.491	0.275	0.262	0.331
Number of observations	18,503	2,163	1,915	1,887
Mean of log monthly earnings	6.58	7.37	7.73	8.21

— Not applicable.

Note: t statistics in parentheses.

Sources: My estimates from 1973 population census; 1975 DANE Household Survey EH8E; 1977 DANE Household Survey EH15; and 1978 World Bank–DANE Household Survey.

The 1973 sample then probably consists mostly of female full-time workers, jand the estimated coefficients are more comparable to the HWAGE estimates of tables 10-3 and 7A-1. If this is the case, then there *has* been some decline in the returns to education for women as there has been for men. Since the expansion of female education has lagged behind that for men, it is likely that declines in the rate of return to higher education for women will also appear with a lag.

Tables 10-1 and 10-2 reveal that the region of origin has almost no effect on female earnings. For men, the effect of these region variables was significant though small. Further, the residential location effects are broadly similar to those for men and similar reasons can be adduced for them; the effect of the rich sector 8 is not as great, but this is explained by the existence of a high proportion of domestic servants in this sector.

The Protected Sector

The effect of the union variable was alluded to above. It seems that membership in a union has a much greater effect for women than for men, producing about a 20 percent premium in female earnings. The level of explanation of the log variance of earnings also increases by about 20 percent. The effect of the SOCSEC and CONTRACT variables is also large and highly significant. Interestingly, these coefficients are fairly similar in the HWAGE equation and the monthly-income equation. It cannot therefore be concluded that these variables are merely picking up the effect of the longer and more regular hours that women with these characteristics are likely to have. In fact, their work hours do not seem to be any different.

It is likely that women who exhibit these formal sector characteristics are those who work more regularly throughout their lives and with fewer interruptions. As such, these variables could be good proxies for labor market experience for women. But union membership for women is correlated with firm size (more so than it is for men), and thus the firm-size effect is also larger than it is for men. These findings indicate that the protected sector is a more relevant concept for women in the labor market. But an element of self-selection could be involved: it is those women who expect to work regularly who become union members. If these conjectures are true, the indicated segmentation in the labor market for women is a result of demand factors as well as self-selection in supply. It may be that employers are willing to pay a premium to women who do not interrupt their careers. Women who have a taste for work are then faced with highly interrelated choices concerning childbearing and market work.

Summary

Estimating earnings functions is intrinsically more hazardous for women than for men, because female participation decisions are more complicated. In general, although all prime-age males participate in the labor force, only a small proportion of prime-age married women do. It is then much more desirable to estimate earnings functions for women that are conditional on their participation decisions. These decisions depend on the number of hours that they can work in a week, together with the costs of entry into the labor market. Although some attempt was made here to account for selectivity bias and for interrupted lifetime careers, it appears even more certain post facto that a further effort should have been made to specify richer earnings functions for women. The few experiments attempted produced valuable results.

It seems that much of the difference between male and female earnings can be explained by the interruption in women's careers and the resulting lower returns to labor market experience; other things being equal, the returns to education are not much lower for women than for men. The dramatically increased participation of women in secondary and higher education also points in this direction. The work in chapter 7 suggested that there is little flexibility in women's working hours, their mean workweek being in excess of 40 hours. Thus it would seem that women have little choice but to withdraw completely from the labor market with the onset of their childbearing years. If women are to compete more equally in the labor market, these results suggest that a more flexible workweek might possibly yield rich dividends. The returns to labor market experience would then presumably rise. More widely available day care for children would also help reduce women's costs of entry into the labor market.

In addition, there is much greater evidence of a protected sector for women than for men. Although elements of self-selection may color this finding somewhat, membership in the protected sector clearly brings high rewards to women.

Table 10A-1. *Matrix of Correlation Coefficients for Female Workers in Bogotá*

Variable	LOGINC	EXPER	EXPSQ	DBOG	DCITY	DTOWN	DURB
LOGINC	1.00000	−0.21309	0.21623	0.14037	−0.00727	0.09293	−0.04619
EXPER	−0.21309	1.00000	0.95273	−0.30293	0.02897	−0.01091	0.18062
EXPSQ	−0.21623	0.95273	1.00000	−0.25355	0.01552	−0.03416	0.15459
DBOG	0.14037	−0.30293	−0.25355	1.00000	−0.10564	−0.22366	−0.52658
DCITY	−0.00727	0.02897	0.01552	−0.10564	1.00000	−0.03109	−0.07320
DTOWN	0.09293	−0.01091	−0.03416	−0.22366	−0.03109	1.00000	−0.15498
DURB	−0.04619	0.18062	0.15459	−0.52658	−0.07320	−0.15498	1.00000
DUMP	−0.11263	−0.07230	−0.10630	0.04144	0.00314	0.02761	−0.01772
DUMS	0.24953	−0.21713	−0.17327	0.18165	0.07133	0.09072	−0.09382
DUMH	0.38125	−0.18741	−0.14862	0.13524	−0.01508	−0.00291	−0.03187
PRIMED	0.30673	−0.45447	−0.45112	0.25744	0.04141	0.09209	−0.06288
SECED	0.51558	−0.40414	−0.34175	0.33607	0.06556	0.10650	0.13361
HIGHED	0.41562	−0.23607	−0.18016	0.16509	−0.01209	−0.00009	−0.04507
POSTED	0.33562	−0.13955	−0.11261	0.14008	−0.01357	−0.02157	0.06451
RSECT1	−0.00908	0.07958	0.07716	−0.02552	0.10829	−0.00039	0.00754
RSECT3	−0.01147	−0.02772	−0.04075	0.04265	−0.02905	−0.03923	−0.03153
RSECT4	−0.01817	−0.03400	−0.03446	−0.00355	−0.01071	−0.01583	−0.00521
RSECT5	0.02032	−0.03695	−0.02205	−0.01653	−0.03303	0.00725	0.00447
RSECT6	0.01837	−0.00781	−0.00756	0.05976	−0.02189	−0.03202	0.03458
RSECT7	0.02628	−0.02443	−0.02820	−0.03664	0.07883	−0.02358	0.01750
RSECT8	0.19555	−0.03125	−0.01982	−0.04268	−0.05998	0.11899	0.02046
UNION	0.33132	−0.12054	−0.12007	0.10269	−0.03681	0.08953	−0.05169
SOCSEC	0.41617	−0.20834	−0.19527	0.22172	0.01793	0.05515	−0.08848
CONTRACT	0.35382	−0.17521	−0.16056	0.17784	0.05394	0.04871	−0.05316
DIST	−0.09109	0.01820	0.01048	−0.01837	−0.06854	−0.09795	0.00320
DTRAIN	0.20440	−0.11909	−0.12395	0.06140	−0.01937	0.06676	−0.03163
FSIZE	0.15704	−0.07251	−0.07954	0.04144	−0.00024	0.03568	0.00209
LOGFSIZE	0.40862	−0.25031	−0.23843	0.22543	0.00454	0.04760	−0.09756

DUMP	DUMS	DUMH	PRIMED	SECED	HIGHED	POSTED	Variable
−0.11263	0.24953	0.38125	0.30673	0.51558	0.41562	0.33562	LOGINC
−0.07230	−0.21713	−0.18741	−0.45447	−0.40414	−0.23607	−0.13955	EXPER
−0.10630	−0.17327	−0.14862	−0.45112	−0.34175	−0.18016	−0.11261	EXPSQ
0.04144	0.18165	0.13524	0.25744	0.33607	0.16509	0.14008	DBOG
0.00314	0.07133	−0.01508	0.04141	0.06556	−0.01209	−0.01357	DCITY
0.02761	0.09072	−0.00291	0.09209	0.10650	−0.00009	0.02157	DTOWN
0.01772	−0.09382	−0.03187	−0.06288	−0.13361	−0.04507	−0.06451	DURB
1.00000	−0.39703	−0.29298	0.50097	−0.21689	−0.34747	−0.18577	DUMP
−0.39703	1.00000	−0.14361	0.24556	0.63475	0.03115	−0.09106	DUMS
−0.29298	−0.14361	1.00000	0.18120	0.46839	0.93321	0.63408	DUMH
0.50097	0.24556	0.18120	1.00000	0.50105	0.21490	0.11490	PRIMED
−0.21689	0.63475	0.46839	0.50105	1.00000	0.55550	0.29700	SECED
−0.34747	0.03115	0.93321	0.21490	0.55550	1.00000	0.59173	HIGHED
−0.18577	−0.09106	0.63408	0.11490	0.29700	0.59173	1.00000	POSTED
0.03134	−0.01334	0.01718	0.02234	−0.01186	0.00749	0.01467	RSECT1
0.10512	−0.00645	−0.05361	0.04957	0.00948	−0.04630	−0.05685	RSECT3
0.01852	0.03347	−0.02820	0.03631	0.02322	−0.00973	−0.03017	RSECT4
0.00878	−0.01294	−0.02212	0.00022	−0.01248	−0.00221	−0.00143	RSECT5
0.06805	0.03371	−0.04793	0.03631	0.02409	−0.05880	−0.07169	RSECT6
−0.05067	0.02822	0.04548	−0.00194	0.03897	0.06357	0.01198	RSECT7
−0.19542	0.03772	0.20884	0.00976	0.10658	0.19558	0.20495	RSECT8
−0.01231	0.14109	0.17359	0.18445	0.32082	0.21617	0.13446	UNION
0.00958	0.28044	0.17020	0.31812	0.46182	0.21674	0.10996	SOCSEC
0.01374	0.22503	0.14857	0.26355	0.38874	0.18323	0.10011	CONTRACT
0.07358	−0.09280	−0.09858	−0.05652	−0.15506	−0.11029	−0.06148	DIST
0.04962	0.12481	0.05931	0.17674	0.21580	0.06390	0.06603	DTRAIN
0.05648	0.09196	−0.00575	0.11740	0.15039	0.00521	0.03172	FSIZE
0.05634	0.21255	0.17475	0.31633	0.42955	0.20472	0.17420	LOGFSIZE

(*Table continues on the following page.*)

Table 10A-1 (*continued*)

Variable	RSECT1	RSECT3	RSECT4	RSECT5	RSECT6	RSECT7	RSECT8
LOGINC	−0.00908	−0.01147	−0.01817	0.02032	0.01837	0.02628	0.19555
EXPER	0.07958	−0.02772	−0.03400	−0.03695	−0.00781	−0.02443	−0.03125
EXPSQ	0.07716	−0.04075	−0.03446	−0.02205	−0.00756	−0.02820	−0.01982
DBOG	−0.02552	0.04265	−0.00355	−0.01653	0.05976	0.03664	−0.04268
DCITY	0.10829	−0.02905	−0.01071	−0.03303	−0.02189	0.07883	−0.05998
DTOWN	−0.00039	−0.03923	−0.01583	0.00725	−0.03202	−0.02358	0.11899
DURB	0.00754	−0.03153	−0.00521	0.00447	0.03458	0.01750	0.02046
DUMP	0.03134	0.10512	0.01852	0.00878	0.06805	−0.05067	−0.19542
DUMS	−0.01334	−0.00645	0.03347	−0.01294	0.03371	0.02822	0.03772
DUMH	0.01718	−0.05361	−0.02820	−0.02212	−0.04793	0.04548	0.20884
PRIMED	0.02234	0.04957	0.03631	0.00022	0.03631	−0.00194	0.00976
SECED	−0.01186	0.00948	0.02322	−0.01248	0.02409	0.03897	0.10658
HIGHED	0.00749	−0.04630	−0.00973	−0.00221	−0.05880	0.06357	0.19558
POSTED	0.01467	−0.05685	−0.03017	−0.00143	−0.07169	0.01198	0.20495
RSECT1	1.00000	−0.06137	−0.03013	−0.03279	−0.05522	−0.04374	−0.05955
RSECT3	−0.06137	1.00000	−0.12772	−0.13902	−0.23407	−0.18543	−0.25246
RSECT4	−0.03013	−0.12772	1.00000	−0.06825	−0.11492	−0.09104	−0.12395
RSECT5	−0.03279	−0.13902	−0.06825	1.00000	−0.12508	−0.09909	−0.13491
RSECT6	−0.05522	−0.23407	−0.11492	−0.12508	1.00000	−0.16684	−0.22715
RSECT7	−0.04374	−0.18543	−0.09104	−0.09909	−0.16684	1.00000	−0.17995
RSECT8	−0.05955	−0.25246	−0.12395	−0.13491	−0.22715	−0.17995	1.00000
UNION	−0.02613	0.05138	0.02050	0.03976	0.11164	0.01255	−0.07689
SOCSEC	−0.03316	0.09851	−0.02799	0.07063	0.07426	−0.01135	−0.09238
CONTRACT	−0.03400	0.02977	−0.02107	0.09161	0.07104	−0.01828	−0.04768
DIST	−0.21467	0.04638	−0.14450	−0.00971	0.30479	0.09273	−0.04630
DTRAIN	−0.00795	0.03027	−0.00692	0.02225	0.06457	0.02958	−0.04953
FSIZE	−0.01383	0.05838	0.04158	0.05016	0.07109	−0.03875	0.08208
LOGFSIZE	−0.02198	0.08964	0.00987	0.09969	0.09083	−0.04210	−0.10518

Source: 1978 World Bank–DANE Household Survey.

UNION	SOCSEC	CONTRACT	DIST	DTRAIN	FSIZE	LOGFSIZE	Variable
0.33132	0.41617	0.35382	-0.09109	0.20440	0.15704	0.40862	LOGINC
-0.12054	-0.20834	-0.17521	0.01820	-0.11909	-0.07251	-0.25031	EXPER
0.12007	-0.19527	-0.16056	0.01048	-0.12395	-0.07954	-0.23843	EXPSQ
0.10269	0.22172	0.17784	0.01837	0.06140	0.04144	0.22543	DBOG
-0.03681	0.01793	0.05394	-0.06854	-0.01937	-0.00024	0.00454	DCITY
0.08953	0.05515	0.04871	-0.09795	0.06676	0.03568	0.04760	DTOWN
0.05169	-0.08848	-0.05316	0.00320	-0.03163	0.00209	-0.09756	DURB
0.01231	0.00958	0.01374	0.07358	0.04962	0.05648	0.05634	DUMP
0.14109	0.28044	0.22503	-0.09280	0.12481	0.09196	0.21255	DUMS
0.17359	0.17020	0.14857	-0.09858	0.05931	-0.00575	0.17475	DUMH
0.18445	0.31812	0.26355	-0.05652	0.17674	0.11740	0.31633	PRIMED
0.32082	0.46182	0.38874	-0.15506	0.21580	0.15039	0.42955	SECED
0.21617	0.21674	0.18323	-0.11029	0.06390	0.00521	0.20472	HIGHED
0.13446	0.10996	0.10011	-0.06148	0.06603	0.03172	0.17420	POSTED
-0.02613	-0.03316	-0.03400	-0.21467	-0.00795	-0.01383	-0.02198	RSECT1
0.05138	0.09851	0.02977	0.04638	0.03027	0.05838	0.08964	RSECT3
0.02050	-0.02799	-0.02107	-0.14450	0.00692	0.04158	0.00987	RSECT4
0.03976	0.07063	0.09161	-0.00971	0.02225	0.05016	0.09969	RSECT5
0.11164	0.07426	0.07104	0.30479	0.06457	0.07109	0.09083	RSECT6
0.01255	-0.01135	-0.01828	0.09273	0.02958	-0.03875	-0.04210	RSECT7
0.07689	-0.09238	-0.04768	0.04630	0.04953	-0.08208	-0.10518	RSECT8
1.00000	0.43171	0.36819	0.01010	0.34111	0.35926	0.53153	UNION
0.43171	1.00000	0.62733	-0.01772	0.25704	0.26487	0.66810	SOCSEC
0.36819	0.62733	1.00000	-0.03555	0.22629	0.20329	0.56796	CONTRACT
0.01010	-0.01772	-0.03555	1.00000	0.05865	0.03237	0.02223	DIST
0.34111	0.25704	0.22629	0.05865	1.00000	0.22267	0.34392	DTRAIN
0.35926	0.26487	0.20329	0.03237	0.22267	1.00000	0.59440	FSIZE
0.53153	0.66810	0.56796	0.02223	0.34392	0.59440	1.00000	LOGFSIZE

Table 10A-2. *Earnings Functions for Female Workers in Cali, 1978*

	Dependent variable				
	Log monthly earnings			Log HWAGE	Log of monthly earnings[a]
Variable	1	2	3	4	5
DUMP	0.0026	−0.008	−0.065	−0.092	—
DUMS	−0.162	−0.154	−0.059	−0.088	—
DUMH	−0.476	−0.359	−0.277	−0.108	—
PRIMED	0.079*	0.090*	0.072*	0.104*	—
SECED	0.133*	0.107*	0.069*	0.106*	—
HIGHED	0.230*	0.204*	0.160	0.157	—
POSTED	0.161	0.163	0.202	0.062	0.068*
EXPER	0.014	0.012	0.005	0.013	0.006
EXPSQ	−0.0003	−0.0002	−0.0001	−0.0001	−0.0001
DCALI	−0.167*	−0.110	−0.155	−0.131	0.139
DCITY	0.286	0.282	0.161	0.168	0.134
DTOWN	−0.034	−0.016	−0.081	0.0001	−0.059
DURB	−0.141	−0.105	−0.095	0.102	−0.060
RSECT1	—	0.345	0.421	0.666	0.389
RSECT2	—	0.339*	0.418*	0.237*	0.413*
RSECT3	—	0.211*	0.174*	0.168*	0.069
RSECT4	—	−0.135	−0.174*	0.093	−0.191*
RSECT6	—	0.064	0.145	0.102	0.201*
RSECT7	—	0.263*	0.227*	0.227*	0.196*
UNION	—	—	0.222*	0.181*	0.238*
SOCSEC	—	—	0.309*	0.360*	0.341*
CONTRACT	—	—	0.073	0.015	0.079
DIST	−0.051[a]	−0.025	−0.030	−0.018	−0.050*
CONST	7.72	7.49	7.53	1.93	7.52
R^2	0.219	0.244	0.301	0.359	0.350
Number of observations	592	592	592	592	592
Mean of dependent variable	8.07	8.07	8.07	2.81	8.07

— Not applicable.

Note: Regression coefficients marked with an asterisk are significant at the 5 percent level.

a. The coefficient of YRSEDU is used as the education variable in regression 5.

Source: 1978 World Book–DANE Household Survey.

Table 10A-3. *Earnings Functions for Female Workers in Bogotá Using Different Experience Variables, 1978*

Variable	EXPER	YRSOCCUP	YRSFIRM
DUMP	0.052	0.006	−0.007
	(0.8)	(0.1)	(1.1)
DUMS	0.106	0.058	0.024
	(1.0)	(0.6)	(0.2)
DUMH	0.075	0.044	0.047
	(0.4)	(0.2)	(0.3)
PRIMED	0.015	0.039	0.038
	(0.7)	(2.0)	(2.0)
SECED	0.068	0.061	0.065
	(5.1)	(4.8)	(5.1)
HIGHED	0.056	0.040	0.037
	(1.5)	(4.8)	(5.1)
POSTED	0.377	0.397	0.385
	(6.0)	(6.5)	(6.3)
EXPER	0.021	0.028	0.044
	(5.5)	(5.8)	(7.3)
EXPSQ	−0.0004	−0.007	−0.0014
	(5.6)	(4.4)	(5.7)
DBOG	−0.075	−0.074	−0.074
	(1.8)	(1.8)	(3.1)
DCITY	−0.0201	−0.194	−0.161
	(1.6)	(1.6)	(1.8)
DTOWN	−0.037	−0.013	−0.032
	(0.5)	(0.2)	(1.3)
DURB	−0.034	−0.034	−0.029
	(0.8)	(0.8)	(0.4)
RSECT1	0.169	0.182	0.163
	(1.3)	(1.5)	(1.3)
RSECT3	0.205	0.193	0.207
	(4.2)	(4.0)	(4.4)
RSECT4	0.168	0.156	0.163
	(2.4)	(2.3)	(2.3)
RSECT5	0.264	0.226	0.241
	(4.0)	(3.5)	(3.8)
RSECT6	0.281	0.249	0.257
	(5.2)	(4.7)	(4.9)
RSECT7	0.287	0.264	0.278
	(5.0)	(4.7)	(5.0)
RSECT8	0.486	0.464	0.486
	(9.6)	(9.3)	(9.8)
UNION	0.204	0.201	0.159
	(4.7)	(4.9)	(3.9)

(Table continues on the following page.)

Table 10A-3 (continued)

Variable	EXPER	YRSOCCUP	YRSFIRM
SOCSEC	0.268	0.256	0.239
	(6.8)	(6.6)	(6.2)
CONTRACT	0.102	0.117	0.102
	(3.2)	(3.7)	(3.3)
DIST	0.015	0.015	−0.014
	(3.1)	(3.2)	(3.1)
CONST	7.39	7.43	7.45
R^2	0.406	0.411	0.418
Number of observations	1,807	1,867	1,866
Mean of experience variable	17.6	6.02	3.83
Mean of dependent variable	8.21	—	—

— Not applicable.
Note: t statistics in parentheses.
Source: See table 10A-2.

Table 10A-4. *Earnings Functions for Female Workers in Bogotá by Education Level, 1975–78*

Variable	1973	1975	1977	1978
DUMP	0.124	0.080	−0.030	0.040
	(6.7)	(1.4)	(0.4)	(0.6)
DUMS	−0.029	0.009	−0.161	0.043
	(0.9)	(0.1)	(1.6)	(0.4)
DUMH	0.067	0.099	0.004	−0.030
	(0.9)	(0.5)	(0.0)	(0.2)
PRIMED	0.114	0.008	0.052	0.030
	(22.1)	(0.5)	(2.7)	(1.5)
SECED	0.224	0.136	0.108	0.116
	(54.9)	(12.5)	(8.8)	(8.9)
HIGHED	0.075	0.097	0.088	0.072
	(5.0)	(2.6)	(2.4)	(1.9)
POSTED	0.266	−0.154	0.193	0.403
	(8.2)	(2.7)	(2.5)	(6.3)
EXPER	0.055	0.021	0.014	0.027
	(44.3)	(5.8)	(3.5)	(6.7)
EXPSQ	−0.0008	−0.10004	−0.0003	−0.0005
	(33.9)	(6.0)	(3.2)	(6.5)
DBOG	0.121	−0.059	−0.042	−0.032
	(11.7)	(2.0)	(1.3)	(0.7)

Table 10A-4 (continued)

Variable	1973	1975	1977	1978
DCITY	0.236	—	—	0.028
	(5.5)			(1.6)
DTOWN	0.147	—	—	0.028
	(6.5)			(0.4)
DURB	—	—	—	−0.015
				(0.4)
RSECT1	0.037	0.365	0.094	0.108
	(1.3)	(3.5)	(1.0)	(1.4)
RSECT3	0.036	0.140	0.147	0.211
	(2.2)	(3.2)	(3.0)	(4.3)
RSECT4	0.083	0.135	0.210	0.154
	(4.1)	(2.5)	(3.2)	(2.2)
RSECT5	0.091	0.284	0.235	0.317
	(4.2)	(4.8)	(3.5)	(4.7)
RSECT6	0.060	0.169	0.131	0.269
	(3.5)	(3.7)	(2.5)	(5.3)
RSECT7	0.083	0.298	0.333	0.237
	(5.0)	(5.8)	(6.5)	(4.2)
RSECT8	0.139	0.418	0.409	0.399
	(7.7)	(8.3)	(8.5)	(7.8)
CONST	5.01	6.67	6.98	7.29
R^2	0.503	0.298	0.271	0.345
Number of observations	18,503	2,163	1,915	1,887
Mean of dependent variable	6.58	7.37	7.73	8.21

Note: t statistics in parentheses.
Source: See table 10-A2.

Urban Poverty, Income, and Employment: What Have We Learned?

The image of Bogotá that emerges from all the studies reported in this monograph is one of a vibrantly growing city that has withstood the challenges of sustained and extremely rapid growth over about fifty years. Much of this growth has been concentrated in the past three decades. During the 1970s, incomes rose significantly in real terms, poverty levels decreased, and employment grew at remarkable rates. Moreover, dualism in the labor market is difficult to find, and even the overall inequality in the distribution of incomes may have declined. Despite high rates of population growth and inmigration, by the late 1970s open urban unemployment had ceased to be a major problem in Bogotá and to some extent in other cities of Colombia.

These upbeat conclusions are in marked contrast to those presented in various writings on employment prospects and urban growth in Colombia and in other similar developing countries during the late 1960s and early 1970s. The 1967 ILO employment mission, for example, found extremely high rates of open unemployment and underemployment in urban areas in 1967; unemployment (including full-time equivalent underemployment) was estimated to be on the order of 25 percent. The mission concluded that, over the period 1970–85, output needed to grow by about 8.1 percent a year and nonagriculture by 8.9 percent a year if previous unemployment and future growth in the labor force were to be fully absorbed (ILO 1970). Similarly, the World Bank's 1970 mission estimated necessary output growth to be about 7 percent per year (World Bank 1972). Although the point was not made explicitly, the tone of the reports implied that such a sustained rate of growth over a fifteen-year period was unlikely, but that everything possible needed to be done to achieve this goal.

As we have seen, the actual rate of growth of GDP in the 1970s was closer to 6 percent, and yet the employment problem by and large disappeared. More recent expectations of continued rapid population growth in Bogotá (for example, Lubell and McCallum 1978) have been belied by a marked slowdown during the past decade. Similar gloomy prognostications have been common for other large cities in developing countries, but most have weath-ered the threatened storm quite well. The various factors that have been responsible for these recent trends in income growth and in the labor market in Bogotá (and Cali) are the subject of this chapter, and I also assess how applicable the findings reported here might be to other cities in developing countries.

In retrospect it turns out that the period covered by the City Study (1977 to 1980) and by this analysis (1972 to 1980) was a remarkable one in recent Colombian economic history. The average growth rate of real gross national product was about 6 percent from 1960 right up to 1980, although it showed signs of slowing down toward the end of this period. It was during 1973–78 that the unprecedented 6 percent annual expansion in employment took place. Although various East Asian countries and Brazil tend to get all the credit for working "miracles" with their economies, the performance of Colombia in the 1970s was truly little short of a miracle. As pointed out by Urrutia (1985), the early years of that decade witnessed a major turning point for Colombia: real wages in agriculture began to rise after stagnating for at least forty years, and the agricultural labor force began to stabilize or contract in absolute terms. Urbanization has now reached about the 70 percent level and its rate of growth is slowing down. If the process of urbanization in general and the growth of the city in particular are regarded as following a sigmoid path, Colombia now appears to be at the turning point of the curve; this means that future rates of urbanization are going to be lower than they have been over the past fifty years. Earlier observers of change can be forgiven for expecting continued faster urban growth, for their expectations were based on experience of fifty years' duration. If the findings in this study differ somewhat from theirs, the reason, at least in part, is that the period over which data were collected for the City Study was a dramatic one.

I will now discuss the policy framework and economic environment in Colombia within which the changes reported here have taken place. This is necessary in order to arrive at some assessment of how fortuitous they were and how replicable they might be. It should be pointed out that, like other countries, Colombia has been quite hard hit by the current international recession. Economic activity has slowed and urban unemployment has again increased quite significantly. It remains to be seen whether the happy results of the 1970s were a flash in the pan or part of a long-run structural change in the growth path of the Colombian economy, with the current downturn representing a cyclical movement of an aberrantly large magnitude.

This study differs from others in a number of significant ways. First, most studies of income, poverty, and employment are countrywide in scope, and are therefore too general to give a flavor of the structure of change at the city level. In this book, I have concentrated primarily on Bogotá and sec-ondarily on Cali in order to develop a detailed picture of the working of specific urban labor markets. Second, most studies depend on a single data set for description and analysis and thus have to draw inferences over time from other studies and can make few tests to gauge the reliability of the data set(s) being used. For example, Anand's (1983) and Mazumdar's (1981) studies of Malaysia and Fields's work on Colombia were each based on a single data source (Fields, for example, used the 1973 population census). I have had the opportunity of using four different but largely consistent data sets over the period 1973 to 1978, and have therefore been better equipped to trace changes over time and to gauge the reliability of both data and results. Third, most studies on labor markets report results concerning male workers only: I have been able to report most results on a comparable basis for both men and women. Fourth, few, if any, studies on urban income distribution, poverty, and labor markets in developing countries have investigated the spatial dimension of these variables within cities. As a participant in the City Study, I have paid particular attention to spatial differences within the city and have attempted to assess the extent and effect of spatial differentiation among urban population groups.

Income and Poverty in a Rapidly Growing City

The evidence examined here suggests both similarities and differences between the structure of North American cities and that of Bogotá and Cali. The stylized facts about North American cities are that they have become decentralized with respect to population and employment over the past fifty years. In fact, central city densities have actually fallen and the growth that has taken place has been on the periphery. This process has been accompanied by the decay of central cities and the flight of high-income households to suburbs. If decentralization is measured purely by declining population and employment density gradients, it is easy to conclude that South American cities are similar to those in the north. The truth, however, is more complex. Although the evidence from Bogotá indicates that the population density gradient has indeed declined, densities have risen all over the city (except in the central business district). At the same time, city boundaries seem to have been extended periodically, with the effect of keeping average population density roughly constant. Rates of growth are clearly highest at the periphery, but the absolute magnitudes of increase in the city's inner rings match those at its outer limits. This is the result of a high-growth situation that, in a sense, has led people to locate wherever space is available. In the United States, movements have taken place from central cities to suburbs, and inner-city populations have declined in absolute terms. What will happen in cities in developing countries in the future when populations begin to stabilize is difficult to predict. The trends in energy prices suggest that transport costs are now increasing—and thus that a long-term decreasing trend is starting to turn around. It is possible, therefore, that the cities of the future will have higher densities than those now observed in rich cities.

The rich in Bogotá and Cali appear to be moving toward the periphery, but only in one geographical direction—a direction that seems historically determined. This pattern is not very different from those observed by Homer Hoyt for many U.S. cities. However, in the current broad pattern of income distribution in U.S. cities, the poor generally live in the center and the rich in the suburbs. There is some concern that, as jobs have moved to the suburbs along with the residences of the rich, the poor living in the center are becoming increasingly disadvantaged in spatial terms. A similar pattern seems to exist in Bogotá, except that income segregation is by radial sectors rather than by rings. Poor areas are short of jobs compared with rich ones, and those living in the former are in that sense spatially disadvantaged. The transport system has, however, done much to mitigate this spatial disadvantage. Further research in other cities would provide a better idea of general patterns in cities in developing countries, but the evidence from Bogotá and Cali indicates that care needs to be exercised in extrapolating trends from U.S. cities to the developing world.

Both cities are highly segmented spatially by income, Bogotá slightly more than Cali, and there is little evidence of any tendency for this situation to change. Although some signs of a decline in overall inequality are beginning to appear, the absolute level of inequality remains very high; the Gini coefficient is in the region of 0.50, whether measured in terms of households ranked by household income per capita, individuals ranked by household income per capita, or earners by labor earnings. At the same time, the spatial contribution to inequality appears to be increasing; each sector of the city, rich and poor alike, is becoming more homogeneous. The city is therefore becoming more spatially segmented by income over time. As noted above, this segmentation is geographically defined by radial sectors rather than by circular rings, as is more common in North America.

As might be expected, poverty is difficult to measure, but the range of estimates developed on the basis of different assumptions is extremely large—from about 18 to 75 percent in Bogotá, for example. I demonstrated in chapter 5 the dangers implicit in measuring a poverty line and making assertions resulting from it. I also suggested, however, that it is possible to derive a lower bound below which it can be asserted with a high degree of confidence that people must be poor and malnourished. In Bogotá this lower bound decreased substantially—from about 25 to 12 percent of the population—during the short period between 1973 and 1978. Real wages at the bottom of the income scale have risen over this period while skilled and white-collar workers' wages have stagnated in real terms. Some of the improvement in income distribution can also be attributed to a dramatic increase in the participation of women during these years, especially since 1977. Much of this increased participation took place among poor women, as has also been suggested by Urrutia (1985).

Although every part of the city has its complement of poor and malnourished people, concentrations of poverty have persisted over time in specific large areas of Bogotá (the south) and Cali (the east). This kind of spatial income segmentation is likely to be exacerbated by the distribution of public services, the quality of which usually follows the pattern of income distribution. This is undoubtedly true in Bogotá and Cali, but the maldistribution of services is not as bad as might be thought. The spread of universal primary education has been complete for some time; it is now the turn of secondary education. The provision of water, sewerage, sanitation, and roads in both cities will also approach universality soon (although Bogotá is better off than Cali). As has been found in a companion study to this book, the transport network is remarkable for its richness and for its high service levels. Flat-rate transit fares also help to reduce the locational disadvantages of the poor in terms of distances from jobs.

Overall, the distribution of public services is probably less unequal than incomes. Selowsky (1979) found that the incidence of benefits from public expenditures was approximately equal across income quintiles in Colombia. Such expenditures were thus quite progressive in proportionate terms, raising the income of each quintile by 25, 15, 10, 7, and 2.5 percent, respectively, in rising order of income. That they can be still more progressive is demonstrated by Meerman (1979) for Malaysia, where similar quintile-based benefits from public expenditure were 50, 36, 27, 24, and 2.5 percent for each successive income quintile. Hence, although government policy toward the poor has probably been quite successful with respect to fiscal public expenditures, much improvement is still needed. Colombia's per capita income is now more than US$1,400; there is little reason for even 10–15 percent of the capital city's population to be almost certainly malnourished and poor.

The potential effectiveness of government policy in this respect has been shown to be high elsewhere. A recent study in Chile, for example, shows that "the decline in fertility, the increase in the supplementary food program, the expansion of medical services to the mother and child, and the expansion in potable water and sewerage availability experienced in Chile in the 1970s have contributed significantly to Chile's infant mortality decline" (Castaneda 1984). In the United States, there has been a long-standing and lively debate on the effectiveness of government action in narrowing black-white earnings differentials. In a careful new study, Smith (1984) gives further historical evidence linking the quality of black education with the future performance of blacks in the labor market. A major relative decline in teachers' salaries that took place in black schools in the south between 1890 and 1915 led to a marked deterioration in the quality of these schools. The effects of this decline reverberated in the performance of blacks in the labor market over the next forty years, as these cohorts went through the labor market. This was in contrast to the improvement that had taken place in black education in the immediate post-reconstruction period up to about 1890.

These examples illustrate the potential power of direct government action to relieve poverty and to affect individuals' labor market performance over a long period of time. They counter the current pessimism about such action. Wherever there is a marked spatial concentration of the poor, as in Bogotá, government intervention becomes easier to target, and analyses of the type attempted in this study become useful. Consider now what this study has found out about the working of the labor market.

Participation and Employment

First and foremost, the empirical work affirms the validity of the standard human capital model (HK) in explaining the variation in personal labor earnings. In comparison with the level of explanation reached in the United States and European countries, where such models typically explain 30–40 percent of the earnings variation, the level of explanation in Bogotá was 50 percent or higher. This matches results for Malaysia found by Anand (1983) and Mazumdar (1981). In those studies, variables other than human capital ones (which essentially comprise education and experience) were found to be unimportant even if statistically significant in their effect. One reason for the relatively high success of HK in developing countries is the relatively high dispersion in education levels found there. Another reason often suggested for the success of HK is the fact that a considerable proportion of employment in developing countries is in the government, where credentialism plays an important role in determining earnings. However, it is not clear empirically that there *is* a higher proportion of government employment in developing countries. Moreover, at least in Bogotá, the HK model also performs well for the self-employed and other nongovernment sectors. Other results support the idea that education is extremely important in the determination of earnings and therefore have major implications for government policy.

During the 1970s the supply of education at all levels in Colombia, but particularly at the secondary and higher levels, increased significantly and deepened. A principal finding of this study is that returns to higher education fell as a consequence of this development. At the same time, however,

credentialism was found to be important: workers received premiums for completing secondary and higher education (but no longer for completing primary schooling). These results strongly suggest that a continuing expansion of education, along with a reduction in the dispersion of completed education, will be quite effective in reducing inequality, at least in personal labor earnings, over the long run. This judgment has to do with the quantity of education; the issue of quality has already been touched on, but will be discussed further below.

Interesting results were also reported for the other main human capital variable: experience in work. Job-oriented training, occupation-specific experience, and firm-specific tenure are widely believed to play an important role in the dispersion of earnings, but in this study they were all found to perform less well than general work experience as measured by (age – education – 6). This finding in turn points to the unimportance of internal labor markets and the existence of quite high job mobility. Furthermore, these results could be said to suggest the usefulness of policies that concentrate on general education (as was also recently documented for Colombia by Psacharopoulos and Zabalza 1984) and that promote job mobility. It may not be very useful for the government to become involved with detailed manpower planning: people can be trusted to train themselves according to perceived demand and to shift jobs when necessary, as long as this is made feasible for them. Job mobility is made easier when fringe benefits such as pension, life insurance, and health insurance can be carried over from job to job, and when retraining is not difficult to find.

The evidence indicates that the labor market in Bogotá and Cali is not characterized by a strong protected sector. Those who work in establishments with formalized employment arrangements (unions, social security schemes, written contracts) and in large enterprises earn only slightly more than others. Moreover, the stability of estimated rates of return to schooling and experience across different occupational and industrial categories argues against the existence of a highly segmented labor market in Bogotá and Cali. Contrary to previous findings, which suggest that union membership raises earnings by as much as 20 percent (Tenjo 1975), the effect of unionism seems to be small in this case. Membership appears to be marginally more important for low-skilled male workers, women, and public sector employees.

Much of the literature on the informal and protected sectors in cities in developing countries is connected with high rural-urban migration. The well-known Harris-Todaro model, which has gained wide acceptability, suggests that migrants typically arrive in cities and "wait" for protected sector jobs while working in the low-productivity informal sector. The results from Bogotá and Cali are not consistent with this view. Migrants are not especially poor; they do not concentrate in specific areas of the city (either the center or the periphery); they are not concentrated in particular occupations or activities; on the average, they are neither less educated nor, perhaps, less skilled than natives. Meanwhile, there are many "second-generation" urban poor among the natives of the city. These features of the City Study data run counter to the popular ideas of poor migrants streaming into the city. Furthermore, there is little evidence that migrants are disadvantaged in the job market. Indeed, both recent arrivals and the migrant population as a whole look very much like natives. The composition of immigrants with respect to jobs and earnings essentially reflects that of the natives. If anything, migrants are marginally more successful than natives.

Much of the literature also suggests that the informal sector consists disproportionately of low-wage service workers and others who work few or irregular hours, in contrast with the formal sector, which is said to employ well-paid production workers who work regular hours. In Bogotá, there is little evidence that production workers are better off than those in other occupations. The only activities that have consistently high concentrations of low earnings are construction and, to a lesser extent, transport. Both these sectors typically employ the most unskilled members of the labor force. Furthermore, with the exception of construction, poor male workers tend to work longer hours than richer ones. Few people are underemployed in the sense that they could work longer hours if more work became available; many who say that they need more work are already working long hours. What they need are jobs that offer higher productivity and earnings rather than more hours.

The evidence therefore shows that there are few structural imperfections in the labor market and that segmentation cannot be held responsible for high or low earnings in any specific sectors. Earnings are clearly related to people's skill levels.

Perhaps the most controversial part of this study is that current location of residence is considered a partial determinant of earnings. The general causation is arguably the other way around; that is, as people become better off, they are quite likely to move to better residential areas. Specifically, the rich generally go to live in rich neighborhoods. I have no disagreement with this view. My results merely suggest the existence of some feedback effects such that the location of an individual's residence may affect his or her earnings potential. These effects are only significant for the better educated: unskilled workers' earnings are similar regardless of the location of their residence. Participation in the labor force also seems to be unaffected by location of residence. My hypothesis then is that the spatial effect essentially captures a differential in the quality of schooling. People living in the poorer parts of the city are more likely to have received a low-quality education, either in their city neighborhoods or in their places of origin if they are migrants. When there is a large concentration of poverty in one area of a city, a person born and raised there will be likely to attend a low-quality school, acquire low aspirations, and develop a poor network of contacts; he or she is therefore assured of a low and flat age-income profile. In such conditions, relatively fewer people continue with schooling to late stages; and those who do so are likely to earn less than their formal equivalents from other parts of the city, because the latter receive superior-quality schooling at all stages.

Some of the problems of the poor but more educated residents of the poor areas of the city also emanate from their relatively deprived home environments. This is reflected in one of the more important correlates of poverty: people with low education and hence flat age-income profiles sink further into poverty during the household-nurturing stage of their life cycles. As the household expands and its income remains the same, household income per capita declines. This effect is measurable and clearly points to higher poverty indices for the 35 – 44 age group and their children. Meerman (1979), in his study of Malaysia, also found that households in the bottom quintile had to spend about 18 percent of their incomes on out-of-pocket expenses for their children's education — even with free primary schooling. The pressures to cease schooling at early ages must therefore be high; those who contribute until later ages probably do so at considerable cost to the household as a whole with respect to extending the period of household poverty. The spatial effect on earnings is therefore twofold. First, the concentration of poverty in an area is likely to perpetuate itself because of its self-reinforcing aspects; second, the dice are loaded against people from such areas who do succeed in acquiring higher education, partly because of low-quality schooling, partly because of a poor home environment, and partly because of the lack of a network of contacts in a deprived neighborhood. The poor would have to face these problems anywhere; the point to appreciate is that when such problems are concentrated in one area, their impact is exacerbated.

The disturbing aspect of these findings is that if deficient environmental factors faced by a poor child are reinforced by higher segmentation, these differences are likely to affect his or her long-term performance in the labor market. Where income distribution is concerned, these effects can reverberate for a whole generation and can be self-reinforcing. Specific policy actions can at least mitigate these effects. It would be idle to suggest that the city should be less segmented; socioeconomic conditions in Colombia make this difficult to imagine. It is practical, however, to suggest that more attention be given to the quality of schooling in these areas, particularly to the facilities and teachers' salaries. Good teachers can even be paid extra as an incentive to work in these schools. Supplementary food programs and better medical services for mother and child would also help. Such measures would be easier to target than is usually the case, because of the existence of spatial concentrations of the poor.

The final issue addressed in this monograph is that of women in the labor market. Women earn less than men in every occupation and industry of activity. The ratio of average female earnings to those of males is between one-half and two-thirds in most developing countries. In Bogotá and Cali it is closer to one-half. The existence of discrimination is difficult to test for because of the lack of data on work experience for women. For men (age − years of education − 6) is a good proxy for experience, but this is not the case for women. What evidence there is suggests that women's rates of return to education are similar to men's but that this is not true for experience. Thus earnings differentials increase with age. The experience results for women are biased since they do not take into account the fact that women typically interrupt their careers because of childbearing. An attempt to estimate this interruption was not successful.

That this is an important issue for the future is borne out by the results on female labor force participation. First, the expansion in the education of females in the past two decades has been so great that access is now almost equal. The results indicate a higher probability of participation with higher education. To the extent that the decision to receive education is linked to the decision to work, this would indicate an even greater intention to participate than is apparent now. Second, the tightening of the labor market in the late 1970s and the consequent increase in real wages at the bottom of the income scale has motivated many poor women to go out and work. Third, measured urban unemployment rates have always been higher for women. Many more women would like to work than now do so; their numbers would probably increase even further should male-female earnings differentials be reduced or removed. Other changes pertaining to day care, flexible hours of work, and so on would also be necessary if women were in fact to participate in much greater numbers than now. The evidence from Bogotá suggests that the unprecedented increases in female labor force participation that have occurred in developed countries are likely to be replicated in developing countries, but perhaps at an earlier stage in the latter than happened in the former.

What Have We Learned?

The overwhelming message emanating from this study is that high urban unemployment, long-run employment problems, high poverty, and segmented labor markets need not accompany rapid urban growth. An appropriate economic environment bolstered by a judicious mix of policies can make better outcomes possible, as was the case in Bogotá and Cali in the late 1970s. It is therefore instructive to conclude this monograph by identifying those factors that were perhaps special and fortuitous for Colombia in the 1970s, together with others that are more replicable.

The economic expansion that occurred in Colombia in the 1970s consisted of increased demand for both rural and urban products. Policy changes that occurred in the mid- to late 1960s, along with specific technical changes that took place in coffee and food crops, induced an environment that did not discriminate against agriculture. Hence, when coffee prices rose in world markets, the benefits filtered down to producers and eventually to labor as well. The 1970s therefore witnessed an increased demand for Colombia's agricultural products. At the same time, major policy changes that took place in 1967 and remained in place for the following decade made Colombia's industrial products more competitive in world markets. An important component of these changes was the institution of a crawling peg exchange rate that was a judicious mix of floating and fixed rates and was administered so as to ensure that the Colombia peso was not overvalued. The result was that Colombia had its first current account deficit in six years in 1981.

The total effect of the policy changes was a continuing expansion in external and domestic demand for Colombia's industrial products: external because of relatively outward-looking policies, and domestic because of overall increases in national income. At the same time, Colombia pursued a responsible but expansionary fiscal policy, and considerable expenditures were made in education, health, transport, and construction. As a result, demand for tertiary-sector "outputs" also rose at a sustained fast pace. During this entire period financial markets were also allowed to operate efficiently and to expand into different areas of activity. A particular innovation special to Colombia was the institution of indexed banking instruments called UPAC, which enabled small savers to save for and invest in housing. Although the overall effect was small, the positive marginal effect of expansion in housing construction is clear.

This expansion of demand in each major economic sector resulted in a corresponding increase in demand for labor in each sector. The rise in coffee prices financed a considerable expansion of the area sown, while technical change, which consisted of the shift to the caturra variety, led to high labor use as well as higher productivity per worker. Since this occurred at a time when the level of urbanization had begun to exceed 60 percent, "surplus" labor became scarce in rural areas!

On the industrial side, monetary and fiscal policy, along with increased exports, encouraged more labor-intensive manufacturing. Thoumi (1979), for example, shows that export industries typically use more labor than import-substituting industries. But the highest increase in employment in the late 1970s took place in the tertiary sector. Part of this was caused by windfall income gains from unprecedentedly high coffee prices, and part came from unaccounted flows from the drug trade. But government expenditure policy also contributed to this increased demand. The government emphasized expenditures on health, education, nutrition, and rural development (all labor-using activities) in the 1970s. Furthermore, wage policy in the public sector was to keep real wages constant but to increase the quantity of services offered and hence employment.

There was some slowing of infrastructure investment in the early to mid-1970s, and some believe that the effects of this dip are being felt now. The combined result of the factors listed above, however, was an increase in demand for all kinds of labor in both the urban and rural sectors. Employment therefore grew in the 1970s, particularly in the latter part of the decade, as did real income. To understand the increases in real incomes that occurred, one must also look at the supply side.

Natural population increases, which had been extremely high in the 1950s and 1960s, before the recent decline in fertility, caused the labor force to expand rapidly in the 1970s. Such high rates of expansion would not normally be associated with labor productivity increases and growth in real wages. But it has been calculated that overall labor productivity improved at an annual rate of 1.1 percent between 1967 and 1973 and 0.9 percent between 1973 and 1980 (World Bank 1984a). The labor share in national income has therefore risen since 1974. Much of the increase in productivity has come from agriculture, where productivity rose at an astounding rate of 3.7 percent a year between 1974 and 1979, although it appears to have stagnated ever since.

Although the driving factor in the growth of labor productivity was the growth of demand, it had to be matched by improvements in labor quality on the supply side. The educational quality of the labor force as a whole is estimated to have grown at an annual rate of 1.3 percent during 1964–73 and 1.1 percent during 1973–80, as measured by comparative enrollment rates between 1960 and 1980 for the relevant age groups attending school. In 1960 the enrollment rates in primary, secondary, and higher education were 77, 12, and 2 percent, respectively; by 1980, they had improved to 100, 39, and 9 percent, respectively — a remarkable achievement. The growth in real incomes, given that the demand for labor was there, was made possible by this major expansion of education — which itself, incidentally, increased the demand for skilled educated labor. One further point of interest concerns the minimum wage. The legislated minimum wage of agricultural workers grew by 35 percent between 1974 and 1980, and it seems to have been complied with in practice. Urrutia (1985) concludes that wage policy must take some of the credit for raising the incomes of the poor. He argues that although demand and supply conditions in the late 1970s made the increase possible, wages would probably not have risen as much in the absence of legislation.

The relatively happy situation prevailing in Bogotá and Cali in the late 1970s that this study has documented—high employment, increased female participation rates, increases in real unskilled wages, a reduction in poverty, and a slight narrowing of the income distribution — has been explained by the larger economic situation prevailing in Colombia during the years under study. High international coffee prices and drug-related income inflows were like manna from heaven that fueled the engine of growth. This should not mask the considerable difficulties that still existed: disparities between rich and poor continued to be wide, and income distribution in Bogotá was still probably among the more unequal for large cities. But the employment-promoting exchange rate policy, fiscal policy, expenditure policy, and social policy have been at least as responsible for the real achievements that were observed in Colombia in the late 1970s. Many of these policies can certainly be emulated elsewhere in efforts to promote urban employment and income growth. Finally, for the sake of Colombia, I hope that my analysis is correct and that the country's economic health will be restored by its own policies once the current international recession is over.

Appendix A

The Data

The City Study has assembled a data bank of existing sources of information on Bogotá and Cali in the form of copies of the original computer tapes prepared by the respective originators of the data. All have been documented in detail by Valverde (1978) and Y. J. Lee (1979, 1980). This study utilizes four of these data sets, all of which were originally collected by DANE. The 1978 survey was conducted jointly by the City Study and DANE.

1973 Population Census

The last two censuses were taken in 1964 and 1973. Unfortunately, the 1964 census does not report incomes. There has been widespread skepticism about the coverage of the 1973 census[1] but Potter and Ordonez (1976) concluded after a careful demographic analysis that the information they analyzed from the advance sample appeared to be of good quality, at least in relation to previous censuses. They estimated that the overall underenumeration for Colombia as a whole was probably about 7 percent. The tape provided by DANE for public use is a 4 percent sample of households. For Bogotá, however, the tape covers all households living in the buildings that happen to house the 4 percent sample. I have used the entire sample for the tabulations in this book, and expanded it to reflect the size of the city's population and estimated underenumeration. Since this study was particularly concerned with spatial distributions within the city, the sample was expanded so that it would be representative of the various subdivisions within its boundaries. (Details of the methodology used are given in appendix D.)

---

1. See, for example, Lubell and McCallum (1978, p. 126), who regard the Bogotá 1973 results as "simply not usable" and therefore do not rely on the census. Their calculations and projections were based on the 1972 Urban Development Study Household Survey covering 4,675 households.

The census contains information on dwelling and household characteristics, demographic data for all individuals, labor force information for workers, and fertility information on females. Although I cannot comment on its coverage, the overall quality of the information in the sample appears to be good and I therefore agree with Potter and Ordonez (1976) in this regard. Nonresponses appear to be distributed randomly; the only obvious bias is that single-person households predominate in the "no information" categories for income and the labor force. One of the most useful distinguishing features of this data set is that the location of respondents is coded down to the block (manzana) of residence in the city. The next section describes the geocoding system used consistently by DANE in all of its work. Income data were obtained from only one question: "What was your income from all sources last month?" Only about 12 percent of the sample did not report income information—a proportion that compares well with nonresponses in the U.S. census.

Appendix C reports the results of an estimation of the income coverage of the 1973 census as well as the 1977 Household Survey and the 1978 World Bank–DANE Household Survey. The aggregation of all incomes reported in the census appears to be no more than 50 *percent* of the estimated total personal income for Bogotá. Various factors are responsible for this underreporting:

- Twelve percent of the people gave no income information.
- When only one question is asked, much of the nonlabor income is probably not reported.
- Income in kind—for example, as received by domestic servants—is probably not reported.
- Many earners receive end-of-the-year bonuses; these are characteristically not covered in one-shot cross-sectional surveys such as the census, unless the question is asked specifically.

In view of these factors, it is not surprising that the income coverage of the census was only about 50 percent.[2]

Household Surveys

DANE has conducted a regular program of household surveys since 1970; the main objective has been to collect information on the labor force. Since 1975, these surveys have been conducted quarterly, alternating between the

2. This may be compared with a recent estimate of undercoverage in the Brazil 1960 and 1970 censuses by Pfefferman and Webb (1979, p. 16), who find that the censuses cover about 57–58 percent of incomes.

four largest cities and the seven largest cities[3] along with an occasional national survey. We obtained the computer tapes for 1972 (Encuesta de Hogares 6, Fuerza de Trabajo: EH 6-FT), 1975 (EH8E),[4] and 1977 (EH15). The 1972 survey was a national one and covered 6,371 households, of which 1,348 were in Bogotá. It contains information on housing as well as demographic and labor force characteristics. This survey does not provide the intracity location of the respondents. The 1975 survey was a special one for the city of Bogotá; it sampled 3,953 households and contains information on demographic and labor force characteristics only. The 1977 survey was conducted in the four largest cities and sampled 6,082 households, 3,161 of which were in Bogotá. Starting with this survey, DANE began to use "rotational sampling" such that 67 percent of dwelling units sampled remain in the next survey and 33 percent are new. Both the 1975 and 1977 surveys contain the location of respondents' residences. The 1972 and 1975 surveys also have information on the number of workers in each respondent's workplace. This question was not included in the 1977 sample.

In these samples, DANE classifies neighborhoods into six socioeconomic strata: 1 low-low, 2 low, 3 medium low, 4 medium, 5 medium high, and 6 high. At the conclusion of a survey, weights are assigned to each of these strata and are then applied to the members of these strata for all expansions of the sample. These "expansion factors" are supposed to take into account the over- and undersampling that may occur over the course of the survey. The expanded sample should then be correctly representative of the city as a whole.

The 1977 survey is unusual in that as many as 20 percent of the working respondents did not report their incomes, a proportion that compares unfavorably with the census. Consequently, a method was devised to impute incomes to them. Appendix B describes the calculation of incomes for all respondents and the imputation method for nonrespondents.

The coverage of income in the 1977 survey is not much better than that in the 1973 census, despite the more detailed questions asked. Labor income and nonlabor income data are taken separately and income in kind is estimated as well. Even when the imputed incomes are included, the survey covers only about 61 *percent* of the estimated total of personal incomes in Bogotá. It also appears that the highest incomes are either underreported or undersampled. If the incomes reported in the 1977 sample are converted to 1973 pesos, there is little real growth in incomes on the average, and those in the highest categories actually decline.

3. Bogotá, Cali, Medellín, Barranquilla, Bucamaranga, Manizales, and Pasto. The first four are the four largest.
4. EH = Encuesta de Hogares; E = Especial (special sample of Bogotá).

The 1978 World Bank–DANE Household Survey

In 1978 the World Bank City Study and DANE jointly conducted a survey of about 3,000 households in Bogotá and 1,000 households in Cali. This was a larger and more carefully conducted survey than previous ones. It had five main parts: (1) household and dwellings characteristics; (2) demographic characteristics of all individuals; (3) worker characteristics, including information on their place of work; (4) information on the unemployed; and (5) information on vehicle ownership and journey-to-work characteristics for the employed.

A few points are worth noting with regard to this survey. A partial recount of dwelling units was done to take into account the expansion of Bogotá since the 1973 census (earlier surveys were all based on a 1972 sample frame). Information on income was elicited more carefully. In earlier surveys, information on earnings of all workers in a household was usually obtained from any available adult respondent. In this survey, all worker information was obtained from each worker directly, even if this required revisits to the household. Furthermore, income questions were asked of all members of the household even if they did not work. Two questions were asked to obtain labor income: the amount and periodicity of wage payments, and total earnings in the previous month. Income in kind was imputed. Various nonlabor sources of income were specifically mentioned to obtain nonlabor income. As a result, the income coverage of this survey is about 90 percent (as shown in appendix table C-1), which is a great improvement over previous surveys.

The percentage of responses giving no information on income was only 3.6 percent, and these have been imputed by the same method used in the 1977 Household Survey. All regressions were conducted after weighting each observation with expansion factors as in the procedure for 1973 described above. These expansion factors take into account ex-post over- and under-sampling as compared with the sample frame.

Household Survey Samples and the Spatial Disaggregation of Bogotá

In map 3-1 Bogotá has been divided into comunas, rings, and sectors, but the basic socioeconomic spatial unit in the city is a barrio or neighborhood, of which there were about 500 in 1973 and about 700 in 1978 as a result of rapid growth of the city. DANE geocodes this unit in a four-digit number of which the first two digits identify a comuna—a collection of barrios. The last two digits identify barrios within the comuna. The comunas were then further aggregated for City Study purposes into rings and sectors. The boundaries of the comunas shown in map 3-1 are the principal streets in Bogotá. The city is bounded on the east by mountains and therefore has an approximately semicircular shape, although the north-south axis is longer. Note that the first digit goes from 1 to 9 and roughly rotates (increasing) from south to north by sectors (or pie slices). The second digit ranges from 1 to 6 and corresponds roughly to rings centered in comunas 31 and 81 and increasing from south to north.

DANE along with the Ministry of Health compiled an inventory of blocks (manzanas) and of dwelling units within the city before the 1973 census, and that inventory has continued to form the sample frame of all subsequent surveys in Bogotá. Thus none of these surveys had sampled the new neighborhoods that had developed since 1972. The sample frame was therefore updated for the 1978 World Bank–DANE Survey. The sampling is designed to make equiprobable the possibility that any dwelling unit in the city according to the 1972 inventory may be selected. The basic sampling unit (*unidad primaria de muestra*) is a block, within which all households in all dwelling units are interviewed. Provision is made for different sizes of blocks. Since all the sampling was based on the 1972 sample frame, it was difficult to trace time trends for changes within the city. Moreover, caution must be exercised in drawing any conclusions about the changing character of neighborhoods. If different regions of the city differ systematically from one another and if one region changes character over time, the later samples will no longer be representative. Sampling is based on the classification of neighborhoods into the six socioeconomic strata. If neighborhoods change character—that is, filter up or down in the socioeconomic scale—the resulting sample will then no longer be representative. Hence, drawing conclusions about fine changes in the income distribution from two household surveys at two points in time is hazardous in the absence of detailed knowledge of the sampling procedures used. If, however, rates of change are not high, such difficulties are minimal—but then one would have less interest in tracing time trends anyway! These remarks can be extended to the coverage of national surveys, where the heterogeneity of regions is perhaps typically more pronounced than within a city.

These details have been offered here since they are seldom given by users of household survey data. They become particularly important when comparisons are made between surveys undertaken in different years; information on each data source is necessary in order to be aware of biases that may arise from differences in survey design and coverage.

Appendix B

Technical Note on the Calculation of Incomes

As indicated in appendix A, DANE household surveys are now conducted quarterly, alternating between the four largest cities (Bogotá, Medellín, Cali, and Barranquilla) and the seven largest (the above four plus Bucamaranga, Manizales, and Pasto). The data are used mainly for the study of urban employment and unemployment and the characteristics of the labor force. Incomes are reported in the following manner.

1. *For employees of all kinds.* First, cash income from employment is reported according to periodicity of payment, which has five categories: monthly, fortnightly, every ten days, weekly, and daily. The multiple used to convert these incomes into monthly equivalents are as follows:

Monthly	1	
Fortnightly (quincenal)	2	
Every ten days	3.04	$(365/10 \times 1/12)$
Weekly	4.33	$(52/12)$
Daily	21.75	

This method obviously overstates income for those workers who are paid at less than monthly intervals and do not work the whole month. However, less than 5 percent of the workers report that they are paid daily (where error is most likely), so the overall effect of this computation is not likely to be unreasonable.

Second, value of income received in kind (food, shelter, clothing) is reported separately. Total labor income is thus computed for employees as the sum of cash income and income in kind.

2. *Employers and self-employed.* The question asked was "Net earnings last month from job?" The answer was interpreted as labor income, although this is not strictly correct for the self-employed.

3. *All.* Each individual's nonlabor income was assumed to comprise income sources (other than employment) categorized as interest, rents, pensions, cash aid, and other such sources. Consequently, each individual reporting any income had two types of income: labor income and nonlabor income.

4. *No information.* A large proportion of the sample—about 20 percent—in the 1977 household survey did not report their incomes but did give all other characteristics. They could not be omitted because they were not uniformly distributed over the sample but were concentrated, as might be expected, among sales workers, sales managers, and proprietors. The method used for imputing income was similar to that used by the U.S. Bureau of the Census. The objective was to impute incomes in such a way that the new distribution retained the "true" mean and variance values.

As the file was read, a $19 \times 4 \times 4$ matrix was created with the following dimensions:

- Workers were classified as employees and self-employed by sex and three categories of place of residence; this arrangement yielded twelve groups.
- Male employers were classified by the three categories of place of residence; this yielded three additional groups.
- Female employers constituted one group and domestic servants from the three categories formed another three groups, for a total of nineteen groups.
- Four categories of years of education (0, 1–5, 6–11, and 12 +) and four categories of years of experience (0–1, 2–4, 5–9, and 10 +) were used.

Each cell of the resulting $19 \times 4 \times 4$ matrix then contained the income of the most recently read record with these characteristics. The records without incomes were then given the income of the most recently read record having the same characteristics.

The rationale behind this procedure is as follows:

Consider the distribution $f(y_t \mid x_t; \hat{\theta})$, which is the estimated distribution of income y_t of individuals, given their vector of characteristics x_t, the estimated vector of parameters being $\hat{\theta}$. Such a distribution may be estimated from the set of individuals with known incomes and characteristics that will give $\hat{\theta}$.

The procedure described above approximates imputing income to the non-respondents by a random drawing from the above distribution estimated from the set of individuals with known incomes from the sample. If n drawings were made ($n = 1, 2 \ldots$), then the average

$$\bar{y}_{t,n} = \frac{1}{n} \sum_{i=1}^{n} y_{ti}$$

could be used as the predictor. But $\bar{y}_{t,n} \to y_t$ as $n \to \infty$, where $y_t = E[y_t \mid x_t; \hat{\theta}]$. Thus, the expected value of incomes generated by the method used (method 1) is the same as the value that would be generated by method 2 where the nonrespondents have imputed incomes given by $y_t = E[y_t \mid x_t; \hat{\theta}]$.

This would be the result if income equations were estimated and then used to impute incomes to the nonrespondents. Method 1 results in greater variance than method 2. Method 2 gives the Best Linear Unbiased Estimator for the missing incomes, but if the nonrespondents with characteristics x_i are given the mean income of respondents with characteristics x_i, then variance of the overall sample is reduced: this is an undesirable result if we are interested in retaining both the central value and dispersion characteristics of the parent sample.[1]

Another way of interpreting this method is to view it as utilizing extra "noneconomic" variables that would not normally be captured in a standard human-capital-type predictive equation.

Further support for this method of imputation is provided by Ruggles and Ruggles (1974, p. 354), in a paper concerned with strategies for merging and matching microdata sets. It is best to quote them directly:

> The use of a matching process has important methodological implications. Imputation by regression would normally result in assigning mean values, whereas the matching technique reproduces the distribution of values in the original data set. For a single imputation the mean value may be desirable, but for repeated imputations the use of mean values destroys the observed variance. The success of the matching technique depends on the data being quite dense, so that similar cases can be found in both data sets. It should also be noted that for matching purposes no specific functional relationship need be determined in advance. Non-linear relationships will automatically be handled as efficiently as linear relationships, without explicit recognition that the relationships are non-linear. This is in marked contrast with the regression technique, which requires determination of the precise functional form in advance. In those instances where the functional form is well known and the data are scattered so that matching is difficult, regression analysis may provide more valid imputations, but with large bodies of data where similar cases do exist, imputation by matching has the virtues of retaining the distributional characteristics of the original sample and reflecting the basic relationship more accurately.

In this case, two subsets from the same data set are being used on the assumption that the "main" data set has many individuals with characteristics similar to those in the smaller "no information" data subset. One further characteristic of this data set, common to most census or household survey samples, was utilized. Data were usually arranged in spatial order: that is,

---

1. I am indebted to Michael Hartley for clarifying my thoughts on this issue, but he should not be implicated in my interpretation of the U.S. census method used to impute incomes here.

households living in sample segment 1 are followed by the next sample segment 2, then segment 3, and so on. Hence under the method of imputing the income of the last entry cell in the matrix, that individual is also likely to be living in a similar area of the city. The result of these imputations is that all individuals who work now have incomes, except for nonremunerated family workers who have zero incomes.

5. *Household income.* Household income was aggregated from the labor and nonlabor incomes of its constituents, but care was taken to exclude the incomes of live-in domestic servants.

Appendix C

The Coverage of Income in Bogotá in the 1973 Population Census and Household Surveys

There is considerable skepticism about the coverage of income in the 1973 population census and the household surveys used in this study. The population census asked only one question: "How much did you earn last month?" Hence one can expect that nonlabor income, transfers, and so on would tend to be understated. Household surveys have more detailed questions: they ask specifically for the periodicity of wages received and wage amounts, wages in kind, and nonlabor income. Thus one expects that they would capture a larger proportion of income than the population census. Since estimates of poverty are often based on these sources, it is of some importance to obtain an idea of the extent to which they understate income. What proportion of personal income can we expect surveys and census to cover? Schultz (1965) estimated that the 1950 and 1960 census in the United States, covered 91 and 94 percent, respectively, of total income as reported by the Office of Business Economics (OBE). The Current Population Surveys (CPS) covered about 85 percent of total income. All of these sources succeeded in capturing about 95 percent of labor income—99 percent in the case of the 1960 census. The error arose from nonlabor income, the coverage of which ranged from 40 to 60 percent. What can then be expected of Colombian surveys if they match U.S. surveys? For Colombia as a whole, approximately 40 percent of total income is labor income and 60 percent is nonlabor income. Hence if we assume that the proportions are similar for Bogotá, and that Colombian surveys also cover about 50 percent of nonlabor income and 90 percent of labor income, expected coverage would be

$$(0.4 \times 0.9) + (0.6 \times 0.5) = 0.66$$

that is, 66 percent. This provides us with an approximate yardstick with which to assess the coverage of Colombian surveys.

The next problem is to define the appropriate concept of total personal income, as given in national income accounts, with which income obtained from surveys can be compared. This note provides one approach for doing this.

The *Cuentas Regionales* (Colombia 1977) provided the first good estimates of gross regional product for Bogotá. For purposes of comparison with income data obtained in a household survey, the gross regional product (GRP) needs to be whittled down to total personal income. This is performed in table C-1 using 1970 and 1975 as an illustration since these are the most recent years available. Note that imputed housing income for owner-occupied dwellings and employers' contributions to social security and other funds are subtracted from the standard concept of total personal income so as to ensure comparability with household surveys and censuses.

Table C-1. *Regional Income Accounts in Bogotá, 1970 and 1975*
(current Colombian pesos)

Item	1970		1975	
Gross regional product (GRP market prices)	25,920		37,671	
+ Subsidies		+78		+573
− Indirect taxes		−3,809		−5,129
GRP (factor prices)	22,189		33,115	
− Depreciation		−2,134		−2,973
Net domestic product factor cost	20,055		30,142	
− Net external income		−795		−577
Net regional product Bogotá	19,260		29,565	
+ Transfer income		+3,525		+4,855
Net regional product Bogotá	22,785		34,420	
+ Interest on public debt		+238		+451
− Government property income		−242		−256
− Corporation tax		−2,169		−2,362
− Retained earnings		−2,289		−3,065
Total personal income	18,323		29,187	
− Imputed housing income		−1,523[a]		−2,188
− Employers' contributions		−640[b]		−1,021
Total personal "perceived" income	16,160		25,978	
As percentage of GRP (market prices)	62.3		68.9	

a. The regional product includes an estimate of housing services that is calculated from an estimate of existing housing stock. Since Bogotá has approximately 50 percent owner-occupied dwellings, I have subtracted 50 percent of the housing services estimate as representing imputed housing income for owner-occupied dwellings, which is not covered in household surveys of income.

b. Employers' contributions to social security are 7.0 percent of employees' salaries in Colombia. Since social security covers about half of the workers, I have subtracted 3.5 percent of total personal income.

Source: Colombia (1977), p. 199.

In the absence of such detailed accounts data for 1973 and 1977, I have approximated personal income for Bogotá as being 65 percent of gross domestic (regional) product at market prices in those years.

	Millions of current pesos, 1973
GRP (1)	54,793
Personal income (2)	35,615 (65 percent)
From census (3)	17,547
Census coverage (3/2)	49.27 percent

The Bogotá regional product is not available for 1977, but we have the following data for Bogotá's GRP as a proportion of Colombia (the 1977 GDP for Colombia is from Banco de la República 1979).

		Percent
	1960	15.4
	1965	17.6
	1970	19.9
	1973	20.9
	1974	21.2
	1975	21.4
Hence, assume	1977	22.0
	1978	22.0

	Millions of current pesos	
	1977	1978
Colombia GDP (1)	718,480	916,500
Bogotá GRP (2), 22 percent of (1)	157,730	201,600
Personal income (3), 65 percent of (2)	102,530	130,700
From survey (4)	62,840	119,634
Survey coverage (4/3)	61.3 percent	92.0 percent

Thus, if 66 percent income coverage might be expected with optimistic assumptions, 50 percent for the census and 61 percent for the household survey are within the range of reasonable expectations, and 92 percent may be regarded as excellent coverage.

Appendix D

The Population of Bogotá and Its Spatial Distribution, 1973 and 1978

Various doubts have been expressed about the coverage of the 1973 population census in Bogotá. One possible cause of underenumeration was a teachers' strike that took place at the time; many of the teachers had been employed as enumerators. The 1972 Urban Development Study Phase II Study and Household Survey was based on a sample frame taken at the time that included dwelling unit counts in the city. On the basis of these counts, the population of Bogotá was estimated at 2.85 million in 1972 in the Phase II study. The manual count of the 1973 census yielded a Bogotá population of 2.499 million. Since attention was focused on within-city distributions in the City Study, I compared the within-city distribution from both sources to arrive at a final estimate of the population of Bogotá in 1973 for City Study purposes.

Appendix table D-1 reports the counts of dwelling units, households, and estimates of population for the 1964 census, the 1972 Phase II Study, and the 1973 census by comuna (see map 3-1 for the comuna divisions). To obtain the final estimate, I generally took the higher estimate from the census and Phase II data, on the principle that dwelling units can be undercounted but not overcounted. I made two exceptions to this rule where the higher estimate seemed far too high for a reasonable population density for the area. The resulting total population for Bogotá for 1973 is 2,877,253, which is the number used throughout this study.

Once the "true" population distribution for Bogotá disaggregated by comuna was decided on, it was possible to expand the public use tape in order to obtain accurate spatial representation of the city. The number of households within each comuna represented in the tape were expanded to give the final count of households by comuna. If it is assumed that (1) the sample households are accurately representative of the true household size in the comuna, and (2) the participation rate of the labor force in the sample is also truly representative of the participation rate in the comuna, then this expansion yields the true population and the true labor force in the comuna.

Table D-1. *Distribution of Population in Bogotá by Comuna, 1973, Different Sources*

Comuna	1964 census[a] Dwelling units	1964 census[a] Population	Phase II report 1972 (F)[b] Dwelling units	Phase II report 1972 (F)[b] Households	Phase II report 1972 (F)[b] Population	1973 census count (C)[c] Dwelling units	1973 census count (C)[c] Households	1973 census count (C)[c] Population	Final population Estimates	Final population Source[d]	Final population Percentage in comuna
11	3,975	32,226	4,170	5,326	37,115	5,145	7,752	40,643	40,643	C	1.413
12	3,008	23,817	5,984	6,241	35,705	5,528	8,269	44,017	44,107	C	1.530
13	5,360	42,898	21,801	33,792	198,053	12,996	20,380	110,660	110,660e	C	3.846
14	5,172	48,950	8,648	9,470	50,505	7,711	12,127	62,060	62,060	C	2.157
21	8,301	68,320	10,753	12,914	75,655	9,224	13,488	67,503	75,655	F	2.629
22	6,485	57,813	11,519	14,813	91,245	7,329	11,588	60,535	60,535e	C	2.104
23	8,201	84,267	15,828	19,395	110,029	9,122	19,433	94,179	110,029	F	3.824
24	6,925	62,171	19,873	28,903	163,918	10,679	21,436	110,520	163,918	F	5.875
25	6,751	61,614	21,259	26,712	152,601	24,177	31,870	169,027	169,027	C	5.875
31	12,917	82,122	7,595	8,727	39,104	12,279	18,192	73,282	73,282	C	2.547
32	7,467	87,857	11,393	12,088	57,389	8,164	14,302	67,197	67,197	C	2.335
41	10,792	86,402	17,638	20,178	107,687	13,011	18,128	89,355	107,687	F	3.743
42	2,318	19,222	8,331	10,321	59,933	7,471	9,790	49,897	59,933	F	2.083
43	4,567	41,851	13,115	15,712	89,903	8,016	14,973	72,636	89,903	F	3.125
44	4,829	35,674	14,666	18,412	112,279	13,322	17,467	101,029	112,279	F	3.902
45	7,311	57,917	29,967	35,621	227,529	24,199	30,847	173,673	227,529	F	7.908
51	3,594	26,969 ⎫	18,471 ⎱	8,414	54,565	7,590	8,084	45,407	54,565	F	1.896
52	6,427	63,660 ⎭	⎰	15,895	84,450	6,672	13,709	66,440	84,450	F	2.935
53	2,730	21,781	6,674	9,664	51,984	4,899	5,262	32,274	51,984	F	1.807
54	3,118	33,660	10,710	18,089	95,713	7,476	13,164	65,967	95,713	F	3.327

55	6,081	50,857	10,524	14,934	88,881	9,197	15,347	87,116	88,881	F	3.089
56	3,108	24,891	27,156	31,831	185,205	25,199	32,960	183,126	185,205	F	6.437
61	6,906	51,245	7,426	8,718	36,647	7,051	9,570	40,602	40,602	C	1.411
62	3,289	23,549	3,889	4,201	25,029	4,575	5,272	23,978	25,029	F	0.870
63	986	13,305	2,708	2,998	19,132	3,414	4,641	25,685	25,685	C	0.893
64	0	23,333	17,161	22,086	120,095	10,071	14,165	74,897	120,095	F	4.174
65	878	6,776	3,202	3,618	19,132	4,093	5,114	28,008	28,008	C	0.973
71	6,130	35,211	6,894	7,556	43,616	6,851	7,105	34,126	43,616	F	1.516
72	8,497	54,069	9,237	9,579	52,088	10,317	10,631	55,512	55,512	C	1.929
73	9,169	67,994	12,752	15,300	81,461	9,160	12,339	59,743	81,461	F	2.831
74	5,428	31,778	7,683	10,011	54,024	5,868	7,738	39,550	54,024	F	1.878
81	3,001	29,012	4,218	4,931	24,849	4,093	4,756	22,445	24,849	F	0.864
82	8,097	48,670	10,754	11,241	58,735	9,921	10,122	50,267	58,735	F	2.041
83	4,778	27,581	7,591	7,688	43,806	7,962	8,712	45,279	45,279	C	1.574
84	130	480	5,633	5,797	36,272	6,395	6,709	40,501	40,501	C	1.408
85	0	0	4,259	4,395	23,622	4,203	4,816	27,515	27,515	C	0.956
91	1,131	5,598	5,893	6,064	37,457	6,155	7,462	42,014	42,014	C	1.460
92	0	0	493	563	3,871	4,639	5,193	29,176	29,176	C	1.014
Total	187,967	1,537,541	405,904	502,801	2,850,014	843,987	479,116	2,499,841	2,877,253		100.000

a. Counts from unpublished DANE sources.
b. Transformation from Phase II zone system made for City Study by Pachon (1979), table A-4.
c. Barrio level counts from unpublished DANE sources aggregated into comunas.
d. C: 1973 census count. F: Phase II report 1972.
e. Lower of the two sources taken.

Appendix table D-2 gives the household counts from the final estimate for Bogotá and from the sample tape by comuna, together with the resulting implied expansion factors used for this study.

As mentioned in appendix A, the 1978 World Bank–DANE Household Survey (EH21) was conducted after the sample frame had been updated in order to account for expansion in Bogotá. A population estimate could then be made on the basis of the dwelling unit count and subsequently the expanded sample. Table D-3 gives the estimated population that emerged from the expanded sample. More detailed estimates have been made within the City Study in order to reconcile different procedures for obtaining city population; these are reported in Pineda and Rodriguez (1982) and in Ingram and others (1983). About the best estimate for 1978 is 3.5 million; this is lower than previous expectations for Bogotá. The population distribution given in table D-3 has been used consistently in this study. Table D-4 gives the resulting population densities by comuna, along with the corresponding ones for 1973, and table D-5 gives the average monthly incomes by comuna for 1973 and 1978.

Table D-2. *1973 Population Census Sample: Derivation of Expansion Factor*

Comuna	1973 count of households[a] (1)	Households in sample[b] (2)	Expansion factor (1)/(2)
11	7,752	787	9.8500
12	8,269	652	12.6825
13	20,380	2,102	9.6955
14	12,127	1,202	10.0890
21	13,914	1,237	10.4853
22	11,588	1,155	10.0329
23	19,395	2,877	6.7414
24	28,903	2,702	10.6969
25	31,870	3,339	9.5448
31	18,192	2,164	8.4066
32	14,302	2,817	5.0770
41	20,178	1,848	10.9188
42	10,321	919	11.2307
43	15,712	1,765	8.9020
44	18,412	1,427	12.9026
45	35,621	2,077	17.1502
51	8,414	467	18.0171
52	15,895	1,954	8.1346
53	9,064	663	14.5762
54	18,089	1,771	10.2140

Table D-2 (continued)

Comuna	1973 count of households[a] (1)	Households in sample[b] (2)	Expansion factor (1)/(2)
55	14,934	1,587	9.1402
56	31,831	2,516	12.6514
61	9,570	1,033	9.2643
62	4,201	479	8.7704
63	4,641	458	10.1332
64	22,086	1,146	19.2772
65	5,114	385	13.2831
71	7,556	383	19.7285
72	10,631	586	18.1416
73	15,300	1,168	13.0993
74	10,011	517	19.3636
81	4,931	570	8.6509
82	11,241	515	21.8272
83	8,712	356	24.4719
84	6,709	307	21.8534
85	4,816	348	13.8391
91	7,462	506	14.7471
92	5,193	279	18.6129

a. From table D-1.
b. DANE census public use sample.

Table D-3. *Distribution of Population in Bogotá by Comuna, 1973 and 1978*

	1973			1978		
Comuna	Estimated population (thousands)[a]	Percentage in comuna	Mean household size	Estimated population (thousands)[b]	Percentage in comuna	Mean household size
11	41	1.4	4.6	22	0.6	5.9
12	44	1.5	4.5	67[c]	1.9	4.7
13	111	3.8	4.7	148	4.2	5.0
14	62	2.2	4.5	110	3.2	4.6
21	76	2.6	4.4	63	1.8	5.4
22	61	2.1	4.5	47	1.4	4.4
23	110	3.8	4.4	65	1.9	4.4
24	164	5.9	4.6	120	3.4	4.4
25	170	5.9	4.7	247	7.1	5.4
31	73	2.5	3.1	82	2.3	3.8

(*Table continues on the following page.*)

Table D-3 (continued)

Comuna	1973			1978		
	Estimated population (thousands)[a]	Percentage in comuna	Mean household size	Estimated population (thousands)[b]	Percentage in comuna	Mean household size
32	67	2.3	3.9	101	2.9	3.8
41	108	3.7	3.9	68	1.9	5.1
42	60	2.1	4.4	51	1.5	5.1
43	90	3.1	4.4	69	2.0	4.7
44	112	3.9	5.0	**184**	5.3	5.0
45	228	7.9	5.3	**379**	10.8	5.3
51	55	1.9	4.7	64	1.8	5.3
52	84	2.9	4.3	20	0.6	4.6
53	52	1.8	4.6	19	0.5	5.2
54	96	3.3	4.4	74	2.1	5.5
55	89	3.1	4.7	112	3.2	4.9
56	185	6.4	5.1	**408**	11.7	5.5
61	41	1.4	3.3	47	1.4	4.7
62	25	0.9	4.0	18	0.5	4.7
63	26	0.9	4.2	34	1.0	4.1
64	120	4.2	4.7	113	3.2	5.5
65	28	1.0	4.9	62	1.8	5.2
71	44	1.5	3.5	29	0.8	3.8
72	56	1.9	3.9	49	1.4	4.1
73	81	2.8	4.0	44	1.3	3.9
74	54	1.9	4.2	43	1.2	4.8
81	24	0.9	3.7	35	1.0	2.6
82	58	2.0	3.8	**115**	4.4	3.9
83	45	1.6	4.2	91	2.6	4.4
84	40	1.4	5.1	58	1.7	5.5
85	37	1.0	4.7	49	1.4	4.8
91	42	1.5	4.7	**86**	2.5	4.8
92	29	1.0	5.0	**54**	1.5	5.3
All comunas	2,877	100.0	4.5	3,492	100.0	4.8

a. Population estimated according to method outlined in appendix D.

b. The 1978 sample has been expanded according to expansion factors calculated for the World Bank City Study.

c. Boldface numbers are for comunas with estimated 1978 populations that are greater than 1.5 times their 1973 levels.

Sources: 1973 population census sample; and 1978 World Bank–DANE Household Survey.

Table D-4. *Densities in Bogotá by Comuna, 1973 and 1978*

Comuna	Area[b] (hectares)	Density[a]	
		1973[c] (population per hectare)	1978[c] (population per hectare)
11	431	94	51
12	223	197	296
13	836	132	177
14	383	162	287
21	251	302	251
22	169	358	278
23	280	393	232
24	1,174	140	102
25	2,190	77	113
31	398	184	206
32	294	229	343
41	381	283	178
42	485	124	105
43	281	321	245
44	588	191	313
45	2,851	80	133
51	881	62	73
52	209	405	96
53	439	118	43
54	442	217	167
55	462	192	242
56	3,679	50	111
61	278	146	169
62	417	60	43
63	1,224	21	28
64	1,147	105	98
65	767	37	81
71	189	230	153
72	270	206	185
73	265	307	166
74	174	310	247
81	215	155	163
82	498	118	311
83	670	68	136
84	1,178	34	49
85	2,076	13	24
91	2,518	17	34
92	1,209	24	45
All comunas	30,424	95	115

a. Calculated using 1973 areas for 1978.
b. Calculated from census map using planimeter (Pachon 1979).
c. Calculated using population data given in table D-3.

Table D-5. Distribution of Monthly Income in Bogotá by Comuna, 1973 and 1978

	1973			1978			
Comuna	Mean household income (1973 pesos)	Mean household income per capita (1973 pesos)	Rank[a]	Rank[a]	Mean household income per capita (1978 pesos)	Mean household income (1978 pesos)	Households in bottom 30 percent[b] (percent)
83	15,069	4,196	1	1	17,960	47,834	6.4
71	7,809	2,781	2	5	7,270	27,102	0.0
84	9,134	2,165	3	4	7,418	38,899	8.8
82	5,850	1,959	4	3	9,530	27,788	6.3
72	6,597	1,915	5	10	4,432	16,794	11.4
51	5,987	1,315	6	7	4,899	24,432	7.9
81	3,194	1,126	7	2	14,499	26,250	12.4
61	2,529	1,057	8	9	4,608	18,529	5.1
53	4,579	1,053	9	32	1,757	9,144	45.2
91	4,628	1,035	10	17	3,198	16,504	24.6
62	4,022	1,033	11	6	5,166	24,382	13.0
74	4,137	995	12	12	3,724	19,348	16.8
31	2,114	884	13	21	2,490	8,343	25.9
63	3,004	794	14	15	3,316	13,944	24.4
73	2,874	794	15	11	4,035	15,027	6.6

12	3,076	785	16	19	2,800	12,179	16.6
65	3,193	753	17	23	2,430	12,262	26.2
85	2,776	737	18	8	4,666	23,758	27.1
41	2,463	714	19	14	3,637	17,292	16.8
21	2,492	645	20	16	3,249	15,674	19.8
43	2,101	577	21	25	2,340	10,439	23.4
55	2,267	572	22	22	2,432	8,655	34.0
42	2,073	570	23	18	2,810	11,185	30.0
22	2,140	539	24	27	2,151	7,335	23.1
45	2,368	528	25	29	1,993	5,661	32.9
44	2,167	515	26	26	2,305	10,802	16.7
14	2,007	497	27	36	1,608	7,153	40.0
54	1,936	477	28	13	3,715	19,564	22.0
52	1,792	469	29	33	1,711	6,625	37.7
64	2,006	464	30	31	1,826	9,655	30.0
32	1,371	448	31	30	1,898	6,216	37.5
56	1,938	435	32	24	2,374	11,323	26.5
23	1,566	410	33	20	2,786	10,152	15.2
11	1,627	404	34	34	1,678	8,346	37.3
92	1,549	361	35	35	1,666	7,398	39.0
24	1,446	359	36	28	2,054	7,844	27.5
13	1,333	337	37	37	1,240	5,706	48.8
25	1,279	322	38	38	1,728	5,971	54.8

a. Ranked by mean household income per capita.

b. This is the percentage of households in the comuna that fall in the bottom 30 percent in Bogotá ranked by household income per capita.

Source: 1978 World Bank–DANE Household Survey.

References

ANIF. 1978. *Marginalidad y Pobreza.* Bogotá: Ediciones Sol y Lunard.

Altimir, Oscar. 1977. "Income Distribution Estimates from Household Surveys and Population Censuses in Latin America: An Assessment of Reliability." World Bank, Development Research Center, Washington, D.C. Processed.

Altimir, Oscar, and Sebastian Piñera. 1977. "Decomposition Analysis of the Inequality of Earnings in Latin American Countries." World Bank, Development Research Center, and Economic Commission for Latin America. Washington, D.C., August. Processed.

Amato, Peter. 1968. "An Analysis of the Changing Patterns of Elite Residential Locations in Bogotá, Colombia." Ph.D. dissertation, Cornell University, Ithaca, N.Y.

―――. 1969. "Population Densities, Land Values and Socioeconomic Class in Bogotá, Colombia." *Land Economics* (February).

―――. 1970. "A Comparison of Population Densities, Land Value and Socioeconomic Class in Four Latin American Cities." *Land Economics* (November).

―――. 1980. "Elitism and Settlement Patterns in the Latin American City." *Journal of American Institute of Planners* (March).

Amemiya, Takeshi. 1981. "Qualitative Response Models: A Survey." *Journal of Economic Literature* 19 (4):1483–1536.

―――. 1984. "Tobit Models: A Survey." *Journal of Econometrics* 24:3–62, Annals 1984-1.

Anand, Sudhir. 1983. *Inequality and Poverty in Malaysia: Measurement and Decomposition.* New York: Oxford University Press.

Ashenfelter, Orley C., and James J. Heckman. 1974. "The Estimation of Income and Substitution Effects in a Model of Family Labor Supply." *Econometrica* 42 (1):73–85.

Atkinson, A. B. 1970. "On the Measurement of Inequality." *Journal of Economic Theory* 2 (September).

Austin, James E. 1980. *Confronting Urban Malnutrition*. Baltimore, Md.: Johns Hopkins University Press.

Banco de la República. 1979. *Colombia's Socio-Economic Indicators*. Bogotá.

Basta, Samir S. 1977. "Nutrition and Health in Low-Income Urban Areas of the Third World." *Ecology of Food Nutrition* 6:113–24.

Becker, Gary S. 1964. *Human Capital: A Theoretical and Empirical Analysis*. New York: Columbia University Press.

———. 1965. "A Theory of the Allocation of Time." *Economic Journal* 75:493–517.

Ben-Porath, Yoram. 1973. "Labor Force Participation Rates and the Supply of Labor." *Journal of Political Economy* 81 (3):697–704.

———. 1967. "The Production of Human Capital and the Life Cycle of Earnings." *Journal of Political Economy* 75(4):352–65 (supplement).

Berry, R. Albert. 1975a. "Open Unemployment as a Social Problem in Urban Colombia: Myth and Reality." *Economic Development and Cultural Change* 23(2):276–91.

———. 1975b. "Disguised Unemployment in Non-Participation? Determinants of the Participation Rate in Urban Colombia." University of Toronto, Department of Economics. March. Processed.

———. 1978. "A Positive Interpretation of the Expansion of Urban Services in Latin America, with Some Colombian Evidence." *Journal of Development Studies* 14(2):210–31.

———. 1980a. "Education, Income, Productivity and Urban Poverty." In *Education and Income*, ed. Timothy King. World Bank Staff Working Paper no. 402. Washington, D.C.

———. 1980b. "Work and Welfare in Colombia." World Bank, Development Economics Department, Washington, D.C. Processed.

Berry, R. Albert, and Ronald Soligo, eds. 1980. *Economic Policy and Income Distribution in Colombia*. Boulder, Colo.: Westview.

Berry, R. Albert, and Miguel Urrutia. 1976. *Income Distribution in Colombia*. New Haven, Conn.: Yale University Press.

Betancourth, Eberth. 1977. *Las Carencias Nutricionales en Colombia, Revisión 1977*. Bogotá: Instituto Colombiano de Bienestar Familiar.

Bhalla, Surjit. 1980. "Measurement of Poverty—Issues and Methods." World Bank, Development Economics Department, Washington, D.C. Processed.

Bourguignon, François. 1978. "Pobreza y Dualismo en el Sector Urbano de las Economías en Desarrollo: el Caso de Colombia." *Desarrollo y Sociedad* (January):39–71.

―――. 1983. "The Role of Education in the Urban Labour Market During the Process of Development: The Case of Colombia." In *Human Resources, Employment and Development,* ed. V. Urquidi and S. Trejo Reyes. Vol. 4. London: Macmillan.

Bourguignon, François, F. Gagey, and T. Magnac. 1985. "On Estimating Female Labor Supply Behavior in Developing Countries." Document no. 103. Paris: Ecole Normal Supérieur.

Bowen, William G., and T. Aldrich Finegan. 1969. *The Economics of Labor Force Participation.* Princeton, N.J.: Princeton University Press.

Bronitsky, L., and others. 1975. *Urban Data Book.* U.S. Department of Transportation Report no. DOT-TSC-OS5-75-45-I. Washington, D.C.

Cain, Glenn C. 1960. *Married Women in the Labor Force.* Chicago: University of Chicago Press.

―――. 1976. "The Challenge of Segmented Labor Market Theories to Orthodox Theory: A Survey." *Journal of Economic Literature,* 14(4).

Calvo, Guillermo, and Stanislaw Wallisz. 1979. "Hierarchy, Ability and Income Distribution." *Journal of Political Economy* 87(5):991–1010.

Castaneda, Tarcicio. 1984. "Factors Determining the Decline in Chile's Infant Mortality Rate." Paper presented at the meeting of the Econometric Society, Latin America Region, Bogotá, Colombia, July.

Chiswick, Carmela Ullman. 1976. "On Estimating Earnings Functions for LDCs." World Bank, Development Research Center, Washington, D.C. Processed.

―――. 1977. "A Procedure for Estimating Earnings of Unpaid Family Workers." *Proceedings of the American Statistical Association.* Business and Economics Statistics Section.

Cogan, John. 1980a. "Labor Supply with Costs of Labor Market Entry." In *Female Labor Supply: Theory and Estimation,* ed. James P. Smith. Princeton, N.J.: Princeton University Press.

―――. 1980b. "Married Women's Labor Supply: A Comparison of Alternative Estimation Procedures." In *Female Labor Supply: Theory and Estimation,* ed. James P. Smith. Princeton, N.J.: Princeton University Press.

Colombia. 1977. *Cuentas Regionales de Colombia, 1960–1975.* Bogotá: Departamento Nacional de Planeación.

Dandekar, V. M., and N. Rath. 1971. *Poverty in India.* Bombay: Sameeksha Trust.

Datta, Gautam, and Jacob Meerman. 1980. *Household Income or Household Income per Capita in Welfare Comparison.* World Bank Staff Working Paper no. 378. Washington, D.C.

Departamento Administrativo Nacional de Estadística (DANE). 1977. *Ingresos y Gastos de los Hogares en Colombia: 1972.* Bogotá: División de Edición del DANE.

Departamento Nacional de Planeación (DNP). 1974. "Plan Nacional de Alimentación y Nutrición: Selección de Alimentos." Documento DNP-UDS-011. Bogotá, October.

Doeringer, Peter, and Michael Piore. 1971. *Internal Labor Markets and Manpower Analysis.* Lexington, Mass.: D. C. Heath.

Fields, Gary S. 1975. "Rural-Urban Migration, Urban Unemployment and Under-Employment, and Job-Search Activity in LDCs." *Journal of Development Economics* 2(2).

———. 1977. "Education and Economic Mobility in a Less Developed Country." Economic Growth Center Discussion Paper no. 263. New Haven, Conn.: Yale University.

———. 1978. "Analyzing Colombian Wage Structure." Studies in Employment and Rural Development no. 40. World Bank, Development Economics Department. Washington, D.C. Processed.

———. 1980a. "Education and Income Distribution in Developing Countries: A Review of the Literature." In *Education and Income*, ed. Timothy King. World Bank Staff Working Paper no. 402. Washington, D.C.

———. 1980b. *How Segmented Is the Bogotá Labor Market.* World Bank Staff Working Paper no. 434. Washington, D.C.

Fields, Gary S., and Nohra de Marulanda. 1976. "Intersectoral Wage Structure in Colombia." Economic Growth Center Discussion Paper no. 251. New Haven, Conn.: Yale University, August.

Fields, Gary S., and T. Paul Schultz. 1980. "Regional Inequality and Other Sources of Income Variation in Colombia." *Economic Development and Cultural Change* 28(3):447–67.

———. 1977. "Sources of Income Variation in Colombia: Personal and Regional Effects." Economic Growth Center Discussion Paper no. 262. New Haven, Conn.: Yale University.

Food and Agriculture Organization (FAO). 1973. "Energy and Protein Requirements." Report of a Joint FAO-WHO Ad Hoc Expert Committee. Rome.

Food and Nutrition Board. 1980. *Recommended Dietary Allowance.* Rev. ed. Washington, D.C.

Frank, R. H. 1978. "Why Women Earn Less: The Theory and Estimation of Differential Overqualification." *American Economic Review* 68(3):360–73.

García, Jorge García. 1979. "Es Importante la Seguridad de Suministro de Alimentos en Colombia?" *Revista de Planeación y Desarrollo* (September-December):129–74.

———. 1980. "La Situación de Desnutrición en Colombia." *Desarrollo y Sociedad* (July) 4:337–56.

———. 1981. "The Nature of Food Insecurity in Colombia." In *Food Security for Developing Countries*, ed. A. Valdes. Boulder, Colo.: Westview.

Gavan, James D., and Indrani Sri Chandrasekhara. 1979. *The Impact of Public Food Grain Distribution in Food Consumption and Welfare in Sri Lanka*. Washington, D.C.: International Food Policy Research Institute.

Greenhalgh, Christine. 1980. "Participation and Hours of Work for Married Women in Great Britain." *Oxford Economic Papers* 32(2):276–318.

Griliches, Zvi. 1977. "Estimating Return to Schooling: Some Econometric Problems." *Econometrica*, 45(1):1–22.

Griliches, Zvi, and W. M. Mason. 1972. "Education, Income and Ability." *Journal of Political Economy* 80(3):S74–103.

Hamer, Andrew M. 1981. "Households and Housing: Residential Mobility, Tenure Choice, and Space Consumption in the Developing Metropolis." World Bank, Development Economics Department. Urban and Regional Report no. 81–19. Washington, D.C.

Hammer, Jeffrey S. 1978. "The Determinants of Malnutrition in Pakistan." Massachusetts Institute of Technology, Cambridge, Mass. Processed.

Harris, John, and Todaro, Michael P. 1970. "Migration, Unemployment and Development: A Two-Sector Analysis." *American Economic Review* 60(1):126–42.

Harris, Nigel. 1978. *Economic Development, Cities and Planning: The Case of Bombay*. Bombay: Oxford University Press.

Harrison, David, Jr., and John F. Kain. 1974. "Cumulative Urban Growth and Density Functions." *Journal of Urban Economics* 1(9):61–98.

Hause, J. C. 1972. "Earnings Profile: Ability and Schooling." *Journal of Political Economy* 80(3):S108–39.

Heckman, James. 1974. "Shadow Prices, Market Wages, and Labor Supply." *Econometrica* 42(4):679–94.

———. 1976. "A Life-Cycle Model of Earnings, Learning and Consumption." *Journal of Political Economy* 84(4):S11–44.

———. 1978. "Dummy Endogenous Variables in a Simultaneous Equation System." *Econometrica* 46(4):931–59.

———. 1980. "Sample Selection Bias as a Specification Error." In *Female Labor Supply: Theory and Estimation*, ed. James P. Smith. Princeton, N.J.: Princeton University Press.

Hoffman, Saul D. 1979. "Black-White Life Cycle Earnings Differences and the Vintage Hypothesis: A Longitudinal Analysis." *American Economic Review* 69(5):855–67.

Hoover, Edgar M., and Raymond Vernon. 1959. *Anatomy of a Metropolis.* Cambridge, Mass.: Harvard University Press.

Hoyt, Homer. 1939. *The Structure and Growth of Residential Neighborhoods in American Cities.* Washington, D.C.: U.S. Government Printing Office.

———. 1966. *Where the Rich and Poor Live: The Location of Residential Areas Occupied by the Highest and Lowest Income Families in American Cities.* Washington, D.C.: Urban Institute.

Ingram, Gregory K., and Alan Carroll. 1981. "The Spatial Structure of Latin American Cities." *Journal of Urban Economics* 9(2):257–73.

Ingram, Gregory K., and others. 1983. "The Developing Metropolises: Lessons from the City Study of Bogotá and Cali." Documento de Trabajo. Bogotá: Corporación Centro Regional de Población.

Instituto Colombiano de Bienestar Familiar (ICBF). 1977. "Recomendación de Consumo de Alimentos para la Población Colombiana." Rev. ed. Bogotá. Processed.

Instituto de Investigaciones Tecnológicas (IIT). 1972. "Metodológias para un Análisis Multidisciplinario de la Desnutrición." Bogotá.

International Labour Organisation (ILO). 1970. *Towards Full Employment: A Programme for Colombia.* Geneva.

Jacobs, Jane. 1961. *The Death and Life of Great American Cities.* New York: Vintage Books.

Jallade, Jean-Pierre. 1974. *Public Expenditures on Education and Income Distribution in Colombia.* World Bank Occasional Paper no. 18. Baltimore, Md.: Johns Hopkins University Press.

Jaramillo, Helena. 1978. "Determinants of Income Differentials after Migration." New Haven, Conn.: Yale University. Processed.

Jen, Li-Ming Caroline. 1983. "Urban Female Labor Force Participation in Brazil." Ph.D. dissertation. State University of New York, Buffalo, N.Y.

Joshi, Heather, Harold Lubell, and Jean Mouly. 1976. *Abidjan: Urban Development and Employment in the Ivory Coast.* Geneva: International Labour Office.

Killingsworth, Mark R. 1983. *Labor Supply.* New York: Cambridge University Press.

Knudsen, Odin K., and Pasquale L. Scandizzo. 1979. *Nutrition and Food Needs in Developing Countries.* World Bank Staff Working Paper no. 328. Washington, D.C.

Layard, Richard, M. Barton, and A. Zabalza. 1980. "Married Women's Participation and Hours." *Economica* 47(185):51–72.

Lazear, Edward. 1976. "Age, Experience and Wage Growth." *American Economic Review* 66(4):548–58. September.

Lee, Kyu Sik. 1981a. "Intra-Urban Location of Manufacturing Employment in Colombia." *Journal of Urban Economics* 9(2):222–41.

———. 1981b. "A Model of Intra-Urban Employment Location: An Application to Bogotá, Colombia." *Journal of Urban Economics* 12(3):263–79.

Lee, Yoon Joo. 1979. "The City Study: The Available Data." Vol. 2. World Bank, Development Economics Department. Urban and Regional Report no. 79-13. Washington, D.C.

———. 1981. "The City Study: The Available Data." Vol. 3. World Bank, Development Economics Department. Urban and Regional Report. Washington, D.C.

Lehrer, Evelyn, and Marc Nerlove. 1980. "Women's Life Cycle Time Allocation: An Econometric Study." In *Women and Household Labor,* ed. Sarah F. Berk. Sage Yearbooks in Women's Policy Studies, vol. 5. Beverly Hills, Calif.: Sage.

———. 1982a. "The Impact of the Female Life Cycle: Time Allocation Decisions on Income Distribution among Families." In *The Problems of Developed Countries and the International Economy,* ed. Burton A. Weisbrod and Helen Hughes. Vol. 3: *Human Resources Employment and Development.* London: Macmillan.

———. 1982b. "The Labor Supply and Fertility Behavior of Married Women: A Three Period Model." *Research in Population Economics* 4:217–35.

Leibowitz, Arleen. 1976. "Years and Intensity of Schooling Investment." *American Economic Review* 66(3):321–34.

Lemoine Amaya, Carlos, and Carlos Becerra Chaparro. 1978. "Ingreso y Distribución Familiar del Consumo." In *Marginalidad y Pobreza,* ed. ANIF. Bogotá: Ediciones Sol y Luna.

Linn, Johannes. 1978. "Urbanization Trends, Polarization Reversal, and Spatial Policy in Colombia." *Raumordnung und Raumwirtschaft,* Arbeitspapier no. 12, des Sonderforschungsbereichs 26, Munster.

Lubell, Harold. 1974. *Calcutta: Its Urban Development and Employment Prospects.* Geneva: International Labour Office.

Lubell, Harold, and Douglas McCallum. 1978. *Bogotá: Urban Development and Employment*. Geneva: International Labour Office.

Maddala, G. S. 1983. *Limited Dependent and Qualitative Variables in Econometrics*. New York: Cambridge University Press.

Mazumdar, Dipak. 1976a. "The Urban Informal Sector." *World Development* 4(8):655–79.

———. 1976b. "The Rural Urban Wage Gap, Migration and the Shadow Wage." *Oxford Economic Papers* 28(3):406–25.

———. 1979. *Paradigms in the Study of Urban Labour Markets in LDCs: A Reassessment in the Light of an Empirical Survey in Bombay City*. World Bank Staff Working Paper no. 366. Washington, D.C.

———. 1981. *Urban Labour Market and Income Distribution: A Study of Malaysia*. New York: Oxford University Press.

Mazumdar, Dipak, and Masood Ahmed. 1978. *Labor Market Segmentation and the Determination of Earnings: A Case Study*. World Bank Staff Working Paper no. 278. Washington, D.C.

McDonald, John F., and Robert A. Moffit. 1980. "The Uses of Tobit Analysis." *Review of Economics and Statistics* 62(2):318–21.

McGregor, Alan. 1977. "Intra-Urban Variations in Unemployment Duration: A Case Study." *Urban Studies* 14:303–13.

McKay, Harrison, and others. 1978. "Improving Cognitive Ability in Chronically Deprived Children." *Science* 200(4339):270–79.

Meerman, Jacob. 1979. *Public Expenditure in Malaysia: Who Benefits and Why*. New York: Oxford University Press.

Merrick, Thomas. 1976. "Employment and Earnings in the Informal Sector in Brazil: The Case of Belo Horizonte." *Journal of Developing Areas* 10(3):337–53.

Mills, Edwin S. 1972. *Studies in the Structure of the Urban Economy*. Baltimore, Md.: Johns Hopkins University Press.

Mills, Edwin S., and Byung Nak Song. 1979. *Urbanization and Urban Problems*. Cambridge, Mass.: Harvard University Press.

Mills, Edwin S., and Katsutoshi Ohta. 1976. "Urbanization and Urban Problems." In *Asia's New Giant: How The Japanese Economy Works*, ed. Hugh Patrick and Henry Rosorsky. Washington, D.C.: Brookings Institution.

Mills, Edwin S., and Jee Peng Tan. 1980. "A Comparison of Urban Population Density Functions in Developed and Developing Countries." *Urban Studies* 7:313–21.

Mincer, Jacob. 1962. "Labor Force Participation of Married Women: A Study of Labour Supply." In *Aspects of Labor Economics*, ed. H. G. Lewis. Princeton, N.J.: Princeton University Press.

―――. 1970. "The Distribution of Labour Incomes: A Survey with Special Reference to the Human Capital Approach." *Journal of Economic Literature* 8(1).

―――. 1974. *Schooling, Experience and Earnings*. New York: Columbia University Press.

Misra, R. P., ed. 1978. *Million Cities of India*. New Delhi: Vikas.

Mitchell, B. R. 1978. *European Historical Statistics, 1750–1970*. New York: Columbia University Press.

Mohan, Rakesh. 1979. *Urban Economic and Planning Models: Assessing the Potential for Cities in Developing Countries*. Baltimore, Md.: Johns Hopkins University Press.

―――. 1980. *The People of Bogotá: Who They Are, What They Earn, Where They Live*. World Bank Staff Working Paper no. 390, Washington, D.C.

―――. 1981. *The Determinants of Labor Earnings in Developing Metropolises: Estimates from Bogotá and Cali*. World Bank Staff Working Paper no. 498, Washington, D.C.

―――. 1984. *An Anatomy of the Distribution of Urban Income: A Tale of Two Cities in Colombia*. World Bank Staff Working Paper no. 650, Washington, D.C.

―――. 1985. *Labor Force Participation in a Developing Metropolis: Does Sex Matter?* World Bank Staff Working Paper no. 749. Washington, D.C.

Mohan, Rakesh, Jorge Garcia, and M. W. Wagner. 1981. *Measuring Urban Malnutrition and Poverty: A Case Study of Bogotá and Cali, Colombia*. World Bank Staff Working Paper no. 447, Washington, D.C.

Mohan, Rakesh, and Nancy Hartline. 1984. *The Poor of Bogotá: Who They Are, What They Do, and Where They Live*. World Bank Staff Working Paper no. 635, Washington, D.C.

Mohan, Rakesh, and Rodrigo Villamizar. 1982. "The Evolution of Land Values in the Context of Rapid Urban Growth: A Case Study of Bogotá." In *World Congress on Land Policy Proceedings 1980*, ed. M. Cullen and S. Woolery. Lexington, Mass.: D. C. Heath.

Morawetz, David, 1981. *Why the Emperor's New Clothes Are Not Made in Colombia: A Case Study in Latin American and East Asian Manufactured Exports*. New York: Oxford University Press.

Morrison, C. 1984. "Income Distribution in East European and Western Countries." *Journal of Comparative Economics* 8(2).

Musgrove, Philip. 1978. *Consumer Behavior in Latin America*. Washington, D.C.: Brookings Institution.

Muth, Richard F. 1969. *Cities and Housing*. Chicago, Ill.: University of Chicago Press.

Nakamura, Masao, Alice Nakamura, and Dallas Cullen. 1979. "Job Opportunities, the Offered Wage, and the Labor Supply of Married Women." *American Economic Review* 69(5):784–805.

Nelson, Richard R., T. Paul Schultz, and Robert L. Slighton. 1971. *Structural Change in a Developing Economy: Colombia's Problems and Prospects*. Princeton, N.J.: Princeton University Press.

Nickell, Stephen. 1979. "Education and Lifetime Patterns of Unemployment." *Journal of Political Economy* 87(5):117–31.

Ojha, P. D. 1970. "A Configuration of Indian Poverty." *Reserve Bank of India Bulletin* (January).

Pachon, Alvaro. 1979. "Urban Structure, Modal Choice, and Auto Ownership in Bogotá, 1972." World Bank, Development Economics Department. City Study Intermediate Paper no. 31. Washington, D.C. Processed.

Pfeffermann, Guy, and Richard Webb. 1979. *The Distribution of Income in Brazil*. World Bank Staff Working Paper no. 356. Washington, D.C.

Pineda, J. F., and S. Rodriguez. 1982. "La Población de Bogotá." Documento de Trabajo no. 26. Bogotá: Corporación Centro Regional de Población.

Pinera, Sebastian, and Marcelo Selowsky. 1978. "The Opportunity Cost of Labor and the Returns to Education under Unemployment and Labor Market Segmentation." *Quarterly Journal of Economics* 92 (August):469–88.

Pinstrup-Andersen, Per, and Elizabeth Caicedo. 1978. "The Potential Impact of Changes in Income Distribution on Food Demand and Human Nutrition." *American Journal of Agricultural Economics* 60(3):402–15.

Potter, Joseph, and Myriam Ordonez. 1976. "The Completeness of Enumeration in the 1973 Census of the Population of Colombia." *Population Index* (July).

Psacharapoulos, George. 1973. *Returns to Education: An International Comparison*. San Francisco, Calif.: Elsevier International.

———. 1980. "Returns to Education: An Updated International Comparison." In *Education and Income*, ed. Timothy King. World Bank Staff Working Paper no. 402. Washington, D.C.

Psacharapoulos, George, and A. Zabalza. 1984. *The Destination and Early Career Performance of Secondary School Graduates in Colombia*. World Bank Staff Working Paper no. 653. Washington, D.C.

Renaud, Bertrand. 1982. *National Urbanization Policies in Developing Countries*. New York: Oxford University Press.

Reutlinger, Shlomo, and Harold Alderman. 1980. *The Prevalence of Calorie Deficient Diets in Developing Countries*. World Bank Staff Working Paper no. 374. Washington, D.C.

Reutlinger, Shlomo, and Marcelo Selowsky. 1976. *Malnutrition and Poverty*. Baltimore, Md.: Johns Hopkins University Press.

Ribe, Helena. 1979. "Income of Migrants Relative to Non Migrants in Colombia: An Economic Analysis of the 1973 Census Sample." Ph.D. dissertation, Yale University, New Haven, Conn.

————. 1980. "The Relative Economic Position of Migrants and Natives in Colombia: An Economic Analysis of the 1973 Census Sample." Paper presented at the International Economic Association, Mexico City, August.

Robinson, Sherman. 1976. "Income Distribution within Groups, among Groups, and Overall: A Technique of Analysis." Discussion Paper no. 65, Research Program in Economic Development, Woodrow Wilson School, Princeton University, Princeton, N.J. August.

Rosen, Sherwin. 1977. "Human Capital: Relations between Education and Earnings." In *Frontiers of Quantitative Economics*, vol. III B, ed. Michael D. Intriligater. Amsterdam: North Holland.

Ruggles, Nancy, and Richard Ruggles. 1974. "A Strategy for Merging and Matching Microdata Sets." *Annals of Economic and Social Measurement* 3(2):353–72.

Schaefer, Kalmann. 1976. *São Paulo: Urban Development and Employment*. Geneva: International Labour Office.

Schiller, Bradley. 1977. "Relative Earnings Mobility in the United States." *American Economic Review* 67(5):926–41.

Schultz, T. Paul. 1961. "Investment in Human Capital." *American Economic Review* 51(1):1–17.

————.1965. *The Distribution of Personal Income: A Study of Statistics in the Size Distribution of Personal Income in the United States*. Washington, D.C.: U.S. Government Printing Office.

————. 1969. "Population Growth and Internal Migration in Colombia." Rand Corp. Memorandum 5765. Santa Monica, Calif.

————. 1980. "Estimating Labor Supply Functions for Married Women." In *Female Labor Supply: Theory and Estimation*, ed. James P. Smith. Princeton, N.J.: Princeton University Press.

Selowsky, Marcelo. 1979. *Who Benefits from Government Expenditure? A Case Study of Colombia*. New York: Oxford University Press.

Sen, Amartya. 1980. *Levels of Poverty: Policy and Change.* World Bank Staff Working Paper no. 401. Washington, D.C.

Sethuraman, S. V. 1974. *Towards a Definition of the Informal Sector.* World Employment Programme Research Working Paper. Geneva: International Labour Office. Processed.

————. 1976. *Jakarta, Urban Development and Employment.* Geneva: International Labour Office.

Shields, Nwanganga. 1980. *Women in the Urban Labour Markets of Africa: The Case of Tanzania.* World Bank Staff Working Paper no. 380. Washington, D.C.

Smith, James P. 1984. "Race and Human Capital." *American Economic Review* 74(4):685–98. (September).

————, ed. 1980. *Female Labor Supply: Theory and Estimation.* Princeton, N.J.: Princeton University Press.

Smith, James P., and Finis Welch. 1977. "Black-White Male Wage Ratios 1960–1970." *American Economic Review* 67(3):323–38.

Srinivasan, T. N. 1980. *Malnutrition: Some Measurement and Policy Issues.* World Bank Staff Working Paper no. 373. Washington, D.C.

Sukhatme, P. V. 1970. "Incidence of Protein Deficiency in Relation to Different Diets in India." *British Journal of Nutrition* 24:447–87.

————. 1977a. "Incidence of Undernutrition." *Indian Journal of Economics* 32(3).

————. 1977b. "Malnutrition and Poverty." Ninth Lal Bahadur Shastri Memorial Lecture, Indian Agricultural Research Institute, New Delhi.

————. 1978. "Assessment of Adequacy of Diets at Different Income Levels." *Economic and Political Weekly* 13(31, 32, and 33—special number): 1373–85.

Summers, Anita A., and Barbara L. Wolfe. 1977. "Do Schools Make a Difference?" *American Economic Review* 67(4):639–52.

Szal, Richard, and Sherman Robinson. "Measuring Income Inequality." In *Income Distribution: Policy Alternatives in Developing Countries,* ed. Charles R. Frank, Jr., and Richard Webb. Washington, D.C.: Brookings Institution, 1977.

Tabares, Henry. 1979. "Población de Cali: Series Históricas y Características." PIDECA Document no. 3, Cali, Colombia: Planeación Municipal. Processed.

Tenjo, Jaime. 1975. "Impacto de la Actividad Sindical Sobre los Salarios: Un Análisis Econométrico." *Revista de Planeación y Desarrollo* 7(2).

Theil, Henri. 1967. *Economics and Information Theory.* Amsterdam: North Holland.

―――. 1972. *Statistical Decomposition Analysis*. Amsterdam: North Holland.

Thomas, Vinod. 1985. *Linking Macroeconomic and Agricultural Policies for Adjustment with Growth: The Colombian Experience*. Baltimore, Md.: Johns Hopkins University Press.

Thoumi, Francisco. 1979. "Estrategias de Industrialización, Empleo y Distribución del Ingreso en Colombia." *Coyuntura Económica* 9(1):119–42.

Todaro, Michael P. 1976a. *Internal Migration in Developing Countries*. Geneva: International Labour Office.

―――. 1976b. "Urban Job Expansion, Induced Migration and Rising Unemployment." *Journal of Development Economics* 3(3):211–25.

Urrutia, Miguel. 1985. *Winners and Losers in Colombia's Recent Growth Experience*. Baltimore, Md.: Johns Hopkins University Press.

Valverde, Nelson. 1978. "The City Study: The Available Data." Vol. 1. World Bank, Development Economics Department. Urban and Regional Report no. 78-6. Washington, D.C.

Velasco, Julian A., and Gilberto R. Mier. 1980. "Valores y Características de la Tierra en Cali." Cali: Planeación Municipal. Processed.

Villamizar, Rodrigo. 1981. "Land Prices in Bogotá between 1955 and 1978: A Descriptive Analysis." In *Research in Urban Economics*. Vol. 2, ed. J. V. Henderson. Greenwich, Conn.: JAI Press.

Visaria, Pravin. 1979. "The Incidence of 'Absolute' Poverty in Sri Lanka, 1969–70." Joint ESCAP–IBRD Project on the Evaluation of Asian Data on Income Distribution, Working Paper no. 6. Washington, D.C.

―――. 1980. "Poverty and Living Standards in Asia." World Bank Development Research Center. Washington, D.C. Processed.

Wagner, W. M. 1984. *Vacant Lots, Land Prices and Assessment Practices: The Case of Bogotá, Colombia*. World Bank Staff Working Paper no. 651. Washington, D.C.

Webb, Richard C. 1977. *Government Policy and the Distribution of Income in Peru 1963–1973*. Cambridge, Mass.: Harvard University Press.

Welch, Finis. 1966. "Measurement of the Quality of Schooling." *American Economic Review* 56(3):379–92.

―――. 1979. "Effects of Cohort Size on Earnings: The Baby Boom Babies' Financial Bust." *Journal of Political Economy* 87(5):565–97.

Wheaton, William C. 1977. "Income and Urban Residence: An Analysis of the Consumer Demand for Location." *American Economic Review* 67(4):620–31.

Wiesner, Guillermo. 1980. "The History of Land Prices in Bogotá between 1878 and 1978." Documento de Trabajo no. 4. Bogotá: Corporación Centro Regional de Población.

Willis, Robert, and Sherwin Rosen. 1979. "Education and Self Selection." *Journal of Political Economy* 87(5):S7–S36.

World Bank. 1972. *Economic Growth of Colombia: Problems and Prospects.* Baltimore, Md.: Johns Hopkins University Press.

————. 1979. *Brazil: Human Resources Special Report.* Annex III, Health, Nutrition and Education. Washington, D.C.

————. 1984. *Colombia: Economic Development and Policy under Changing Conditions.* Washington, D.C.

Yap, Lorene. 1977. "The Attraction of Cities: A Review of the Migration Literature." *Journal of Development Economics* 4(3)239–64.

Index

Ability, earnings and, 242, 243, 245
Age structure: earnings and returns to education and, 261–62, 276–77; demographic structure of Bogotá and, 27–28, 54; labor force participation and, 184, 185, 186; labor market segmentation and, 297, 306–07; malnutrition and, 105, 107–09, 123; of poor workers, 115–16; worker profile and, 142–48
Agriculture, 358; changes in, 13; income distribution and, 63; labor productivity in, 16; productivity and, 359
Alderman, Harold, 96
Amato, Peter, 71, 272
Amemiya, Takeshi, 197
Anand, Sudhir, 75, 239, 247, 301, 308, 311, 350, 353
Atkinson index, 59, 60, 86–87

Background variable: as determinant of earnings, 242–43, 276, 277; as determinant of labor supply, 202–03; of prime-age women, 205–06
Becker, Gary S., 238, 383
Ben-Porath, Yoram, 239
Berry, R. Albert, 3, 18, 61–63, 300
Bhalla, C., 95
Blacks, 352–53
Bogotá: boundaries of, 24; in Colombian urban system, 9–12; demographic structure of, 27–29;

earnings and returns to education in, 248–56; growth rates in, 22–23; historical overview of, 22; income distribution in, 33–41, 64–69, 71, 74, 75, 77, 79; labor supply in, 220–23; land values in, 41–54; population in, 24–25; population distribution in, 29–33; poverty in, 111; spatial disaggregation of, 364–65; spatial growth of, 25–27; zoning regulations in, 26–27
Bourguignon, François, 216, 247, 256–58, 260
Brunner, Arnold William, 26
Business cycles, 188

Cali: earnings and returns to education in, 248–56; growth rates in, 22–23; historical overview of, 22; income distribution in, 64–69, 71, 73, 74, 75, 77, 79; land values in, 41–54; population in, 24–25; population distribution in, 33; poverty in, 109–10; spatial growth of, 26
Calorie intake, 93–98, 101, 103, 123–24, 127–33
Calorie price calculations, 103, 137
Calorie requirements, 92, 96, 125–26
Calvo, Guillermo, 242
Census reports, 5, 6, 361–62; income in Bogotá (1973) and, 370–71
Childbearing, 328, 329, 339, 357
Children: demographic structure of

The most recent World Bank publications are described in the catalog *New Publications*, which is issued in the spring and fall of each year. The complete backlist of publications is shown in the annual *Index of Publications*, which contains an alphabetical title list and indexes of subjects, authors, and countries and regions; it is of value principally to libraries and institutional purchasers. The continuing research program is described in *The World Bank Research Program: Abstracts of Current Studies*, which is issued annually. The latest edition of each of these is available free of charge from Publications Sales Unit, Department B, The World Bank, 1818 H Street, N.W., Washington, D.C. 20433, U.S.A., or from Publications, The World Bank, 66, avenue d'Iéna, 75116 Paris, France.